SELECTED WORKS OF
SACHEVERELL SITWELL

SELECTED WORKS

WORKS

of

SACHEVERELL SITWELL

ROBERT HALE LIMITED

63 Old Brompton Road London S.W.7

First published 1955

MADE AND PRINTED IN GREAT BRITAIN BY
WILLIAM CLOWES AND SONS, LIMITED, LONDON AND BECCLES

CONTENTS

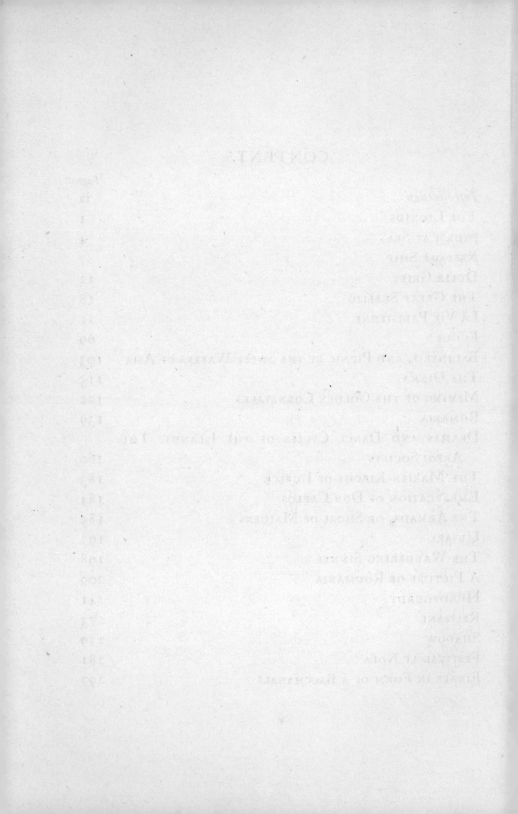

CONTENTS

LIST OF ILLUSTRATIONS

ACKNOWLEDGMENTS

THE thanks of the author and publishers are due to Messrs Colnaghi for permission to reproduce *A Turkish Lady and her Attendant*, by Liotard; to Picture Post Library for the portraits of Don Carlos and Offenbach; to the Rijksmuseum, Amsterdam, for the three paintings of scenes in Istanbul by J. B. Vanmour; and to the Musée Van den Bergh, Antwerp, for permission to reproduce *Dulle Griet*, by Brueghel.

INTRODUCTION

In preparing this volume of *Selected Works* I have had the ambition before me of making the book readable, as far as possible, with changes of scene and subject in order to avoid monotony, while conforming at the same time to some general, overall design and plan. It must be borne in mind that many of these pieces were written during the six years of the Second World War, and they carry the imprint of that, though it may be that they are no less contingent to the present time. But it is probably better to follow them through in the programme, and arrive at my conclusions, later, when more expedient.

The Leonids was chosen for opening because of its strange effect which is that of a curtain drawn suddenly back; or, rather, it is like a window thrown open. You stand in the window and look out on to the night, and are participant in the procession that sweeps across the heavens, noiselessly, and will not pass again in a lifetime. One does not know whether it would be more wonderful to see this strange sight as a child, or as an old man.

Descriptions of cliff scenery and stormy seas follow, a device used in order to awaken feelings of uneasiness and anxiety. Most readers will be familiar with the nightmare of falling over a precipice, and it is a common sensation to have a dread of looking down from heights. My machinery for producing neurosis is exactly to that formula; and *Storm at Sea* with Othello driving before the tempest into the harbour of Famagusta, as in the marvellous opening of Verdi's opera, is followed by the *Refugee Ship* carrying Roumanian Jews from a Black Sea port to Haifa. Close upon this *Dulle Griet* begins, which is a fantasy upon Brueghel's painting in the Musée van den Bergh at Antwerp, a picture more familiar to the English public of recent months, because it was exhibited last year in London. Contemporary material has been added to this, in the way that one of Brueghel's sons might have put additional figures into his copy of the painting, by an interpolated account of a Home Guard "exercise" and of the "blitz" at Nuneaton. It ends in smoke and flame, and fantasy.

The Great Skellig is a penance, a stony Thebaid. It is a strange thought that the Irish monks or Culdees penetrated in their ecstasy for solitude as far as rocks and islands at which, even now, it is nearly impossible to make a landing; to St Kilda which was an easy stage in their progress, but to the awful Rockall rising steep out of the Atlantic main, to Zuliska, and it is said to Iceland before the Northmen got there. The monks of the nitron desert were, comparatively, in luxury beside them.

Following immediately upon these bony heels is the light-hearted *La Vie Parisienne*, written, and intended, to be the recreation of an hour. Starting from drab mid-Victorian London where there were no cafés and hardly, even, a restaurant but only eating-houses, it attempts to recapture the glitter and gaiety of the Second Empire. It is a tribute to Offenbach, the genius of comedy in music, but something more than that with his haunting and nostalgic tunes.

The piece which follows is the best thing which my only amateur interest in music has achieved to date. *Fugue* is an essay on Bach's organ music, which I have tried to describe visually, yet, were that possible, in the formal language of the fugue. Above all I have tried to apprehend the "meaning" of the music. I hope and believe that my analysis of the Fantasia and Fugue, the tremendous and awe-inspiring Prelude and Fugue in C Major, the Passacaglia and Fugue, and the terrific—there can be no other word for it—Prelude and Fugue in E Minor, a work of art equivalent to a "one-man" Chartres Cathedral, may not be wholly inadequate to their subject. It is only a pity that there is no room, as well, for a study of Bach's Goldberg Variations, published elsewhere. I think that being a practised writer upon architecture helped me to describe Bach's organ music. I am fully aware that writing such as *Fugue* is a little difficult to read, and should be followed for the health and calm of the reader with lighter passages, if mental indigestion is to be avoided.

Badinerie, and Picnic by the Sweet Waters of Asia is, therefore, an interlude, and I borrowed part of the title for it from the name of a movement from one of Bach's Suites for Orchestra. That is a dialogue, or more accurately, general conversation of a gay, bantering character, between the wind instruments, and in my own version not a *chinoiserie*, but what used to be called a *turquerie*, moving from the highlights on Meissen and Chelsea porcelain to the ceremonies of the Tulip Reign.

A piece appears next which has only been printed in a small collection of essays called *Touching the Orient*. It was written for introduction to a long poem, a Seventh Canto of my *Doctor Donne and Gargantua*, but the poem was only half completed and has not been published. I had been up the Blue and White Niles, as far as Sennar in one direction towards Abyssinia, and down to Er Renk in the other, which is where the Nilotic tribes begin, the Dinka in plenty, and the first sight or inkling of the Shilluk. Their extraordinary stature puts these tribes into a canon apart, and they would provide a subject for a great painter. But the huge Watussi of the Belgian Congo are more gigantic still, and a fantasy upon them forms the Epilogue to my *The Hunters and the Hunted*. A friend of mine who was in Northern Rhodesia during the last War has told me of the visit of the King of the Watussi and his orchestra of giants to the Governor, and one has only to read the account of this tribe by a German prince who was the first European to have sight of them.* It reads entirely like a fairy story. They advanced towards him, the nobles and their retainers, seven feet or seven feet six inches tall, in long, patterned gowns, leaning on high staffs or wands, attended by Pygmy servants. Their wealth is in herds of immensely wide-horned cattle, of lovely markings. Such a spectacle out of the antique pastoral world was reserved and kept waiting for us until the turn of the last century. The Herreros of South-West Africa, cruelly decimated by the German colonists, made a kindred subject, tall of stature, also, with red-gowned women reputed to be the most beautiful of all African races, in horned head-dresses of peculiar aspect. All the tall and thin races are themes for sculptor and painter, and *Dinka* could have been written, had it ulterior purpose, in order to induce someone of talent to undertake the journey to the Sudan.

A "peasant piece" follows upon this, written in the

* Grand Duke Adolphus-Friedrich of Mecklenburg-Schwerin in 1898.

language of Delibes' *Coppélia*, and opening with that mimosa-laden waltz the strains of which could have been written by no one but a Parisian. But the stage directions read, "A square in a little town on the borders of Galicia". It has to be remembered that in the days when this was written, just after the fall of France in 1940, *Coppélia* was far from being the familiar commonplace it has become to-day. It was given by one of the Russian companies before the War, which had been the only opportunity of seeing it in a London theatre, for Diaghilev never included it in his seasons. Stray performances of *Coppélia*, and memories of the great revival of *La Belle au Bois Dormant* at the Alhambra in 1921, were the only taste, therefore, of what have now become the classics. *Coppélia* is written of, here, with more than a little of that awe and reverence with which one enters for the first time—and more and more impressed upon every subsequent occasion—into the Cathedral of St Mark's. *Coppélia* is one of the holy places of the dance, with all the lightness and inconsequence demanded for serious performance of its *csárdás* and *mazurka*. The action I transferred bodily, with poetic licence, into that "square in a little town on the borders of Galicia", allowing my fantasy full play upon and around the person of Swanilda. It is a *realization* of *Coppélia*, as though the lovely glamour of the footlights, that false sunlight of the theatre which is, yet, so warming and inspiring, has removed itself, entire, into that wonderland of Hungary, of distant Transylvania, of Galicia, of where you will, and you find yourself walking by the cornfield with Swanilda in her *tutu* as though come out through the stage door, between performances, for a breath of air. It becomes, therefore, like a festival performance of *Coppélia* in a far-off and foreign town where one has never been but in imagination; or been once, and longed to go again. It is possible, for instance, and I have done it, to write poems in imaginary celebration of ballet performances in the Fenice Opera House in Venice, "the theatre of green lacquer", with the arrival of the ballerina by gondola, supping afterwards with Swanilda on melon and red foaming wine of Valpolicella, opening, thereby, a world of poetical imagery and experience which could extend through the heat of August and its thunderstorms to the green waves lapping on the palace painted with the white clouds of Tiepolo, his turbaned, moustachio'd Orientals, and damasked models who were a gondolier's daughters; or to the Venetian dancer Barbarina in her black domino as in the pastel by Rosalba. Here, it is the Hungarian plain, and we hear the cymbalom or Hungarian dulcimer. I have tried to give it all the colour possible, so that it is a performance of *Coppélia* in the "little square".

The haunting strains of Delibes' music give place to *Romaria*, an evocation of Portugal written in the form of a fantasy upon the Convent of Jesus at Aveiro. It is an excursion or country picnic of the nuns. Two or three of the convent chapels in Portugal are fantastically beautiful. Indeed, that of Santa Clara in Oporto is, literally, *rutilante de dorures*, and of a quality to which the Convent of Jesus does not aspire. But, at Santa Clara, the convent is secularized and you are only admitted into the chapel. The rest of the nunnery is not shown. Also, it is a town convent. The romantic interest of the convent chapels is enormously heightened by the device of screens and lattices to conceal the Abbess and the nuns. But they were not entirely hidden. You caught sight of them behind the golden grilles. The nun's choir at Santa Clara is as distantly ravishing as a view of the Seraglio and its inhabitants. Any and every stratagem is used in order to add to the excitement; and, where not deliberate, it has been done unconsciously. Also, to see the nuns moving behind their grille is to assist at the rehearsal of some sacred masque or ballet to which the public is not allowed. Or, again, in convent chapels in Bavaria and Austria the nuns may hide themselves in opera-boxes in order that the theatre imagery should play both ways. The golden lattice, which must have been the nearest that either the nuns or their audience reached to the theatre, reached to its ultimate heights in Mexico. In all this it is impossible not to be reminded of the stratagem by which Venetian courtesans of the sixteenth century made themselves more conspicuous and more interesting, which was to walk upon high pattens or *chioppines*, a fashion of Turkish origin still lingering two hundred years later, where we can see it in Liotard's paintings. In another Oriental country, Japan, the "screens of State" behind which the Court ladies passed their lives played so large a part that it would be no exaggeration to say they were the plot or action of the whole drama, as can be read in Lady Murasaki's novel

The Tale of Genji, which was written in the eleventh century. With such things in mind, and not forgetting accounts of the Venetian convents during the century of carnival, I have taken the nuns out of the Convent of Jesus at Aveiro for a picnic or *romaria* in the pinewoods.

I hope that this piece of almost a theatrical association will lead on easily and naturally into *Dramas and Dance Cycles of the Islands*, which is perhaps a prime instance of nostalgic writing, composed during one of the worst and longest stretches of the War years, when it was a memorable treat to get as far away as the next village, and a rare visit to London was as audacious as a journey across Siberia. The full rigours of that long imprisonment, and the absolute cessation in most of those things that made life worth living, must have pressed hard on and spurred the imagination. In the result, this piece of un-ashamedly "escapist" writing pleases me more than anything else printed in these pages. Written in the manner of Gaugain's paintings, it is a fantasy on the South Sea Islands. I took immense trouble with the fruits and flowers, and with trying to get the colours of the landscape. When the Royal Academy held their exhibition of a hundred years of painting, a year or two ago in London, pictures were on view by William Hodges, who accompanied Captain Cook on his second voyage. "On his return", according to the *Dictionary of Painters*, "Hodges painted for the Admiralty some views in Otaheite (Tahiti) and other islands in the Pacific Ocean." His pictures of the huge war canoes of the Oceanians, full of tattooed warriors, with the high hills of the islands rising at the back tufted with strange palms, could have been another inspiration, but at that date I had not seen them. In one detail I have been inaccurate, for it appears that the narwhal is an inhabitant of the Northern Arctic Seas. Shortly after writing it, a friend told me of his experience during the First World War when he met a man —I think a Scot—who made his living by going every year, as his father and grandfather had done before him, to buy narwhal tusks—"sea ivory" as it was called—from the Eskimos in Baffin Bay and Greenland. This must have been the most unlikely and picturesque of businesses to remain in private hands. To those persons who have had the opportunity of going to Tahiti, or Fiji, or to Samoa, reported to be the most beautiful of all the islands, I hope my Oceanian chapter will not come amiss. Even while writing this, my brother lately returned from Honolulu tells me of the wonders of the climate and landscape, and of seven hundred varieties of hibiscus growing in the gardens, floating, as is their wont, upon the sunlit airs.

The Marien-Kirche of Lübeck comes after, deliberately as must be obvious, and on purpose because of its difference. How calm and beautiful it was, with tombs and wall tablets to forgotten burghers and their families—totally destroyed, now, I am afraid, or terribly damaged—and I can never forget the silvery organ! But it is of no use to write of that again. At the Reformation the Lutherans did not pull down or deface the monuments in old churches, with the result that this church seemed to be, not a charnel house, but something alive out of the fifteenth and sixteenth centuries. I imagine it must have been even surpassed by the wonderful old Marien-Kirche of Danzig, which I have never seen, but that had not the golden association with music. Bach never climbed into its organ-loft. Lübeck is Baltic and North German. It is a brick building in the Baltic style, and therefore different from such another, if little known, place in which to study the old German atmosphere as the chapel of the "German Nation" in the church of San Domenico at Siena, which contains and is indeed entirely hung with tombstones of German students at the University in the sixteenth and seventeenth centuries, with their coats of arms in the style of Dürer, that is to say, the style of Nuremberg. Why there should have been such mortality among the students I do not know. The old German heraldry is most wonderful, and the long names. But how much variety there can be in brick building! How different again is the Marien-Kirche from the marvellous old Pieterskerk of Leyden, in Holland! That, for it has been cleaned and the whitewash removed, is a rose-petal brick interior; it is like a tent or pavilion of cloth-of-roses, for there could be no other name for it, and I so described it in *The Netherlands*. But in the Marien-Kirche at Lübeck you cannot forget something a little sinister as well as old. Could it be that Doctor Faustus, "blasphemer and nigromancian", entered here, who had studied magic in the schools of Cracow?

Embarcation of Don Carlos is like a little footnote to long experience and love for Spain. How pleased I am that I saw Don Carlos! It could have been a little play staged particularly for my benefit! And this is followed by another memory from childhood, of peculiar and memorable importance to myself, but it is, in fact, of some little interest because it is a record of the great invasion of Britain by the Gypsy coppersmiths in 1910-12, of which warning was given by Mr Augustus John who had come across them at Marseilles and elsewhere. No one knows where they had started from, but study of their language undertaken by Gypsy scholars revealed many Russian and still more Roumanian words in their dialect. The families of Tschorons and Demeters were of a picturesque wildness of appearance that would have delighted Callot. Their extraordinary invasion of these islands at so late a date (passports were not then required!) is one of the most interesting chapters in Gypsy folk-lore. For myself, I can never forget that part of my initiation into the secrets of life was due to the Gypsies. For when I was about eight years old, and at school at Reigate, I saw a Gypsy woman suckling her child under the long wall of Reigate Priory, and it was my first intimation that human beings are like the animals of the field. The Gypsy theme is further pursued in *Wandering Sinnte*, where I might have said that an interesting theory of Bataillard is that the Gypsies come round again at intervals of long years and seem to have some instinctive or traditional knowledge of where to find their camping-places. They are, in fact, migratory like the swarms of birds, and it must have been in obedience to some instinct that the coppersmiths came to Britain, thanks to which I was lucky enough to see a family of the Ursari while I was at school at Eton.

In *A Picture of Roumania* the survival into modern times of the equivalent of an outlying province of the Byzantine Empire is the topic. Bucharest and its polyglot population, its bastard churches, its Gypsies and Sephardim or Spanish Jews are described; and there is a study of the Skoptzi, who were droshky drivers of the Roumanian capital. All this reads, now, as if it were remoter even than the pantomime splendours of the Turkish Sultans; it seems, indeed, as though it were a study of life under the Comnenoi or the Palæologi; yet it was written in 1937!

In the piece called *Hurdygurdy* my ambition was to take the opposite pole of music and write a pendant to the episode called *Fugue*. Both were, in fact, printed together in the first place. For a long time I had played with the idea of making either of the Hungarian Gypsy musicians Czermak or Biháry the hero of it. Any reader who remembers *The Visit of the Gypsies*, or *The Wandering Sinnte*, different episodes I have written, will know of my interest in the Gypsies and their music. This goes hand in hand with a love of virtuosity for the sake, it could be said, of the virtuoso, as proved by a book on Liszt and many pages therein on Paganini. Musical dictionaries, the perusal of which was a pastime while waiting for other books to be brought round in the Reading Room of the British Museum, at length gave me what I wanted in the person of Gusikov, an impromptu player of Russian-Jewish origin, now forgotten entirely—indeed, no one has heard of him—but he would seem from contemporary accounts to have been the greatest of all musicians of his kind.

Part of the fascination of this particular subject is in its Russian or, rather, Ukrainian background. In order to achieve it I had to steep myself in accounts of childhood in the country, out of Russian memoirs. I can see the traces in it, too, of my reading of *Pan Tadeusz*, the Polish epic of Mickiewicz, which has beautiful and poetical accounts of the rye-fields, and of picking mushrooms in the forest. Also, of the ceremonial dancing of the *mazurka* in the evenings, with the Polish nobles holding their ladies by the hand, and with their other hand twirling the long ends of their moustachios, as they processed to music down the long halls of the castle. The town of Mohilev, where our Russian-Jewish musician passed his childhood, I described from personal knowledge of near-by Hotin, a town with a Jewish population on the Dniester, formerly Roumanian and now in Russia. I tried to get into the soul of the Russian folk music, carrying its sophistication a little further than it can ever have got in the time of Gusikov, by following the strains of Gypsy orchestras into the Novo-Troitski Traktir, and the Moskovski Traktir, Moscow restaurants famed for their Gypsy bands and Gypsy singers. Tunes were played there such as the famed *Zigeunerweisen* of Sarasate, heard by the Spanish violinist in Moscow and written down by him.

Similar tunes, one or two of them by bandmasters, but in the Hungarian idiom, were used by Brahms for his *Hungarian Dances*. The peculiar nature of the special instrument played by Gusikov, and the wonderful effects drawn by him out of its slender structure, made me think, inevitably, of that magical clavichord player Violet Gordon Woodhouse, whom I had known from childhood, and my account of Gusikov ends with what is, in fact, her playing of Mendelssohn's *A Midsummer Night's Dream*, a musical experience of immortal and breath-taking loveliness, only the more immortal because it perished so completely at her lamented death. In this episode, as in several others, the reader will notice undercurrents of the War and of the dread and apprehension of those six years of isolation.

The haunting strains of Slav music give place to one of many studies of beggars that I have written, companion pieces to my writings about Gypsies. On this occasion it is reprinted from *Touching the Orient*, and is a description of Relizane, a horrible little colonial town in Algeria. Horrid it certainly was twenty years ago, and there is no reason to think it is better now! The only material for the artist in such a town as Relizane was to be had from the beggars who found easy accommodation beside their parents and confrères in paintings by Hieronymus Bosch. It is followed by *Shadow*, which is a portrait, if no more recognizable than a shadow on a wall.

Festival at Nola is written in Neapolitan style, inspired, that is to say, by the climate, the architecture and the music of Naples, the one town in Italy which has come down to us with a large population from classical times and conveying, therefore, in its vociferous hurlyburly something of the ancient world of Greeks and Romans. Rome itself is for ever, now, the ecclesiastical city; and it could even be true that at certain periods in the Dark Ages its population was outnumbered by its statues. The scene of the festival is not Naples itself; but the near-by town of Nola, in the Campania, where what is nothing more nor less than the Festival of Adonis is still celebrated, doubtless with ever-diminishing resemblance to its original, but still an extraordinary living relic of the ancient world. This is a crowd piece, as are others of my writings descriptive of the market-place of Marrakesh and the Feria of

Seville. I spent several winters at Amalfi, near Naples, as an appreciative onlooker of the Southern scene and used to know well the country round Naples, towns like Torre del Greco, Torre Annunziata, Nocera de 'Pagani, Sorrento and all those places, actually or in spirit on the slopes of Vesuvius, and warmed by volcanic as well as solar fires. This was an occasion, then, to give free rein to fancy in a description of a fiesta in a Southern Italian town. Only a few miles away from Nola across the Campania, where the vines are trained on trellises as high as trees, and ever in sight of Vesuvius, lies Aversa, a town built nearly on the site of the ancient Fescennia where the Roman comedies were born. Aversa was to the ancients what Bergamo was to the Italian *seicento*, for it was from Bergamo that the Commedia dell' Arte came. Is there not a Bergamaske dance at the end of *A Midsummer Night's Dream*? But Aversa was famous for the broad licence of its comedies, and Callot called his little books of woodcuts of the Italian Comedy the *Balli di Sfessania*, after the ancient Fescennia. *Festival at Nola* was written in full knowledge of this, as though the *Balli di Sfessania* were playing in the next town and waiting to come to Nola for the second night of the festival, which is to-morrow night.

And we arrive at the Finale, which is the ending of my *Sacred and Profane Love*, and which it is not difficult to deduce from the last movement of Beethoven's Seventh Symphony. This is said by some authorities to be based upon a Cossack tune, yet it is unquestionably a bacchanale. Bacchus or Dionysus, Dr Lempriere tells us, invaded India in order to teach the inhabitants "the use of the vine, the cultivation of the earth and the manner of making honey". This is the sense in which I interpret the bacchanale, and it is used here for a happy ending.

In reading through these pages one is aware of certain discrepancies which have crept in during the course of years. It is inevitable that this should be so when it is considered that some of the extracts are taken from books written as long ago as 1934, and that others date from immediately before or during the Second World War. An amusing instance of the "time signature" which falls, eventually, upon everything that is the work of human hands will be found on page 42 of *La Vie Parisienne*, which is obviously the first reaction of having experienced a colour film. I have left it unaltered in its naïveté. An anachronism of rather the same order may be noticed on page 147, where travellers who know Portugal may be surprised to read of the Convent of Jesus at Aveiro being "two days' journey from Oporto". I can only assure them that this was certainly true if you tried to travel by road in Portugal in 1926. A little further on in *Romaria* there is a description of going through Seville, without stopping there, on the second morning of the Feria (page 158), for it was not until 1947 that I saw this glorious spectacle close to, and could write of it in full. Similarly, on pages 136 and 138, there are inaccuracies in my account of the ballet *Coppélia* due to unfamiliarity with this well-worn classic of the dance. Finally, on page 172 and thereabouts, it should be remembered that I was writing in 1941 before the start of the war in the Pacific, when some of the islands were less familiar and less bloodstained names.

There are no doubt very many other slips and omissions, mistakes and misapprehensions. The first thoughts of any conscientious author are of his own shortcomings. These are hideously and woefully apparent when he reads his proofs. Nothing, ever, is the equal of his expectations. Proof reading can take on the aspect of an eternal and perpetual wet day with no sun and, as day fails, but a weak bulb in the electric light. Nevertheless, I have tried hard for warmth and clarity. I have mentioned that *The Areöi Society* is my own favourite among these pieces, precisely, I think, because of its warmth and clearness. But there are many other pieces, not presented here, with which I could wish to tempt the reader. In this last moment I would only ask for the lack of continuity which is inevitable in any selection of writings not to be held against me, and that I should not be reproached for putting Bach's fugal music and the lightness of Offenbach's *La Vie Parisienne* within the covers of one book. The intention is a collection of pieces to be read in themselves, and not necessarily the best, or the worst, of what there is to choose from. Many books are not quoted here at all. Yet there is enough, I hope, to satisfy most tastes.

SACHEVERELL SITWELL

7 *March,* 1955.

THE LEONIDS*

My father, when a little boy, was woken up one night, and dressed, and taken to the window. Upon a summer evening, I think, in 1867. It was to watch a shower of meteors fall into the sea. They may have driven in a carriage down to the Foreshore, or along the Esplanade. I do not know. That would seem more likely, upon a summer night, than to stay at a window.

The shower of stars had been announced beforehand by the newspapers. To take place for three nights together. And never again in a lifetime? Once more I am not sure. Something tells me that it happens every eighty years or so; that it is nearly impossible to see it twice; that the Leonids are coming near again. There will be another summer evening, I believe it is in August, when the three-day spectacle is at its climax. What does it portend? And what does it mean to have a lifetime dashing in fire across the windowpane, and falling out of the night sky into the sea? How wonderful and terrible it would be to see it twice, in the beginning and the end! How full of meaning; and in a sense how meaningless! For their fire is extinguished before they reach the earth. Except for their punctual timing, they have no bearing upon us. Unless there is truth in the horoscope, and fortunes can be told.

The Leonids fell on this occasion out to sea. I do not know the exact nature of their display; whether they came at hazard from all quarters of the heavens; like pouring rain; or one at a time as though a hand shook the bough. More probably it was like a hundred shooting stars, so fast that the eyes could not follow them. I have been told of this since childhood and cannot remember now whether they fell outside the atmosphere, or really reached the sea and spattered on the waves. It is possible I imagined that, for I have met no astronomers nor anyone whom I could ask. All I know is that they were seen by everyone and will come again. Not, it cannot be, the same

* From *Primitive Scenes and Festivals*, 1942.

I

falling meteors; but they must derive from a fountain of fire that flows for ever and is, itself, moving through space.

Upon an August evening in 1867, and again soon! The discrepancy or little likelihood is obvious. How curious to stand at the same window, but the house is deserted now, and watch fire fall for the second time across the Valley into the sea! Then, it was the hand of God; now, it will be the Great Anarch!

But the spectacle, if it is a clear night, will be no less tremendous. The Leonids are heavenly bodies. They are fiery particles that vanish utterly in space. Nothing is left but the memory of them. When we consider the extraordinary bodies seen in the sky during historic and all prehistoric time, meteors with tails stretching half across the firmament, maned heads, phantoms in the form of golden swords or arrows, and so forth, and if we accept that, rightly or wrongly, the majority of the human race have acknowledged the influence or the portent in such things, then the Leonids are of plain symbolic meaning. The name given to them is significant of this. They are the signs of genius. Young and ardent spirits, for they are quenched so quickly. They are burned up before their time, and by a fire within themselves. Long ago, the portents were more visible. Out of our teeming millions few, if any, can dash themselves like torches upon the ground. But, taken through all time, if not falling like a shower, it is at least as though a hand—whose hand?—shook them from the branches.

What, in fact, are the Leonids? We do not know; but we can create them for ourselves. In the first place, by listening to the music of their name. The Leonids are the young or little of the lion. A name, also, for a dazzling display. They are of tawny or golden colour, which may mean many things, according to their race. For it is an universal symbol. Kings in golden armour, such as are buried underneath the hill? It should mean much more than that. They are divers or acrobats of the golden skies. And we are to imagine them, since all things tangible have an earthly body, with long hair—is that not implicit in their name?—and clothes that fit tightly to the frame. Spangled they may be, but it does not impede their action. Their dwelling is a tent or hut beside the megalith. No other building, made with hands, is timeless. So they live in the green plain of the dolmen or stone circle. When the stars of the morning sing together, it is they. For the dawn is neither for young children, nor old men. Figures in human form, but never in the act of walking. They recline, or slumber, or go quickly; for, like Mercury or Harlequin, they must be volatile and moving. They are dæmons or fiery spirits. Above them, the starry sky is in continual display, ever cloudless, to the zenith, and all round, for there are no hills. The only shadow is the white megalith.

Here is the arena for the chariot race. Or for the funeral games. All round it is smooth driving ground. The horses are white stallions. And from this eminence the constellations can be seen in movement, but never swifter than the fingers of a clock. Even when they fall in fire. The whirlwind is a figure with outstretched arm who appears to write his name. One of the winds of space who blows between the planets. And now the word comes, and the Leonids fall from heaven through the night. They reach the ocean; or are snuffed out above the mountains. But they presage events: or lives of promise. Here are, yet, no cottage windows where they can be seen past the honeysuckle or between the lilies. Neither the slum, nor the palace has been built as yet. But they fall past the sheepfold. Once, in a lifetime, the man with a scythe looks back over his shoulder and sees the Leonids in an empty heaven dropping towards the cornfields. And, when he reaches the village, the old women have brought out their grandchildren to watch the mystery. No one wants to sleep that night, except the puking babe.

They fall so violently that they could strike the fishing nets. But where the boats are, we are told next morning they fell much further out. And all listened, but could hear no sound. In another district, persons come back a week later from the forests and describe to us what they have seen. In the huge plain they fell far off, and at the same time, it thundered in the mountains. In another place nothing at all was seen or heard. Someone, at a deed of darkness, saw those golden lights and put down his hand. All over the world men listened, but heard nothing. The meteors are aloof, and burning only for themselves. There is no other meaning. The dæmons, who are snuffed out so soon, were formed for the display. It is all in the flame and fury.

3

STORM AT SEA*

THE howling of the storm is let loose as though to the lifting of a hand.

It is as if, coming round the corner of a street down by the harbour, we are hit by its full, mad force, shrieking and raving in from the sea. Doors and wooden shutters are wrenched open. The windows are pointed arches, or the bifora, a pair of lights with a stone pillar in between. And the street, all of stone houses, leads down into the gale.

The long clouts of rain beat like the ends of ropes. Listen to the roar of the wind! It could be the wailing of seabirds flying in their millions, inland from the storm. Great bodies of them could be passing overhead. That might be the beating of their wings. It blows through the flesh and bones. It is a storm in ten thousand: in a lifetime. And a night when much will happen. Not yet sunset: but the livid evening.

But the rain has stopped. You can hear nothing but the wind and waves. A pause, as though for living things to hide themselves. Suddenly, lightning flickers like fire set to the entire firmament. There is utter silence. A rushing, tearing sound. Then a wild leaping, and one tremendous boom of thunder. It hits, at the end of that, like a whip that lashes upon metal. The next moment striking full upon that, shuddering and shrinking, while it rolls in triumph and booms above our heads.

Growing darker, ever darker. It could be something animal and gigantic. But it rises into a wild and endless shrieking. A huge engine or machinery is working in the storm. Or a rhythm. For it is blowing in from sea. And no one has run for shelter. A crowd of persons is waiting on the quay. As though their help will be needed. They have hurried out from their houses because, storm or no storm, the hour has come. For all we know it may have been delayed for weeks. But now it is imminent.

The whole air is shaken and beaten in the gale. But there has

* From *Splendours and Miseries*, 1943.

4

been a message: or some signal has been seen. It grows dark and darker; and still the howling of the storm. Those low clouds could be seabirds flying south out of the white or polar darkness. The lightning plays again upon the leaden waters. Thunder booms and rattles: and then hits with all its force, close by, as though some building has been struck. Dry thunder, now, without a drop of rain. So that the emptiness is sinister and lies like tinder for the fire to fall. Imagined lightning flares every way you look, as those eyes of fire within the eyelids upon the middle of the night. The leaden air is incandescent and could be lit with flame.

There are frightful pauses between the lightning and the thunder; and again, no interval at all, but the crack of doom at once after no warning. And the yelling, howling tempest multiplies in detail. It has interior rhythms. This is a night when there will be knocking at all doors. No one will forget this storm. There come sudden furies: spates in the whirl of waters: the ghost-fire of St Elmo will burn at the masthead. A wet and shining thing, but faintly glowing, and difficult to see, as it might be a seabird, fainting from exhaustion, that clings to the rigging.

We are waiting with the crowd for someone to arrive. By sea: or it could be by air. It does not matter. Someone is coming in a storm of wind and thunder. There has been an escape from a lost cause; and danger all the way. Until the last moment.

No time for more while the thunder cracks and booms. For it rises to a hurricane. The tornado shrieks and roars. One tremendous boom of thunder shakes above, below, and in the hollow caverns of the earth and sky. It runs every way at once, thundering this way and that, and then in one point only where it breaks into the leaden chambers, loud and enormous, in the livid cauldron of the storm, thrashing the metal, and shuddering upon the walls like a spirit dying.

But there is a closing of wings. Something descends, or comes down into the water, not far away. It could be a huge seaplane landing in the harbour. A sail has been sighted, and in incredible speed it comes up out of the darkness. The persons waiting come running out from the shelter of the harbour wall. It is known immediately and recognized. There is a moment of danger while the sails are lowered. We hear the sound of that, and of the sailors shouting. And then the gliding, past the pier, into the calmer waters.

Othello's vessel has come safely into port.

Where do we find ourselves? It could be upon the quays of Famagosta. There are—there must be—golden stone and sand dunes. But it is no hour to watch the painted sails and painted prows. This flight, or arrival, is in the imagination. For we speak in symbols.

There is a fanfare of trumpets as Othello steps ashore. His friends welcome him, and he enters the castle with Cassio and Montano.

REFUGEE SHIP*

WE hear the barking of the dog Cerberus, or the echo of it in the orchestra.

It could be many other things. Distant gunfire: "after one of the heaviest bombs had been dropped, a whole built-up area appeared to boil." We hear the cries of terror of the multitude, like a raging beast trapped in the fire. It is chained up, and has no escape. Humanity is being roasted on the spit, and the dog Cerberus guards the burning bodies. We hear the buildings crunch down, while whole factory walls "come up at you", hundreds of feet into the air, as though they took to flight. No! No! that is the Inferno of the living. We have to pass through this. It is no use to look the other way. There are bodies underneath the houses. It will grow worse and worse. The big fires are coming. A black pall of smoke hangs over the town, and the dog Cerberus barks from out of it. Yes. It barks. Those are guns barking. Those are not drums. They would not beat at such intervals. It is the dog Cerberus who guards the Stygian shore. Throw him a bone to gnaw, and he will pick it up, and let you by.

But the winds have not died down. How long, O, how long will it be before they settle! There are a hundred fires left burning and they light the sky. You could see to read a newspaper. And what will the headlines be! What city, or country, has fallen? Or can it be the end of all things, the final night edition! No! There is ever another dawn. That is the bitterness of it. There must be daylight by which to see the comedy, and the paint upon the dead men's faces. By to-morrow there will be more sights to see. The brains are seething in a head which is on fire. There is a skull which you could poke with a stick and which would fall to ashes. Limbs drop easily out of their sockets. A foot juts up at you like a foot out of the bottom of a bed. There is someone talking, and groaning, in that dark

* From *Splendours and Miseries*, 1943.

7

corner. And a body is carried out that is like a plaster cast, like the "living statues" of the old music hall, it is so thick with dust.

The angels have plaster wings and lie upon the chancel steps. Some tombs are blown open and the bones have rolled about for dogs to play with. A winding sheet could be the table cloth spread upon the grass for a picnic. But the printed slogans of the vicar are not even torn down from the announcement board. The dead enter into the next world with a burial service. They are put into one common grave, as though it were the hundred men shot down by the firing squad. All the clergy of the town take part. Of all denominations. There are long lines of weeping men and women, and children led by the hand.

It is here the myth begins, among the black-clad mourners. It is here we wander, lyre in hand.

The dog Cerberus barks in every suburb. Or is it thunder? Listen! listen! that was, surely, lightning. Or is it no more than an electric train? The last train home: down to Hammersmith, or Putney. Down to Blackheath: down to the Isle of Dogs. They flash in that manner on a frosty night. No! no! something is coming. It was a train, after all. There was a tremor in the earth. It must be the underground. But look! There can be no doubt about it. They have come back. They are dropping flares. The whole sky is as light as day. But it is not London. The suburbs have no names. Nor has it London's heart. Piccadilly, with its name like a coster's dance, all pearly buttons. Not Lambeth, round great Bedlam. Not gas-lit Pimlico. Not Soho, of the foreign tongues and newspapers. Not Bond Street, nor the Strand.

For we have gone past the postern. Cerberus barks behind us. Those were dead men whom we passed. They were dead bodies. Did you see their hands? Why are we here? It is because the lost years can be found again. Also because we look for someone. And for the arts of a lost world. Someone is dead. Something has gone and cannot be recovered. It has been necessary to descend into Hell in order to bring it back. We took the occasion of so much misery to join the mourners and follow the dead bodies. For there have never been such spectres of hopelessness and doom. They have lost their homes and are in lodgings and in hostels. In prisons and in concentration camps. When new houses are built they will have nothing to put in them. They have lost their hearts and found they have no souls. What has gone is more important than the mere body. There can be corpses, in plenty, and nothing to save. Neither more, not less, than from the living person. Their deaths have made no difference. To themselves least of all. They are unwanted children, conceived because there was no better amusement on the drunken Sabbath. Worse still, on a sober Sunday with its lifeless streets. For drink is too expensive. There is never a bacchanalia in the suburbs, at the terminus of the tram. Or at the detached villa, with its own front door and garage. At the Tudor (two-door residences) and baronial halls. Where is the painter of the arterial roads and avenues? They are roads of triumph leading to the town hall. Past mansions of the dead, all in ruins. Past the police station and decontamination centre. Past the cottage hospital.

Cerberus is chained at every door, like the dog outside the department store, except that his owner will never come back again to fetch him. At any moment we may hear his bark, for it is a moonlit night. It is full moon, but the moon has gone behind a cloud. There is a "black-out" here upon the shores of Hell, purely as a measure of precaution. Leaflets have been printed, and will be distributed through the post, or from your nearest Labour Exchange. And the paper upon which the leaflets are printed must not be destroyed or thrown away.

Only upon this one shore. The other bank is neutral territory. But we have only this means of communication between here and there. By the small ferry boat. Not at stated times, but irregularly. There is no priority. All must wait their turn. So it is said, but this is not true. Some of the living have been known to reach the other side. We will give instances of this immortality. Others are detained under no warrant. They have become wanderers along the shore. The vast mass of humanity takes nothing with them, and leaves nothing behind. We hear no more of them than their laughter, or their cries of terror. Some persons have become immortal by their sufferings.

We began with a storm. We have been born in stormy times. And, indeed, the winds blow us to the banks of Styx. It can never be calm again in our lifetimes. Those, who die, have the roaring of it in their ears. It can be continual as that held

9

note which musicians have heard, and which has made them lose their reason. A howling or moaning, or a high pitched interrogation. A perpetual question, a riddle or a mystery. The stupid and uneducated have heard it, too. The saints and witches had their "voices." So had common lunatics. Fantasies of the subconscious, but this is not enough in explanation. Their disease has given them this flowering season. These are monstrous fruits, Dead Sea apples, flowers which are striped and freaked with colours. We shall touch all these, and taste them, even if we spit the poison out.

But we arrive in the full shrieking of the gale. We would sooner be wrecked than have to wander on that shore. The floating hulk, to starboard, is a refugee ship bound from a Black Sea port for Palestine. Of such are the phantoms of our own time. It is raising anchor. The seagulls ride near to it upon the swell. It could be a ship from the guano islands. It has become like a rookery, where you tell the nest by the white droppings at the tree foot. There are stainings of white lime upon the ivy, and looking up, the rooks are cawing in the leafless boughs. This, too, this ship is like a town or settlement. They have turned it into their village. Not worn or rubbed away, but clotted or coagulated by months and months of misery. Who would dare go down into the ship's galley? Into the sleeping-quarters, where there are salted herrings, eaten and thrown down upon the tables, on the floors? The ship's bread is too nauseating to be touched. It was kneaded in that cloacal tunnel, upon a table that is like a clotted altar stone.

No one wants these fugitives. They have been driven from every port in turn. Many children are on board, of a strange pallor, with a tinge of blue like the paste of fine porcelain showing underneath their skins, the same colour as the blue of the eyeball, and as though washed upon their wrists and faces. All are dressed in black. Children, who, anywhere else but on this ship, would be playing games, are held in their mothers' arms, or sit, huddled, in their laps. Like the young leaves they are withered on the stem. Men and women wear shabby shoes, and shuffle, without lifting their feet, but only to that side of the ship which faces to the shore. None of them look out to sea. And, in fact, the further coast is invisible. Hidden in a Channel fog. They hear the church clocks and the clanging of the trams.

Sometimes, an engine whistle. Or the shouting of the evening papers. Nothing from the further shore. Not the mournful tolling of the bell buoy, stroke after stroke, as it lifts upon the waves. No message. Nothing. There is no sign. But the anchor is hauled up. The winches groan and pant. A huge wave comes up and hits the ship, like a blow before there is time to put the arm up to the face. The entire ship shudders. And all on board cower as it heads out to sea, into the storm.

DULLE GRIET*

PERHAPS it is better that this should be written in a time of rampant madness. For it imposes order.

The Old Believers are driven out in bands into the forests. That has happened before, and it happens now. We could have heard them singing in their choirs, while the torch was put to the wooden buildings and all the living fell down into the flames. Now they suffer meekly and are inarticulate. The drones fly into the bonfire and are suffocated in it. Indeed, it has been lit to smoke them out. The fires are red, red, red.

But, first of all, we will have a woman running from the flames. A mad or half-wit woman, by the name of Dulle Griet. She has a man's steel helmet and steel breastplate buckled on her breast. There is blood upon her helmet and it has run down upon her nose; she holds a sword in her right hand and a basket is upon her other arm filled with pots and pans and every kind of kitchen utensil, some of which, by accident, have formed themselves into a human face. Or it could be a fish's nose and eyes and mouth. She carries everything except her eyeshades, gas ointment, and her respirator. Except for those, Dulle Griet is one of ourselves fleeing from the flames. In any tongue of the five continents.

The horizon soars and pants with fires, and at this moment is poppy red, but dulls down. Not for long. It is white hot, and burns up again behind a hill. We do not know, at present, whether it is town or country. It could be leagues of burning forest, or a hundred thatched villages on fire in the plain. A huge city, too, or just the fires of Hell. Let us try to determine where we are. An object like a huge jug belching smoke, that could be a gigantic incinerator on the outskirts of a town. Something extraordinary stretches straight into the distance; and this might be the moonlit runway of an aerodrome. Over there are sheds with wheels on the top, like those above

* From *Splendours and Miseries*, 1943.

12

Dulle Griet,
by Brueghel

Part of the
Northern Face
of one of the
Shiant Isles, by
W. Daniell

the shafts of coal mines, and some of the hills are clinker heaps. There has been a battle among the collieries, in and out of the mine buildings, but they are pyramids and Roman ruins. For a time, only. There is the mast of a ship with all its rigging, and at the top a wheel like a ship's wheel, and a great bell attached, that is ringing. A man, carrying a ship's boat on his shoulder, is making off as fast as he can go and rides upon the thatched roof of a house. One of his starved and emaciated limbs, the leg of a deformed cripple, lies straight out before him upon the roof, and in monstrous parody he beats himself along with a saucepan as though he were a hobbyhorse. The boat is full of minute persons, variously occupied, and floats in a sort of bubble or vacuum, as though all contained in a soap bubble, through the concave sides of which we see a little landscape in a prism.

There is a brick tower, something like a Kentish oasthouse, that has a mouth and nose and eyes, and a birdcage hanging from its apex, which is curved into a peak. Out of this mouth or tunnel a lot of frogs come somersaulting or playing tricks. One of them offers the madwoman its head which it holds up in a hand. Near to it, there are other nightmare forms. Frogs' legs with a skewer stuck in them; a barrel creeping forward contrariwise to its rolling motion on four hands, with a face, and since it has no head, a Slovak peasant's bowler hat upon the barrel's rim. Nightmares of the frog's anatomy; for instance, the front legs and shoulders of a frog with its long and skinny hands, a saucepan instead of a head, and that holds in correct position a fishing-rod and line upon the hook of which a huge egg is caught, filling an entire nest, and the egg has been chipped open and holds as many embryos as the ship's boat has persons in it.

There are, also, crayfish forms come to earth; and a creature like a beaked frog, the intestines of which have been gutted. In the foreground it is a fantasy upon the egg, the frog, the tadpole. We may be reminded in this of a curious old German book, *Historia Naturalis Ranarum*, by A. J. Roesel von Rosenhof, Nuremberg, 1758, for that work is a fantasy upon the dissection of frogs. In its handcoloured plates, that are incredible in detail, we see the frog pegged down to be opened with the knife. In every case it is as though the frog was

3   13

crucified; not raised upon a cross, but pegged out upon the ground. Its four feet, which are so like hands, are drawn out to the full extent of the limb and lashed down to four heavy iron pins or staples which are driven into the dissecting-table. The frog's belly is uncovered in its pathetic nudity; we see its head laid back and the underneath of its pathetic, frog-like chin. The markings and stipplings of its skin are rendered in every particular; but the dissection has begun, and in every succeeding plate the viscera, down to the skeleton of the frog, are given in the same painstaking manner in all their colours. So are the angles and shadows of the dissecting-table, and, sometimes, the knife and scapel are laid beside the frog as instruments of this long-drawn passion that worked the flaying and withering of this humble creature. There are, also, the skeletons of frogs, that have the look of fourfooted birds, standing or crawling with the penthouse shadow of their ribs attached, at an angle, to them. The complete skeleton, in every articulation of its bones, may be at the foot of the frog that is bound upon the cross. In that we get the contrast of the grey bones of death, that have no colour, with the livid and expiring hues of the living.

The execution is as startling here, as we see in the brickwork of that oasthouse face, with the many marks or blemishes upon it, and the outline of a tree in early leaf shown against it. An awning is spread out upon it instead of an eyelid to one eye; there are little nightmare figures that have no point at all, but are pure fantasy, particularly where a ruined house becomes a watermill and creatures akin to the animal phantasms of the spiritualists walk along the walls, or warm their hands at a red cloak hanging up, instead of at a fire. At their back there is a wall through which the branches of the tree obtrude, emerging above three copper pots which are fixed up on the stones to fill with rain.

But attention wanders to the red horizon and its panting fires, over a morass where two human beings are stranded on a sandbank. A huge ovoid form, like an egg set up on end, is a tower, also; but its masonry is shattered so that we see the yolk inside, from out of which what appears to be an immense harp tilts forth, but its strings are a spider's web, and we see the spider in the middle of it. A cage rises above this, which is thatched, and upon that thatched roof four or five mice are dancing, but they are the mouse homunculus, like the mice of children's toys that are dressed up in little coats and jackets, and there is a smaller roof of thatch above them. It even becomes a thatched pagoda, for there is still another thatched roof, smaller still, but making three in all. Behind them the whole horizon is red, red, red with fire. What can the meaning be? In the market towns of China, far in the interior, there are men to be met with whose livelihood consists in carrying round a wicker cage. Inside the cage there is a rat. The trick they play is, for a coin, to push a burning brand or a straw dipped in paraffin between the bars, in order that the rat should dance and run about the cage, and cower in the corner.

But the spate of frogs or tadpoles is not done. It could have rained with them. A high ship's mast rises up out of a turret, above another building, with masthead and long bannerol that floats from it, and in the rigging and upon the turret there are frogs that climb with pails upon their heads, holding with one hand to the ropes. A frog stands upon its head with the staff of a rope walker or equilibrist in its hands, upon a chimney pot. Behind that is a white haze of molten fire, and a perpetual tocsin of bells ringing away into the distance. No doubt, the alert, too, upon the screeching sirens; while the wardens sound their rattles for gas.

In the foreground it could be a modern battle training school. Hand-to-hand fighting is continuous, between men and women. Faces are blacked, with dirt from the exhaust pipe of the motor engine. It is unarmed combat, but for the knife; and perhaps housewives have an advantage for they are used to trussing ducks and chickens. Would it interest you to hear some stories of what happened during the preliminary bombardment from the air?

The eighteen-stone woman who lived next door was lifted a hundred yards out of her bedroom, when the roof came off, and was stuck, flat, high up upon the wall of a public house. She is still there. They have not moved her. As to someone's mother-in-law who lived, here, in this house, she went entirely. Nothing was left of her. We found her brains, the day before yesterday, and buried them in the back garden.*

* The "blitz" at Nuneaton.

The hand-to-hand fighting is in progress upon a causeway between the houses. A little black devil, like a newt, clings to the parapet and watches it. His two front legs and one hind leg grip the top, and he can balance with his tail. In the bed of the river, or it is probably a canal, a number of persons are coming out of an archway in a brick building. There is fighting down in the town sewers. A number of the enemy have climbed down the manholes in the street pavements. It may go on, down there, for days. The reinforcements coming out from the archway all wear the old fashioned, hooded respirators. They could be brothers of the Misericordia in their cowls. But not dressed in black. Members of the cofradía forming up for a paso or procession in the Semana Santa? Dressed all in white from cowl to foot; or like the Dominicans in black and white. They are carrying the Virgen del Gran Poder. We shall hear the harsh trumpet and the drum, and the wailing cry of the saeta as the statue is borne past. Those are Gitanos of Triana, which is the Gypsy suburb.

The cranking, just now, was like a tank column, down, next to Marks and Spencer's. Yes! that is it. Opposite the bronze statue of Queen Victoria. Near the granite lavatory upon the island in the middle of the street. Where the Green Line buses stop. These women fight like tigers. They have fairly got three men down, and are finishing them. A Home Guard is jabbing with his bayonet at a pig with wings. In midst of it all a man sits at a table playing cards. The whole air smells of fire. Wherever you look, in the distance there are blackened stumps of towers. But the Battle of the Bridge goes on. If we call the battle by a name in the newspapers, we are sure to lose it. There will be a big announcement in the news to-night, at nine p.m. Be sure you listen! We shall all be tuning in. All doctors and nurses are ordered to report immediately for duty. In fact, the balloon has gone up.

And, having gone up, the balloon is coming down.

It was unexpected, at least, that we should have to fight animals. A number of persons have been caught on their way home from work. And a woman has given birth to a baby in a tram. They are dropping flares and incendiaries. This is just to light the fires, many of which were left burning from last night. The big stuff will come later. One family has fled in safety to an islet in the duckpond in the public park. They have rowed out to it in the park keeper's little boat and are hiding in the thatched hut among the mandarin ducks and carolinas. Many others have been trapped and drowned in cellars, when they hit the water mains. Gas and electricity are cut off; and there is no answer from the telephone. How can one keep calm and think of other things?

THE GREAT SKELLIG*

BEYOND the wood, that primitive land lies clear in every detail into the prodigious distance. A wide river or estuary flows into the world and out of it before the eyes, not being out of view for as far as the sight can carry. The sloping meadows sweep down to the water and the world is divided, but the meadows stretch on again at the far side of it with no difference in their green dominion. That other world is out of earshot; no voice can carry across the waters. The far bank of the river is a mystery only reached by the coracle, but the same flocks of geese move in armies over the plain. The unreal colour of this pastoral kingdom comes in part from its own emptiness of not a wall, nor hedge, and no barrier until the far-off mountains. But it is raining in a dozen places at once under the wide sky, so that the clouds move in shadow over the open land.

And now, a goosegirl can be seen, near at hand, in a hollow of the meadow, while a shoulder of the sloping field shows beehive huts and a rough stone cell. This is the oratory of the saint, and a round tower stands above it, tall as a minaret and capped with stone. The only entrance to this is by a doorway high up in its circumference, so that the ladder lifted into the inside makes the tower impregnable. It is their belfry and watch-tower; and before climbing like Stylites into their column the monks look for distant flames over the inarticulate plain, and, at sight of them, retire into that pillar.

In its pristine state this land was on the extreme edge of the world, lapped by the surges. The mountainous lift and swell of ocean spoke of its ubiquity out of the unbroken vast. In winter, the howling and roaring of the winds told the sphere of waters. And there were valleys or points of land near the sea that, even in the storms, had their peculiar warmth of clime, as under shafts of sunlight, so that they were little tropics and in their luxuriance of growth foretold the promise of the warm islands

* From *Dance of the Quick and the Dead*, 1936.

18

of the ocean. For this reason, and for its utter solitude, this far edge of the world had become a second Thebaid. It had more anchorites than the Nitrian desert. But the physical appearance of these ascetics is even more unknown to us than that of the monks of Egypt. Something of those phantoms of the hot sands, who were as hairy as the satyrs, is preserved to us in mosaics. But of this second Thebaid, and of the Culdees who were its monks, nothing is left but the bare stones of their cells. They must be pictured from conjecture, red bearded, and wearing robes of tweed that were dyed with seaweed and with the seashells of the bare rocks. These athletes in privation and self-denial spent the whole winter in the darkness of their cells. When they emerged into the spring light they must have come out like bears from their caves.

The monastery that we have described is that of Clonmacnoise, looking over the wide waters of the Shannon, but this was among the most accessible of their hermitages. The true character and extraordinary distribution of their Thebaid is to be found at the world's end, remote from these green meadows. They built their cells on islands among the reeds or, not contented with the misty inland seas, sought the ironbound coast. The holy men must have crowded in a drove, to the exclusion of all other inhabitants, into the Dingle peninsula, for it is more thickly strewn with ruins than any of the sites of classical Europe. Here is the oratory of Gallerus, no larger than a stone hut, but of distinct and peculiar architecture. More numerous, still, are the ruins upon Inishmore, the greatest of the Aran Islands, under the shadow of Dun Aengus, the cyclopean fortress. This was the work of pagans; and the terror of its antiquity, five hundred years old or more at the coming of the monks, must have haunted, even then, its tremendous cliffs, sheer above the ocean.

Here, at least, the anchorites had for company a large concourse of their fellow monks, but the extremity of their fury of escape is to be found in such frightful retreats as that of the Great Skellig. This appalling rock lies nearly ten miles out to sea. The ocean sinks suddenly to a depth of ninety fathoms before it, and the rock is almost impossible to land upon because the Atlantic swell rises and falls twenty feet at a time in the calmest weather. The rock is only half a mile long and a quarter of a mile broad; but it rises sheer out of the sea, and the cells of the anchorites, in order to have enough level space to stand upon, had to be built at a height of six hundred feet above the waves. The unimaginable noise and tumult of the storm, in its effect upon the nerves, all the long winter through, makes one of the most extraordinary chapters in the whole history of asceticism. Probably not more than six or eight anchorites, at a time, supported this living hell of wind and cold, but it is evident from the remains of no less than five cemeteries that the Great Skellig had its permanent population who passed their lives upon the rock. During the winter, in the violence of the gales, it will often have been impossible to stand upright and the anchorites must have crawled to their chapels through the frightful voices of the wind. Their provision during the winter depended upon two deep wells of water, and it is probable that they must have kept a flock of goats to feed upon the lichen and the salt grasses. There were, also, the myriad eggs of the sea-gulls; but the anchorites can have had no other food than the dry bread, or biscuit, of the summer's baking, and often they must have been starving when winter was over and the first coracle came out to them. It is difficult, indeed, not to look upon these hermits as spiritual ancestors to the lighthouse-keepers who are stationed upon the same rock and condemned to identical conditions. But, at least, their existence is the guarantee that there are ships passing, while, save for a raid once in a century by the Northmen, there was never a sail and summer was lonely as winter. Theirs, in fact, was one of the extreme situations, the posts of honour, as it were; and the whole of these scattered communities, down the rocks and islands of that iron coast, belong in spirit to the ascetics of the Eastern Church and have no parallel elsewhere in Europe. For emergency of site and drama of isolation there is nothing to choose between Aran or the Great Skellig and the rocks of Meteora or dales of Athos. And there were other posts just as perilous in the seas; Tory Island, off Donegal; High Island, off the coast of Connemara; the lonely and fearful Teach Molaise, on Inismurray in Sligo Bay; or the Great Blasket, of stupendous cliffs and terrific in grandeur; yet, of all these, none is dramatic as the Great Skellig. It is in the cauldron of the storm.

MÉTELLA

Nous sommes dans le restaurant à la mode, mon cher, et minuit vient de sonner.

Rondeau

A minuit sonnant commence la fête;
Maint coupé s'arrête,
On en voit sortir
De jolis messieurs, des femmes charmantes
Qui viennent, pimpantes,
Pour se divertir;
La fleur du panier, des brunes, des blondes,
Et, bien entendu, des rousses aussi...
Les jolis messieurs sont de tous les mondes;
C'est un peu mêlé, ce qu'on trouve ici!
Tout cela s'anime et se met en joie;
Froufrou de la soie
Le long des couloirs!
C'est l'adagio de la bacchanale
Dont la voix brutale
Gronde tous les soirs!
Rires éclatants, fracas du champagne,
On cartonne ici, on danse là-bas,
Et le piano qui grince accompagne
Sur des airs connus d'étranges ébats!
Le bruit monte, monte, et devient tempête;
La jeunesse en fête
Chante à plein gosier.
Est-ce du plaisir ou de la furie?
On parle, l'on crie
Tant qu'on peut crier!
Quand on ne peut plus, il faut bien se taire;
La gaîté s'en va petit à petit;
L'un dort tout debout, l'autre dort par terre,
Et voilà comment la fête finit.
Quand vient le matin, quand paraît l'aurore,
On en trouve encore,
Mais plus de gaieté,
Les brillants viveurs sont mal à leur aise,
Et dans le «grand seize»
On voudrait du thé.
Ils s'en vont enfin, la mine blafarde,
Ivres de champagne et de faux amour,
Et le balayeur s'arrête, regarde,
Et leur crie: «Ohé! les heureux du jour!»

21

LA VIE PARISIENNE*

IT is the last day, but one, of October 1866.

Yesterday, London seemed dark and interminable through the windows of a four-wheeler cab. The area of bright lights reached to Piccadilly and no further. For one must think of oneself, on that evening, as the hero or phlegmatic Englishman of Jules Verne, dining early in—would it be the Reform Club —dining early and not speaking to his neighbour. This is a typical figure known to all who have read *Round the World in Eighty Days*. For that book of adventure begins and ends, it will be remembered, in a club in Pall Mall.

Dinner, at half past five or six o'clock, consisted of mutton soup, a cutlet—only, due to Soyer the famous chef, it would be a cotelette Reform—roast partridge and greengage tart. Afterwards, it was a matter of smoking and reading the papers. For a moment we may consider that interior of Roman architecture, its arcaded court, the whiskered waiters and still more hirsute members, the solid bookshelves and chairs of solid mahogany. The frock coat was ubiquitous and a top hat hung on every hat peg in the hall. Each of these members, this was the symbol, had his chambers or his home, inviolate and unmentioned by him. But, now, having slipped into the clothes of this strange top-hatted individual, we ask for a cab and drive home slowly through the night. Pall Mall and St James's Street are deserted. Military tailors, Lock's the hatter, wine merchants, shops for sporting guns and for fishing tackle, line both sides of the street. It is a world of men. But there are lights at the corner, looking along Piccadilly. Down there lay the heart or lifeblood of the town. It was burning, burning, in a yellow incandescence. It had a million gas lamps and a million oil lamps.

In all this immense town, the big city of the world, there are few theatres and little gaiety. Down in that direction, the huge

---

* *La Vie Parisienne* was first published in 1937.

glass lamps flare outside the public houses; the prostitutes wait on the wet pavements, prostitutes in bonnets, straw bonnets that frame in the face and make it virginal. Gin and whisky are the vices of the town. But, of its squalor and immorality there is nothing left. No one is alive, now, to tell us. We have to guess at the saturnalia of the slums, at the blind drunk Saturday nights with every penny spent and nothing left for the home.

But, instead, our way leads down Knightsbridge or the new South Kensington. The streets of blinds and curtains come. There are long enfilades of stuccoed porches, all alike; so identical, indeed, that upon a Sunday morning, you can watch every family as it goes to church, or comes back for its Sunday luncheon. These churches, as frequent as the mosques of Cairo, or Stamboul, are of pattern Gothic, in grey stone, with no aim at beauty. To-night, the grey stone spire loses itself in fog. The first of the winter fogs is coming, and the church is dead and empty till next Sabbath. But, in view of to-morrow's foreign clime, we have a vision of this square in summer, on a morning when the chestnuts are in leaf with every candle lit, and lilac, dark red or white, blows above the railings. Then, there were striped awnings, carriage wheels flashed by like spokes of gold, the painted railings glittered. That was not long ago; but, now, it is darkening into winter. And here, at a porch, or any porch, we part, for we are to meet again in the morning. It is Paddington or Pimlico, Belgravia or South Kensington. It is all the same. They are all alike. But there is packing to do, for, to-morrow, we start early. To-night, if you open your bedroom window over London, there is a reddened sky, red as if with Bengal lights, and the roar of the town. And, now and again, from nearer, the clop clop clopping of a horse and cab. This only; and the tapping of the window blind.

In the morning, it is a drive of forty minutes to Charing Cross to take the train to Dover. We move out at a snail's pace on the iron bridge above the river; we see suburbs, apple orchards, and the oasthouse like a dovecot, a beehive, like a cowled kitchen of some medieval monastery standing in the parabolas among the hop poles—down the twinkling lines of them, for ever changing. Then, the white cliffs, two hours on the Channel, and the sandy dunes of Calais. And, after this, the endless plain of Picardy, Amiens and its smoky station, and, at last, Chantilly, green woods and viaducts, a château to one side or the other, Creil and more woods, and then allotment lands. This is a sign that Paris is near. There are market gardens, more houses; we cross a bridge above a street of little shops. The black walls of the Gare du Nord begin, black with soot and steam. They hide houses which are drab white and paper thin. Their thinness, in fact, gives a nervous horror of what the noise must be within, the din of the trains and depression of the thin, thin rooms. But the houses fall back to either side. A platform like a long thin spike advances. Its roof comes out to shelter us. The main roof opens and the train stands still. We have arrived in Paris.

It would be easy, now, after disputing with the porters, to drive into the lit streets to a hotel. But, instead, we change the station. It is the Gare St Lazare and no longer the Gare du Nord. There is reason for this, as there is for every folly. The platforms are crowded; but at the exit of the station, close to the booking office, a space is cleared. And it is here that the action begins.

At once, this mere transference from one station to another gives the unreality that we want. It is no longer a particular station but the pattern of arrival. Also, its translation out of reality on to the stage gives it a ghostly or intermediate existence in the sphere of time. It is the night of 31st October, 1866, the first performance of *La Vie Parisienne*; but, also, it is the summer day of that same year depicted in the action. In this way we have the freedom of reality and unreality. We both witness this Scene One in the station and are participants as well. Our comment or ornament to the action is, therefore, comparable to the music that will soon begin. And just as the plot was contrived for music, so must our adaptation travel to its own advantage from the one day to the other.

Bright sunshine, therefore, floods the platforms. Every moment more trains are bringing visitors to Paris. They come in from every direction, after all-night journeys which began a moment or two ago in the wings, from foreign capitals, from watering places, Vichy, Trouville, Biarritz, or from a quiet day or two, incognito, in the country. By the exit, and waiting for

24

an arrival, two young men, Bobinet and the Vicomte Raoul de
Gardefeu, pace up and down in front of each other, strutting in an exaggerated manner like a pair of turkey cocks.
They try to avoid each other's glances; and very soon it is
apparent that they have come to the Gare St Lazare in order
to meet the same person. Nor are they silent, but talk rapidly
in short, clipped phrases, pouring out their grievances. Nothing
could be more characteristic than their dress. Gardefeu, who is
the elder of the two, has the tall stove-pipe hat, the "cylindre",
pomaded hair, a monocle, a walking-stick with a tassel, and
wears the latest elegance of a short brown coat, trousers of the
same and a fancy waistcoat. Gardefeu is the man of the world
of forty, bien rusé, and deeply in debt. Bobinet, "petit Bob",
is very small and dapper, in a "cylindre", of course, and wearing a short coat that is like an Eton jacket. He is the little,
clipped poodle of the trottoir. Gardefeu has to hurry his steps
in order to keep up with his strut and patter. His voice is high
and shrill; and Gardefeu is the person who, in every instance,
will be the successful lover. It is just this that has happened.
This, indeed, is the trouble between them.

"*Bobinet* (à part). C'est M. Raoul de Gardefeu. Je ne le
salue pas, parcequ'il m'a joué un tour.

Gardefeu (à part). C'est le petit Bobinet. Il ne me salue pas,
parcequ'il nous est arrivé une aventure.

Bobinet. J'étais un peu plus que du dernier bien avec Blanche
Taupier. Tout Paris sait que j'ai été un peu plus que du dernier
bien avec Blanche Taupier.

Gardefeu. Blanche Taupier m'a aimé, comme elle sait aimer.
. . . Tout Paris sait que Blanche Taupier m'a aimé.

Bobinet. Un matin Blanche Taupier et moi demeurions alors
tous les deux à Ville d'Avray. . . . Blanche me dit: 'Petit Bob,
si nous invitions à dîner ton ami Gardefeu.'

Gardefeu. Blanche était à Ville d'Avray: elle m'écrit, 'Venez
demain à une heure, il n'y sera pas; en sortant de chez vous,
recommandez à votre domestique de dire que vous devez bien-
tôt rentrer.'

Bobinet. Je réponds: 'Soit, invitons Gardefeu.' Elle me dit:
'Va le chercher à Paris, il est chez lui à une heure; ne reviens
pas sans lui' . . . je pars.

Gardefeu. J'arrive à Ville d'Avray; je trouve Blanche; je ne trouve pas Bobinet; je lui dis: 'Comment avez-vous fait pour l'éloigner?'

Bobinet. J'arrive chez Gardefeu . . . son domestique me dit: 'Monsieur va rentrer à l'instant.' Il était une heure; j'attends, deux heures arrivent, puis trois heures: j'attendais toujours. . . .

Gardefeu. Blanche me répond: 'J'ai pris un moyen très simple . . . j'ai dit au petit Bob d'aller vous chercher à Paris, et de ne pas revenir sans vous.'

Bobinet. Enfin, à quatre heures, je me décide à m'en aller tout seul, je retourne à Ville d'Avray, et je le trouve installé.

Gardefeu. Vers cinq heures il est revenu; je lui ai dis, 'Tiens, pendant que tu étais chez moi, j'étais chez toi; c'est très drôle!'

Bobinet. Je ne l'ai pas trouvé drôle.

Gardefeu et Bobinet (ensemble). Et voilà pourquoi nous ne nous saluons pas.

L'Employé. Le train de Rambouillet, messieurs, le train de Rambouillet!"

At once the platform fills with passengers. It is now that the air becomes magical and charged with meaning. And, in a moment, the music will begin.

Métella comes walking past. She has been in the country with Gontran, her lover, no further than Fontainebleau or Chantilly—or was it Rambouillet?—summer names like bands playing under the trees, like drives in the forest, a picnic, a "Robinson", or a trip upon the river. She is twenty-five years old, with short fair hair quite different from the fashion, a little hat, a pillbox hat not covering her curls, a black close-fitting bodice and a rose pink crinoline, not bell-shaped, but straight and of the rigid sort, with simple lines like seams of the same black on it. In one hand she holds her green parasol. Her walk has great attraction and you can see the curious points of her boots, black kid boots they might be, and that she wears white stockings.

But Métella, leaning on the arm of Gontran, passes them by. She ignores both Gardefeu and Bobinet, though they have come to Gare St Lazare to meet her. "Connais pas!" is all she will say as they step forward; and then, when safely past them, she turns and smiles. But it is too late. It has this effect, though, that their quarrel turns into reconciliation. They quarrelled over

Blanche Taupier and, now, become reconciled when Métella pretends not to know them.

After this, the plot can unfold itself without interruption. The Chœur des Voyageurs starts off with the speed that only Offenbach can communicate to a chorus. Its rhythm is made out of the name of every nationality that comes to Paris and from the name of every station on the line. It quickens and quickens its pace until, at a turn, the orchestra begins the breathless and headlong tune to which its preliminary speed has been but the prelude. This is long and open and comes to the clension or gathering up of its ends when the brass instruments rally, as it were, and with short and stabbing blasts bring back the verse, sung, now, like a strophe, antiphonally, or to right hand and to left, in reserve of breath, till the chorus comes back again, more headlong than before, and the music ends like the conclusion of a dance in a coda of short, separated notes.

This Chœur des Voyageurs is, perhaps, the quickest and most brilliant of Offenbach's choruses. We write this, moreover, in full knowledge of many others and, not least, the wonderful military and concerted finales of *La Fille du Tambour Major*, written in 1879 just before Offenbach died; written, in fact, when his hand was cramped in agony from gout, and achieving in this finale to the last creation of his comic genius, a sort of apotheosis or return to pride of the French military spirit which pervades Offenbach, as it does Berlioz, or, indeed, most other patriotic Frenchmen of the Second Empire. Into this finale the Chant de Départ is introduced with most thrilling effect; but we must return to the Chœur des Voyageurs with no more than this mere allusion to that opera of Vivandières, of Zouaves, of Spahis, of Chasseurs, Cuirassiers, Tirailleurs, Grenadiers, a comic opera, in fact, which calls out for a splendid revival.

The first hearing, then, of this Chœur des Voyageurs is an experience that no one who loves music will forget. It is Offenbach at the height of his comic genius. But nothing in the world can be wholly original. Its superlative speed and dash are derived from Rossini, who, in his turn, was based as to this side of his genius upon the old Neapolitan school of opera buffa. Offenbach is, in this respect, the last flowering of that tradition.

It was founded upon the quick inflections, the lightning moods of the Roman or Neapolitan crowds. Mozart, in the *Nozze di Figaro*, neither achieves, nor seeks for, such street effects. It was Rossini, deriving from the school of Naples, who excelled in this direction. The opening chorus in the *Barbiere*, where the linkmen dispute for their tips with Count Almaviva, is an instance of this. But those persons who took the opportunity, three years ago, when *l'Italiana in Algeri* was revived for Mme Supervia, at Covent Garden, will have heard the finale to the first act of this comedy. It is, indeed, the best thing in all that opera which, from that moment, declines in inspiration, until, in the end, the plot becomes quite unintelligible and this piece which opens in such brilliance and sparkle finishes, in fact, not far from bathos. Nothing, though, could equal the speed and brio of this finale. It is as original in conception as any finale to a Haydn symphony; but with character and demonstrable purpose, or meaning, added to its speed and patter. Nothing, in this miracle of lightness, is inappropriate or unintelligible in sentiment. It would seem, from this finale, as if the coming act must be one of the wonders of music; but the genius of Rossini stops short of this and finds its limits in this final chorus to the first act. Half a century, and more, separates *l'Italiana in Algeri* from *La Vie Parisienne* and, perhaps, any convention or tradition must have that lapse of time in which to work if it is to exploit its possibilities to their full advantage. During that interval of fifty years it would be invidious to mention Donizetti, in his *Don Pasquale*, a comic opera which has more poetry, more beauty of phrase, than Rossini ever aspired to; and there are, as well, in minor excellence, the operas of Auber, *Fra Diavolo*, for example, but the culmination of Rossini in his comic genius is surely, as we have said, to be discovered in Offenbach. No one, now that another sixty years have elapsed, has the correct art of singing this music; nor is it possible, or even conceivable, to translate Meilhac and Halévy, his librettists, into any true resemblance to their original. It is to be remembered that his contemporaries found the serious, or lyrical side of Rossini fully equal to his comic genius. He was, to them, the master of all styles, serious and comic. The opera buffa was only a half, if that, of his genius. But Offenbach, with the assistance of his incomparable librettists, Meilhac and

The Shiant Isles, by W. Daniell

Cove in Malbay, by W. H. Bartlett

The Clett
Rock, by W.
Daniell

Halévy, concentrated his energies upon the comic side alone. Rossini, who seldom, if ever, found a good book to set was scarcely ever upheld in his inspiration by librettists who could make for him the opportunities in which he excelled. But the collaboration of Offenbach and his two inveterate assistants was able to produce success after success in ease and assurance. This is not to suggest that the genius of Offenbach, for a genius he was within his limits, is ever of the first order; but Offenbach is one of those lesser men, a Chabrier, a Johann Strauss, a Rossini, in fact, through whom more frequent delight is to be obtained than from their more austere betters. And, of this, there could be no more conspicuous truth than in the case of *La Vie Parisienne*.

We have, indeed, in another moment, as the plot proceeds, the entry of the Brazilian. This decidedly "rasta" personage, who has arrived this moment, by this train, in Paris, with his pockets full of gold to spend, is preceded by an elaborate orchestral introduction, or comment, à la Figaro in the *Barbiere*, which surpasses the "Largo al Factotum", that song with which Figaro comes upon the scene, in fantastic or personal effectiveness. It has set out to compete with Figaro's song; and it excels it. A moment later we have the unfolding of the whole plot with the arrival of the Baron de Gondremarck. He has come from his native Sweden bringing with him his young wife, the Baroness, and also a letter of introduction in his pocket addressed to Métella, whom he is most anxious to meet. This is the opportunity for which Gardefeu has been waiting and no sooner has he set eyes on the Baroness than he offers himself as guide to the Baron and his wife during their stay in Paris. He takes them quickly to his own flat or apartment which he indicates to them as the Grand Hotel, that new hotel on the Boulevard des Italiens, at which they had reserved rooms. They see through this deception; but Gardefeu promises to effect that introduction to Métella; and, as for the Baroness, she is more than content to have Gardefeu for her guide while her husband attends to the many business matters which have brought him to Paris. In the meantime, before they leave us, and while we are still at the Gare St Lazare, we have a trio of Gardefeu and the Baron and Baroness upon the attractions of Paris.

4   29

Her words are:

Je veux, moi, dans la capitale
Voir les divas qui font fureur:
Voir la Patti dans Don Pasquale,
Et Teresa dans Le Sapeur.

The lines that we have quoted convey, in the space of a breath, the whole glitter of the contemporary scene. But now, the act ends with another chorus, a finale, of frenzied gaiety: "Tous les étrangers vers toi s'élancent, Paris!" and the curtain falls.

We will, now, descend into this double or multiple world, of which we have the temporary liberty, while it lasts. We go, in fact, from the stage into the audience. This first night has attracted to itself a public that is as varied and cosmopolitan as those figures we have left. In the stalls and boxes are sitting the Duc de Mouchy, Prince Murat, Khalil-bey, the Duke of Hamilton, Pietri, the Dukes of Sagan, Richelieu, Cossé-Brissac, the brothers Ezpeleta, Prince Troubetzkoi, Emile Augier, de Gontaut-Biron, Vacquerie, Daru, Narischkine, the Marquis de Caux, Nigra, Camille Doucet, etc., etc., . . . and Cora Pearl, Leonide Leblanc, Silly, Anna Deslions, Leontine Massin, Caroline Letessier, Giulia Barucci, Constance Rézuche, Lucile Mangin, Marguerite Bellangé, Adèle Courtois, and others.* The import of these names comes from their association, in turn, but omitting those that are less interesting, with the marriage of the first-named Duc de Mouchy with Princess Anna Murat, great-niece of Napoleon I, a wedding that took place less than a year before this, while Princess Anna Murat survived until 1924 to be mentioned by Marcel Proust; with her father, Prince Murat, the son of King Joachim and Caroline the sister of Napoleon, who was born at Naples in 1801, while his father was King, and was brought up there, who emigrated to America, after Waterloo, and was postmaster for many years at Tallaharsee, in Florida, who married a great niece of Washington and, returning to Paris after the coup

* This audience, with the exception of Cora Pearl, was present at the first performance of *Orphée aux Enfers* by Offenbach, Meilhac and Halévy, given in the following year, 1867, at the Bouffes-Parisiennes, cf. *Offenbach*, by Louis Schneider, Paris, 1923, p. 137. They had come to see Cora Pearl as Cupid on the stage. This public we have repeated for the present occasion, excepting that we have placed Cora Pearl among the audience.

30

d'état, was recognized by Napoleon III as of imperial blood, had his debts of two million francs paid, was granted a generous allowance from the civil list and, surviving the fall of the Empire, died in 1878, being the father of the Duchesse de Mouchy, just mentioned; in the case of Khalil-bey with the extravagances of the Egyptian Khedives, the shuttered berlins and daumonts in which the ladies of the harem drove through the streets of Cairo, the opera house with boxes guarded by gilded lattices and a posse of black eunuchs, while music of Verdi was played to the orders of the Khedive Ismail; with the Duke of Hamilton, grandson of William Beckford, son of Princess Marie of Baden and cousin, therefore, of Napoleon III, for whom Napoleon had, in 1865, in the year previous to this night, restored the Dukedom of Châtellerault granted to his ancestor, who was guardian to Mary, Queen of Scots, by Henri II, in 1548, this young man with the auburn curls and florid face being a prodigious rake, the patron of the Café Riche and the Maison Dorée and host at supper parties beyond number given for the ladies of whom we have written the names in midst of this paragraph; then there is Pietri, an Italian cousin of the Emperor; the Duc de Sagan, descendant of Talleyrand, inheritor of a principality in Prussia through his mother the Princess Dorothea, the last of the family of Biron, Princes of Courland, Semigalle and Sagan, who had their origin through the favours of the Empress Elizabeth of Russia; the Duc de Richelieu, descended from the sister of the Cardinal, a youth of twenty, kinsman to that émigré duc de Richelieu who founded Odessa and was the ablest man in the Russia of Alexander I, kinsman, also, to the Duc de Richelieu, who, born in 1696, was a page to Louis XIV, and two years before his death, in 1788, married a girl of fourteen that she might have a state pension as his widow, this woman, in her turn, living to be so old that she was presented to Napoleon III and Eugénie at the Tuileries, while her relation, the young man whom we are discussing, married a niece of the poet Heine, who was known personally to the writer; the brothers Ezpeleta, of whom we know nothing, though their name, which must be Basque, suggests the silver mines or ranches of Mexico or the Argentine; Cossé-Brissac, Troubetzkoi, de Gontaut-Biron, Narischkine, the Marquis de Caux, husband of Adelina Patti, names

31

which evoke faded elegancies, shadows of the "cylindre", the stove-pipe hat, curious details of their shoes, so different from ours, their opera cloaks, their glasses, their ties and waistcoats, their carriages waiting for them till the play was ended, their bedrooms, their nightwear, our curiosity as to all these things being aroused as we watch them in the theatre, or in the foyer during the interval, persons who because they are just so far removed from us in time, where our grandparents could touch their hands, are further from our reach or knowledge than the figures in more distant centuries. Also, these men are in the near pattern of ourselves, they travelled by steamer and by railway; their clothes are but little different; they are even so near to us that we could see the family resemblance between them and their descendants; and could, in fact, by searching our memories, think of some person to mention to them whom we knew and whom they would remember. Talking in this trivial interval between two acts of the play, none of these persons, had we this gift of immortality in our possession, would have the seriousness to listen, it might be. And yet, if drawn aside and convinced by some proof or token, what is there that anyone in this thronged hall or foyer would not want to know! Not alone the fortunes of his own descendants, but news of his friends and loves, how their end came, and news of the living; what time it was:—not, as looking at a clock or watch, but as though finding an old newspaper in a drawer and searching, at once, through its headlines for its date, as though this person, or any and all of them, knew beyond the futility of the moment and that our interruption came only from a further halt or station in time and not from the ends of it, where we find the truth.

The thought of such a mission as this gives a curious thrill or tingling to the skin. All these persons who are whiling away this interval, talking till the next act begins, are in our power, to be told their fate. Not that their characters are pleasant. There is hardly a person here whom we would choose for a friend. They are the "hommes du monde"; and their only appeal to our interest lies in their elegances and their associations. Those who could recognize Leonide Leblanc, Silly, Anna Deslions, Leontine Massin, Caroline Letessier, Giulia Barucci, Constance Rézuche, Lucile Mangin, Marguerite

32

Bellangé, Adèle Courtois, while they were sitting in the stalls or boxes would know them, here, in the interval. The hetairae of the Empire were of a type to themselves as can be seen in the unflattering photographs which are all that is left of them. It is, even, an extraordinary thought to consider the hopeless search that we might make for their graves. These women, who were so well known in their time, are not to be discovered in death. Many of them would be buried under their real names: others, retiring in poverty or riches from the scene, would take another name and die in it. And not only their deaths are interesting, in this sense; but, also, the start of their careers: the first betrayal, and how soon another followed on it. But the beginnings and ends to so many lives of pleasure must not interrupt this heyday or flowering of their beauty. And it is in the women that we see the difference. Their dress is as elaborately improbable as in any print, by Utamaro, of the "green mansions". The crinoline, which had gone out of fashion with the Empress Eugénie and her Court, two years before this, in 1864, was still worn in greater fantasy than ever by demi-mondaines. This gave them a hieratic distinction and made them, as indeed they were, the priestesses of a cult to be known, at once, by this insignia. Perhaps, under this general listing of their names, we may allow imagination to play upon the diversity of attractions. Leonide Leblanc and Leontine Massin, for instance, two names which, together, have a distinct and travestied echo in our ears, in parody of a great choregraph of our time, these, in their names of Leonide and Leontine, must represent the maturity of that visual moment.* In their persons they are that epoch and none other. They must be seen in

---

* These names, so typical of their time, are to be compared with those of their equivalents, a decade later, after the fall of the Empire. For the hundredth performance of *La Fille du Tambour Major* a supper party was given by Offenbach, on 7th March, 1880, at the Hotel Continental. The guests included, as well as the actresses of the piece, Rose Thé, Humann, Humberta, Bade, Bertha Legrand, Becker, Rivero, Ghinassi, Lavigne and also, it is only fair to add, Leonide Leblanc, by then somewhat of a veteran. With her exception, these are the names of a new period tending towards the age of Toulouse-Lautrec. After the supper an orchestra played a quadrille on motifs from Offenbach's operas, but he was too ill and feeble to recognize all the tunes. He had written more than a hundred operas and operettas. Offenbach died a few months later, on 4th October, 1880. *Les Contes d'Hoffmann* was produced after his death, 10th February, 1881. *La Goulue, Jane Avril, Nini patte en l'air,* were the favourites of the fin de siècle, the period of Toulouse-Lautrec and of Beardsley. They are removed by two generations from Leonide Leblanc and Leontine Massin.

33

red velvet mantles trimmed with black lace, in black tulle dresses with gold lace, in caracos of red satin studded with gigantic steel buttons, or hung with cut glass, or wearing the Diana bodice which left one shoulder uncovered. They are to be thought of, naked, as the Olympia of Manet; but with figures pinched in by their corsets, and little, or Celestial feet as if still wearing the boots of black kid which were the fashion. And their bodies, according to the same convention which makes a dancer in the wings much smaller than her height upon the boards, are little and puny taken out of the great cages of the crinoline. Giulia Barucci, an Italian, is the contadina of the vineyard, but a blonde Italian; Adèle Courtois, another name of the day, not beautiful, but dressed as no one else could dress; Anna Deslions, famous for her figure; Marguerite Bellangé, to whom the Emperor drove, in a closed berlin, passing the afternoons of a year or two ago with this languid, or Creole beauty; Silly, a shape of fantasy or artificiality, a griffon bruxellois, so small as hardly to be considered, but with every artifice of veil and parasol, a drive with whom in her carriage through the Bois must have had the poetry of l'Escarpolette of Fragonard; and, most of famous all, Emma Elizabeth Crouch, i.e. Cora Pearl.

This daughter of a wandering and drunken Irish musician, who wrote one beautiful song, Kathleen Mavourneen, could never learn to speak French correctly. Her Cockney accent was her charm. She has a round face, a skin of dazzling innocence, and matchless teeth. Her hair is blonde and cut like a little girl's. When she opens her mouth she may say anything under the sun and is completely and absolutely shameless. Her appearance of a virginity which is too good to be true, which has been trained in every viciousness, but the final and essential one, until the last moment, which is to be the prerogative of every fresh lover that she takes, this is her fascination. A depraved and arrested childhood which has still preserved its youthful health and high spirits, has been the means by which she has grown rich. She has a luxurious house hung with silks and tapestries, an onyx bath, and the finest horses and carriages in Paris. Her pointed naïveté in all her dealings disconcerts and conquers men. She is twenty-three years old, with nearly ten years' experience behind her. Cora Pearl may have appeared

34

as English to her French or cosmopolitan lovers, but we have no evidence as to the impression she produced upon an Englishman. To our ears it is probable that she would have lost her nationality without assuming another, as if, in our day, she had lived for a long time in Hollywood. She spoke French, as we have said, with an atrocious intonation, while her English was a little in front of, or behind, her understanding, being no longer her second nature but something, once learned, and now forgotten. Since the age of fourteen, according to her memoirs, which are not necessarily apochryphal, she had earned her living. Before she was twenty she had become established on the scale in which we now find her. The diamonds upon her neck and wrists are in proof of this. She seems to shed forth an aura or glamour of dissipation, like that given out—and there is no doubt of this—by Gaby Delys. It is, in part, physical but also, she has a quality which makes her the centre of attention. Her career is neither entirely her own fault, nor that of her pursuers. She was created for this purpose, and to this end. It is as if she were intended for it, as others are impelled, in spite of every obstacle, to act, or to play the violin. The decrees of providence have set her apart and given to her, in so doing, an evil radiance which is only in variation upon the talents bestowed on others. It is probable that the Duke of Hamilton, perhaps accompanied by a friend or the trainer of his race horses, were the only Englishmen in this audience, but Cora Pearl, who may have been born in either Dublin or Exeter, will have spoken to them, if speak she did, in the same atrocious French in which she talked to all comers. In public, here in the foyer, as well as in private, she was surrounded by a circle. We were told, only a few days before writing this, of an old gentleman who, were he alive now, would be about ninety years old. He used to describe how, one Sunday morning, Prince Paul Murat called and said he would take him and his little brother for a walk in the Bois. When they had started he said the Bois was not very interesting and he would take them to see a friend of his instead. So, in their sailor suits, gloves, sticks and "melons" (bowler hats) they called at a large house and were shown into a salon, where Cora Pearl was lying on a sofa, the focus of a hemicycle of diplomatists, senators and academicians, all seated with their chins leaning on gold knobbed walking-sticks, their yellow gloves placed in the "cylindres" at their sides, upon the floor. The Prince presented his "jeunes amis", M. Alfred L. and M. Alphonse L. and they joined the hemicycle. When they returned home their mother asked if the Bois had been nice and whether they had seen any animals, to which their reply was "Mais non, Maman, beaucoup plus que ça: une femme toute nue!" This story, which could only be true of the period in which it occurred, for, if young children had been offered similar adventures in the time, say, of Louis XV, the nude woman might be lying on the couch but there would not be the hemicycle of diplomatists, senators and academicians, gives us the apotheosis of the Empire. It is the painted ceiling of that gilded time. Heavy draperies, the velvet curtains of Garnier's Opéra, descend from the cornice. This naked goddess, and it is necessary to think once more of the Olympia of Manet, has the curves and contours which present taste does not admire. She is sunning herself, like a lioness, and is silent and impels silence on those around her. This is not the nudity, as now, of an outward and athletic body, nor the nudities of Tiepolo or Boucher who could ride without restraint upon the clouds. Instead, it is a secret thing to be unveiled, unwrapped. When it is finished, like the lioness who has performed her trick, the silence ends. Her maid brings in her light and silken underclothes. It is the beginning for the hoop or crinoline. Every hand reaches for its "cylindre", and the morning's done. We can think of this as we see her, now, surrounded, as ever, by men who wear their top hats, their "cylindres", in this interval and are as difficult, indeed, to separate from their stove-pipe hats as the Chinaman from his pigtail, or the Bedouin from his beard. And now, in its turn, this interval is ending. The theatre attendants announce the dying gaslights and the raising of the curtain.

When there is so much to claim the attention, alike on the stage and in the audience, it is no longer necessary to follow every detail of the action. Often before it has been with a wrench, a breaking or rupture of reality, that the real world is left for the world of artifice. The first spoken words, when the curtain goes up, are ever a disillusionment. It is not so, or never to the same degree, if music is the medium between the true world and the false. But already, the orchestra is playing. It is effecting this transition as we pass down the row of stalls to take our seats. We are being transposed into the world that we left so short a time ago. The Baron de Gondremarck, Gardefeu, Bobinet, and the strange figures, the "fantoches" that surround them, become the reality that we are watching. At once, we are plunged into an intimacy with their actions.

The Baron and Baroness are settled comfortably in the apartment of Gardefeu, which it still pleases them to pretend is the Grand Hotel. The Baroness, with Gardefeu, as her guide, has entered upon an orgy of shopping. Gloves, shoes and hats begin to arrive. There is a delightful duet, sung by the shop assistants who have come with their parcels. This introduces the character of Gabrielle, the gantière, to whom Offenbach has given music in foretaste of other lovely moments that are to come. It is at such times that Offenbach approaches near, again, to Rossini, as will be plain to those who remember the little song in the third act of the *Barbiere* which is sung by the old housekeeper. This is often omitted in performance; but it is a small masterpiece of melody and characterization. Only, there, it is an aged character who is portrayed: here, it is a young girl and her song is tender and gay; in fact, it is her personality and appearance, even when the music is heard alone and without her. This is a true case of portraiture in music. Her air is the portrait of her; and this is a faculty which has been given to but few composers of music.

But this beautiful air, thrown so liberally to the audience, and then forgotten, is followed, in a moment or two, by the famous duo of the Baron and Gardefeu, a duo which has been cast in the form of a bolero. Its theme is the Baron's letter of introduction to Métella: "Portez la lettre à Métella." The Baron sings of his austere upbringing in Sweden, and the coda or quickening of the verse comes with the mention of Métella: "Je veux m'en fourrer, fourrer jusquelà." There is nothing Spanish in this bolero, unless it is a sort of fantasy of elaboration, a note of melancholy turning into the delights of expectation. This is, indeed, that part of this comic opera which is most full of inspiration, not the frenzied dances and drinking songs of the orgy which is to come. Here, there is song after song which is an independent creation, a poetical entity, living

37

within the bounds of its own imaginative existence and, if torn from its context, still surviving as the comment of a great satirist upon the peculiar times in which he lived and, also, as a work of art in itself. Such is the song of the Colonel's widow, sung by Gabrielle, an absurdity of a really high order of invention and a tribute, in this, to the intelligence and quickness of wit of its audience. No public of fools could appreciate this.

But there are better things to come. For now we have the "Couplets de la Parisienne", sung by Gabrielle. The talents of Offenbach, at their most copious and fecund, had that felicity of melody leading into melody which is characteristic of Mozart. Also, the mere physical length of his harmonic genius is a thing remarkable by itself. Nowhere is this more manifest than in the "Couplets de la Parisienne". The verse, which is a caricature, but an affectionate one, of feminine conceits and foibles, dressing, shopping, promenading, then turns into an extraordinary picture of the times. It gives us the noise and movement of the crinoline as they are portrayed nowhere else in art. And, not only that, but why the crinoline was worn, what its charm was in the eyes of those who wore it, how it felt to wear a crinoline, in what lay the fascination that could be achieved by it, all expressed in the foaming, bustling, trembling advance of it, in the progress of the tune, going forward by little rapid steps with the tap tapping of her shoes upon the pavement. If the "Couplets de la Parisienne" were described as having the elegance and fragility of a figure of Chelsea or Meissen porcelain it would give only a part of the quality of this song. A Meissen figure is a china marionette but with only one pose or movement, fixed until the figure is broken. It is a dancer in the end or attitude of her dance. But, here, it is the figure in movement, a living body, and the only work of art in which the crinoline of the 'sixties is really portrayed. That it should possess those qualities that have been named is thrown into the isolation that it deserves when we think of the typical things of that period, of the brassy coils of Meyerbeer, an orchestration like a great chandelier in blaze, the marble and gilt and ormolu of the opera house of Garnier; or, nearer home, the Ruskinian Gothic that was to give us the black and yellow Natural History Museum, South Kensington, or the red brick of Keble College, Oxford. The "Couplets de la Parisienne" is a song that, in silence and when it is not heard, stands under a glass shade. When that is lifted from it, the figure comes to life. Trembling its flounces, the cage or crinoline comes on. Nothing so artificial has ever been imagined. And the sound of it creates the person who is in this cage. It is what is hidden, so elaborately hidden, that is the fascination of the crinoline. We hear the tap tapping of her black kid boots; and, since this gives her no ankles, must think of her white stockings, the flashing white stems of them seen once in a dozen paces, and hope for a tilting of her crinoline. For it can lift like the glass shade itself. Then we shall see her twin knees against the rills or foamings of that huge white shell, the living thing hidden in the crinoline.

The beauties of *La Vie Parisienne*, such as this song that we have described, exist, side by side, with the grotesque or "fantoches" of the piece. These are conceived of in a vein of invention to which the only parallel is in the caricature statues of Dantan. One or two of these, that, for instance, of Paganini, are familiar to most people; but a glance through the Musée Dantan, a book of woodcuts in silhouette of admirable execution, depicting most of the figures carved by Dantan of which replicas were sold at his studio, will reveal live characters who are the exact embodiment of the grotesques of Offenbach. In fact, this nearly forgotten sculptor, Jean Pierre Dantan (1800–1869), is the nearest equivalent to this aspect of Offenbach. Dantan, the inventor of this genre of caricature sculpture, exists in a solitude by himself, and is the only person who ever practised the art. And so it is with Offenbach; he has no parallel in music, where this line of grotesque invention is concerned. It begins, soon after the opening of the piece, with the song of the Brazilian and is, by this stage in the evening, well advanced upon its course. But the full play of his "fantoches" does not come until the next act so that we leave our analysis of their effect until that moment comes.

In the meantime, we have that exquisite lyrical invention, the "letter song" of Métella. This is the moment when she reads aloud the letter of introduction sent round to her by the Baron de Gondremarck. It is in the writing of Frascata, who was her lover last summer. It is tempting to quote a few lines

39

of this beautiful thing; but we must be content with its opening words: "Vous souvient-il, ma belle?": Such is the start of the "letter song".

The operatic cliché of reading aloud a love letter has nearly always, for some reason, an inspiring effect upon the composer. It is a convention like the serenade, or the music lesson. In fact, it is the serenade, not as sung, but in its reception by the person to whom it is addressed. Perhaps the letter song in the *Nozze di Figaro* is the most lovely thing in the whole of that opera! But, in intention, it is not quite the same as this song of Métella. Countess Almaviva is telling Susanna what to write down in the letter. The song, which is flawless in shape, has even the rhythm of someone saying aloud what is to be written down. But it is at least, and this is our purpose in the comparison, in the feminine and not the masculine psychology. It is, thus, that women think of their lovers; in a different mode therefore, from that of the serenade. So it is with the "letter song" of Métella. The greatest artists, in their lyrical moments, possess this power of changing their sex. Shakespeare, in *Antony and Cleopatra*, would appear to be in love himself, with first the one and then the other. This is the gift, also, of the great novelist. Where Madame Bovary is concerned, it is no longer Flaubert but this woman with whom he has completely identified himself, as we have evidence in the symptoms of poisoning that he developed, when writing of her death. The "letter song" is, therefore, shall we say, in intention the opposite or passive to a serenade. But, here, in the song of Métella, we have first of all, in sentiment, the feelings and memories of Frascata, her lover of last summer, upon which is imposed the tender but only half-regretful mood of Métella. Gardefeu and Bobinet have occurred since then, if not before; there has been Gontran, on whose arm we saw her at the Gare St Lazare; and, soon there will be Gondremarck. Métella cannot be expected, therefore, to feel sentimental about Frascata. At the same time she has pleasant memories of the summer they spent together; and the words of Frascata are certainly strong in sentiment; he is unhappy, as well, at being so far from Paris. The half-sentiment of a moment is often more moving than a burst of tears. It is genuine and felt; and is not hysterical or adolescent. So this "letter song" is serious and considered. It is an instance in which Offenbach exhibits the extraordinary powers that were his. This composer of more than a hundred operettas could achieve moments, like the "letter song", which have the purity, the clean jet of inspiration, of Mozart. This is no audacious comparison to anyone who knows enough Rossini to compare him with Mozart, and enough of Offenbach to think of him as close to the comic genius of Rossini. The *Contes d'Hoffmann* is in vindication of this coupling of their names. And it is more than probable that Mozart, himself, could we have seen it, would prefer this opera to a "music-drama" that lasts for four evenings and has never a light or lyrical moment.

At the same time, it is to be understood that we do not attribute to the composer any deliberate method by which he has reached the results that we have described. It is a matter of instinctive technique, like the processes by which poetry is written. No one can suppose that the choice, for instance, of vowel sounds in poetry is undertaken upon any principle but that of inspiration, that is to say, of subconscious creation. The writing of such music as the "letter song" must very nearly correspond to the composition of a lyric in poetry. The time for discussion is after it is finished and not while it is being written.

This opera reaches its moment of beauty in the "letter song" of Métella. The rondo fulfils its shape and, once again, there comes the introduction, the first few lines of the verse: "Vous souvient-il, ma belle?"; and it is done. But, as a curtain to this act, we have the Tyrolienne of Gabrielle. This is in parody of a German waltz. It begins with a slow schühplatter dance, a mountain waltz meant for the stamping of heels. The entire company joins in this, and they sing words of an inspired silliness to which the music could not be more appropriate.

Then, always with Gabrielle to lead them, the tune becomes a yodelling song. This is orchestrated in masterly fashion so that, as a parody, it is really thrilling in effect. And it becomes frenzied at the end, where the waltz turns and turns like a great wheel in midst of the yodelling. The coda comes, with everyone shouting "Ohé, oha", and the orchestra spinning its circles to the fortissimo of every instrument. It has a pompous and almost military termination and then the curtain falls, falling, indeed, upon this brass band waltz of waltzes.

41

The scene ends, in fact, upon a high pitch of fantasy. The châlet summerhouses are invoked, and the absurdities of the Tyrolese beer garden. It is a parody of diabolical force and adroitness; a humour, to which other humours of comic operas, before and since, are as the films of Walt Disney in colour compared to those that are in black and white. This parody of the Tyrolese mountains has every fire of colour. It is the most exciting, and most absurd, curtain that could be imagined. The strains of that yodelling waltz linger in the ears. Nothing could be more appropriate to come before the orgy scene that will be played in a few minutes' time. Its sardonic strength is in anticipation, as it were, to this banqueting or orgy that is to follow.

And now, during this interval, let us come out of the theatre into the street. We will treat this pause or rest like the relâche upon the stage. It will give us the day in Paris.

When we get into the air it is a fine morning in May or June. The play, you will remember, was in October; but its action was in the summer. The characters of the piece, and those men and women whom we have mentioned in the audience, are not the only persons to be met with. That would be to say that the world of the footlights was no more than a gigantic mirror reflecting the same figures. If that were so, we have been, in a sense, the audience of both bodies; and it is, once more, in the quality of witness that, bearing the time and date in mind, as though to set our watches, we walk out into the daylight.

Or it is the person who left London for Paris who has come back. For it is necessary to point that contrast. The morning air must have the smell of Paris. This is another mode of life. It is the Imperial capital in splendour.

From the Grand Hotel, where Gondremarck and the Baroness think themselves, or pretend, to be, we come out into the street, it is as easy as to leave the theatre, in the entr'acte, for a breath of air. And now we are ourselves, looking with curious eyes; and yet it is the authentic brilliance, of sunlight on the "cylindre" and the crinoline. But the word "cylindre" is to be disliked. It is the stove-pipe hat, the tall top hat of the Emperor, worn by all classes, and in symbol, to ourselves, of the age of smoke, of the chimney and the funnel. The buildings of the capital are the same: it is the persons who are different. And not only the persons, but every detail of their lives.

We first see it in a barber's shop. This has wax busts, immaculately suave. There are weeping whiskers, falling in two drifts below the ears; the Dundreary, but redeemed and made Parisian; and the Imperial, beeswaxed to a point and with pointed moustachios, so exaggerated that they might be the antennae of an insect. The chief part of a hairdresser's work, moreover, lay in the making of wigs and toupés. No one would admit to baldness. Perhaps the daily life of a fashionable hairdresser would give us a characteristic picture of the time. His clients were not only the "hommes du monde" of the boulevard; but, also, we should go with him into the ugly houses of the day, the newer and richer the more ugly, where hair was curled or wigs tied on before the mirror, catching in this manner a hundred details of those lives that are lost to us. For who is there to tell us of these things! Even any one of those men mentioned in the theatre, at the moment of his leaving his house or apartment for the play, would be standing in the doorway about to step into his carriage, and the exaggerated height of him, wearing the inevitable tall hat, is as distant from us, though so near in time, as the mitred priest in a temple of Isis or Osiris. The moment has gone, and it will never come again.

But now we are at the Tuileries, named like the shining of light upon tiled roofs and turrets. It has lately been joined by the Emperor to the Louvre and stretches its over-loaded fronts into eternity. Within, it is said to be dark and uncomfortable, with long corridors, windowless and lit by lamps. The decoration is in official styles and without interest. But it is out of this mingling of all the worst tastes that Napoleon III and Eugénie come forth into that world of silks and silk hats, of crinolines and carriages, that is our present interest. And the Cent Gardes à Cheval, at least, are of this time and none other. As their name implies, they form a squadron of a hundred men, drawn from the cavalry regiments. They are quartered at 37, rue de Bellechasse, in a building which had been a convent and now (1937) belongs to the Ministry of War. In this house their Colonel had an apartment which he seldom used, and the unmarried officers had their quarters which were furnished from the garde-meuble. Their mess was a big room decorated in white and gold, where they were served on silver plate by a maître d'hôtel and servants in livery. Every morning, a maréchal des logis, two brigadiers and a dozen men, under the command of an officer, went on guard at the Tuileries. Until 1858, an officer of the Cent Gardes slept at night outside the door of the Emperor's bedroom. Their full dress uniform consisted of a sky-blue tunic with red and gold epaulettes, white breeches, high boots, a breastplate, and the helmet designed by Eugène Lami, with a white horsetail and a red plume. The Cent Gardes only rendered military honours to the Emperor, the Empress, the Prince Imperial and foreign royalties. During the State Balls at the Tuileries, a Cent Garde stood motionless, like a statue, on every step of the great staircase. This immobility was, indeed, the subject of many jokes and much bewilderment. They were chosen specially for their great height belonging in this, as it were, to an extinct kind of Frenchman. Most of them wore the imperial and the great moustaches of the Emperor and were gigantic effigies, therefore, of the deity in little.

It might be said that no palace, of whatever architecture, is to be considered in the true picture of itself without a mention of the uniforms that brightened its doorways. But, in the case of the Cent Gardes, this is of more than usual importance. The Tuileries has gone, and the Cent Gardes have gone with it. They were the corps d'élite of the revived Imperial Guard. In this respect they were one of the sights of the capital. The Baron de Gondremarck, in that legendary North from which he came, from the remote province, it is likely of Dalecarlia, will have heard of the Cent Gardes and have gone to watch them, on his first day in Paris, as they mounted guard. I remember, myself, long accounts of them from my old tutor, and his remark that their absence from Paris, after the siege of 1870, and the destruction of the Tuileries, left it no longer a capital.

But the Place du Carrousel, the interior square formed by the Tuileries and the Louvre, was the scene of the military reviews of the Empire. This custom had been inaugurated by by the great Napoleon. It was in the Place du Carrousel that he reviewed the Old Guard who, in order to take up their

positions in the square, had to march under the triumphal arch
of Percier and Fontaine, which was then surmounted by the
bronze horses of St Mark's. These horses, which had formerly
adorned the triumphal arches of Nero and of Trajan, in Rome,
and were, then, taken by Constantine to decorate his new
capital, whence, after a thousand years they were removed to
Venice by Doge Enrico Dandolo, had been brought to Paris
by Napoleon. They were returned to Venice after Waterloo.
Their place above the Arc du Carrousel was occupied by a
poor copy; but, in other respects, since the joining of the
Tuileries to the Louvre, this centre of the capital had a more
splendid effect under Napoleon III than in the time of Napoleon I. A review of the Imperial Guard under Napoleon III,
with the veterans of the First Empire grouped round him, had
the most imposing effect. It was the sort of military occasion
for which music should have been commissioned from Berlioz.
This was not done: but, at least, the military music that Berlioz had heard in his childhood, half a century before, under
the great Napoleon, sounded forth again from the massed
bands. The Chant du Départ was to be heard, and that fanfare
with which the Emperor appeared to his troops. It is described
by Balzac, who, also, remembered it. "A son aspect, les tam-
bours battirent aux champs, et les musiques débutèrent par une
phrase dont l'expression guerrière deploya tous les instruments,
depuis la grosse caisse jusqu'à la plus douce des flûtes. A leurs
sons belliqueux les âmes tressaillirent, les drapeaux saluèrent,
les soldats portèrent les armes par un mouvement unanime et
régulier; des mots de commandement se répétèrent comme des
échos, et des cris de vive l'Empereur furent poussés par la
multitude enthousiasmée . . . l'Empereur resta immobile sur
son cheval. . . . Aucun trait de son visage ne s'émut." These
scenes, if they lacked the imperishable glamour of their original had, now, even increased in military splendour. It would
be a delight to us to attempt some description of the Imperial
Guard, as they appeared under Napoleon III, in the period
at which military uniforms attained to their most far-reaching
lengths of inappropriate fantasy. No fewer than thirty-three
battalions of infantry and thirty-seven squadrons of cavalry, a
total of some forty thousand men, were comprised in the
Imperial Guard. But we must be content with no more than a

mention of the Cuirassiers of the Guard, the Hussars, the Grenadiers, bearded and aproned, and the Zouaves. These last will be remembered—shorn of their splendour, but still dressed in their baggy red trousers and armed with their excessively long and thin bayonets, bayonets, if I remember rightly, that were three sided and like a long skewer—before the War. They were the ordinary Zouaves of the line; their equivalent in the Imperial Guard were that much more ornate and fantastic in finish; brave men, who perished nearly to a man in the fearful war of 1870.

But, if this masculine side of sartorial fantasy is insisted upon, however lightly, its equivalent in feminine vanity was of a variety that defies description. This is to be seen in any fashion plate of the period; while the better ones, such as those drawn by Compte Calix for *Les Modes Parisiennes*, or those of Jules David in *Le Moniteur de la Mode*, form an extraordinary panorama, or a promenade, as it were, by the side of romantic summerhouses; at the foot of the cliffs, near the bathing-machines which a horse is dragging into the shallows; under the sides of the mountains, close to a village of Savoyard châlets; in an ivied arbour whence the turrets of the château can be seen; in a church, at the première baptême; or in a box at the opera, where the attention of all is turned in our direction and the lorgnette is in universal use. Such are the fashion plates; seldom justified, perhaps, in actual fact, but presenting the possibilities, at least, in their most attractive aspect. There is a whole repertory of poetry, even, an "Elegy of Dead Fashion", composed out of the names of the materials employed, "Blue Louise, gris bois, grenate, myrtle green", to quote one line from this enchanted past. But that world, indeed, is of a richness of imagination that is incredible. Nothing more far fetched or remote from reality has ever been created into fact than these fashion plates that are still to be bought for a few pennies on the book-stalls. And the truth or interpretation of these visions is to be seen in the paintings, by Boudin, of the Empress Eugénie on the sands of Trouville. Her hooped red crinoline is wider than those worn by her ladies and is looped up from the ground to show the black boots, the black kid boots of the 'sixties. It is as if Eugénie in her magenta crinoline is going to dig upon the sands. But, as well, we have a description of her on the sands at Biarritz, only a few miles from her native Spain, an account by a malevolent diplomat who pretended that he mistook Eugénie and her ladies for a group of the wives or mistresses of some Spanish matadors on their way to a fight at Bayonne, the point of his pretence being their scarlet crinolines and the crimson paint upon their faces.

To return to Trouville, there is more than one painting by Boudin of this subject. Sometimes the Empress and her ladies are looking out to sea in what must have been an exquisite ennui for, at Trouville, there was nothing, absolutely nothing to do. The ladies were, as it were, imprisoned in the sea air by the caprice of their mistress. They hold parasols over their heads; or are armed with long, thin walking-sticks. In another picture, the group comes drifting towards us over the sands. They appear to be floating in their short, or country crinolines and are walking far out at the margin of the sea. We wonder, bird-like, what footmarks they will leave upon the wet sands. And their crinolines, seen against that emptiness of sea and sky, have the sharp unexpectedness of an image in Rimbaud's *Les Illuminations*. But the genius of Rimbaud was too impatient to dwell for long in a world of fabulous elegance. His poetry has only the hint of this and no more. Perhaps that world lay in wait for a wandering and feminine touch to seek out its colours again and give them life.

It is tempting to dwell for a little longer among these elegancies of Compte Calix, or of Jules David, who are always drawn, two together, in a pair. White doves are ever in a pair, and so, too, are the milkwhite oxen of Tuscany, working among the vines, by the banks of blue iris. Their dual presence gives these elegantes a sort of virginity of reputation and, also allows an echo of their conversation to reach our ears. The topic is fashionable intelligence. It is more easy, in the light of this, to enter after them into the shops that we read of in the monthly summary or causerie of *Les Modes Parisiennes*. We hear of dresses worn recently by the Duchesse de B. . . .—or, sometimes, such a person is actually named in full—at the Opéra, during a performance of *Vespri Siciliani*, or Bellini's *Beatrice di Tenda*. A moment later we are asked to look inside a coffer which les demoiselles Noël are sending to the Court of Russia. The demoiselles Noël are the fashionable shop for hats and

47

bonnets. Or it is a consignment, also destined for the Russian Court, of the parures and garlands of artificial flowers made by Constantin, a famous artist in his line. With true Russian prodigality these orders are of the most expensive sort imaginable. The Grand Duchesses will wear these wreaths and garlands at the State Balls in the Winter Palace, where every supper table is built round an orange tree in fruit or blossom, where the mazurka is danced, and the uniforms of the Cossacks and Circassians transport this winter elysium to even greater distances than is the truth.

But indeed, these parures and bonnets of Constantin and the demoiselles Noël are of the utmost elegance, as we can see them in *Les Modes Parisiennes*. Headdresses are composed of sheaves of gilded corn; there are purselike, openwork caps made of red and gold filigree; wreaths of white fuchsia for the hair; garlands of lilac, cananga and syringa, of white nympheas, of heliotrope or geranium, even of the spikes and flowers of cactus. The drawings of these headdresses, delicately coloured by hand, are one of the delights of *Les Modes Parisiennes*. Their effect must have been beautiful on the hair and framing in the face. Also, the straw bonnets of the time are inimitably drawn. Their yellow straw, the "paille blonde", is bent into every form that a bonnet can take; or it floats out far and wide, with flopping brims, in summer parody of the peasants in the fields. And, always, the hand of Constantin has left his touch of virtuosity upon the curve of a feather, or the placing of a flower.

But, also, the taste of this person, of whom it would be interesting to have the portrait, for he was the prototype of so many things that are typical of the time, had an influence in the interior decoration of houses. We read, in the fashionable intelligence, of an immense ball given by Prince Napoléon at the Palais Royal. A huge buffet decorated with silver bowls, amphoras and cornucopias, was decorated with an arrangement, by the hand of Constantin, of Asiatic and tropical plants: "These cactuses, nymphæas, China roses, drew the sense of smell and even satisfied it. The flowers trembled under the lights of the chandeliers and seemed to yield up their souls; here the geranium and carnation breathed, and, here, the heliotrope. The women surrounded the buffet, bending their lovely necks into the bouquets of flowers and seizing ices and sorbets with their beautiful and admirably gloved hands. It is with gloves as it is with shoes, they give distinction to the whole art of dress. Gloves, then, must be irreproachable, they must lie on the hands without a crease or wrinkle, they must show the fingernails, and the skin must be supple, glistening and perfumed. After long search it is only the old established house of Privat who can supply gloves that fulfil all these conditions. As to Constantin, there is no doubt that he has surpassed himself on this evening." Such, in paraphrase, for its refinements of language are impossible to reproduce, is an account of a ball at which Princesse Mathilde acted as hostess. Her dress, for we can translate no more, was "une robe en tulle bobin à cinq volants, sur lesquels était brodée une guirlande d'épis de blé et de mignardises rouge du plus charmant effet. Un collier de cinq rangs de perles fines de la plus belle eau entourait le cou splendide et les blanches épaules de la Princesse. Sa coiffure (des demoiselles Noël) se composait de fleurs des champs mêlés d'épis et de mignardises." Her brother, Prince Napoléon, who was in the exact likeness of his famous uncle, only in the Mussolinian canon, moved about from group to group of the guests, parading his Roman profile. And there was present, as well, Comte Walewski, a natural son of Napoleon, being, were it possible, even more in the image of Cæsar. This imperial likeness in many of the Bonaparte family is important enough to be noted. Napoleon III, who, it is to be argued, was not a Bonaparte at all, had his own distinctive appearance, which became the model of the Frenchman of the Second Empire. We have already seen it, reproduced to scale, in the Cent Gardes; and it was to be recognized in the baggy trousered Zouave, in the boulevardier and in the blue bloused workman. But, Napoleon III apart, there were many of the family and, especially the branch of King Jerôme, whose features were in the classical or Cæsarian mould. This was of the finest or Dantesque type of Italian and it is to be remembered, in connection with this, that the Bonaparte family was of ancient and noble origin. Their resemblance, therefore, was to the Augustan line. An Italian dictator of our own time, if he has this likeness, is more related from his peasant birth to a Cæsar raised out of the legion or cohort to the purple. Their marble pallor, their green eyes and small, white hands were the distinguishing marks of the true Bonaparte. It is in this manner that we must think of them moving among the hothouse flowers so dear to the 'sixties. Princesse Mathilde in her five-tiered crinoline with its design of ears of barley and with golden corn sheaves in her hair; and Prince Napoléon and Comte Walewski, the nephew and son of Napoleon, in the black tail coat and trousers that seem so remote from Austerlitz or Marengo, and yet, though in the image of our own, have the subtle changes, the archaisms, of three generations dead and gone.

While the waltzes of Waldteufel or Olivier Métra ring against the walls, this paradise of flowers, real and artificial, yields to us its identity in time. This was the epoch of petunia, of gloxinia and calceolaria. Every season saw new varieties, speckled, mottled, dappled, all shrill and violent in hue. They loved the flowers of Mexico or Borneo, to be grown in steam heat, under a Latin name that might have been the name of a scent invented by a perfumer, or, more simply, the name given to any one of these crinolined women under the glittering chandeliers. The boldness of their extravagant conceptions found its counterpart in such names as oppoponax and mesembryanthemum, and in the uncompromising colours of the petals. The geranium or pelargonium was trained into its shrillest and most blatant tones. Paris, in this time, was renowned for the forcing of hothouse flowers and for stove plants; these latter, natives of Borneo and of the tropical jungles of the East Indies, plants with variegated leaves and names longer and more complicated than the dogmas of the Eastern Church. The descent of these principles from the Parisian gardeners and nurserymen of the Second Empire is still to be seen in the Corporation gardens of watering-places, even in England. But the supreme example of this style is the "tapis vert" of Montecarlo. This is in exact period sense with the façades of the Casino, with the decoration of the older rooms in the interior, and with Garnier's delightful little opera, or salle de théâtre. Only, in the gardens of the tapis vert, the palm trees and the luxuriance of cactus and agave take an almost unfair advantage of the conditions. Nevertheless, the grass, grown blade by blade, and the flowers potted out and renewed every few days, make the perfect specimen of a garden of this sort.

Such is the application of its principles to the open air; but, indoors, not in the salons of the Palais Royal, but in private apartments and modest rooms we would find its equivalent artifice in hanging baskets and jardinières. More than all else, though, this is the age of ivy. This plant was made use of for purposes that are forgotten, now. They trained its tendrils into pyramids and parasols; and, as a pot plant, made round balls of it, clipped like a bay tree. It was formed into firescreens, an idea so characteristic of the 'sixties that it could have been invented in no other period. It was trained upon the backs of sofas and couches. In a monograph devoted especially to the ivy it is written: "But it is not alone in windows that you see the ivy trained. Ivy often forms a green and fresh screen across a room, being planted in boxes, and its sprays trained over rustic framework. Ivy often casts its pleasant shadow over a pianoforte so that the musician may sit before his instrument as within a little bower. Ivy may be seen adorning the shrine which hangs upon the wall, or dropping its sprays above the lady's work-table. The staircase in the house of a great painter here is a complete little bit of fairyland, thanks to his love of ivy, which festoons the balustrade of the polished oak stairs, and strews forth its kindly leaves among the rarer beauties of palms and myrtles, which rise grove-like upon the landings. I know an apothecary's shop which is rather like a bit of wild wood, from its growth of ivy, than a shop of physic. I was told, the other day, of a studio, here, equally sylvan; and I know an old cobbler who could not mend his shoes without seeing his ivy bush daily before him as he works." When reading these sentences, we become completely immersed in the period of which we are treating. That book is as true of its time, as Pepys was of his. We are to think, then, of an ivy-screen in its brightest terms; not of the dark and cobwebbed leaves that grow upon the walls. The firescreen will have shimmered like green water; but the staircase festooned with ivy, and the "pleasant shadows of the ivy cast over the pianoforte" are of a horrid fantasy which it is impossible to contemplate with a calm mind. We, therefore, bid farewell to this tendrilled interior and seek the light of day.

The Grands Boulevards are no more than half finished.

Their alignment is complete but there is scaffolding every-where. The whole city is rebuilding. This is the first town of the modern world, and there is still no city to compare with it. Yet Baron Haussmann was no genius in architecture. Paris is beautiful through consistency, in conception but not in detail. This morning, in the summer of 1866, it shows in telling contrast to the London we have left. The Seine runs through Paris and is not, as is the Thames, a frontier dividing the capital from what is no better than a long-drawn slum. The stucco deserts of Paddington and Pimlico, of Belgravia and South Kensington, have no equivalent here in Paris. But, hav-ing spent the morning, we can eat our luncheon in the Boule-vard des Italiens, at the Café Riche or the Maison Dorée. In London, there is nothing but the chop house. The Café Riche or the Maison Dorée, as well as the excellence of their food, have a name for gaiety and enjoyment that is comparable to the reputation of an operetta of Offenbach or Johann Strauss. This is very different from the oyster rooms of London. They consist of small rooms, much gilded, and with low ceilings, of the sort, in fact, still to be seen at Florian's, in the piazza at Venice. Upstairs, there are the famous salons privés which played so large a part in the scandalous history of the Second Empire. Here, were held supper parties after the play; or, indeed, the final scene of *La Vie Parisienne*. Those rooms, with their characteristic gilding and their mirrors, all destroyed long ago, have for ourselves the dissipated glamour of a little ridotto of the Settecento, the Casino Venier, for instance, in Venice. The delicate stucco ceilings and walls, the inlaid floors, may cause those little rooms to be haunted by ghosts in mask and domino, but not even the figures whom we know so well in the paintings of Guardi, the gamblers with bird masks and with fur muffs for their hands, are more remote from us than the patrons of the Café Riche or the Maison Dorée. Any old gentleman sitting in the room with us at luncheon may have been a soldier in Napoleon's wars. But it is not the old so much as the young who are conspicuous. The spread of a crinoline occupies the whole, and more, of a doorway. Because of its shape and size it is always framed for us in the lines of wall and ceiling; it over-laps from the edges of the tablecloth; it obscures the chair or sofa on which its wearer is sitting. It moves in its own scale of sound, which those who have heard it will never forget and which has become, for them, an integral part of the fascination of women. The drawbacks of its size make the measure of technique in its wearers. It is a disadvantage willingly embarked upon, one of those handicaps, like riding side-saddle, which finds its reward in an incomparable attraction. The discrepancy between the crinoline and what it hides is the secret of this. It is a cage, and you must guess between the bars. The art of enticement through concealment has never before in history had such pains devoted to its perfection. Such dazzling orna-ments and arabesques, the shot taffetas, the damask reps, the merveilleux, clouded, spotted, checked or marbled, the gold and silver brocades, the lampas figured with golden palms, all the ostentation of these shapes and patterns is but the glass shade, or bell, to hide the figure that is known within.

Perhaps the mere dimension of a crinoline is more impressive in the small rooms or cabinets of the Café Riche or Maison Dorée. Outside, in the afternoon sun, those trembling pyra-mids, advancing or retreating, have the even and gliding mo-tion of an engine, a very slow engine moving on its rails. This peculiar effect is because you cannot see their feet. The crino-line glides or trembles on its way. Thus, a wide street, or the Boulevard des Italiens, presents an animation which is more slow and deliberate than any street scene that our eyes have witnessed. But whenever it was possible, the crinoline wearers did not walk. They drove. This was the age of carriages. It was a side of sartorial elegance in which they copied England. The best carriages were built in England; and the horses and the grooms and coachmen came from England. Into this forgotten art it is impossible for us to enter. We can only be witnesses to this elegance; and it will take us away from the crowded boule-vards towards the Bois.

It is now, and in connection with this, that we meet with Constantin Guys. Our picture of a summer day in Paris in the 'sixties has had no mention, till this moment, of any of the contemporary painters whose names are now famous. This is because they were in revolt against their age. There is only Manet of whom this is not absolutely true. His painting of a summer afternoon in the Tuileries Gardens, now at the National Gallery, with its portraits of himself, Baudelaire and Théophile

Gautier, is no less than the document of those long dead summers. No one can look at this picture and not feel the sentiment of that hot afternoon. You can hear the brass band playing under the trees. But, with the exception of this painting by Manet, there is none of the great Impressionists who would be in sympathy with our object. We must be contented with the lesser men: Boudin, who painted the Empress Eugénie and her ladies at Trouville: Eugène Lami, who is described by Baudelaire as "an artist almost English in his love of aristocratic elegance": the fashion artists, Compte Calix and Jules David: and now, in this phase to which we have come, Constantin Guys.

This greatest of all amateurs there has ever been had his rôles of dandy, military spectator, and witness of the low life of the cancan and the "maison close", but our only present concern with him is in his drawings of carriages and horses. In the 'thirties and 'forties Guys had lived a great deal in England. He dressed like an Englishman and affected English words in his conversation. He must have begun drawing at this period. Guys was a Frenchman upon whom the luxury and elegance of English life had profound effect. The portraits of Sir Thomas Lawrence, who was not long dead (he died in 1830), had restored the tradition of Van Dyck that England was a land of fabulous wealth, and of equally fabulous elegance and beauty. In outward sign of this were the equipages, which had not their like in Europe. It was these that Guys set himself to draw, not uninfluenced, it is obvious, by the contemporary Ferneley and Herring. Until the 'fifties it was London, and either Spain or the Orient, that Guys drew. Those of his drawings which have Paris for their subject seem to belong, almost entirely, to the 'fifties and the 'sixties, to the period, shall we say, when he had returned from the Crimean War, where he had made sketches for the *Illustrated London News*, acting, in fact, as one of the earliest of war correspondents. He was, by now, over fifty years of age, but his best work was to come. It was, now, that he began to make hundreds of drawings of the crinoline and the stove-pipe hat. In the 'sixties he attains to the height of his talent; and, after that—though he is abroad in the streets of Paris till he is knocked down and has both legs broken by a carriage, at the time of the carnival of 1885, and lingers for another seven years, till 1892, in a nursing home, the Maison Dubois—during all this time, from 1870 till 1885 it would appear that he had ceased to work. There are no drawings by Guys that can be referred to any date subsequent to the fall of the Empire. It is as though, after the 'sixties, Guys had ceased to be interested in contemporary life. The 'sixties was his golden period. The strange habits of this recluse who would never sign his drawings, who beneath his mask of a man of the world and dandy spent all his days and nights in observation, and came home in the late hours to his garret, where he drew, this nocturnal worker had an output of drawings which could be numbered by the hundred. And, among them, if, sadly, we remove ourselves from all his other phases, there remain drawings which represent the side of fashionable life that is our subject.

For, now, we are drawing near to the Bois. It is the afternoon; and even, at that, an afternoon in autumn. This is the time of *La Vie Parisienne* and we advance the date of this, for it will run all through the winter, to an afternoon when there is bright sun and it is intensely cold. Even so, the afternoon is the hour to go driving. The big, new houses, near the Bois, have carriages drawn up before their doors and many a scene is playing that has its counterpart in Constantin Guys. It is only Guys who has fixed that moment when the lady, in her immense crinoline, comes out of the house on to the doorstep at top of the stone stairs. The calèche or brischka waits for her, below. A pair of horses are harnessed to it. A footman holds the door open and the groom stands by the horses. The lady has to hold up her crinoline with both hands in order to descend the steps; and then like a cloud, she climbs into this boat or skiff and seats herself. The groom has his box seat at the back of the calèche. He holds the reins high above her head, and the calèche goes forward as easily as a gondola and much more swiftly. The lines of this carriage are of an incredible lightness and elegance. Paint and leatherwork are impeccable, for it is Baudelaire who comments upon the artist's remarkable knowledge of accoutrement and coach building. "Guys", he says, "draws and paints a carriage, and every kind of carriage, with the same care and ease with which a consummate marine painter treats every kind of craft. All his coach construction is perfectly orthodox; every part is in its right place, and nothing needs correction."*

There are many other kinds of carriages. The calèche that we have described is the lightest and quickest of them all. It is meant for one person only and is overloaded with a friend to sit beside her. But there are, also, the daumonts and the carriages in which it is invariable for a pair of persons to be sitting together. To be alone in the swiftest and most skiff-like of carriages is not indelicate; but, to the sensibility of the time, there is something indecorous in sitting, alone, in a carriage where there is room for two. The more solid pace emphasized the impropriety. But a young woman could even drive herself, so long as her equipage went fast enough. On the other hand, the actresses and demi-mondaines no less than advertised their charms by the manner in which they were driven. There were ways of sitting in a carriage. The implications of this dumb language may be lost upon us, now. But, indeed, the crinoline might have been specially designed for the display of its folds and billows in an open carriage. Driving in a light pony chaise the crinoline would fill the whole body of the carriage. Were this the summer—and, for a time, again, it is—an open landau with two ladies seated in it, in bonnets and with open parasols, comes past us and the billows of their crinolines, like waves upon the shore, beat high up against the coachman's box. Not only does the landau glide past us like a caïque or a gondola, but the billowing of their crinolines is as though the ladies, who lazily recline in it, were marine bodies allowed their convention in this covering of foam.

The capitals of this carriage life during the nineteenth century have their peculiar romance which attaches to them. We may mention the Steyne, at Brighton, with its glaring chariots and curricles of the Regency; the Achilles statue and its purlieus in Hyde Park; Seville and its mule-drawn carriages in which the "vanilla coloured ladies ride"; the Toledo at Naples, a narrow street with open carriages going in solid procession, every evening, at a walking pace; the Prater with

* This quotation, and any others that follow, are taken from *The Painter of Victorian Life*, a translation by P. G. Konody, of Baudelaire's *Peintre de la Vie Moderne*, 1865. This edition, with many illustrations of Constantin Guys, was published by the Studio Ltd., in 1930.

its Hungarian equipages of Esterhazy and Batthany; and the Champs Elysées leading towards the Bois. We could wish for drawings of all these scenes from the hand of Guys. But, having noticed the start of the afternoon drive, we can do no better than follow it into the Bois. It is a slow and gliding procession; there is but little passing or overtaking. On its way, other carriages join in from every direction until the wide avenue, striped with the shadows of the trees, becomes no more than a stream of traffic. It ends on the banks of the lake.

This is one object of the promenade. It is to the lake in the Bois that the Empress drives, on most afternoons in her daumont. Sometimes, while going round the lake, the Emperor meets her in his phaeton. He holds the reins himself; an aide-de-camp sits beside him, and two grooms with crossed arms occupy the back seat. On such occasion he asks her to drive with him for a little while and this does not always please her. But it is not, necessarily, those melancholy tours of the lake that we need follow. Our pleasure in the carriages and their occupants will be more intense if we are lost, as it were, in the main stream or body of their progress, not knowing whence they come or whither they are going. Then, we may find ourselves in what Baudelaire terms "a halt or encampment of carriages". It has a fantastic improbability. Phaeton, daumont, calèche, clarence, coupé, berlin, barouche, britschka, the grande duc and grande coureuse, the charàbanc and four-in-hand, in their galaxy of paint and varnish all but touch upon each other. Baudelaire notices the "slender young men and women, attired in the eccentric costumes authorized by the season, standing on the cushions, on the seats and on the roofs, witnessing some event of the turf being decided in the distance". But our own preference is for the slow advance of this encampment, for the rolling of its wheels.

It must not be so hot that we are in a swoon or dream of heat. Under the trees, the top-hatted dandies are sitting, cigar in mouth, straddling on a chair, or with legs extended and their feet upon a second chair. They prefer their own company and make remarks upon the passing carriages and their occupants. Their very attitudes bespeak the lazy hours that lie before them. It is deep summer; and these tyros are the mayflies of the day. This is their place of gathering; or in the foyer of the theatre.

57

It seemed to be for ever and has quickly passed. This leisurely pastime of the hot afternoons has gone for ever. It is incompatible with the motor car. An age cannot but seem remote in our eyes that could do no better than use trained animals for locomotion. This may have been the ultimate elegance of horse and carriage but that mere fact relates it into the general or universal past. The afternoon encampment of these carriages, in all their different forms, has the strongly marked marine analogies that we have noticed. It might be an assembly in the halls of Thetis, in those blue bowers open to the skies. And the men and women of the "cylindre" and the crinoline are as improbable as triton or mermaid to our disillusioned gaze.

But it is necessary to correct this focus in order to look upon them with eyes that can praise their elegance and be unaware that it is fading. We see the carriages break up that encampment and glide slowly home, down the even waters in between the trees. It is turning to autumn. Already, we have left the melancholy contours of the lake and its white swans. The quickest of the daumonts comes past, and, in the words of Baudelaire, who must have seen this, "the Emperor disappears in the midst of a vortex of light and dust down the avenues of the Bois de Boulogne". The days are shortening.

This reverie of summer on a winter day brings us, with the fading of its images, to our winter of 1866. It is that afternoon on which we started, when there is bright sun and it is intensely cold. The crinolines no longer fill the carriages with their billowy clouds. Heavy, fur rugs now wrap them round. The Emperor and Empress are skating in the Bois. Every afternoon, for ten days, they have driven in their daumont to the Cercle des Patineurs, in the enclosure of the Tir aux pigeons.* There, we are told, the "lac gelé se transformait en grand salon". Hundreds of persons are looking on. The Emperor skates in a calm way, in a close fitting long coat, or paletot, his tall top-hat glistening in the sun, his long moustache blowing on the wind, with an air as if he is pursuing some abstract thought, and paying no attention to the moving and tumbling throng around him. He is a good skater, and, quite often, takes one of the young ladies of the Court with him on his arm. The

---

* This took place in the hard winters of 1866–67, and 1869–70. Cf. *Les Tuileries sous le Second Empire*, by Jacques Boulenger, Paris, Calmann-Lévy, 1932, pp. 136, 137.

Empress, dressed in dark colours and wearing a veil, does not skate so well as her husband and leans heavily on the arm of her cavalier. Once or twice she has a fall and the crowd, many of whom disapprove of the shortness of her crinoline, are not pleased to see her on the arm of a man and falling, in this way, in public.

To this scene, with its echoes of "Les Patineurs", that familiar waltz by Waldteufel, the early darkness descends. And, now, all the gas lights are lit. The whole city is glittering with lights through glass windows. Cafés on the Grands Boulevards are thronged with people: string bands are playing. It is easy to pass an hour, or two hours, in this way, listening to music. It has long been dark. People are dining; or have dined, and are, now, waiting, as if for time to pass. Many of them are standing. It is the bar of the Bouffes-Parisiennes. A bell rings, and another act begins.

This third act is the Festin. It has been organized by Gardefeu in honour of the Baron de Gondremarck and his wife. A salon of the Café Anglais is the scene but, just for the sake of appearances, Gardefeu gives the Baron to understand that the Swiss Admiral, to whom he has lately been presented, is the host. Whether the Baron believes this or not is of little importance. He is enjoying himself too much, in any case, to protest. The guests are valets-de-chambres, concierges, maids, shop-girls, all in their best dresses, and alive to the occasion. They can be called anything they like—Madame de Folle-Verdure, Madame de Quimper-Karadec. All the "fantoches" of the piece are assembled.

This festin, it will be realized, has been given nightly for many weeks on end. It is curious, therefore, to think of its original actors. Zulma Bouffar was the gantière Gabrielle; Céline Montaland, as fair as a Scandinavian, was the Baronne de Gondremarck; Mlle Honorine, than whom, apparently, no choice could have been better, was Métella; Léontine Massin, whom we have met before, was Madame de Folle-Verdure. As for the men, Brasseur played the Brazilian and, such was his versatility, Frick and Prosper, two other small rôles, as well; Hyacinthe was the Baron de Gondremarck; Priston was Gardefeu; Gil Pérès, Bobinet; Lassouche, a famous actor, contented himself with the part of Urbain, a head waiter who, in the last scene of the play, has one of the best songs in the piece. It has a chorus of young waiters and consists in the advice given to them by Urbain, their chief, upon how to conduct themselves in their responsible situation in the Café Anglais. They must be discreet: "Fermons les yeux" is the burden of his song: "Ne gênons pas les amoureux." And the orchestration of this song has more than a suggestion of the cancan in it. This music, in fact, is the sublimation of the cancan. No music is more instinct than this with the measure of its period in time.

We are to remember that every morning, for many months on end, this company of actors had woken from the festin of the night before into a new day that would end in this identical manner. It is more than seventy years ago. We have to consider the dawn of a winter day for Mme Zulma Bouffar, Céline Montaland, Honorine, Léontine Massin, and for Brasseur, Hyacinthe, Priston, Gil Pérès and Lassouche. It would come with the first foot upon the creaking wooden stair. Coffee and a petit pain are upon the way. We can see the folded clothes upon the chair, the exiguous washing-stand, letters in the slanting French hand, the shoes with pointed toes, the fiacres and horse-drawn buses, the red, red bricks and polished pitch-pine. And so another day would pass, with a call at the theatre for a message or for letters.

In the evening this festin of *La Vie Parisienne* came nearer and nearer. The shuddering of the batterie de cuivres proclaimed its coming. For this real gaiety, this diction in which the word "champagne" is heard as often as you can hear the three syllables of "vendetta" in any opera by Verdi, has its apotheosis, here, in this third act of *La Vie Parisienne*. The project is to entertain the Baron de Gondremarck while Bobinet and Gardefeu can amuse themselves with the Baroness. An intoxication of pleasure is the purpose and this is induced, in the audience, by every device in music. The scene must be a painted room blazing with chandeliers and girandoles. It requires a big stage, larger than any private room at the Café Anglais; but this is a necessary convention, it is the heightening of the illusion. We have to believe in this, just as, when the theatre orchestra enlarges and exaggerates the beauty of letter song or serenade, when the harp or the harpsichord assumes the whole body of the music and contradicts, in this, every possibility of fact, it is of no point to cavil at the enlargement of the truth. Instead, this is the golden moment. It's an intoxication such as circumstances can never allow in life. Neither can present-day popular music, an importation into this continent and a mating, at that, of the negro and the Jew, ever achieve this inebriation from pure sound. The words, now, are too idiotic or too sentimental; they are sophisticated, even, into a skilfulness in rhyme which only slurs and embarrasses the ruder melody. But, with Offenbach, and in the hands of Meilhac and Halévy, the wit of the words and the rhymes is in exact accord with the music. Neither can outpace, nor be any detraction from the other. The scene begins with the song: "Son habit a craqué dans le dos." It is the chanson à boire, the drinking song. Later on, this is to become intensified out of all proportion to its original. That will be in the quadrille. But this chanson à boire, has its rhythms of the cancan. Indeed, the whole of the music for *La Vie Parisienne* stands in relation to the cancan as does the music of the Rosenkavalier to the Viennese waltz. Its insistence, or dominance, is always in the background of the tune. And, at moments, it will hold the whole scene.

The grotesque characters at the festin cannot be too exaggerated in their oddity. Anything, or everything, may be worn by the Swiss Admiral. It is, however, essential for him to wear immense golden epaulettes and carry a telescope or a speaking trumpet. The fact that it is a fancy dress ball for all concerned except the Baron de Gondremarck doubles the gaiety; and this is true of it in the sense in which a doubling of the brass instruments in the orchestra increases the fire and brilliance of the sound beyond all precedent. The best proving of this is in the case of Berlioz. On occasion, when one of his greater works, the Grand Messe des Morts or the Te Deum is to be performed with an augmented orchestra the opportunity has occurred to give, as well, his military marches, the Rakoczy or the Marche des Troyens, with these increased forces. Then, the effect is exciting and intoxicating beyond the imagination. So it is with this festin of *La Vie Parisienne*. It should always be done with particular regard to the effects of the brass instruments. If these are added to, and it would be more effective, still, were it for this scene only, then there is nothing in all theatrical music to compare with this. *Fledermaus*, which was given eight years later, in 1874, apart from its overture, the masterpiece of Johann Strauss, has too much dialogue and too little music. The dialogue, moreover, being in German, could not but appear to disadvantage by contrast to the French of Meilhac and Halévy. *Fledermaus*, it is needless to remark, has some music that is immortal. The writer has, on another occasion, been taken at fault for saying that Mozart, could he have heard it, would prefer the *Fledermaus* of Johann Strauss to the *Ring of the Nibelungs*. This truism is more especially applicable to the overture. The speed of inspiration that this seems to foretell for the rest of the opera is to some extent belied by the slow action of the piece and its long spaces of dialogue. *Fledermaus* is music written about gaiety: it is not gaiety itself. But for the Franco-Prussian War, and the splitting of the French and German-speaking worlds into two irreparable parts, there might well have been, in the 'seventies, a closer rivalry between Johann Strauss and Offenbach. The French and Viennese schools of comic opera might, then, have surpassed themselves in direct competition with each other. There is, however, in parenthesis, this one interesting detail that is concerned with *Belle Lurette*, an operetta which is the last work of Offenbach, written during his finishing strokes to the *Contes d'Hoffmann* and left uncompleted by him. Léo Delibes, in fact, added the final touches to it and orchestrated the overture. The interest of *Belle Lurette* lies in the parody of The Blue Danube waltz that it contains, a parody that might be added to this banquet scene of *La Vie Parisienne* after the manner in which the tunes of other composers are admitted, at one moment only, in *Don Giovanni* and in the *Barber of Seville*. The historical anachronism of adding a parody written in 1880 of a tune composed in 1874, to a scene of an opera dating from 1866, would excuse itself in this instance because of exceptional circumstances. It should, and it must surely be, most appropriate to *La Vie Parisienne*.

The chanson à boire comes soon after the opening of the scene. It is unfortunately true that no translation can ever give the effect of these songs. They have to be, and can only be, sung in French. It is, also to be remembered that, excellent as the revivals may be of *La Vie Parisienne* that are given, from time to time, in Paris, the original art of the opéra bouffe no longer exists. Its actors and actresses are dead and their tradition has died. A performance can be given that relies upon old memories and has the authenticity of early photographs of the company to proceed upon, but all this can be no more than a faded copy of its pristine force. An opera which was written in the 'sixties in order to be exactly typical of its time, even of its particular year, cannot expect to survive three-quarters of a century and still remain entirely accurate to its purposes. It is of the original performances, then, that we must think. This was the apotheosis of the Paris of Napoleon III, of Baron Haussmann. Paris was the first modern city of the world, of a modernity which, now, is old-fashioned and antiquarian. But the race of boulevardiers, all dead, is the proof of this consciousness. Their boast was that they never left Paris. Its improvements brought the whole world to the capital. Anyone who left it retired into the mists of the past. This was the first modern city since the Rome of the Cæsars. Speed, we must remember, had only just been invented. It took Napoleon I as long to go from Rome to Paris as it did Julius Cæsar. In two thousand years the rate of travel had not altered. The change had only just come. It had only been in operation for twenty years. You could travel in a train all through the night and wake up halfway across Europe; but, in the minds of the boulevardiers, all travel was in a subjective direction, towards Paris. We have a confirmation of this state of mind in the characters of Baron de Gondremarck and the Brazilian. They have made their way from the ends of the earth in order to reach Paris. And so, we may add, have the ancestors of Offenbach and of Ludovic Halévy. Only they are there already; they have anticipated Baron de Gondremarck and the Brazilian.

It is apparent, by now, that the Baron bears no ill will for the deceptions that have been practised upon him. There is no malice or cruelty in this piece, but a condition, it must be admitted, of complete immorality. But it is the same Elysium, for all that, which reigns in the *Nozze di Figaro*. Nobody is left out. Everyone is involved so that it weighs equally upon all. Baron de Gondremarck has his recompense in the company of Métella; while, had it not been for his own importunity to have his letter of introduction delivered to her, the situation would not have developed into its present complexity. It was Baron de Frascata, his predecessor with Métella, who made the suggestion and let loose this avalanche of intrigue. Frascata is now, we are given to understand, far away and thinking all the time of Paris. It is not his fault that he is not here, enjoying "les flons-flons de l'operétte et les refrains du café-concert". For, after all, this is only the theatre; not life itself but a mirror held up for it to look into and see itself. Métella has nearly forgotten Frascata, with whom she spent the summer days of the year before. Soon, she will have forgotten Gondremarck.

All the illusions and half-illusions of the piece are made manifest in the chanson à boire. The words "Son habit a craqué dans le dos" should give the clue of falsity to everyone, Gondremarck included. But Gondremarck, on the contrary, is to be observed making fun of the Swiss Admiral and not in the least influenced by his fictitious importance. Meanwhile, the tables are brought forward laden with bottles of champagne and the scene continues. More and more fantastic figures are introduced. Madame de Folle-Verdure and Madame de Quimper-Karadec, in their immense hoops, fill a long sofa between them. Gabrielle and Pauline and Métella wear crinolines as wide as the round sofas of the time, or as wide as the circumference of the crystal chandeliers. A numerous chorus should accompany them, in whom all the vagaries of fashion as portrayed by Compte Calix or Jules David, by Constantin or the demoiselles Noël, can be displayed. This is, in short, a wonderful opportunity for the costume designer. The men of the piece, who are not "en travesti", wear the evening clothes of the date, which are not so much altered from our own. They only have that amount of difference which is necessary in order to turn them into ghosts of the present. They have the black trousers and black tail coats of our own day, only different in cut. The trousers nearly cover the tops of the shoes, which are pointed. And the waistcoats and collars and ties, the white shirt fronts still with a suspicion of the earlier frills about them, are subtly different and changing in a hundred ways. Also, for the men in the original production, fashionable correctness could not have been possible. Even in those days Savile Row found a poor substitute in a French theatrical tailor. Their clothes will have been full of incongruities. They will have been wrong in all the little details. This of course, combined with the exquisite precision of the women's clothes, designed by the best houses, will have furthered the extreme fantasy of the play.

The champagne is poured out, glass after glass. Toasts are drunk and every character lifts the champagne to his lips and puts it down empty, to be filled again. This is the moment at which Offenbach excels himself. It is necessary for Baron de Gondremarck to become a little drunk. Toast after toast is proposed and, as well, Gabrielle or Pauline, and, most of all, Métella, ply him with drink and, themselves, drain their glasses and call for more. The piece becomes vertiginous and drunk with tunes. In Viennese music it is the strings that are vehicles for intoxication. The violins intone the Viennese waltz, or it is preluded by the cymbalon. But, with Offenbach, inebriation of the senses is brought about by the brass instruments which sound out in the light rhythms, strongly accented, that have never, before or since, been given such a daring treatment of the dance. Also, the incredibly quick patter of the choruses brings about a vitality that no other light music possesses. Such choruses are the special genius of Offenbach, who could write them down, no two alike, in the distraction of a roomful of people, or even at the last possible moment, while driving in a cab to the theatre. The chanson à boire becomes distorted and different in meaning when it is taken from the Swiss Admiral and given to the chorus to sing. Soon, it will undergo still further transformation. Meanwhile, the attitudes and utterances become more and more intoxicated. A general dance begins. The stage is a whirlpool, turning, turning in a hundred convolutions, for the great width of the crinolines fills its space twice over. This is more exciting, even, than the Tyrolienne of the previous act. And, by now, the characters of the play have become impossible to part from. They are as indelibly remembered as the persons on board ship during a long sea voyage. The moment of parting must come; but the climax is not yet reached. It is possible to bask in the certainty of that, knowing it is not far off. For the excitement gathers and gathers. It is an orgy to which only the Banquet of Trimalchio can be compared. Both of them are orgies of an imperial capital. That was Rome, and this is Paris of the Second Empire, the city of pleasure of the modern world. But the Banquet of

Trimalchio had no music. It was an age of flutes or pipes. This has all the battery of the brass instruments, inventions which daze and bewilder and bemuse the senses. It is the speed of the modern world in a tangible form sharing the quickened wits of the metropolis, the town of a million souls. It is the whole town turning, turning in the dance.

But, now, another music begins. This is the play within the play. The dances traditional to the third act of an opera are about to start. Gondremarck and Métella, Gabrielle and Pauline, Madame de Quimper-Karadec and Madame de Folle-Verdure, the Swiss Admiral, Prosper and Gontran and Garde-feu and Bobinet, are all of them of secondary importance, now. The divertissement of *La Vie Parisienne* is the culmination of its wonders. We are given, one after another, all the popular dances of the day. Waltz follows on waltz and the polka comes after it. These dance tunes are an extraordinary embodiment of their age. They are the clothing of its bones with flesh and blood. Every phase in them is like the turn in a familiar conversation, or they create, at a stroke, the dresses of the dancers. This scene, or this moment of the divertissement has, in truth, a resemblance of spirit and of matter to the banquet scene of *Don Giovanni*. Its tunes have that same action upon the skin of the sensitive listener, that tingling effect which in the lore of ancient India signified the presence of the god. It is, in fact, the descent of genius upon the earth, for that can manifest itself in moments such as this when time is held back and the past stands still. A sort of immortality is conferred so that, during those long and lengthening periods when the music is not given, it has, yet, an independent existence apart from its closed prison within the pages of the printed book. A moment in the past, if no more, is given back its breath to breathe.

These tunes are the popular dances of 1866. Among them is the Redowa, a peculiar and characteristic form of waltz, of which the name alone, is redolent of that particular time. The very sound of that title, quite apart from the music of which it consists, seems to convey this feeling. It is danced by the principals of the corps de ballet, perhaps by two pairs of them, and could be described as a spinning and well-emphasized waltz, danced with much reversing, which makes it entirely different from the graceful or languorous waltz, as it is differ-

ent, again, from the German waltz. In fact, it was too special-
ized a form of dance to remain long in favour and, within a
year or two, had lost its fashionable glitter and sunk down
lower in the social scale to become the prize event in popular
dance halls. This is the fate, it must be admitted, of most of the
tunes that were once fashionable. When Estudiantina, the
waltz in Spanish time by Waldteufel, is heard in the circus or
the music hall it is difficult to believe that this was the fashionable tune of 1865 or 1866. And the same thing can be said of
Les Patineurs, also by Waldteufel, of which the distant echoes
have already been heard in these pages in the enclosure of the
Tir aux pigeons, when "le lac gelé se transformait en grand
salon". But Estudiantina and Les Patineurs, perhaps, also, the
beautiful Les Sirènes, have survived all the changes of fashion.
Their virtual immortality has already lasted them for three-
quarters of a century. The Redowa, which is not less characteristic, is untarnished and uncontaminated. It will be the first
time most persons in the audience have ever heard it.

After the Redowa comes the quadrille. This has been formed
by Offenbach out of some of the principal tunes in the piece,
only, to this purpose, they have had to be slightly altered in
shape and, therefore, in meaning. It distorts and changes the
themes so that they become sardonic and are, as it were, in
caricature. This transformation of character is of most peculiar
effect. The altered forms of the tunes in this quadrille have an
analogy in the last part of Liszt's Faust symphony when the
themes that had sounded innocent or pleading and had made,
in fact, the portrait of Gretchen become converted into sneering
and sarcastic forms. It is, indeed, a study in demoniac possession and, here, in this quadrille of *La Vie Parisienne* a comparable transmutation has taken place, only its purposes are those
of drunken gaiety. It might be said that there has never been
music so suggestive of this as the dances that are under discussion. The quadrille is constructed in the first place from
the chanson à boire, only its emphasis is given to the trombones
who, for effect, might indeed in added number, be placed in
the stage boxes. It becomes a cancan of delirious intensity, is
given part of one of the choruses with which to fulfil its pattern
and then, with many stabbings of the brass, returns again and
again into the deliberate cancan. After this comes a part of the

quadrille which is more conventionally itself, except that the refrain, or second half of that, has the turns of the tarantella, a dance which was a favourite with Offenbach, who wrote some inimitably witty music in that measure, and then the chanson à boire comes back once more, augmented, if that is possible, in its crude and angular violence.

After the end of the quadrille this orgy or festin goes with such a speed and force that it is impossible to follow its order of events. The dancing becomes general. Baron de Gondremarck should, at this point, be crowned with a wreath of roses. Then, in his antiquated evening clothes, which have a hint of the diabolical, of the gentleman in black about them, he becomes the statue of a satyr. The effectiveness of this is that you can almost see his goat feet hidden in his patent leather shoes. His hairy goat legs are where his calves should be. His wreath of roses, or of eglantine, hides the sprouting horns upon his forehead. He is the goat king, or satyr king, the Priapus of the Festin; or even Offenbach, himself, as the devil at the feast. And then, as suddenly, he is the actor playing Baron de Gondremarck.

For, now, there is a tremendous and final chorus of vertiginous speed. "Tout tourne, tout danse", is its refrain. This is of a rapidity to which there is no parallel in the arts; nor is any other music, than this, the music of real frenzied enjoyment. The whole company are whirling, whirling, glass in hand. A moment later the final strophe comes, ever quicker, quicker, and ending, as ever, in the movements of the cancan. This is the last time we can see the painted scene for that private room at the Café Anglais, the chandeliers, the girandoles, the crinolines, that evening of 1866 blazing in its lights. For the delirium ends in military precision with full forces of the orchestra, till the last final shuddering of the brass. And the curtain falls.

It may be lifted many times; but the music has gone and, without that, the figures have no life. These few moments, then, are our tribute to Offenbach who made them live. But, of his hundred operas and operettas, *La Vie Parisienne* is but one instance and, that, not necessarily the best. Such, at least, in one solitary phase of his creation, was the comic genius of music. And no one who has ever heard *La Vie Parisienne* can deny this title to Offenbach. It is a world that he occupies to himself, and in which no other man can approach him.

FUGUE*

THERE has been demonstration of the universal truth by fugue, and it may be that more wisdom is to be found in that than in the religions, and religious books, of all the world together.

But the one genius, Johann Sebastian Bach, was master of the fugue. Even in his hands the form was not always obedient. It might take a direction that, mathematically, was imposed upon it; be deflected, by new material, from the argument; or become redundant. But his was the supreme intellect in music. He had most, but not all, of the other wisdoms. Therefore, at times, a purely musical virtuosity creeps in. Technical skill in surmounting difficulties becomes an end in itself; or, even, he celebrates his faith, by that, as though he had come to believe that the ordering of his giant ingenuity was expected of him by his god.

Nevertheless, he is the huge grammarian. No other genius stands beside him. He frames the laws. His language is of a majesty that none other can approach. He is, all things considered, probably the greatest artist there has ever been. There is only Shakespeare to compare with him. Shakespeare, indeed, is so extraordinary a phenomenon that we are hardly interested in his person, and accept the obscurity of his history as part of the miracle. He was a poor actor, who wrote immortal plays. But the personality of Johann Sebastian Bach is of another sort. It is physical; in the sense that he inhabits, physically, his music, and however little we may know of him, we feel his presence in it. This is a question, more than anything else, of his characteristic weight, by which we intend solemn and serious from his first tread, but moving, when it suits him, in every mood of the heart or soul.

We are concerned, here, only with his organ music. Not with the Chorale Preludes: only with Toccata, or Fantasia and

* From *Splendours and Miseries*, 1943.

Fugue; Prelude and Fugue; and Passacaglia. In these we hear the full flood of his genius in its architectural forms; not interpreting the sacred text, as in his Cantatas, nor in the rôle of primitive, as in the orchestral Suites or Overtures and the Brandenburg Concertos, where the germ of symphonic shape is not yet developed, and these limitations leave him on a par with his contemporary Handel in the Grand Concertos. The giant hand of Bach and his divine intellect are to be heard in the Forty Eight Preludes and Fugues, as much in the first set as in the second; in the Goldberg Variations; in the Chaconne for violin solo; in the Chromatic Fantasia and Fugue; in the Cantatas; and in the Mass in B minor. But more than anywhere else, it may be, in his organ music. This is because, upon that instrument the performance depended upon himself alone. Until the coming, in fact, of the great pianists, and the emergence of conductors who were virtuosi, the organ was the vehicle for the greatest triumphs of instrumental music, and this was true until the time of Mendelssohn. The clavichord and harpsichord upon which Handel and Domenico Scarlatti were rivals to Bach were not suited by their nature to be heard by an audience of more than a roomful of persons. But in Northern Germany where attendance in church was nearly compulsory, there could be a public of many hundreds, or more. That this music owing to its intellectual content can have meaning to but few persons makes an empty, or nearly empty, Gothic church with Renaissance monuments, the setting in which we would listen to Bach's organ music. So it begins; but soon, very soon, it lifts us from the cold stone vessel into eternal time and space.

The Fantasia and Fugue in G minor can be our first experience of these wonders. Its rhapsodical opening puts it among the bravura pieces. Indeed, it starts after the manner of an improvisation, like a flourish to impose silence and impel attention. The Fantasia is of some three or four minutes in length and the huge personality, the giant hand, are apparent in it. Like so much of Bach, its eternity is achieved by retrogression. This is, in fact, not music of the eighteenth century at all. It belongs to an older and more serious epoch, though its content is musical, and only musical. Religious thought does not enter into it; still less into the Fugue that follows. The scope is only for musical display, but of the ancient or Northern school of Hamburg, where music was still influenced by the Netherlands composers of the sixteenth century. According to tradition, Bach composed the G minor Fantasia and Fugue for a particular occasion, his visit to Hamburg in 1720, when he played to the organist Reinken, who was ninety-seven years old at the time. The old man is supposed to have remarked that he did not know such players still existed. It was, therefore, not a revelation of something new in music, but the survival of the old which Reinken considered must have died away.

The story may be apocryphal, but, none the less, it tells the truth, for inspiration came to Bach, often enough, from dried up and disused sources. To the detriment of his eyesight he was, all through his days, an inveterate copyist of the works of lesser men, of small musical stature, necessarily, when compared with himself, but it was as though he had a particular affection for the old grammarians. They were his quarry in which he found unworked or forgotten seams. We know, too, from personal testimony that, in his own home, he would always go to his instrument and play some piece of music by another composer, as though that released in him the springs of inspiration, before he played any music of his own. This is an indication of his character and method and it proves that, like other great artists, he would turn to advantage anything and everything that came to hand. He needed, also to be put into the mood or trance, the fixed focus, or the "step" on which the speed boat moves across the waves. That must be the nearest physical analogy to the act of inspiration and it requires, in every instance, an auxiliary, a vehicle for the intoxication, for the spontaneous flowing of the numbers. It was provided, in this supreme example of the mystery, by the playing of some small piece of music from another hand.

But the Fantasia continues upon its way. There are passages of meekness or humility, developed out of the texture, which could be interpreted as deprecation of what is to follow; or are they no more than incidental, part of the musical pattern, as it were? For this is not, yet, the mighty and supreme genius of music. That is to come. And soon. The Fantasia ends with a thunderous and martial decision, a formal termination which tells plainly that it is done and ended. This is so different, too, in phrase or architecture, from the Handelian termination which is a magnificent conclusion. That, also, expresses itself in full-blooded architecture, shall we say of the Venetian order, of Venetian door and window and mounting stair, more splendid, indeed, than any buildings in that floating city, but this decision in the Fantasia implies that more is coming. That we have reached the Fugue: that what has gone before has been but Prelude.

The fugal subject plays itself, for the first time, like a story or a narrative that has to be listened to in full. It must, and can only be, a moral tale, some sentence full of meaning, the titles of God, it may be, as they might be called down from a high tower, not by human voice, but by a peal of bells upon a clear morning. The material, or the tune, has been said to be an improved version of a passage from a sonata by the nonagenarian Reinken; and again, it is claimed as a Dutch folk tune, being probably the one and the other combined and altered into its present form. But the effect, as we listen to it, could well be that of a Dutch popular song of the seventeenth century, or earlier, played upon the carillon. It has the substance of a carillon, as though arranged for that in the foundry when the bells were cast, while suitable tunes to exploit their possibilities were discussed.

At first hearing it is like a rustic merrymaking, a kermesse among the canals and watermeadows, not in the opening phrase of the Fugue, which, we have said sounds like the names of God; but in the second half, only, of its first line or sentence; after which, with the miraculous changes of which music disposes, the answer or remainder of the whole theme comes back, bound in and staved for treatment so that it is obvious the fugal voices will begin. It turns, then, at once and immediately, abstract and not pictorial, as it divides. The second time the theme is played it has changed again, miraculously, in meaning, and is organ music, pure and simple, sounding high up among the rafters of the ceiling, played clearly and conspicuously by the person in the organ loft. In silvery and piping tones, and we shall find that it differs in suggestion and meaning each time we hear it; now, less energetic and less dulcet than before, but adapted to endless variation in the hands of genius.

The derivatives of the theme seem to grow, organically, out of the stem as though this was natural to them and not the fruits of his abnormal skill. It is because the theme has been tried and tested in every possible way until it has been shaped into the long melody of the *andamento*, from the Italian *andare*, to move forward or go on, for that is the type to which this Fugue belongs. There can be *andamenti* which have been built, purposely, so that they divide into a pair of sections in order to give the composer every opportunity for full development and the complete exhibition of his powers. Shorter themes, not complete as tunes, were termed *soggetti*, meaning subjects; while, in the grammar of the fugue, a theme which was so brief that it consisted merely of a musical figure was given the name of *attaco*, from the Italian *attacare*, to tie or bind together, or combine.

The G minor Fugue then, is an *andamento*. It is not of that type which is just a subject suited by its nature for fugal treatment, as in Bach's Art of Fugue, where an apparently dull or simple theme was chosen, deliberately, because it was capable of so much development. Nor does it belong to that order of themes, dating from the last period of his organ compositions, written at Leipzig when he was in the full maturity of his intellect, the feature of which is that their content is that of an aphorism or an epigram. This is, definitely, a tune, so much so, that no one who hears it can forget it.

From its sparkle and liveliness a popular origin is quite probable, while, though Northern and not Italian in phrasing, it is not specifically Teutonic in feeling, but could easily be Dutch, a burgher or folk contemporary of Sweelinck, a Dutch tune that had been heard in Hamburg, which is nothing unlikely. Perhaps the ancestry of this tune or its connections are to be traced by analogy with the career of the great English composer of the previous century, John Bull, who, when he left the service of James I in 1617, and took up the post of organist at Antwerp Cathedral, not only formed a friendship with the Dutch composer Sweelinck and wrote a fantasy upon one of Sweelinck's Fugues, but wrote, also, a "Dutch Daunce" and folk song variations upon the Flemish or Dutch airs "Ein Kindeken ist uns geboren" and "Den Lustijken mey" (The Merry May). We would imply that the Dutch folk tunes upon which John Bull wrote his variations were of the same character and origins as that which served as theme for Bach's Fugue in

G minor, and that, perhaps, the presence of such tunes in Holland was as much a tribute to the importance of Sweelinck as it could be argued, in a parallel sense, that Italian melody and the beauty of Italian singing in the streets was due to the great Italian schools of music and singers of the past. These were, in fact, relics of a golden age of music in the North, of which the organists, Reinken at Hamburg, and Buxtehude at Lübeck, were the living survivals.

When the tune or song comes back again it is played reflectively, and in a kind of purposeful solitude, which gives to it, once more, another and a different meaning. More silvery and piping, yet, while this particular register isolates the melody, and we hear it up near the ceiling, breaking from the flutes; the treble pipes of the organ, one after another, being brought into play as though the strict harmony was a game among them, while the air climbs in and out and wreathes itself upon the pipes. The pace, even, is slow and rambling, for this setting forth of the tune is deliberate so that we can listen to its message. If such there be? Or is it music, pure and simple? Certainly, unlike the other fugal music that we would examine, this has no theory of Creation. It does not breathe terror. The huge rolling figures of the organ Toccata and Fugue in F major are not present. Nor the lightnings and thunder of the Toccata and Fugue in D minor. This is more purely musical in meaning because of the long melody of which it is born, and which is treated objectively by Bach, in the sense that the voices of the Fugue are derived or developed from out of it, and not imposed with superhuman ingenuity upon it. But now the voices of the Fugue begin to turn in upon themselves, and alter in intent by doing so. There is an analogy in this to the animal that rolls upon its back and shows its belly. The great hounds of the chase do this in play; so does the spaniel, and all other dogs. It is with them a gesture of surrender, an offering of their vital parts, so that they may die quickly, but it has become a convention in their play, as much so as when they bite the hand but do not close their teeth. In proof of which, the humble rabbit turns on its back to let the fox or greyhound kill him. By some humanity, or animal feeling, that inhabits the cold numbers or the architecture of the Fugue, this is what happens. Or it is some gesture of the composer's mind, as though he looked down in that moment from the organ loft, while the huge fabric of the Fugue slows down and steadies, and is done.

The organ Fantasia and Fugue in G minor of Bach is of an immortality that never tires, although it is among the most familiar of all his works. It is so cheerful and good humoured that we would listen to it as humanity or human feeling. It never makes the skin tingle or the hair stand on end, in that way which only Bach and Berlioz and Beethoven, in their different individualities, can achieve. Each time we hear the Fantasia ending, and the beginning of the Fugue, we hear the shadow of the giant in that formal clension, as though he showed his huge hand, and his powers, for the moment. It is a bravura ending, though less so than another that we shall remember; and after a moment's pause we hear the tune in its wonderful components, interlocking and returning in its phrases, chiming like a peal of bells, compact and fitting, made perfect in shape by the hand of the supreme master, so that its descending phrases are exact in cadence with the opening and it is set forth as a living entity with breath and animation of its own. The perfect balance of its syllables is so mysterious. What does it mean? What is its intention? This is no accident, like the pearl in the oyster shell; like the lump of amber borne to land in the floating seaweed, after a high wind, while the strand-rider patrols the lonely Baltic shore; nor any other of the happy freaks of nature. This is deliberate: not found by chance, but made by skill. Invented in the one place, and then made anew, like the turning or polishing of that drop of amber. And, in fact, it could be, in substance, a gathering or coagulation of goodwill or sweetness. Its burden is of bene-volence, set forth in an ingot that is imperishable and, like amber, warm to the touch; that is no bigger than the one breath only, and then divides or sheds its sweetness, which is diffused among the various voices and gathered up into the whole body of the fabric, so that it informs the argument and points the message.

But, immediately, and with only a pause of a moment in between, we hear the organ Prelude and Fugue in G major of Bach. This is of another character altogether, being one of his lesser masterpieces, and not to be numbered among the huge and triumphant demonstrations of his intellectual beliefs, though he believed with heart and soul as well, but it was his intellect that proved it to him. In the opening of this Prelude and Fugue, which are not so little in length, he does not tend the vine; he does not reap the golden field; there are no voices of God, nor rushing winds; instead he is domestic and genial; and in the Prelude it could be that he is watering a windowbox, in his dressing-gown, with a painted can. It is a demonstration, from trivial and little things, of the wonders of the world. We would number this with his domestic music, which exists in quantity. Not in scale, for, necessarily, this is bigger in scope than his Sonatas for a solo instrument, violin or violoncello, his flute and harpsichord Sonatas, lovely though they be, or the vast body of his keyboard compositions, but this organ Prelude and Fugue is domestic, surely, in its content. It breathes domestic or family contentment, and in the Prelude sets out to prove nothing, but is happy in its surroundings.

The opening is a set of brilliant and gay flourishes, not of triumph but of contentment, with a rocking or rolling upward rhythm, ending like the notes of a fanfare, almost, but this is only imitated or suggested, the pipes breathe neither defiance nor exultation, it is no more than the climbing of the fingers, one over another, upon the keyboard. After these flourishes the main theme appears, which is no more than a rising sequence, something which by its fluency can be suggested and hinted at, and even imitated indirectly, like its own echo or shadow, so that the pattern or message is repeated, but in outline only. There comes a moment when this theme proclaims itself four times over upon the manual, given out in ascension, after which it disappears and yields place to ghostly suggestions of itself in harmony and rhythm. But the capping of the theme, which is equivalent to an answer to the riddle or question which it poses, is a marching or a treading of the grapes, for the structure of the Prelude has changed in mood, and becomes positive. It enunciates the truth in this marching rhythm, which ends the first section, when the whole form is recapitulated for further argument, but ends with a most lovely phrase of exit or termination, through which the melody is led, to open again in fresh and tireless discussion of moral principles. It would be beyond our powers to enter into technical details of its structure, but a mind which has dwelt for long among the other arts, and lived in music as an amateur, may make a contribution that lies beyond and outside the absolute musical analysis, and yet brings other lights to bear upon this miracle of mortal origin.

Indeed, the particular miracle consists in the animation of an inanimate structure, if it is conceded that any piece of music, for instance this organ Prelude and Fugue, has one existence, on the paper upon which it is written, in however many copies, and another which only comes into being in performance, and is, therefore, intermittent. But this latter is its true life. Beneath the rules and complications of its formal structure a heart is beating and a mind is working, as though we could impute this same possession of the human faculties to the elaborate mechanism of a clock, to some mathematical calculation, or other co-ordination of minute and lifeless parts. The utmost endeavours of human craftmanship are, nowhere, stricter or more exact than in the Fugue. But those others effect no more than their purpose. They have no ulterior meaning. They advance no argument and pursue it to the end. Their life is intrinsic and not independent. Bach is the only master who can animate the Fugue. The subject, upon this occasion, comes from the opening chorus of his Cantata "My spirit was in heaviness", but the theme has been transposed from minor to major, and lengthened in the process. It has been suggested by Dr Sanford Terry that the Fugue was written ten years after the completion of the Cantata, which was an early work. In form it belongs to that type of theme which was called in Italian musical language a *soggetto*, shorter, therefore, and less of a tune than the subject of the Fugue to the Fantasia in G minor. In meaning it would appear to be an ecclesiastical reiteration. Some inevitable truth, which does not dull by repetition, but even, as the sacred formulas of the Buddhist church, confers immunity. At first hearing there is, certainly, a threat in it, an allusion, it may be, to death, which is unavoidable, and a state which was as important, in the mind of Bach, as the living world. But the theme coils in upon itself. It is not a melody but a sacred formula. It has a pushing rhythm, which pulls its conclusion after it, and begins again. Belonging in spirit, to an earlier century, to a hundred years, at least, before the period of its composition. It has, in this beginning, a grimness which appears nowhere else in its own time. But soon relieved, and as though that threat was no longer necessary turning to a gaiety in the exhibition of its own powers, but little and unimportant in locality, as though this was a morning spent happily with Bach during years when he was unconcerned with the world and living outside it in some small contented place.

The liturgical voices have become secular. We are in the pastoral or idyllic world; and it would have many parallels, we do not doubt, did we but know his Cantatas, where it is certain more beauties lie concealed than in the whole body of music that is unfamiliar and but seldom given. There is, indeed, the same feeling in the Cantatas as in this organ Prelude and Fugue, that the music does not care whether it is performed, or not. This is not the case with an unfamiliar work by Berlioz. Upon such rare occasions as those are given, they call aloud to be repeated. But the Cantatas of Bach were composed in the routine of his duties, and would seem content, as it were, with the date of their original performance. This makes them immortal, but ephemeral. A series of masques, but without action, and played without scene or dresses, such are the Cantatas of Bach. In many of them the splendours and miseries of the world are not the theme. So it is with this Prelude and Fugue. It is concerned with quite other things. We hear that in the opening flourish of the Prelude, and it continues within the Fugue. For the burden of this music is affection. And by what miracle is that expressed in fugue? Not the lifting of pain, as in "Es ist vollbracht" from the St John Passion; not the broad flowing Arcadian vale of "The sheep may safely graze", both of which breathe thankfulness and peace, in their kind; nor is it the reflective picture, complete in itself, that Bach could evoke from the three words "Et in Unum", in the Mass in B minor, which is among the most lovely of his inspirations. If we are to imagine these, for a moment only, as though their idiom expressed itself in painting, they are revealed as timeless in their greatness, but old fashioned in their time. The design is as copious as in a tapestry or picture of the Middle Ages. Let us name no names of painters, but affirm that, in these, he is a master of before the date of Rubens, untouched by the Renaissance and drawing most of his imagery from the Bible. In the particular works that we have mentioned there is nothing, as painting, that is later than the time of Luther, and it is, in

78

fact, that contemporary vernacular in music that he has extended and made into his own. It is possible, therefore, to be timeless, and two hundred years behind your time. And, if as great as Bach, to be appreciated only in part after two more centuries have gone by. The curious isolation of this Prelude and Fugue in G minor in space and time, and what we have called its happy indifference to its fate, are confirmed in the odd modulations of the ending, which are even oriental in sound, in the sense that all early music, and most early works of art, have an Eastern accent. It can be no more than an accident, unless the imagery in which it deals comes from the Bible. It is suddenly wafted away from the landscape into contemplation, or into prayer. Without doubt, it is a religious ending, and it seems to express some mystery which it does not understand, but which must be accepted implicitly by a world which is not old enough to comprehend. What has gone before has been child-like in confidence and serenity. What follows is certain, but must not be argued. There is much, in fact, that cannot be explained. And the Fugue ends on that mystery.

The melody of Bach, when it is idyllic, must be based upon the visual surroundings, which will include the books and music that his eyes had seen. In another instance, it is impossible to believe that Handel, in spite of his notorious indifference and apathy towards the other arts, does not reflect the Roman and Venetian travels of his youth. Handel composed in the grand or classical manner, not because of his robust physical frame only, or because of his Gargantuan appetite, but for the reason that he was a cosmopolitan, imbued with the urbanity and humour of a world that we have lost. His music is the mirror of that civilization, just as the beauties of his musical structures, composed in England, are as though Brunelleschi, Bramante, Sansovino, had built upon English soil. "Ombre mai fu" depicts ilex or cypress, the shade of Soracte or of Vallombrosa, not the wood of Dunsinane. His Water Music comes from a gilded barge moored at Hampton where the Thames flows past villas and soft lawns. What an era of visual perfection is to be perceived in the organ Concertos of Handel, where all around is new and splendid! And the rolling organ leads the eye to new statuary and painted ceiling.

79

But the melody of Bach goes deeper and concerns the whole of life, in an older world, apart, where the values are more permanent, and there are no coats of gilding. In order that this should not be transitory it has been fixed in time. That is to say, it is eternal because it deals with things that do not alter. But it speaks a ritual language, not in modern speech, but in an universal language which is, at once, old and new. With no grand buildings, or classical façades, but of timber-frame houses out of which you can step directly, and look up into the sky. Because he needed nothing more, but was contented. The musical facility had been developed in him through all the generations of his family. They had been peasants and artisans, organists and town musicians throughout Thuringia. The names of more than sixty members of the Bach family who were connected with music have been preserved. He spoke, musically, in a vocabulary that was their own. There was no need for him to invent an idiom. It was born in him. Perhaps there may even be some obscure natural reason for his genius in that the father of Johann Sebastian, Johann Ambrosius Bach was twin brother to Johann Christoph Bach, and that they were identical twins, both of them violinists, alike in thought and speech, and so similar in appearance that their own wives were unable to distinguish between them. It would seem, in Johann Sebastian, to be equivalent to a double transference of talent, resulting in an endless multiplication of the family abilities. A phenomenon which has appeared, perhaps, but this one time in history. By a freak of nature, or a rule which we do not understand, the uncle had a greater talent than the father. But, again, the sons of the uncle, in their turn became, the one, an obscure violinist, while the other abandoned music and went into the grocery business. The balance of genius righted itself and regained its level of normality. Of the twenty-four children of Johann Sebastian three or four were remarkable for their musical talents, but if positive genius had appeared again we should expect to find it, not among his offspring, but in the descendants of his brothers Johann Christoph, or Johann Jacob. With so many known individuals of the one family it could be possible to draw up a graph or chart showing the direction taken by their talents, and even, what would be, from conjecture, the path of probability. But this excessive blossoming was not to come again. Nevertheless, its reasons are apparent. It flowered, as we should expect, upon one of the least likely of the stems. The seedlings showed promise, but Philipp Emanuel, Wilhelm Friedemann, Johann Christian, never approached their parent in his genius, and the phenomenon expired among them.

We are now to hear this greatest of all artists at his fiercest and most tremendous fire of mind. What has gone before has been, by comparison, but the gentle warmth. This particular work is the organ Prelude and Fugue in C major, one of the five great organ compositions of his Leipzig period, written, probably, about 1735, when Bach was nearly fifty years old. This is important to remember, while we listen, because the reader who is not professionally interested may not realize that the bulk of Bach's organ music, which, in any case, represents a much smaller part of his output than the layman might imagine, was written during his early life, chiefly at Weimar. This Prelude and Fugue in C major represents Bach, then, in mental and physical maturity. It is, in fact, an extraordinary work, as physically exciting as any music ever written, and to which belong many implications. The theme of the Prelude, and of another figure that occurs in it, are closely related to the opening chorus of his Epiphany Cantata "The Sages of Sheba", No. 65, written ten years previously, in 1724, and having, perhaps, some special association for his mind. Certainly the character of this Prelude suggests that the theme has not been chosen just because of its musical possibilities, because it was so hard a core or germ of melody, nor for the converse reason that being, superficially, meaningless or like a riddle it lent itself readily and pliantly to his designs. On the contrary, from the opening bar of the Prelude its soaring and ascending energy is apparent. It has been described by one writer as pastoral in character; while another critic interprets the Prelude as the vociferous welcome of the population to a reigning prince. Probably it is nearer to the truth to point out again that it is an Epiphany Cantata from which the theme, in reminiscence, has been adapted and that, therefore, it is more likely to have a Pentecostal meaning. Bach felt so powerfully the power of words, and gave to them so literal and pictorial a setting that the clue to the meaning of this Prelude is probably to be found in the exact words of that first chorus of the Cantata, and again in the precise mood of that other coincidental figure which immediately precedes, so it is said, the entrance of the voices and concludes the movement when they have done.

The prevailing tone of the Prelude is harsh and strident, to the point, nearly, of being frightening. In effect it is a whirling and spiral climbing, which it is impossible not to associate with the Pentecostal winds and fires. This is expressed, so to speak, upon the trumpets. None of the dulcet shades of the organ are required. Nor is it a rolling figure, for the sake of rolling, as in the organ Toccata and Fugue in F major, where it is the play of a mighty strength, an infant strength, even, as though it were possible to conceive of a youthful creator who is making order out of chaos, and whose intentions and movements are depicted in this rolling figure, and in its constant clensions, which are as though things had been put to rights, and then he sets out again with more tasks to do. But in this Prelude the flames do not catch instantly or consume entirely. They return again and again. The succeeding subject, that comes after the soaring and ascending fire, seems like an expression of pious wonder at the miracle, not in surprise, for it is implicit that it is expected. Definitely, this calm and thankful return which prepares for the fire and the fearful winds to come back again, can mean nothing else, if music has a meaning. And in fact, the ground is set and ready. It returns. The succeeding stages of the miracle, or just its repetition, are depicted in the music. The second reappearance is more terrifying still, accepted, once more, with pious and deprecating confidence, which is nothing else than a message that all is believed in and credible, but the tones of the organ, thereby, suggest in some way the empty vessel of a church with all the ornaments of devotion. And then, when all is ready, the winds and fires begin, for the last time. But, for this occasion, they catch; and their whirling, soaring fury makes the hair stand on end. There can be nothing else like this in music, for its terror. It gets right away, with the ground cleared for it, in a manner of physical excitement or inspiration that can only be compared with the enormous acceleration of some engine, or the drop from the minor into the major key, as when, in that simile we used before, the speed boat rises on its "step", and roars away, or the aeroplane alters its note of menace to die down into the distance behind a cloud.

This concluding part of the Prelude becomes more and more like the cranking of some gigantic engine. It is to be more formidable still. But there is one more return of the subject in a changed tone, as though in worship of the power that sent it, almost as though the flames were bowing low, or kneeling at the altar stone. And they are lifted, suddenly, dying or diminishing. The gigantic engine beats its flails and ploughshares into trumpets. The flames are quenched. The giant power intervenes and orders. There comes the tremendous ending, in three phrases, like words of two syllables upon the trumpets, so peremptory that it is not credible this should be the triumphant proving of the problem. They are, in fact, three blasts of the trumpets, at sound of which the whole world falls down, in the name of the Holy Ghost who worked this miracle of the tongues of fire. It is the voice of God, and no more is said.

The Fugue which follows is built upon a theme so short that it is a phrase or little more, and only occupies one bar. By nature, therefore, it belongs in fugal language to the type of Italian *attacco*, a subject which in the literal meaning has needs to be combined or bound together. This is a Fugue in five voices, and the mysterious subject is repeated so constantly in different forms that, in effect, it is never absent from the structure. An unfortunate resemblance between this figure and the Prelude to the *Meistersinger* is no fault of Bach, and probably an accident on the part of Richard Wagner. But the coincidence is soon forgotten. At first hearing this phrase or theme of the Fugue, as is so often the case with Bach, comes out of the remote past. It is archaic; and if, superficially, it has some resemblance to the Prelude to the *Meistersinger* it could, as well be said to be nearer in spirit to the opening notes of *Le Sacre du Printemps*. But the voices of the Fugue, one after another, break in upon its ritual phrases, and in a curious way they are so suited to a fugue that each entrance sounds like the introduction of new material. That is to say, the figure, in itself, is little more than an entrance. It exactly suggests that, and no more; and for a while the Fugue employs itself with the accumulation of its parts, until all have entered. To this point the Fugue has but little other meaning beyond the ancient liturgy of the phrase itself. But there comes an augmentation of the subject.

upon the pedals, by which it is altered in character, at which time the whole complex machinery of the Fugue is set in motion and that figure has become menacing, and as it were, proved in action, and not awaiting contradiction. In reedy tones and with a gathering speed it enunciates the sacred apothegm, and states it again more positive still. The entire Fugue moves with assurance to a foregone conclusion. It is as though this were some Euclidean problem to be solved, which will be proved by logic, without argument. But now the parts are quickened, and the turning, whirling of the Prelude comes back, with less intensity, it is true, more resembling a cloud of incense as that seethes and swirls up from the censer, and conceals, it may be, some miracle or transformation that is taking place, that occurs regularly and is part of the ritual. Or the ritual itself, the Communion, the miracle of transubstantiation, it could be. Whatever that thing may be, it has happened, and is over. The ending of the Fugue is concerned only with the conventional dying of its voices, while the music lifts up its eyes, as it were, towards the heavens. And when the voices have stated once more what they have to say, the Fugue slows down, and dies in full diapason against the mortal walls and ceiling.

In this organ Prelude and Fugue in C major, in particular, Johann Sebastian Bach is the greatest of the Ancients. Of none other of the great artists is this so true. It is because his concern is with the ancient truths. He does not belong to his own century at all, but, being rooted in eternity, has a meaning for all times, and speaks, therefore, in an ancient voice out of the universal and omnipresent past. Probably, in order to be numbered among the Ancients it is necessary to be peculiar or uncomprehended in your time. Johann Sebastian Bach is not the last of that race. Beethoven, obscured, but happy in his deafness, and William Blake are two others. They are approached by Cézanne; and there have been no more. These are not of the race of Watteau, Chopin, Keats; of whom, down perpetuity or in purgatory, the youthful ghosts wander among the myrtle groves.

But Bach is most Ancient of them all, before, in his old age, he withdrew into the mazes of the Fugue, and concealed himself where few could follow. That technical obsession betrays the Teuton in him, of which, despite their separable beauties, the Musicalische Opfer and Die Kunst der Fuge are the exemplars. Probably, also, another work unfortunately inaccessible to us, the Canonic Variations for organ on the Chorale "Von Himmel hoch, da Komm' ich hier", composed in the last years of his life. Sir Hubert Parry, in his account of this work, describes how, in the last of the eleven variations, the canons come tumbling out one after another, close upon each other's heels. It may be that these Variations in canon are more readily appreciable than the many difficulties of the Musical Offering or the Art of Fugue. They were handed in by Bach, as an exercise, on joining the Mizler Association for Musical Science, in Leipzig, and were composed in 1747, only three years before he died. In thinking of his final contrapuntal masterpieces, of which this is to be numbered as the third, we must express gratitude, in our admiration for him, that he lived too early to become involved in the arguments for symphonic form. Too much of his Germanic energy and thoroughness might have been wasted upon the orchestra. The Suites or Overtures and the Brandenburg Concertos are sufficient. Those are enough to show that the orchestra of the eighteenth century was not suited to his genius. That he was too big for it. That, in fact, its restrictions, into which he could not fit himself except in a string of dances and *galantieren*, impeded his greatness and brought him inferior, in this respect, to Handel. The orchestral music of Bach is even provincial when it is compared with that of Handel, if we except such a masterpiece as his Concerto for two violins. Where his forms had room for their natural growth he is supreme. That is why he is to be preferred on the organ to in the orchestra. That is why, not the Forty Eight Preludes and Fugues only, but the six French and the six English Suites, which are heavier in texture; the seven Partitas, more lengthy and important still; the Italian Concerto; the Chromatic Fantasia and Fugue; are so imperishable as works of art. That is why the stray Fugues and Fughettas; the Six Little Preludes; the Twelve Little Preludes and Fugues, are so individual in experience. That is why short pieces, such as the Fantasia in C minor (with an unfinished Fugue), written in Italian style, and so purposely bringing in the crossed hands that it is meant, evidently, as a pasticcio of Domenico Scarlatti; or the little Marches and Polonaises found in the notebook of his second wife, Anna Magdalena Bach, are so perfect as small works of art.

The drums and banners of one of the little Marches, in particular, and its turkey step are realized in so small a space that it is as simple as a folk song, and yet is the epitome of parade and pipeclay. We see the parterre of soldiers in their red coats, white leggings, and high, half sugarloaf caps, planted like flaunting tulips in rows, flamed scarlet and white; and after a little manœuvring they dismiss, but, for another moment, the drums taps on. Bach brought as much skill and workmanship to these miniature pieces as to the greatest works of his intellect.

But upon clavichord or harpsichord Bach has one rival, Domenico Scarlatti. For it might be possible, after a lifetime at this music, to prefer Scarlatti. That much must be admitted. Domenico Scarlatti was a supreme artist, and a specialist. His physical energy and vitality were given to this one task only. His intellect was not quicker than that of Bach, but it was more human, in the sense that he was more sophisticated and of the world. He had elegancies of manner that were below the contemplation of this other, with his provincial background in a small North German town. At the same time, what might have been superficial in Domenico Scarlatti was redeemed by his exquisite taste and sense of poetry, having been brought up, too, in music, in the strict school of his great father. Domenico Scarlatti had in him the virtues of Italy, while it is difficult to find in him an Italian fault. Bach had in him the German virtues, a humanity and genius which belong to all time and to the whole world, but the German prolixity, and on occasion only, the faults of their thick speech. At the back of him there was the shade of Veit Bach, his ancestor, who was a miller and baker, and there were the shades of the Thuringian town musicians.

But few persons are privileged to know in entirety Bach's organ music, while those who have written upon it are concerned, naturally, with its technical analysis. Thus it comes about that some of the supreme works of the human intellect and imagination have to depend upon occasional performance and have been left unrelated, in æsthetics. Even Dr Schweitzer, who can explain the musical imagery of the Cantatas, being an organist himself, seems to consider that the organ works are accessible and makes little or no attempt to group them according to their form and meaning. When removed from their purpose in a transcription, these pieces take on lesser and diverted values. Their ancient language is translated into that of the concert hall or drawing-room. But of Bach, at least, there need never be an end. He has, ever, something new to say. His old and familiar music is reborn with a different meaning; or some tremendous work by him is heard for the first time. This could happen until the end of a long life, so that it becomes a positive benefit that so much is hidden. The organ compositions are the great works of Bach as a solo player and his only opportunity to appear in that character to a big audience, and above all to himself, for they were written, we may be sure of it, for his own pleasure.

In the result we have such works as the Passacaglia, which take their place with the most superb creations of the human spirit, with the greatest poetry in any language, and with the most sublime in painting or in architecture, but which, hardly yet, have been judged along those parallels. The Passacaglia, because it is the unique work by Bach which bears that name, is even in a favoured situation for discussion. What can be done, though, if only for purposes of identity, among the three Fantasias and Fugues, five Toccatas and Fugues, six Trio-Sonatas, seven Fugues without introduction, and twenty-six Preludes and Fugues? The six Trio-Sonatas can be reserved, at least, as chamber music for they can be played upon the harpsichord or pedal-piano. Of the Preludes and Fugues there are those which are early works and can be set aside; and, again, there are, among the rest, the eight Short Preludes and Fugues, leaving, in all, some twelve organ Preludes and Fugues to rank with the Passacaglia and the best of the Fantasias and Toccatas. This is an opus which, given the opportunity, it would not be difficult to discuss in the manner which we should wish for it. Their basic principles, not technically but in imagery and æsthetics could be assembled and compared. We could class them according to their moods of pleading, rolling, dancing, gliding, soaring, marching, according to the architecture of their entrances and terminations, according to the mingling and intonation of their voices. There is that step which, in the words of Dr Schweitzer, is like the treading of the grapes; and another which depicts a heavenly exultation, or indeed the footsteps of creation, for life springs up where it has trodden. The Passacaglia would seem to consist of many poses or arrangements of a pleading figure, in which affection is touchingly portrayed, and the acceptance, also, of whatever may be coming. But the phrase or figure is in double profile, as it were, for, as well, it expresses infinite love and compassion on the part of the creator. The same figure, with a little difference, conveys the one or other. In the form of the Passacaglia this is all clothed in springtime beauty as are the personalities in an Italian painting of the Quattrocento: that is to say, the exquisite pathos and loveliness of the phrasing and the modulations make the wild flowers of the foreground, so that the forms are advancing through a flowering meadow and the repeats and interweavings of the shape confine the valley and carpet it with flowers. Are they the living or the dead? They have their children with them, and they are holding flowers in their hands. The form sways and dances, slowly. It is almost a Sicilienne. But the intonation is always upon the pleading. And the Passacaglia is followed by a Fugue in which the authentic voice of God is heard, in linked or joined syllables, in the form of a chorale with which the strains of pleading are combined, conveying the answer or assurance. This fugal portion of the Passacaglia is inexorable, and even terrifying. It mounts to a climax, though the voices of pleading and of pity are still heard in it, and the whole passionate and gigantic structure manœuvres for its ending, throwing out buttresses, tying itself with ropes, moving bodily forward, and dying away in pious wonder. No musician, beside Bach, has been able to build up these formal shapes with so full and fiery an intensity, to render them so completely the vehicle of creation. His Chaconne for solo violin is a parallel instance. Again, its close-knit form, without the returns and shackles of the Sonata, allows him to build up a drama that is nearly unbearable in poignancy and depth of feeling, and which is so miraculous in conception and so gigantic in scale, of such mortal meaning, moreover, that it is utterly incredible, and makes all other music whatever, except, perhaps, that of the passing moment, to sound trivial and false. We have called attention, already, to the rolling figure of the organ Toccata and Fugue in F major; and we would compare the opening of another organ Toccata and Fugue in C major, an effect which is strong and magnificent, almost beyond credibility, in its expression of masculine force, like the sudden view of some fantastic architectural frontispiece, approached by processional staircases and flanked by towers, so high and old that the weeds and flowers grow from them, the western façade or El Obradoiro, as it is called, of the Cathedral of Santiago de Compostela, shall we say, seen, suddenly, in the sun after a shower of rain, in all its ancient and quasi-Indian magnificence, to which succeeds a flowing melody that depicts the laughing valley and the loaded vines. Or again, the Organ Prelude and Fugue in E flat major, another late work of the Leipzig period, which opens didactically, like a lesson in the catechism to a small boy,* until after a bar or two, wonder and astonishment supervene at the length and breadth of the divine exposition, and it comes to its masculine conclusion and begins once more. It has completed the argument, and now gives proof as it progresses on its way. If you listen you will be convinced. Of what? That there are purpose and design. That there is benevolent intention; but that humanity must help itself. That the masculine will can bring order into the world. And the argument is repeated with overwhelming emphasis, and is indisputable, at the end. The Fugue that follows is of a primal simplicity, it would seem, until its tremendous nature becomes apparent. It is concerned with dogma, as though setting forth to give theological proof by mathemetics: that is to say, it is one of the deepest, musically, of all the Fugues of Bach and at first hearing, therefore, dry and, we have said so, dogmatic in effect, until the passionate ending and the problem proved. Such is this tremendous and cataclysmic work, for it is no less than that. As serious as the paintings of Michelangelo in the Sistine chapel, as tremendous in scope as Dante's *Purgatorio*, but devoted, as it were, to the spreading of light, to the diffusion of day, of logic, into the primal darkness.

* I may not be believed when I state that my clue to the meaning and import of this Prelude in E flat major was written before reading in *The Art of Bach*, by A. E. F. Dickinson, 1936, that this Prelude introduces the Catechism Preludes. Nevertheless it is true, and perhaps some more of my imagery may be confirmed by such an instance of intuition on my part.

But we have kept, till last, what would seem to be the greatest wonder of the whole. We intend the organ Prelude and Fugue in E minor, again a Leipzig work. This begins, impressively, as any organ Prelude of Bach, and probably of intention, or in order to give itself the time to climb into its dizzy height, relaxes somewhat its hold upon our interest, until it has prepared its place of advantage, and is ready. This wonderful work of art has no less than five themes that rise spontaneously, as it were, from the structure and rhythm of the Prelude, two of them being more important than the others, although it is true to say that all five are not audible to the amateur at every hearing. But the visual knowledge that they are there must add something to the enjoyment of the professional musician. The structure seems to rise up or lift itself into the immortal air with much evident soaring of wings, and upon a series of steps or paired notes, infinitely varied, but recurring continually, sometimes in a marching or a dancing rhythm, and at other times like the coupling of a pair of pillars or columns, when in fact, these are the props or stays of this universe, for it is too great in scale to be mere architecture. They are more comparable, then, to the parts of some immense engine, being, certainly, the means or machinery of its propulsion. And it circles in the distance. It is climbing steadily, and will come back.

The sensation is as though some enormous subject was banking out of the clouds above our heads. It is only to be indicated in terms of the aeronaut; in fact, of those who gaze into the heavens. It comes steep down from a steep height, and like in sound to those organ pipes of Spanish cathedrals that point out horizontally over the heads of the congregation, ending sometimes in the carved head of a Moor in his turban, as though they were the medieval artillery or culverines, comes down with cannon blazing, and having reached the bottom of its trajectory, just over our heads, soars up again into the empyrean. This process is accompanied by the steps or paired notes which, now, are definitely the scale motifs that commentators have identified in Bach as being associated in his mind with ideas of rejoicing. After this climax there comes another period of preparation, an interval which is filled with religious contemplation, almost as though in excuse for the unearthly excitement of what has gone before. But it comes back again. The return is more thrilling still. From a steeper height, and still more tremendous in its dive down above our heads. Once more the process is repeated. The religious interval, and then the terrific descent or entrance of the theme, which steadies, now, for the conclusion, and like the great white cumulus, cloud-like, sails levelly away.

The Fugue begins at once, seeming, by some illusion in space, to come after with scarce a pause at all. Its theme is a handful of notes, indeed a scale passage for the fingers, up and down, like "chopsticks", of little significance in itself, but leading to a stupendous counter-subject, the irruption of which can only be compared, in simile, to the descent of an angelic Michelangelesque figure with knit brows, employed upon some process of thought which has become action, a young male angel, or more properly, the face of creation itself, and therefore, the countenance of God. This revelation comes again, and more than once; but now the Fugue sets off at a tangent, in a new direction, a thing for which it is condemned by the purists, as also, because this middle portion of the Fugue continues on its way for a hundred and twenty bars, which is as long as the beginning and end of the Fugue put together. It consists of a huge treading or skirting, or a system of manœuvring for play, into which that magnificent counter-subject breaks in, with superb utterance, while the ascending scale passages prepare its entrances. After each appearance the rhythm steadies itself a little, and a quiet or pause comes in the measure, to allow time for the mind to wonder and prepare for more. The whole of this section, allowing for those intervals, is miraculous in its energetic strength, rising to tremendous climaxes that are foreshadowed when the onward march of the entire structure is broken by the fluttering of great wings as the force of creation, fearful but benevolent, comes down again upon the Pentecostal gales. A huge agitation or churning of the airs precedes each appearance, while, if we study its successive entrances, they are accomplished like a *tour de force* with manifest difficulty, which enhances the miracle; or it comes down, triumphant, like the lightning of the storm, in a splendour and terror that take the breath away. After this tremendous passage, whatever it presages, the strict Fugue returns again, and having stated the argument, dies away in wonder, and the Fugue is ended.

The fugal subject of this terrific work has been characterized as meaning nothing in itself. It is not a tune at all; nor yet an epigram; but, more accurately, a rhythm, merely, balanced by a trill. But it is enough; being as indefinite, for a germ of creation, as the faces and figures seen by Michelangelo upon the plaster of the wall. It would not sound, even, to have particular musical possibilities. There has, merely, to be a beginning. No mental message is attached to it. But inspiration comes so closely after it, that it could almost be that Bach, having devised the wonderful figure which follows, prefaced it, on purpose, with this nondescript opening, which is no more than the grinding of the engine's wheels, as it begins to move. A fugal subject, just as short as this, but, for contrast, full of meaning, is that of the Fugue following upon the E flat Catechism Prelude, for again this is, quite obviously, of purely religious significance. That is proved, if tunes mean anything at all, by its chance resemblance to the hymn tune of "O God, our help in ages past", from which circumstance it is known in England as the St Anne Fugue. There can be no doubt, then, as to its meaning. A tune, needless to say, can be parodied or distorted. A hymn tune, for instance, can be played in waltz time; but, when identity is so close as this, the meaning must be as though we had the same text in a different translation. That must be the limit of divergence. The only changed sense is in the ending, which, with Bach, portends not sturdy defence but abstract meditation. In the beginning, the invocation is the same, that is to say. The identical God is addressed in it, but the melodic line is inward and falls back upon itself. As to the meaning of a phrase in music there could be no more clear example than the organ Chorale "Ein' feste Burg". We need not to be told that this is a setting of Luther's anthem; or that the same melody is to be heard again in the Chorale Cantata (No. 80) written by Bach for the Reformation festival of 1730, which was the bicentenary, as well, of the Augsberg confession, for the tune is Teutonic, of the century of Dürer and Lucas Cranach, as much as the "sea tunes", "Rule Britannia", or even "Hearts of Oak", are Britannic, of the age of Nelson, breathing as they do, the salt airs of Trafalgar, Greenwich,

Offenbach, a caricature by Thomas

The Arrhuba, by T. Allom

Portsmouth, Plymouth, or The Nore. It was Wagner who said that the national character of the English was portrayed in the opening bars of "Rule Britannia". To a like extent, the German Reformation is apparent in "Ein' feste Burg". The Chorale Cantata, with accompanying drums and trumpets, is overwhelming in grandeur of effect, with alternating chorus, strophe and antistrophe, given forth and answered by the voices, culminating in the open, foursquare rendering of the Chorale hymn in four parts.

The Cantata "Wachet auf" (No. 140), known to the English audience as "Sleepers wake", which is another great masterpiece in the old German mode, the tune having been composed by a priest, Philip Nicolai, in 1599 after a plague in his parish, should be heard sung by the Catalan choir of Barcelona, because the nasal, Spanish voices of the boys add still further to the ceaseless and imperturbable surging of the sacred rhythm. It goes on its way, supported, as in some great procession, that is spiritual and not physical, by the phrases of the chorale. Never, indeed, can there have been such rhythm. And the voices surge up into it in a manner that stills the blood, but rubs its hands upon our hearts to bring the life back. Voices cry down from the watch tower till the whole heavenly city of parable is awake. We may use our own discretion as to whether we hear in the opening, with Dr Schweitzer, the virgins starting up from sleep to wake each other, and the preparation for the coming of the Heavenly Bridegroom; later, a dance of the virgins who strew flowers before His way; or, in the end, where the Chorale is sung in plain chant, unadorned, the music of the Heavenly wedding feast. The images cannot be decided in precise terms. All that is certain is the surpassing wonder of the music.

The Easter Cantata "Christ lag in Todesbanden" (No. 4) should be heard, also, sung by the Catalan choir, for it is unforgettable in majesty, proceeding at the same slow pace of ceremony, to the wonderful and solemn plainness of its end. Here, again, the Spanish voices, with their addition of Latinity, increase the warmth and fervency of the music so that the starched ruff and plain dress of the Lutheran pastor are not present, and we are in the Middle Ages. Particularly, we say, when it is performed by Spaniards. For it is interesting to

8

compare with this any good rendering of the Cantata "Gottlob! nun geht das Jahr zu Ende" (No. 28), in which comes the Chorale written by Kugelmann about 1540 and known in this country as the Old Hundredth, phrase by phrase, verse by verse, delivered, commented upon, and then resumed, by strings, oboes, trombones, and organ. Old German melodies by Martin Luther and his contemporaries form, of course, the basis for Bach's Chorale Preludes for organ, and supply the material for many of the great choral movements in his Cantatas. Of that incredible total of a hundred and forty-three Chorale Preludes for organ in their three different modes, plain and reflective in the style derived from Pachelbel, the decorated or coloratura in the style of Böhm, or treated in fantasia fashion in the manner of Buxtehude; of the three hundred and nineteen Chorales harmonized by Bach; and among the two hundred and eight Cantatas, and the hundred or more additional Cantatas that are lost, making three hundred, perhaps, in all; as to two-thirds, it may be, of this total, Bach was working in the old German manner. Among the incunabula. For that is how we would consider it. These are the incunabula of Northern music, corresponding to the woodcut pictures of the Reformation period. But the music is greater than the draughtsmen. Or is it that we only hear it through the mind of Johann Sebastian Bach?

The early German masters, in music, those we mentioned, together with Heinrich Schütz and Samuel Scheidt, were men of the seventeenth century, spread over three human generations, but all born after the Reformation. They invented the art form of the Chorale Preludes, but, mostly, did not compose the Chorale tunes. The greatest name among them, and the foremost German composer before Bach, was Heinrich Schütz (1585–1672). Closer knowledge should enable us, at once, to recognize the influence of Böhm or Pachelbel, of Scheidt or Schütz or Buxtehude, Reinken, or indeed of others who have been long forgotten. Not that the Chorale Preludes of Bach are consciously archaic, but he takes in them, the current pabulum, tunes which were a hundred or two hundred years old and known to all the population, and gives to them their Germanic setting. In this way, and in part through his own forebears of the same name, was the old German style of Bach invented.

94

Bach is computed to have written the Cantatas at the rate of one a month for twenty or thirty years of his life. In spite of their sacred purpose there can be no doubt that he regarded them as music of occasion, for passing performance, and felt no scruple in detaching portions of them, or otherwise altering and incorporating where it suited him. The Secular Cantatas, few in number (there are only twenty-three), could, on the same principle, be convertible, from Profane to Sacred. The Dresden Court Cantata "Die Wahl des Hercules", the giant being an Electoral Prince who was eleven years old, had most of its music embodied a year later, in the Christmas Oratorio. Another of the Secular Cantatas was used, as well, for the same purpose, while a chorus from yet another Cantata was employed by Bach for the Osanna of his Mass in B minor. But it so happens that two of the most lovely and well known of all his melodies occur in a Secular Cantata, afterwards to become immortal in their sacred setting. One of these, moreover, is in the pastoral style and the other in the old German manner.

Their occasion was the "Hunting" Cantata, "Was mir behagt". The year was 1716, so that it is the first and earliest of these secular compositions. Bach went with his master, Duke Wilhelm Ernst of Saxe-Weimar, upon a birthday visit to Duke Christian of Saxe-Weissenfels-Querfurt, whose remote capital lay a day's ride of thirty-five miles away, through the Thuringian forest. A great hunt was to be held. The Duke's birthday was 23 February, when the deciduous trees would be leafless, but the hunt will have been chiefly in the pinewoods. In the landscape, as it might be, of Dürer or Altdorfer, passing through the magpie villages of black and white. Near Weissenfels the country becomes more hilly and, according to an old guide book, "the vine is cultivated with some success". It is this contrast that we find in these two airs, one romantic and the other pastoral. The Cantata was given, we suppose, upon the birthday evening, and the musicians, presumably, had been brought from Weimar. Salomo Franck, of whom the name is the most poetical part, had written the libretto. The characters are Diana and Endymion, Pan and Pales. Dr Lemprière, whom we have consulted, tells us in his *Classical Dictionary*, that Pales was the goddess of sheepfolds and of pastures. Her festivals were called Palila. The ceremony consisted in burning heaps of straw, and in leaping over them. No sacrifices were offered, but the purifications were made with the smoke of horse's blood. The purification of the flocks was done with the smoke of sulphur, of the olive, the pine, the laurel, and the rosemary. Offerings of mild cheese, boiled wine, and cakes of millet were made to the goddess, and it was during the original festival that Romulus first began to build the town of Rome. Such was the curious occasion for these two immortal airs, for the two songs of the goddess Pales were that known, in translation, as "The sheep may safely graze", or "Flocks in pastures green abiding", and that which, twenty years later, in 1735, reappeared in the Sacred Cantata "Also hab Gott die Welt geliebt" (No. 68), from which it is familiar as "My heart ever faithful".

No description could exaggerate the beauty of this pair of melodies. When we remember their occasion it may remind us of the immortal tunes in *Figaro*, were it not that those are tainted with the theatre. We have to recall, again, the hunting party for the prince's birthday, and the bucolic setting. At the palace of Herrenhausen, outside Hanover, in an upper room, there are paintings by a Dutch or Flemish painter that depict Ernst Augustus, the first Elector and father of our George I, with his hawks and huntsmen. They are probably the most detailed pictures of this subject that were ever done, in large cartoons that call for tapestry, and that could be illustrations for a treatise on falconry. The hawks are on the wrist, in their hoods and chains, and there is much delight to be had, besides, from the horses, the liveries of the huntsmen, their horns and equipment, and the curious portraits. It could be, with little difference, the hunt of Weissenfels, and it should be in this spirit that we listen to "The sheep may safely graze" and its companion air "My heart ever faithful". Behind that, with only the subtle change of Sacred to Profane, there is the hunting party. The first mentioned of these tunes is broad and flowing, with all the physical healthiness of Handel, preceded by a recitative of heavenly beauty, to which the lapping rhythms of the pastoral succeed, vale upon vale, among the wattle fences of Virgilian calmness and serenity, tinged, though, by the radiant clouds and rounded shades of trees, till we are reminded, perforce, of "Opening the Fold", "The Bright Cloud", "The Rising Moon", and the pastorals of Samuel

Palmer, painted at Shoreham, when he was under the influence
of Blake, and the lovely melody becomes English in this
association.

The other tune, which has been more familiar for many
years, is more pointed and angular in its beauty. There is more
in it of the German primitive. This is great music because of
the world of purity and faithfulness in which it moves. By some
miracle it is, musically, the whole expression of its text, so much
so that it is, spiritually, a tune that could be offended against,
and that, in certain circumstances, we would not dare to remember, or to sing to ourselves. Of no other music could this
be true, except of some simple tune remembered from childhood with poignant or particular association. It is the answer
given in the second half of the first phrase of "My heart ever
faithful" that lays bare the humanity of this far away but ever
youthful tune. It repeats again, and then lifting itself upon
what has been said and settled carries the mood a little further,
and stating it once more until we are in that landscape of long
ago with the steep houses, up the stair into the many windowed
attic where the red apples lie, gives to us the little village or
Thuringian town, it does not matter where; for it could be in
Hungary when Veit Bach lived there as miller and baker, or in
one of the Saxon towns in Transylvania. Certainly there is a
winding street of steep houses that leads up a hill. This is an
instance, in analysis, of the rising figure in Bach's music that
Dr Schweitzer interprets to mean the lifting of the human heart.
We are in that world of musical images that he describes, and
of which he was the first serious interpreter. He remarks the
notes, in repetition, that mean spiritual crisis; the toll of funeral
bells, in warning, but sometimes welcomed, and even, in the
Cantata "Christus der ist mein Leben" (No. 95), insisted upon,
in a tenor aria that calls repeatedly for the bells of death, which
are imitated in the bass.

There are the sounds, as well, of knocking or hammering,
like the midnight knocking at the door which awakes the porter
in *Macbeth* and brings him to the gate; or less intermittent,
with quicker blows, it means divine judgement; or, with a
figure of wild trembling, the last, dread day of all. There are
the rhythms, again according to Dr Schweitzer, of running and
following. Paired notes can mean a heavy, dragging walk;

while a weary, limping rhythm portrays fatigue and the approach of death. Running is closely echoed by a running figure,
and following by an imitation in two or more voices. The
marching rhythms can be grouped according to their different
meanings; in degree of pride and confidence, exultant or in
triumph. There is that measure which Dr Schweitzer identifies
as the treading of the wine press, according to an image from
the Old Testament; pictures of storm, and of the calm of
evening; the coiling of the serpent, portraying evil; or the
silvery, captivating laughter of the angels. Paired notes, in a
light and dancing rhythm, intend running water; while quick
scales, ascending or descending, mean clouds or waves.

If such be the musical language of the Cantatas, first translated and described by Dr Schweitzer, who had the curiosity,
also to follow it out among the Chorale Preludes by tracing and
comparing the same figures as they occur in both, then there
must be meaning elsewhere, when there is occasion for it. Not
in the dances and *galantieren* of the French or English Suites;
not in the Brandenburg Concertos; for their frame and purpose
do not allow of that. But this incredible genius was the master
of all styles. In this respect there is only Shakespeare to compare with him. What is the intent of the Chromatic Fantasia
and Fugue? The Italian Concerto, on the other hand, has no
need for any further meaning. Its late date (1735), infers, in
all probability, that Bach had come across the Sonatas of
Domenico Scarlatti. Certainly, it is identical in manner with
the Fantasia and unfinished Fugue in C minor for harpsichord,
in which the crossing of the hands betokens the Italian influence, and which was a late work composed in 1738. We could
call them Venetian or Neapolitan according to our mood, not
in the shallow effects of Italian opera, but they are Italian by
their light and shade, of deep cornice and pediment, as though
in a dramatic lighting that never was in the little Thuringian
towns. This Concerto "in the Italian style" has an opening
theme derived from Georg Muffat, one of the many forgotten
composers of whom Bach made a study, but the answer to it is
so skilful in construction and so perfect in idiom that the work
is in a category to itself. This is not in the "Italian style" of
Vivaldi, but of a different character altogether. Bach knew the
music of Vivaldi very well indeed; to the extent of arranging

sixteen of his violin Concertos for harpsichord. But there is no evidence that he had come across more than a stray Sonata or two by Domenico Scarlatti, and we are left to infer that the Italian Concerto of Bach is, therefore, "Italian" in an ideal sense, but that, by intuition, it approached the style and mannerisms of Scarlatti, who was, by turn, Venetian, Neapolitan, Portuguese, or Spanish, according to the vicissitudes of his career; but, in fact, in all things, Mediterranean or Southern. The slow movement of the Concerto, though beautiful in itself, is of another identity, not Italian in texture or sentiment, but the mood returns and we come, too soon, to the last cadences of the sparkling, exhilarating Italian scene. We would attach no other meaning to it than that of light and colour.

Very different in intention is the Chromatic Fantasia and Fugue, gigantic in scale, within its compass, and descending to the very depths of feeling. We feel, not that it is one of many works by Bach, but that it is the entire creation of a great master in itself, as though there was no need of anything further from his hand and all he had to say is expressed in it. The Italian Concerto, by contrast, is an extra work, or something added, as when we discover with delight some picture by a favourite painter, and its size and importance come as a revelation of a fresh side of his genius. One of the chief pleasures of painting is derived in this manner, since few but the expert will keep in mind the printed measurements in books and catalogues. How often have we known this happen: in Venetian and Toledan churches, in Italian palaces, in the picture galleries of Europe, mostly dispersed, now, in precaution against bombing! The Italian Concerto is when the master worked directly under Italian influence; but the Chromatic Fantasia and Fugue are in no Italian convention, however lightly worn. In some three or four of the wonderful Goldberg Variations we detect the Italian hand, for its late date, 1742, makes it more than ever likely that Bach has seen Sonatas by Scarlatti, or, by that alchemy of human instinct, through long reflection had approximated to the unknown truth. By these three works alone, the Goldberg Variations, the Chromatic Fantasia and Fugue, the Italian Concerto, Bach is evident in his stupendous greatness. But when we think, as well, of the Forty

Eight Preludes and Fugues, of the eighteen Suites for harpsichord, other Preludes, Fugues, Fantasies, and Toccatas,
realizing that this is but Bach's clavier music, and not even
the main ocean of his genius, which was for choirs of voices
and for organ, then it is to know in him the master of all
masters, and, with Shakespeare, the greatest light of the
West, dimming the Latin glitter of the Mediterranean. All
other composers are, compared with him, like lesser poets
of the Elizabethan age. They worked in the same medium, but
can but be mentioned with him. Their whole universe is music,
but this is its fountain. He is past, future, and recurring present.
Beethoven, not always, only now and then; Handel, at his most
superb; and Mozart, always Mozart, are all that are left beside
him. And that natural music which is anonymous; the airs or
folk tunes which are the emanation of the soil, and that, even if
their authorship be known, remain no less a mystery. The wild
flower can be as beautiful, and as richly scented, as that to which
humanity has put all its pains. In no other music, but that of
Bach, can a portentous complexity wear a calm and smiling
face. The Goldberg Variations are in proof of this, for their
beauty can be appreciated in ignorance of the canons at every
interval from the unison to the ninth, and twice in contrary
motion, which is to say, the subject is answered by its inversion.
Most perfect instance of all is the quodlibet, that forms the
thirtieth and last of the set of variations, for the four popular
songs which it presents, in combination, at one and the
same time, coalesce in their fragments into a miniature that,
in its robust manliness, is an epitome of the burgher tunes that
it conceals. The enormous hand of Bach has, in this, descended
into microscopic detail. He is the master of all proportion, as in
the little Marches and Polonaises copied into the notebook of
Anna Magdalena Bach. The surface melody, so to speak, of the
quodlibet is equivalent to those. The quodlibet could be four
of the little Marches wrought together into one.

But the mighty hand of this Ancient intones the language of
the Fugue. In the words of one who heard him at the organ:
"his fist was gigantic . . . his hand was never weary and lasted
out through a whole day's organ playing. The comic style was
just as familiar to him as the earnest". That phrase may be
puzzling, until we remember the Fugue subject of the organ

Fantasia and Fugue in G minor; or again, the Fugue alla gigue in G major. "Comic" is intended in the lofty style; and in the sense that figures from the Italian Comedy appear in Watteau's paintings. Those are not less serious because comedians form their subject. There can be little doubt that both theme and treatment in the two organ works that we have mentioned are in the "comic style". Not the light *badinerie* or *galantieren* for harpsichord; but in the manner of the greatest architecture, as though Vignola or Palladio had been called upon for buildings in the "comic style". This is conceivable at Caprarola or Villa Lante, or in the villas of the Venetian terra firma. The comic vein of Bach was, by nature, Northern and old fashioned, if things that are eternal need not be ephemeral and absolutely of their day. Let us think of this as Dutch or Hanseatic humour, lying from the North Sea to the Baltic, and not influenced by Italian skies, but characteristic of the high gabled buildings of the Northern Renaissance, anywhere from Brussels or Antwerp, across Germany, to Danzig, or beyond. The Fantasia and Fugue in G minor, we suggest, might be called, architecturally, a work of the Netherlandish Renaissance, coincident with late Elizabethan or with James I, and therefore, about a hundred years earlier than its actual time. Not medieval; nor having lost, altogether, the effects of that; but older, certainly, by a century than the date at which it was composed.

The other organ works, or a few of them at least, are too gigantic to be classified. They are only to be listened to, and wondered at. Such, truly, are works of a huge fist. This is the Ancient of all time; and musical genius has no existence by the side of him. He is the only one. The others have but little meaning. Compared with his solid sculpture they are but arabesques in stucco. It is because he, only, speaks the fugal language and moves freely in it. No other can manipulate its difficulties and make sense of them. It is too old and formidable; but, in his hands, it is the secret language of the soul and mind. It expresses what has never been expressed again. It improves at every hearing, and it never stales. At the end of a lifetime all has not been said. There is ever something new; and so much of it that no one living can have heard it all.

His giant form emerges out of the Biblical past, quickening the shades of old polyphony. His sources are forgotten men. The

Biblical Sonatas of Johann Kuhnau; the organ works of Fres-
cobaldi; the Toccatas of Froberger and Merulo; Pachelbel, of
whom the name, for an organist, is as suited as Thomas
Tompion to be a clockmaker, for it suggests the syrinx and the
dulcet tones of the organ; Schütz and Böhm and Buxtehude;
such are his origins. They are his primitives. It happens, therefore, that the supreme genius of music springs from a forgotten
soil; and, in view of his family history, an exceptional flowering
or a hybrid that has never come again. Perhaps this analogy is
not applied enough in explanation. But, possessed of it, many
mysteries in the arts may yield their secret. We see the *Nozze
di Figaro* as all comedy and music resumed in one, and even the
side comments of farcical situation given the line of beauty.
But there are artists, like Chopin, who cannot be explained at
all; whom no one could prophesy, unless we consider that the
invention of the new instrument, the pianoforte, made it certain
that he would appear.

In the case of Bach there are almost too many reasons why he
should have been. He had all the past behind him. We hear that
in the pleading phrases of the Passacaglia. For the rest, it is a
language and an architecture for all time. But the true secret is
his Christianity. It is upon that assurance that his rolling
phrases mount into the heavens. Such are the truths that his
Fugues set out to prove. And there is more wisdom in him than
in religion; more of truth and beauty than in all the prayers
and aspirations. Many faiths; but only one true Ancient, of
whom we hear the huge fist when the formal language of the
Fugue begins.

BADINERIE, AND PICNIC BY THE
SWEET WATERS OF ASIA*

My first object is the head of a masked girl not more than three inches high. You could look at her for a long time, or for ever. Because, in herself, she has immortality, but can be shattered to bits in a moment, and become but broken china.

Instead of hair, her head is dressed with flowers. That is to say, her hair is brushed up above her ears and temples, but where her curls should be, they are metamorphosed into flowers. Into a tower, or nosegay, of little precise petals that would snap quickly, or would chip their edges. Roses, pinks and daisies: painted in gay colours, and that have all but scent.

But now, she turns from nature into comedy.

Her forehead is completely right. You would know from her forehead what her face must be. A moment ago it was as though you held a lovely head up by its hair, which had been transformed into flowers, but now it is a face hidden entrancingly, and on purpose, by a mask. And not an ordinary mask. This is cut differently. It is as fanciful as the cut leaf of a tulip tree.

The cheeks or fesses of her mask are nearly swallow tailed. Like the wings of a swallow tailed butterfly. Not so large as a swallow tail, not forked, or like long coat tails, for they curve round, they are cheeks or fesses moulded to the curve of the cheek bone. The fascination of this mask comes from the white lights of china upon its black contours. Indeed, the curves of her mask make the two halves, or separate beauties, of the whole. And her nose is where the body of this butterfly should be.

Her eyes are green or hazel, like eyes seen from an inch away in the strongest light. Whether sunlight or candlelight, it does not matter. But they are enclosed, surrounded, in the black of the mask. And again, they are a pair. You can look closely, and see the mock suns and the iris. She has painted

* From *Splendours and Miseries*, 1943.

eyelashes. Her eyebrows you cannot see, for they are hidden in her mask. So that they are a pair of black cheeks, with the white and carmine of the flesh shown only round her mouth. The scarlet of her lips is as though in reply to this concealment. Ready to speak, but rather full with silence or disdain.

We have said that her nose is the body of this butterfly. And, by its angle, it bears out the simile of flight. For it rises, in enchantment, from the face, between the black wings of the mask. But its light or comedy character, borne out by her red lips, is contradicted in her mitre of little, formal flowers.

She turns from comedy into nature, and is the head of Ceres. A head of Ceres, or a caryatid. A figure that carries flowers: a garden term. And a goddess of Comedy again. The stopper of a scent bottle; or a little patch box.

There are other things; the handles of walking-sticks which are masked faces. A masked beauty: or the head of Harlequin. Sometimes Janus-like, with heads that face both ways, so that you see the beauty, in profile, both sides at once; or, if it be Harlequin, one face solemn, and the other smiling. A seal of Harlequin in a sentrybox, not more than an inch high. Another stopper can be a white swan with a golden collar shaped like a golden crown, worn at the middle of its lovely neck. And a group of Cupids, clothed or naked, building a house of cards.

But here is something beautiful, and more full of meaning.

A big and placid face, which is expressionless, and not higher than the finger.

A man's head, clean shaven, round as Phœbus. But the curious point is that it is a moonlight face taken out into the day. For the head is shaven. It must have close cropped hair. It is the head to wear a nightcap. For, in fact, it belongs to the time when wigs were worn. Without their wigs they wore nightcaps and dressing-gowns. That is why we say this is a physiognomy for candlelight taken by surprise out in a summer morning. In fact, a theatre face. It was conceived for artificial light. It has paint upon it. Round patches, or almost round, upon the cheekbones, so that they are like a hectic flush, except that there is nothing feverish, all is placid and moonlit in expression. Indeed, the face is quite blank and mask-like, but for its colour, and for the eyes, which are light brown. They are the eyes of a man who would have light brown hair. Who is highly intelligent, and who plays a part.

The eyes are used to a strong light. He has not been taken out of the dark into the sun. He is accustomed to as bright a light as this, but of another sort. That is why he has paint upon his cheeks.

Does he wear a cotton nightcap; or a kind of turban?

He has the most poetical of headdresses that has ever been invented. It is turban, ruff and nightcap, all in one. It has, also, something of the chef's cap, or the scullion's, and could be worn by the doctor, the peasant, or the lawyer. By the Chasseurs Alpins, even, in the mountain villages. And yet, it is as simple as a folded handkerchief. It is rayed or striped in three colours, red and green and yellow; and they are bright colours, not violent, so that their effect is pale. The shape is a ruched cap, or ruff, with the stripes running each in its turn from his shaved head, which is like a mask; but the form of the whole cap is that of a Swiss Guard's cap, worn to one side, and fuller on that side, falling to the ear. In fact, a beret; but not the cloth cap. For this is silken; or it is striped cotton.

But the beauty of this headdress lies in its pleats, or ruchings, and in the rayed stripes, like moonbeams, that follow on each other like the colours of the spectrum. The face of the comedian is the full moon. And he wears a cap of moonbeams. They are lights on water, or on a moonlit land. But the form of the cap is, also, like a ruff; like that of a ruffed lizard, or of a bird of paradise. In fact, he has a ruffed head. We catch the bright lights of china on each ruching of his cap, and see how the moonbeams waver, but are in regular order, while they break or tally with the folds.

His placid face is quite unmoved by this. But remark that he has no pallor. There is paint upon his cheeks. Not, therefore, a mask of melancholy. He is, more, that sort of musician who plays in the classical manner, without expression, whose features never alter while the music lasts. Not, indeed, a mask of restraint. For it is all in the music. It is his convention not to be affected by it, but to embody it. And his instrument will be the mandoline, or guitar. The sling may be upon his shoulder, now. But we have only the head of Mezzetin. His striped dress we do not see. This is nothing but his head and ruff.

We know the dress of Mezzetin. His striped shirt and trousers; white stockings and black, square-ended shoes. Often, he sits cross-legged for convenience of his guitar.

We know him, too, with his mandoline slung upon his back. Like that, he is the tramp or straggler. He is like a soldier with his gun. Or a vagabond with his pots and pans. He wanders along, slowly, perhaps with a blade of grass or a flower between his lips. Cigarettes are not known yet; and a tobacco pipe is as rare a thing as a pipe of opium. But he has only to unsling his mandoline, and we shall have music in a moment. The gesture is as simple as putting on your gas mask.

But a word about the dust upon his shoes.

For it is the dust of the theatre, not the mud of the roads. Indeed, it is the dust seen in a beam of light. If you open your window when it is full moon. Or if you come near to the shaded candle. Or below the girandole. Night dust: the sacred dust of the old theatre, which is as holy as the dust of churches. It comes up between the boards.

This is no statue that has suffered mutilation. That has no arms or hands. Not dug from the soil, or dragged up in the fishing-net. It is whole and entire. It is the head: and the head only. But a head: and not a bust. It has no neck. It stands, directly, upon the shelf or table, and can be taken up in the hand.

Ah! I have seen him when I was a child. Looking down from the asphalt of the Esplanade. At the age when shepherd boys, who spend the whole day alone, see visions upon the green hillside. I saw him upon the sands: and in Catlin's Arcadia. That was my education all the summer. Now, he will be as old as Pantaloon. Walking with a stick. But he is dead, of course.

I only knew his shadow. But a shadow that had colour; not, therefore, quite a ghost.

And, later, in the lands of music. . . . And in imagination.

What a lovely thing! But, to tell the truth, I would sooner that he did not sing, or touch his mandoline. I prefer the god when he is silent. As he is now, with closed lips. A Turk's head, almost. But he could be no one else than Mezzetin. By the double white lilac. By the mock orange.

Ah! what a breath of milk and honey. In a land of milk and honey.

An enclosed land, a walled garden near to the Milky Way. For such is the philadelphus or mock orange. It is a constellation or a starry bush. The creamy flowers are in myriads. You can shake the rain from them and smell the mock orange in the raindrops.

The white lilac is more melancholy, more nostalgic. But how it snares the senses! Somehow the mock orange is more suitable to Mezzetin. Because it is a scent, an echo, of the warm South. In name only? The white lilac, jasmine, roses, stephanotis, are in another mood. But the mock orange is a whole milky constellation. Not hanging in pale racemes or snowy trusses; not like the lone meteor in dark leaves; not like the rose; not like the jasmine; but clouding the branches with its cups of milk. It is the ghost of the orange grove; a phantom from the citrus lands. The mock moons of the Milky Way. And the soil is white with the shed petals.

The scent of the mock orange is creamy white, like curd, and you taste, in it, the honeyed anthers. For his whole figure.

For the head of Mezzetin, the single flamed tulip. That is to say, we would have the body of Mezzetin by the milky branches, for his striped suit. But his bust should be put beside the parrot tulip. They are flamed red and yellow, with veins or bracts of the leaf green, and there are so many other colours. Feathered purples, crimsons, golden browns. One at a time. A tulip for every morning. For the tulip has the lights of china on it, and is as high as the bust of Mezzetin, if it is just the head and not the stalk.

It is like a lovely cup put down beside him, that is never touched by lips, and that each night is thrown away. And you can compare the featherings and flamings. But the tulip is warm to the touch. To the quick of the fingernail it feels like living flesh. It is alive. It is composed of airy cells. It is a creature of the sun. But this piece of china is completely cold. More like moonlight. The white paste is like the substance of moonlight. That is to say, it is flat and has no depth. So must the insect feel that strikes upon the windowpane.

For the blank white of the porcelain has some quality that is invisible about it. Or shall we say that it is dead, and has been fused in the fire! A dead substance, not organic. Moonlight, therefore, compared to sunlight. Where Mezzetin is a nocturnal creature, chameleon of the waxlights, whom it has been our inspiration to stand by the white lilac. And, now, by the painted tulip.*

But the cosmogony increases. It is a whole world in miniature. Or the genius of Johann Joachim Kändler.

Here are white horses led by blackamoors. They are milk white Lippizaners, with long tails. Their milky bodies are naked as Venus, with no saddle or stirrups, taken out of their stalls or riding school into the sun, with an Aethiopian at the bridle. We see them, in imagination, by the pillars of a Doric colonnade, near to a rainbow fountain.

Or it is a blackamoor standing by a fruit basket.

Here are Orientals holding lutes. A Turk with a guitar: a Turkish woman who holds a zither, or a shell. A Janissary, chamberlain to King Dodon, in high peaked cap with a veil that falls behind. A kneeling Turk, with his wares spread out beside him, becomes a silk-clad figure with a sugar bowl. We are taken into an Orient of the fancy, which, in fact, had existence, not so long ago. The shell could be one of those giant clam shells from the Pacific, used for holy water bowls in the gilded churches of the South, and taken, now, inside the gilded lattice. As for the Heyducks or Janissaries they are the curious, neuter guardians of the Seraglio. Their long gowns and conical or peaked hats relate them to beehive or antheap.

We will have a picnic along the Bosphorus. Down by the Sweet Waters of Asia.† Those who resort from the European shore come in caïques; those from the Asiatic in the arrhuba. It is a Friday or the Turkish sabbath; and a golden evening. Among the fruit sold is the grape, or yellow chaoush, which

* The two pieces of old Chelsea china, here described, are the head of a masked girl, and a head of Mezzetin. They are illustrated, in colour, in *Chelsea Porcelain Toys*, by G. E. Bryant, the Medici Society, London, 1925; and are the work, probably, of the Flemish modeller, Nicholas Sprimont, who came to Chelsea from Liége, and managed the factory.

† The Sweet Waters of Asia are on the far or Asiatic bank of the Bosphorus, about half-way between Constantinople and the Black Sea. The Sweet Waters of Europe are beyond the Mosque of Eyoub, at the end of the Golden Horn. Both were celebrated, under the Sultans, as places for picnics, and the inhabitants of the Turkish capital and its suburbs, in Europe and Asia, resorted there on days of holiday. All travellers describe the scene, down to Théophile Gautier and P. Loti. It was the embodiment of the rococo Turkey of Liotard and of the Dresden china figures, and as such I have tried to add my description of it to the rest.

The Sweet
Waters of
Asia, by T.
Allom

Banquet to the Dutch Ambassador, Cornelis Calkoen, by Sultan Achmet III of "The Tulip Reign", by J. B. Vanmour (1671–1737)

tastes of dew and honey. For there is a great concourse of persons from both continents, divided by the narrow straits, and a multitude of veiled women.

Moving among them we see the vendors of sweetmeats and confectioners, with tables set up beneath the plane trees. They are selling sherberts. Of raisins, pears, and prunes and quinces, cooled with ice. Many other sweets, as well. A confection of rice, boiled down into a jelly, which is cut into squares or slices with a brass shovel, and has attar of roses dropped upon it from a perforated silver vessel. A sweet, too, which is made from honey and almonds; another of walnuts; and another of honey and the juice of fresh ripe grapes, which is formed into large square dice. Besides, there is the water seller, moving in and out among the crowd, with his glass cups and long spouted jar. When called, he attaches a mass of snow to the spout, and the water comes forth cool and limpid through the pores.

Wherever we look there are veiled women. They are sitting in long rows upon the ground; or walk slowly, leading their children. A negress or two are among them. All are alike as nuns. In black dresses, mostly, some in white; but all with the white headwrapping, which covers the face and conceals all but the eyes. It is, therefore, like a nun's picnic, but for the plane trees and the fountains. But for the stork's nest upon the minaret. We can see the balcony for the muezzin, and hear the clacking of the stork's beak.

But, too, for this fountain. For it is a kiosque, or an arabesque. A square pavilion of marble, with the wide roof of all Turkish fountains, and a bason to which gilt cups are chained, with a dervish or other person to dispense the waters. There is a Turkish café, too, where coffee is drunk, interminably, as though it were potent as opium. Other buildings show, mysteriously, between the trees. In every direction there would seem to be the carved balcony, or gilded lattice.

The forms of the turbans are as elaborate as in a fairy story. After a few years they will be forbidden, and it will be as though peony or tulip were banished from the flowerbed. For this is a land where the arts are sumptuary. If we follow one of these turbaned merchants to his house, it will be a mean dwelling, with nothing in it. No furniture; for they sit, and sleep, upon the floor. All their magnificence is in their clothes. And only with the men. The women are like veiled nuns, until they go back to their bare walls.

The Sultan has a pavilion in this valley of the Sweet Waters, where, Tartar fashion, he shoots with a bow and arrow on these summer evenings; or watches the play of marionettes. Ah! what a golden evening. Of the Sweet Waters of Asia. But the shadows lengthen. The painted caïque waits with gilded oars.

They return in the arrhuba.

Here come those carriages, slowly, slowly, at the pace of the white oxen. For the arrhuba is a chariot drawn by buffalos. The thick locks between their horns are stained with henna, like the ladies' fingernails, and below the dyed hair they have amulets of beads upon the foreheads. They are longhorned oxen; but it is only now we see the beauty and peculiarity of the arrhuba.

For it is all curves and arches. The carriage, itself, is gilded and floreated, in arabesques, and has oval windows on all four sides, filling the whole space, but for the gilded frame. It is more open than a gondola, so curved and rounded that it appears to float upon its wheels, although it has no springs. One after another the arrhubas come into view, each with four ladies in it, who sit upon the floor. The curves of their cowled heads, their full sleeves and wrists that hold a fan, fill the gilded cabins. And they are led along, so slowly, with eunuchs walking at the sides, and a man who holds each buffalo by the curving horn.

But another singularity of the arrhuba is still to come. The carriage is all curves and ovals with its windows and its wheels. And there is a peculiar ornament which enhances this. The tails of the white oxen are fastened into a long and lofty wooden bow extending from the neck yokes, and projecting over their backs. This arch is hung with chains of gaudy tassels, so that they sway and dangle, and, in the mind, usurp the place of carriage springs. To the slow treading of the oxen, and the shaking of these golden tassels which could be antennæ, some limb or part of which the function is imperfectly understood but which is in connection with the guarding of the women, the arrhuba comes past, and we see the veiled sultanas and hear their muffled voices, hidden in the silks with which their heads are wrapped. One, and then another, the pastoral carriages come by, under the plane trees, with their curious tasselled ornaments dangling from as high up as the carriage roofs. Those coaches could be the howdahs upon elephants, or the wicker cages in which Moslem brides are borne upon the backs of camels.

It is but a short journey out of Asia, under the plane trees, down to the water where the caïques wait. But, in a sense, the procession comes from far away, out of antiquity. This suburb of the Sweet Waters is where Asia ends. But the waters are metropolitan, and face the Golden Horn. How slow, how slow the past dies, and how quickly it is ended! Like this golden sunset. It is borne away from us by the milk-white oxen, at the pace that a man walks. Ah yes! this happened, not once, but upon many summer evenings. They must have thought that it would last for ever. Now, all are gone.

We make no excuse for this picnic. It imposed itself. And now we would see gardeners, goose sellers, Savoyards, Tyrolese. A woman with a hurdygurdy, and a Polish lady in a crinoline. Beggar musicians, and a Hussar who plays the bagpipes. Little, longhaired, red and white dogs, Bologna terriers; salt miners; a tailor riding upon a goat; and a lady singing, while a fox sits at the harpsichord. Busts of laughing Chinamen, as though the faun lay under the yellow skin. Pandurs or Circassians, and Japanese.

Or take the "Swan Service" of Count Brühl with its nymphs and dolphins, in allegory of water; its tritons and nereids holding shells. Some of the plates of the "Swan Service" have ghostly swans raised or embossed in the snow white paste, so that they are just the necks of swans and the ghostly reeds or bulrushes. The great dishes and tureens are too elaborate, it may be, with their naked nymphs and sporting dolphins. They are too copious for the fragile porcelain. But the lesser pieces are as fanciful as Bernini's fountains. Yet another imagery, which is Northern, and not Roman. The swans belong to the Baltic. Swans of Denmark, of Livonia, Courland, or Elsinore: of the Goths and Wends. We are reminded of the chapel of Knights of the Order of the Swan, at Ansbach, in the church of St Gumbertus. Built by the Margrave Albrecht Achilles, with its medieval tombs and hatchments of the Swan Knights. The "Swan Service" is like the poetical expansion of this theme, but without its chivalry. It is meant for pleasure.

But we return to the "crinoline" groups, which are characteristic of Kändler. Young women in great panniered skirts; pairs of lovers, sometimes in Spanish costumes of the stage. And to the porcelain groups, generally. A group of Cupids hairdressing, where the curiously big heads of the Cupids relate them to the mandarins, or "Malabars", as they were called; and Cupid as Harlequin. He has baby legs, a dunce's or a Pierrot's cap, the curls of a little boy, a white mask with slit eyes, a Pierrot's white ruff, and the chequered coat of Harlequin, but fitting like a baby's suit. A two year old Harlequin, who is, in fact, Cupid, or a cherub. But again, his large head relates him to the Chinese boys with big heads and hats of cabbage leaves.

Or we find the pair of "Morlacchi", who, in prosaic language, are a man offering ham to a woman under a tree. But they are "Morlacchi" by their costume, and called accordingly. For the "Morlacchi" were a tribe of Dalmatian mountaineers, Illyrians or Albanians, famous for their ferocity, a kind of mountain pirate when most of Dalmatia was Venetian. They but seldom came down into the towns, but had cherry orchards near their villages, from which the cherry brandy of Zara was distilled, so much so that "sangue dei Morlacchi" was the local name for this cordial in all Venetian territory.

We could argue, also, an Albanian origin for Pierrot. In this way. The Albanian was zany of the Dalmatian seaports, hanging about for hire, and speaking no language but his own. His white fez and white clothes, his doltish or country manners come down from the mountains, made of him a rustic stranger who could be impersonated and played upon the stage. Certain it is that Pierrot wears the white cap and trousers of the Shqipniter or Albanian. The ill or malarial Albanian who is longing for his native land. He cannot be understood. His long sleeves and ruff are the licence of the theatre, and this gives us Pierrot of the Venetian stage.

And now for the Harlequins of Kändler.

No two of them are alike. In the colours of the cherry orchard. Masked, of course; sometimes, half Pierrot, in Pierrot's ruff and his white buttons, with a white mask and a black hat like a priest's biretta. Holding a dog, a Chinese pug dog, but wearing breeches and not Pierrot's trousers. Or sitting upon a tree stump, holding a mug of beer. Crouched, in fact, like a many-coloured panther, all lozenged and diamonded, his arms and body in one colour scheme, and his legs in another. In a dancer's white shoes. Sometimes in a mask, half white, half black; or all in white, with a white mask, and a white coat which has black seams down the sleeves.

In which case, he is only known for Harlequin by the playing card upon his coat. It may have been Kändler's particular invention, but it had its origin and meaning. For the parti-coloured suits were sewn like patchwork quilts, with the aid of playing cards, in order to get the diamonds or lozenges into their proper order. This will have suggested leaving a playing card among the other diamond shapes; and, in the end, only a few out of a pack of cards, in elimination of all the other checks. One playing card upon a suit of white, and the comedian turns from Pierrot into Harlequin. And particular cards, of course, had their esoteric meaning.

Such Harlequins out of a pack of cards have the eight of diamonds, perhaps, or the five of hearts, upon their coat sleeve. Sometimes, upon one arm, or one side only, the other half of the body being blank. It is enough, so long as the coat and trousers have black seams. By a kind of poetical economy, the entire Harlequin is suggested by just the one card showing. He wears a white ruff, and has the ace of spades above his heart; an undress Harlequin, the scullion of the castle kitchens; or the Court Jesters, Joseph Fröhlich and Postmaster "Baron" Schmiedel, for the British Minister to the Saxon Court tells us that the King (Augustus III) "always dines with company, and his buffoons make a great noise and fight with one another during the whole repast". But, in truth, this particular Harlequin of the playing cards is found nowhere else, and may have been an invention of the Saxon-Polish Court. There are, even, instances where his red and white cheeks and flaxen, wig-like hair relate him to the peasant dolts or knaves, and to the Four Ivans of the Russian legend.

We hear the echo of this pandemonium and laughter, and of the rattling plates, in the group of a seated lady with a cavalier kissing the hem of her dress, a servant carrying fruit upon a dish, and Harlequin teasing "Baron" Schmiedel with a mouse. Or it is a lady and gentleman, seated, with a pair of Harlequins, one offering them a plate of fruit, and the other hiding behind their backs. Or Harlequin crouches upon the ground, at their feet. Or sits at a table beside another man, and holds a monkey; or holds a monkey's tail and blows a horn. Or but bows low, mockingly, and is about to spring. Columbine pushes away Harlequin; or her lover is on his knees before a lady, Cupid brandishes his bow and arrow, but Harlequin leers sardonically.

But we come back to the cherry orchard, because a woman is sitting underneath a little tree, with a bowl upon her lap, near a little table with cups and saucers standing on it. A pair of parrots are in the branches, and she is offering them cherries. Behind her stands Harlequin. He has white trousers, a white ruff, and lesser white ruffs upon his sleeves; black dancing shoes, with buckles; a black hat like a Pierrot's hat; and a mask in natural colour, which is to say, red and white, with flaxen hair that is certainly a wig. We can tell that he is an actor by the gestures of his hands. He is calling out to the parrots, probably in a voice that they will imitate. And his red coat is completely covered with the playing cards. All at different angles, and all high in their different suits; sixes, fives, or eights. His hands, in his white gloves, so near to these, are part of his mocking attitude.

It means much, or nothing. Probably nothing: it is, even, part of the quality of porcelain that it is so fragile. If it is broken, which card will lie uppermost ? Perhaps his head and white ruff will have rolled a little way ? Or his white gloved hand ? Perhaps the room will, suddenly, darken while we look at him? For, all this time, something has been preparing. We hear a grinding, screeching. Of brakes. Of some engine broken down, which tries to start up again.

Turn over in your sleep, and dream another dream.

THE DINKA*

*(This essay is in preface to a poem that has not
been published.)*

In the spring of 1931 I was given an opportunity of going to
the Sudan. This was, at the first, a project of no great interest
for someone whose ambition to see the Tropics was concerned
more with India and the East Indies. All the greater, for this
reason, was the revelation of British rule in that immense land.
For the whole of this huge territory is run with Roman modera-
tion and sense by a mere handful of British officials.

The twenty-four hours in the desert express from Wadi-
Halfa to Khartum are exciting enough. And, below Khartum,
there is Omdurman, a negro metropolis with a hundred
thousand inhabitants, drawn, it would seem, from every tribe in
Africa. Khartum itself was laid out by Lord Kitchener on the
plan of a series of Union Jacks, with large open squares and
broad intersecting streets. And, of an evening, the drums of
Omdurman, played with savage intensity and in wild variety
of rhythm, roll out their music from five miles away, up the
Nile, in prelude to the true Africa that lies behind them.

But the real interest of the Sudan only begins beyond Kosti,
two hundred miles south of Khartum. Here, the Moslem Arabs
are left behind, and we come to the tribes of pagan negroes.
The crocodile sprawls on the sandy islands: the hippopotamus
cools himself in the river, and only his two little disproportionate ears announce that enormous lumbering body hidden
in the water. The birds are indescribable in beauty and variety.
The golden-crested ibis preens herself in the rushes: storks and
cranes are as numerous as the dwellers in great cities: magnificent eagles soar overhead. There are other birds, nameless,
because never seen before. The river-banks, to either side, are a
park of game. Deer, in their hundred kinds, can be seen in

* From *Touching the Orient*, 1934.

herds. The ostrich is but one among a line of ballerinas. Zebras seem to wait to be harnessed for the chariot of a princess in a fairy-story. Zebras for her summer-chariot (their antipodes, the reindeer, draw her sledge in winter). There is the giraffe, more fanciful still. The lion has his lair in the long tawny grasses. The ruin of certain red trees, on which they love to feed, betrays the elephant. If, far off, certain small towers, like the periscopes of submarines, turn round and round, as in the wind to sniff the airs, it is his herd advancing in a trampling thunder.

These are the animals, and men are no less interesting. One morning we saw a naked figure, more black than charcoal, wading down the shallows. He was waist-high in the river; and passed the reeds with flashing trident looking for fish to spear. He was the first true savage we saw. That afternoon, landing at a great village of huts, we saw one negro a head and shoulder taller than the others. He was the first of the Dinka; and by the next evening we were in their midst.

Their home is the east bank of the White Nile. What especially distinguishes them is their inordinate, stork-like length of leg, in which they fully equal the extravagancies in physique ascribed to the negroes by Leo Africanus. They are as peculiar as the pygmies, or as the race of duck-billed women from the Congo. The Dinka, as often as not, are six feet six inches in height, and, on occasion, as much as seven feet.

They are a pastoral people, and the purpose of this great stature is that they should look out over the marshes upon their herds of cattle. This they do in a characteristic pose, standing on one leg, with the other foot, akimbo, to their knee. Long hours they pass like this, motionless as a statue, and leaning on a long spear. The silhouette of a Dinka, on sentry against the evening sky, is an unforgettable sight.

They are unclothed and naked save for a rust-red cloak that they wear with the dignity of a Roman warrior, giving to this simple cloak the air of expense and elaboration of a dress from the *grandes maisons* of Paris. Their pride, and their carriage, are ineffable. They wear tight-fitting skull-caps of bright blue, or white beads; inlaying them, as it were, into their woolly hair; and fashions are changed in this, so we were told, every year.

Bracelets and anklets of beads point, still further, their naturally slim wrists and ankles. They wear an ostrich-plume in their hair and carry a high, knobbed walking-stick.

These are their men. The women are more naked still; but no more magnificent nudity could be imagined. Their every movement is a revelation. If these are savages, then what are the dwellers in our own poor streets ? The women of the Dinka are, at once, the statues of a golden age and the models of our own contemporary standard of looks. Their small heads, crowned with little caps of beads, their thin hips, the slimness of their limbs, everything about them is of the present, as it is of the antique past. Their features, it must be added, are small and neat, with none of the grossness of the real slave-negro.

Finally, there are the adolescent warriors, who need to be thought of in a class to themselves, because, by the extraordinary manner in which they decorate their faces and bodies, they have ceased to be negroes and have become something quite different. They paint themselves with wood-ashes and with certain kinds of clay so that nothing of their porphyry skins is left. In general, their bodies are of an unreal green, a grey-green, like green under the most violent light of electricity. Their faces, under the elaborate *maquillage* to which they are subjected, are products of the circus and the limelight. With this, they go entirely naked, carrying, perhaps, a bow and arrows, or a spear and shield. They have a knightly elegance, a softness of tread, and seem, really, to be creatures of another world.

Such are the Dinka, so far as their physical appearance is concerned. Let us consider their history and their environment. They were lost in the world until some ninety years ago. It was the search for the sources of the Nile that first brought the white man into contact with them. Of their own history they know nothing; and their memory extends no further back than the limits of their own personal vision—to grandfathers and great-grandfathers remembered out of their own childhood. They have a vague tradition of having come out of the south. The Dinka were never slave-fodder, like the tribes living nearer to Abyssinia, or the negroes of the Gold Coast. It was from those that the harems of Turkey and Arabia were filled and the plantations of America and the West Indies received their store of black labour. The Dinka were warriors and not slaves; and they are part of the great negro race which includes the Zulus, the Matabele, the Basuto, the Masai. So their tradition is correct. They came up into the Sudan from the south, probably, according to learned opinion, at the end of the fourteenth, or beginning of the fifteenth, century. During the five hundred years that have elapsed, since then, they have accentuated their own peculiarities by intermarriage, and by the laws of nature. And they have ceased to be warriors and have become cowherds.

In their relatively small vocabulary there are no less than five hundred different words with which to describe every variety of marking to be found in the cattle. The exact shade of colour, the precise spotting or shading of their coats, the particularities of horn and muzzle, all have their name. And, where they have neglected their own history, the Dinka know by heart the generations of their herds, and can recite them back into the mists of the past. Their lives are, therefore, exclusively pastoral. Their diet is milk, and, scarcely ever, meat; a fact which may account for the slimness of their physique. In summer, they live in little towns of tents among the water-pastures, at a day or two's distance from the Nile; and, in the winter, when the floods have dried and there is no grazing left, they repair to their permanent settlements upon the river-bank. The summer-villages are rings of a dozen or twenty huts, with low doors through which they have to crawl. Briars are torn up and built into a hedge around them, and they sleep safe from lions and other marauding animals, with their herds, lying down among the huts, under the vigilance of the fiercest dogs imaginable, who bark at every footfall outside the rampart. The permanent villages are much bigger and more elaborately built. They are the size of small towns, having, perhaps, four or five thousand souls dwelling in them.

It is the perfect picture of pastoral peace to think of the Dinka living for so many centuries untouched even by the rumours of any world but their own. Across the Nile live the Shilluk; and that is all. But the Shilluk, a tribe of nearly similar origin to themselves, are more fierce and a degree more barbaric in culture. They know a little more than the Dinka, not of the outside world, but of the arts of life. And they provide the element of terror, the background of war, without which it is safe to assume that no human beings have ever existed. They go naked, like the Dinka, and are even more elaborately painted. A stature of seven feet is more frequently met with than among the Dinka, and they wear a towering, high coiffure to accentuate it. Often, their hair is raised into a crown of seven points and dyed a bright and fiery red.

As it is, the Dinka are the most beautiful race I have ever seen. It is a wonder to me that no painter, and, still more, no sculptor, has gone among them to seek perfection. Their every attitude is a revelation. I have never seen anything to equal their walk; and, in the furnace of midday heat, when they come down to the river-bank and bathe, the beauty of the sight is indescribable. The young maidens bathe in one place and the warriors in another. They offer the perfections of masculine and of feminine beauty. There is enough material, here, to occupy a great artist for the best years of his life. And no one has yet attempted to take advantage of this opportunity. Human beings are here to be seen in all their pristine and un-spoilt beauty, uncontaminated, and without the constriction of clothes. Arcadian peace reigns, undisturbed; and, if painting and sculpture are to be found in it, there is, also, poetry.

The Sudan is virgin ground, so far as any attempt at serious writing is concerned. And its beauties have the most poetical force to them. This was my temptation; and I resolved to make some attempt at a description of the scene. More particularly was I impressed with the first direct contact with the savages.

This can be best portrayed in the sublimated description of a long walk, begun before dawn. The path led down a beautiful valley, and, crossing this, so that they would intercept our path, two figures appeared. They were painted in the fashion of green that has been described; and, together, they formed the most extraordinary apparition it has ever been my good fortune to see. It took one back five thousand years. We might have been walking in the fields below Mycenæ; for this pair of negroes—I believe they were brothers—were a knight and his page. They paint themselves in this manner when they are courting, and this young knight, accompanied by his page to carry his finery of beads and feathers, was on his way to some neighbouring village. They walked hand in hand, as is the custom with negroes, for I have seen them do this in Morocco. They came up and spoke to us, not greatly astonished, and went on their way again, without looking back, not in the least surprised that we were unable to understand their words.

Later on in the morning, we heard loud and persistent barking of dogs, and found ourselves suddenly close up against one of their villages of summer tents. The hedge of thorns rose, waist-high, and over it peered the adolescents of the tribe in their full *maquillage*, for we cannot call it their war-paint since war was not in their minds. Their faces, painted with red and green and white, and their bare arms and waists, suggested the actors at a country fair called from their tents at an alarm of fire or the escaping of a tiger. But, at the same time, there was the god-like certainty of their movements to account for, and this removed them from the tinsel. The whole ring of tents was no bigger in extent than a painted cloud, or the circle of a painted dome. They, themselves, were painted with the bright colours that merge into each other at a distance. So are frescoes, seen nearer to the eyes than was intended, or with the power of glasses. And this scene recalled one particular fresco, in the church of San Giovanni Evangelista, behind the Cathedral in Parma. The dome is painted by Corregio with a rampart of clouds, over which angels, who are wingless and of the age of these adolescents, peer down, or are at play hurling what would appear to be snowballs at each other, or they may be some concentration of the sunlight that is so strong and violent that it litters the ground and can be gathered up and compressed by the hands. This Dinka village had the indifference to the white man that is a great part of their dignity, even if its real meaning is no more than a stupid lack of curiosity. As soon as they had satisfied themselves as to why the dogs barked and gave them warning, the disturbance had no more interest in their eyes. They went about their business and looked at us no more.

For all the rest of that day I lamented the absence of the painters and sculptors who should be established in these great natural studios—not only in the Sudan, but all over torrid Africa. The negro Sultanates of Bornu, Ashanti, Nigeria; their warriors in quilted armour; the dazzling dyed stuffs that they make; great mud-cities like Kano, or Sokoto, with a hundred thousand inhabitants, or more; Djenné, with its echoed architecture, its pylons from old Egypt; Dahomey, where shipwrecked mariners from Portugal taught the art of bronze-casting and the great schools of negro sculpture arose; the Congo, where ivory was carved with such subtlety and sense of beauty; what is the Nile, in its infancy, and the Nilotic tribes, to this?

These same qualities must be even more vigorously present in the Zulu, who are the parent-stock of the Dinka and the Shilluk. The Zulus had a great military history, under the famous Tchaka, who is said to have been responsible for the death of a million persons, an achievement that might be the envy of certain of our own politicians, were it not that the losses were on the enemy's side, and not on our own. Everyone has read in his childhood of the Zulu Impis, the black legions; of their Spartan discipline; and of the terror that they spread. They deserved a better fate than the pen of Rider Haggard and the pencil of Caton Woodville! It was the Homeric Age, existing almost into our own times. But it is probable that their sons are now quickly degenerating. The white man is too near to them, and there is not the same benevolent Government to watch over them that there is in the Sudan.

The Dinka may be the attenuated ghosts of what negro warriors may once have been, but at least there are no signs of their decline from this, and these curious refinements in their appearance are due, not to the decadence of the race, but to a change in their manner of life. They have ceased to be soldiers and are become shepherds. They live in true Arcadian simplicity, such as the pastoral poets of Alexandria and Syracuse had never seen.

The Sudan is a furnace, with the furnace-door opened for the draught at the hour of sunset. It is difficult to conceive how the Occidental can live in it. It is artificial, for him, as life in a submarine or an airship. But these are the very contrasts that give it interest. And, having spent a mere three weeks in that extraordinary land, I am moved to prophesy that it will find, one day, the painter or the sculptor who is worthy to celebrate its peerless qualities. If it fails at the hands of poetry, the fault is mine, for this first attempt.

MIMING OF THE GOLDEN CORNSTALKS*

I

THE clock strikes six. It is a summer afternoon.

A square in a little town on the borders of Galicia. The high
wooden houses with pointed gables are painted white or wild
rose pink; yellow as primroses or powder blue. A young girl
looks out of a window. A moment later she appears in a doorway and comes out into the square. Immediately the sunlight
bursts into flower. That is to say we have music. This hanging
of the golden air with flowers is like a seemingly innocent, but
artful music. Its prelude is the opening of the waltz, the preliminary beats to give the rhythm. When the tune comes, it is
so familiar we can scarce believe our ears.

The young girl is about fifteen years old; and in this peasant
land of many petticoats wears, audaciously, a short ballet skirt,
tights, and ballet shoes. It is the convention. And her hair is
dressed, formally, to go with it. But listen to the waltz! The
waltz of Coppelia! And watch how she makes sure that she is
not seen, and runs across the square, through and across the
music, as it were, pausing opposite, before a certain house,
poised on the waltz, and looking up into a window! A second
young girl sits there, and apparently, she reads a book. She
never moves: and never lifts her head. The other, in time to the
music, makes many signs to her. But in vain.

But the drama becomes more interesting. A young man
enters, as though to sing a serenade. In every movement and
gesture it is obvious he is a lover. Also, by the pantomime,
that the first young girl is jealous of the second. Just now, he
only sees his sweetheart at the window. The other, whom we
watch, hides in the shadow.

At this moment, but only for an instant, an old man in a
musty coat and wig appears at a low window of the mysterious

* From *Primitive Scenes and Festivals*, 1942.

house. Part of its mystery, in fact, is this haunting but banal waltz, coming from nowhere. The old man moves away from the window, and the young lover at once runs forward and kisses his hand to the girl above.

Then something curious happens. We hear, from within that room, a little mechanical and tinkling air, in time to which the girl seems to raise her head and make some gesture of reply; but then, abruptly and jerkily, sits down again.

And now the door opens and the old man comes out, stick in hand, with his hat upon his head. He is off, on some business, into the town. With a huge key he turns to lock the door behind him; but, in another moment, has dropped it on the ground. He is Coppelius, the toymaker: Doctor Bartolo: or Doctor Hunius, the dear old Balt, whose garden at the back of his house is full of plums and apples.

We hear that little tinkling tune again; but there is no one moving at the window. We are living, none the less, in a world of beloved shadows and enchantments. What magic in their names! How much of romance rings in our ears, and tingles on our skins, now that there are no theatres playing! We said Doctor Bartolo; so the girl could be his ward, Rosina. In another moment we will hear the serenade, sung by Lindoro, for Rosina knows Count Almaviva only by that name. But listen to the waltz! And look at the painted wooden houses! This town is not Seville.

Or the doll or automaton sitting at the window could be the lovely Olympia, made by Spalanzani, with Coppelius helping. We shall see the doll-like movements of Olympia as she sings her song. Ah! how magical that banal music! Or it could be Giulietta, in Venice, with her lover, Peter Schlemihl, the man without a shadow, for he has given it in exchange to the sinister Dapertutto. Or again, Antonia, whose death was brought about by Doctor Mirakel, when he called up the ghost of her mother, who had been a famous singer, and bade her sing before her. The song, too, of Antonia where she accompanies herself upon the harp.

It is enough. There is no need for more.
We come back again into the square.

123

The ballerina runs after the butterfly, feigning to have seen nothing of the drama at the window. Frantz joins in and catches it, and pins it to his collar. This is Swanilda's moment. She tells him he has been unfaithful to her. Does he prefer Coppelia? He shakes his head. But Swanilda will not listen. She tells him she loves him no more.

The square, so the programme reads, fills with a happy crowd. The burgomaster makes an announcement. A bell has been presented to the town by the lord of the manor, and there is to be a festival because of this. Young couples are to be married, and will be given dowries. From noon to midnight there will be dancing. It is our opportunity.

Now for the pigheaded peasants. And we leave the world of Leo Delibes for that of Dvořák, or Béla Bartók. This is a little town, remember, on the borders of Galicia! Now for the re-dowa, polka, dumka, furiant. Upon the borders of Galicia; somewhere, that could mean, near to so many other lands. Music in the Magyar rhythm. We shall listen to the csárdás. Our subject is the peasant world between the Black Sea and the Baltic, in form of a divertissement, for the sake of brevity, or an air with variations, after which we come back within the conventions of the stage, and behold the Miming of the Golden Cornstalks.

We will have dances of spinners and harvesters. That happy crowd are the occasion, as though it is only necessary for them to change their dresses. It is a summer evening among the groves of sunflowers; in the mountains, the High Tatra or Carpathians; and along the plain. Not in any one place; but, for convenience, in a square in a little town. The whole of this peasant world is sublimated in their dances. Their primitive beliefs and legends; those, especially, that are pre-Christian and come down to them from pagan times. Not that, in bucolic reckoning, it was so long ago. Where shall it be? Would you have the music and the Căluşari dancers from Ca la Cinturoiă, near Craiova? It is better to be lost entirely, as though it is a holiday without guide or map. Only listen to the music, watch the spectacle: do not bother about time or place!

Here are the places of forgotten music. A village, a landscape, in a song. Or dance. The bagpipes, the cymbalon, the violin. Here the tunes are collected and written down. For

every one saved how many more will have been forgotten!
Abstractions of the sharp air in the mountains. Of the fiery
plain: the haunted forest. Green rivers: fields of rye: images
of the performing bear: village dramas: the maiden at the well:
of the fair, with a thousand waggons and ten thousand horses:
folk memories of when the Turks came by, and of the towers
of skulls: of a young child eaten by the wolves: prophecies
spoken by the jackdaw: princesses of the wainscoting: of the
tree that spoke: of all birds and animals given words to say:
and mere tunes which have no meaning but entrance or
intoxicate in themselves, and linger in the memory.

Bare bones that clothe themselves with flesh. Airs that are
archaic, and discordant in their harmonies. Played and sung
according to the ancient mode, while sunset lit the whitewashed walls. Pantomimes of fife and drum. Dances of the
Dacians. Of the white shirt and Phrygian bonnet, worn at the
carved and painted porch. For these primitive tunes are entire
in their simplicity. Nothing can be taken from them. A catch
from some broken instrument: and that is all. Without Gypsy
ornament. Not needing the clashing of the Berecynthian rattle.
The broken cymbalon is enough; and the violin and drum.

We reach the rustic scene and hear, in epitome, a little air.
That contains the whole race. The same language may not be
spoken a few miles away. It can be the pocket of a distant
nation; or a whole people scattered in confusion among their
enemies. It has the accent of its tongue or language. Part
rhythm; and part intonation. And how magical the change of
key! It is now it runs in the blood. It is the psychic turn from
feminine to masculine. This is the magician's secret.

Now come the Căluşari dancers with their hobby horse.
They have fasted for several weeks, and their leader has kept
a vow of silence. It is a dance of exorcism. A panic, or nameless
fear, like that which routs the herds. It is the horned god who
runs among the flock. At another village the god has come up
from the field of rye. His name has been forgotten, but all
know him. Or he hides like Vertumnus in the plum boughs;
and must be tempted down.

There was once a witch who is, now, a long legged mare.
What was the fox that looked in at the window? Which was
the silver maiden in the stream, beneath the stone? Is every

goddess dead? What of the gentle birch trees? There comes a sighing out of the orchard. It is too beautiful to be but rain. And look! the sunflowers do not bow their heads. Ah! now it steals along the ground, like something that would crawl up to our feet. It slips out of the branches. You can hear a door and window bang. It is within the house.

Some tunes come like a moment with half-closed eyes, in which instant inspiration descends. Their birth is from a sip of honey: not through long reflection. Ah! now it comes. A blind man, or one who cannot read music, may be the godhead. It is a sacred trance: in utter simplicity. And it ends, roughly and awkwardly. Did we not say these are the pigheaded peasants! Their music grunts among the acorns. And in the next moment, it is instinct with poetry. Unless we think of it as a run of numbers, found by divination. Villages scenes and festivals far removed from anywhere, in the immense peasant lands.

Listen! that is a little csárdás. I have heard it upon the virginal, soft as a mouse's movements, but sunburnt as the plain. With a *glissando* at the end, as though upon the cymbalon. A little Children's Piece by Béla Bartók. How poignant are its turns and modulations!*

Some of the tunes are dry and brittle as a wooden toy. But it articulates: it has joints that move. The melody is four-square, like the script of an antiphonal. It has no date or time. And it hardens into a portrait. There are tunes that can be like melodies worn inside out. And, suddenly, a form will catch fire. A rondo upon a folk tune is an example.† They are village scenes or tableaux, complete in themselves, with no external influence. All is in the timing, with no opportunity for expression; percussive or droning, like the village band. But always, sooner or later, the village fair.

At present, we are among the Dacians. How to bid farewell to the cosmogony of peasants! This is a moonlit hora in the time of the golden harvest. A hundred larks are singing in the cloudless sky. The black hats and long white shirts worn outside their trousers, in the Wallachian fashion, make the hora dancers akin to Pulcinella, but the music has style and rhythm

* Played by Mrs Gordon Woodhouse upon the virginal.
† Three Rondos upon a Folk Tune, by Béla Bartók, 1931.

of its own. It is danced in a circle, hand linked in hand; or the young men and the girls dance, side by side, as though it were a promenade, a ceremonial walk. Music and dancing are in *moto perpetuo*. They need never end. Till we hear the Ciocarla, which mounts and rises like the lark.*

Here are performing bears from the Carpathians. That dance, but such music is intrinsic. It does not depend upon the execution. But there is a tune, here and there. Distant villages are the most likely; or then, again, in the outskirts of some little town. So that there is no pattern by which they can be found. At the horse fair: or by the cemetery wall. At a wedding: or where the dead woman lies with her face uncovered. There is a song from among the rose trees, for it could be in Bulgaria within sight of Rhodope. Or out of the willow forests in the Danube delta. Far distant, are we not, from the borders of Galicia? In so many rhythms. And of so many nations. From all the great Balkan, far from the redowa and the furiant. We hear the gentle love songs of the Bosnians, savdelinkas of Turkish sort, from Sarajevo's gardens, in view of the plane tree and the minaret.

Villages near the Jugoslavian border show the influence of that proximity. The inhabitants, even, may be partly Serbian, and it is revealed in the women's costume with their full skirts and simple headdresses, consisting of no more than a shawl or handkerchief folded into a turban. At Décs, which is not far from the battlefield of Mohács, they wear pleated dresses without pattern, but daring in their colours; while at Alsónyék, in the same neighbourhood, it is cretonnes and chintzes, all of flowered pattern, like the milkmaids of pastoral poetry, and in fact, their milk pails are brightly painted. Here, in Southern Hungary, the folk music is rhapsodic in character, the land of Liszt's Second and Twelfth Hungarian rhapsodies with their frowning or heroic tunes in all their force and blatancy. Near to the scene of Turkish massacres, and of epic or dithyrambic import.

For a difference, here are the Pan pipes. The true syrinx only blown in the one region of the Danube, where cranes and pelicans populate the water meadows. Not music, but a comment or an interjection, though the tones are honeyed. Now

* Ciocarla is the name of a popular Roumanian tune.

and again there is a virtuoso on this instrument. But it has to
be bird like. It leads and dominates: it interrupts. Not the
sweet notes of the shepherd. But a river flowing into Tartary.
It has the water qualities of that; and is not of the earth or
air. And since it is inhuman, it is not archaic. It is from
before history began.

But we will come down to the Banat. Where Roumania
was entered, formerly, from Yugoslavia, beyond Timişoara.
We would see the mountaineers of Hatzeg. To what race can
they belong? The men wear sheepskin pelisses and shoes of
sheepskin. But it is their physiognomy which is peculiar, as
much so as that of the Crow Indians who had the semi-lunar
outlines to their faces. To begin with, their heads are so deeply
lined and marked, riddled, in fact, and creased, and with men
of middle age, more often completely bald and hairless. Like
the head, therefore, of a tortoise, and with a tortoise's creased
neck.

These are not the fox-masked Mongols with pointed chins
and little tufts of beard, the men of Tamerlane, who, himself,
was a Mongol of that type according to the portrait drawing
of him by the Persian painter, Bihzad. They are, therefore,
Mongols of an earlier invasion. Of Central-Asian ancestry;
but not of the Golden Horde. Their big outstanding ears are
those of the Buddha, but without the long lobes that were the
mark of longevity and wisdom. Also, the eyes are not slanting.
And the taint of their skins is not yellow. It is, rather, red or
tawny. They are related, not to the Chinese, but to the Red
Indian in the Mongol. Red Indian warriors, shaved for battle,
but not warriors any more. Mere mountaineers and shepherds.
Of prehistoric Mongol origin, for that blood is not to be
mistaken among them. They are pastoral Siberians, settled
near Danube's banks in a range of lonely mountains. We
would seek out their priest or Shaman, for in customs as well
as facially they are pre-Christian. They stand in their locks of
wool outside their cut log cabins. No people of Europe are so
primitive of aspect. The Buriats come immediately into mind.
The home of their race must be behind the Altai. They
reached this solitude after some frightful cataclysm, the survival of a scourge or epidemic, one of the flails or scorpions
which fell upon the West. It will have been a flood of barbar-

ians, coming out of the fires of sunrise and burning all before them. Sordid as an invasion out of the slums. This terror of the ancient world is preserved for us in the countenances of this little remnant. From how long ago, we cannot tell. But, once, they swarmed.

We have come to the huge plain of mirage. Fata Morgana plays along the endless air. Miles from anywhere, in midst of this, sits a shaggy bear. A man, crouching on his heels, and wrapped from the ground up to his eyes in a coat of sheepskin, so that no more than the top of his head is to be seen. Upon horseback he will be like a bear riding a wild horse, for he keeps his heels so much in play that the horse jumps at every moment.

Soon we come to a water well with a great pole above it like a gallows, and to more of the shaggy bears grouped round it in their unshorn sheepskins. Here, too, they wear the Hungarian cloak, or szűr, with the sleeves sewn up and used for pockets. It is a cloak of white woollen felt, embroidered at its hems and edges; the motif, often, being a garland of red roses, but with the flowers so disposed and eyed that they would be taken, superficially, for a design of peacock's feathers. There are ornaments, based on sprigs of rosemary, between the roses. Often these leaves are blue or yellow, or any colour but what is native to them.

Another cloak is the suba, worn by both men and women, of sheepskin, with the fleece inside or out according to the weather. They reach from the shoulders to the heels, and as many as fifteen whole sheepskins are required to make them. The dressed skins, with the fleece inside, hang in long straight folds or pleats, with much embroidery round the shoulders, down the pleats in floreations that expand into a formal flower; and many embroidered fringes round the hem. The effect is magnificent, for the suba sways and dangles. It has something Mongol or Turkish in its pastoral finery, an air belonging to a race of horsemen, for they are plains of cavalry. No one has ever walked. Their ancestry of the Orient is attested by the name of szűcs attached to the guilds of tanners and dressers of skins in Hungary since medieval times, in echo, as it were, of the legendary souks of the Eastern world. Until the end of the nineteenth century there were in the Alföld hundreds of makers of the szűr and suba, the design and pattern of which differed in every region. Now, it is doubtful if more than one or two masters of these ancient crafts could be found. But this vision of the shaggy bears fades like the mirage. Or it is another act: a changing of the scene.

It is no more the puszta. Here are villages, where the streets at certain festivals will be carpeted with flowers.* They will celebrate the winter solstice with mimes and processions, the actors being known as regos in Hungary, turony in Slovakia, and turka in Roumania, feasts in honour of the victory of the sun god; and games and pantomimes of carnival, with shouting to drive away evil spirits, loud and discordant drumming, a relic of the ancient Shamanism; and in remote districts, cere- monies to do with the fertility of women, based upon magic, and which may include flagellation of the young brides and unmarried girls.

But we arrive among the Matyós, who inhabit a few villages in Northern Hungary and Mezőkövesd, famous for its costumes. The Matyós are different, ethnographically, from the Hungarians, and it is probable, of Tartar origin. The men wear small felt hats of black or green, perched at an angle, held in place by an elastic band; long white linen gowns like sur- plices, with laced sleeves; and a shirt which is thick with colours and presents roses and tulips. The married women have rich embroidery upon black; sometimes a worked cap or helmet with short ostrich feathers, dyed red, surmounting it; but, more often, black feathers to match the blackness of their dresses, which, in some curious manner, suggests an equine ornament, as though the women, in symbol, were mares. They are, in fact, maned headdresses; and the image might be taken from the fringe of hair, between the ears, across the horse's skull. But the characteristic, so far, of the Matyó costume is the long white surpliced men's dress and their small round hats, so that they look like choristers or ecclesiastics, but obviously are also dancers, with something, almost, of the dervishes' long gowns that swing and fill with air as they swirl round and round in ecstasy.

* Budaörs, a village near Budapest. But this custom exists in other places; in the Canary Islands; and at Barlow, in Derbyshire, where, also, the well head is garlanded with flowers.

The ragyogó is a headdress worn only by the bride upon her wedding day, a crown like that of the May Queen, composed of artificial flowers. The effect is extraordinary for its poetry. These Tartar villagers, the Matyós, have embodied in this, as in a ballad or a legend, the beauty of the harvest and the flowering fields. The outer edge of this crown or diadem is a convention of ears of corn which wave and tremble as the virgin walks. It is worn with a white pleated dress and sleeves, or rather, shoulders that are as light and loose in filament as the crown above, so that the whole effect is that of white flowers. They are, themselves, bridal bouquets. And yet, in imagery, it is Mongol. It is to Mongol women that these virgins are related. The maidens of the Siberian tomb mounds are no different.

Their wedding ceremonies are much concerned, also, with pillows and fine linen. With feather beds stuffed with gooses' down, and painted wooden furniture. But before Christmas, near the winter solstice, a crèche or presepio is set up in the houses, and before these the young girls kneel, wearing special clothes and a peculiar headdress that is yet more mysterious in origin. It is a high steeple hat, immensely thin and long, like a horn or a cornucopia, but with the esoteric meaning hidden behind its medieval aspect, for it is the hat of a court lady of the fifteenth century. The young girls wear wreaths of flowers across their foreheads downwards, to behind their ears, and a frontal of flowers upon the hat itself, and twining up its height. There are flowers, too, at the apex of the hat, and two folds of a veil or wimple descending from the crown, and from behind the head. These hats are tilted at a slanting angle. They are made of coloured paper, red and pink and white, and bear some affinity to the towers and buildings, likewise of coloured paper, made by the peasants of Zakopane and the Tatra mountains, work of the Slovaks and the Polish mountaineers, part, also, of the celebrations of Epiphany. Those are, in fact, set scenes for the presepio, but their fanciful architecture fulfils the only background that our imagination could project for these kneeling virgins.

It is the imagery of the sugar cone, the dunce's cap, existing in an ambience that is entirely of its own. Utterly capricious, for it has no relation to the buildings of their daily lives. This, too, which we apply to the wooden cabins of the Tatra, refers again to the Matyós for it is to be noticed that the houses of Mezőkövesd are whitewashed, plain and dull, and that this fantastic enrichment of costume is, as it were, in supplement or recreation upon the ordinary visual circumstances of their lives. It is the art of shepherd or sheepshearer, as much concerned with threads and stitches as that of the nomads in whose tents the rugs were woven. As though confined to a barge or to a circus tent the Matyós do no more than ornament a wooden board, a milk pail, a wooden chair, or table. The rest is what they wear upon their backs.

This country, of which we are speaking now, is the land of Brahms and Dvořák. It can only be considered, æsthetically, as the great peasant region, without respect to history, or to present frontiers. A world where humanity has flowered in music and legend, and in the arts of costume. What else could be said of a Magyar village, lost in the woods, where the women's hats are made from the skin of a great fungus or toadstool that springs up in the rains!

However characteristic of the Magyars it is continued over the border in Slovakia. Here upon a Sunday, or on a day of pilgrimage, you may see a whole village dressed in shades of pink and rose; children's dresses, in a village close to, that are like Tudor portraits; and a few miles further on old ladies in caps and ruffs resembling the mezzetins of Watteau. The country will be cultivated like a patchwork quilt, in long thin strips. Ethnographic frontiers in this region of the old Austria-Hungary were, perhaps, purposely obscured. Because of this confusion, when Brahms composed in Hungarian idiom, it could be called in stricter accuracy his country or idyllic style. For it was a poetic diction, almost, by which he was inspired, but only, loosely, of Magyar origin, for it is, as often, Slovak in character. How lovely are those moments! But we would listen to the peasant composer in this land of peasants.

This year, in the centenary of Dvořák, we would honour that neglected genius. Forgotten, although his music was played in London sixty years ago. To those who love Dvořák he can become one of the pleasures of a sunlit world. Listen, if you may, to a golden age which was without war or persecution. Bohemia and its forests stretch out to the horizon. The sky is cloudless. It could be some summer pilgrimage in the countryside, and the music speaks a language which is more simple than the Slavonic patois. It is the universal peasant tongue. The harvest has started. Plums and apples have begun to fall. The beehives make the orchard loud. There is honey in the new hayrick and along the loaded bough. Inspiration came easily to Dvořák, who composed quickly and had not to meditate.

How beautiful are the Slavonic Dances, one and all of them! Music which, like Casse Noisette, can never tire. In our time of confusion how reassuring are his beauty and directness. Much of his chamber music, two works for pianoforte and strings, especially, and a string sextet, are written, throughout, in the Slavonic rhythm.* They may be among the most lovely of Dvořák's works, and have a quality of sunny spontaneity which is unique among the Slavs. In beauty of melody they are not inferior to Schubert. It would seem extraordinary that melodies of such loveliness should not be upon the lips of everyone. They are a part of the world's inheritance, but shared by few. In the case of tunes, such as these, doubts must exist in the mind as to whether the necessary combination of notes lay there, to be put together by mere science. It must be, as we said before, more in the nature of a lucky run upon numbers. It is a break, or graph, traced like lightning through them. The great composers of popular or cheap music work in the same laws, which are suddenly relaxed for them. And it is obvious that in the case of Schubert and in that of Dvořák, their surpassing gift for melody places them among that category. Nevertheless, Dvořák is likely to remain for ever neglected. His fame is static: and he is passing out of history as quickly as the peasant world of last century from these villages that we have seen. Of the peasant Dvořák more than a half lies in oblivion. But that which remains, long after his oratorios and other works of convention are forgotten, brings back a golden age.

The scene is a village street of thatched and whitewashed houses. It is immensely wide, and the one-storeyed houses

* Quintet in A major, *op.* 81; quartet in E flat, *op.* 87; and string sextet in A major, *op.* 48.

stand sideways, with their gables showing. There has been some great religious festival. Everybody has come out of church, and is walking in the same direction towards the pilgrimage. It is a crowd, though, and not a procession. Rain has fallen, and the road is deep in mud. To one side, the wooden structure to draw water from the well could be a great gallows, or a huge whip resting in a wooden socket. No shops: nothing but an ugly row of lamp poles and some telegraph wires.

But it is the land of Coppelia. We must be near the borders of Galicia. The women and young girls are in ballet skirts. From behind, they look like ballerinas who have thrown a shawl across their shoulders and are hurrying through the draughty wings into their dressing rooms. It could be the corps de ballet after the last call in front of the curtain. And a number of young children with them will have had their places in the apotheosis, or the transformation. Even, for their gay colours, in the harlequinade.

For it is the land of the peasant ballerina. As many as seven or eight starched skirts are worn, one above another, and all of different colours. Their length is to just below the knee. Each skirt, too, is tightly pleated, so that the effect is that of a bell of clay or china. And the hems are all embroidered in many colours; while bright silk ribbons, woven with flowers, and made at one time in Lyon especially for these villages, to the point that the name "Lyon" is their synonym for silk, are fastened round their waists so that the long ends hang down, close together, over the backs of their ballet skirts, and down to the parti-coloured rims.

It would be as difficult to give the key to all these colours as to describe those pretty and expensive ribbons, for their quality lies in the subtle differences. But the top skirt can be bright scarlet, or gentian blue. If it be red, it will have a border of green, or white, or blue. If blue, the red geranium will edge the gentian. No two dresses are alike. Their fronts may be white frills or aprons, white bodices; or black, as the case may be. No headdresses; but the hair worn in long plaits or ringlets. Such is the costume of the Mátra mountains. In a particular village.

In another, the unmarried girls in their ballet skirts have white frilled sleeves, white aprons of heavy, open lace, like a bedspread or a counterpane worked with patterns; a silken shawl across the chest; and crowns of embroidery and gold and silver paste, with the flowered silk ribbons hanging from them. Sitting there, a few of them together, upon a Sunday afternoon, they could be Berber women. It is due to the conventional designs in black and red upon their aprons; and although, sitting down, their ballet skirts are not in evidence, they have the air of dancers. In this village the colours are worn alike. The difference is in the detail. That makes them, again, into a troupe of dancers. In fact, they are village maidens of Kazár, in Northern Hungary, near the Slovakian border.

But it is more fanciful, near by, at Buják. This is the region of ballet skirts and Russian boots. Here, the effect dwarfs the wearer. They are authentic ballerinas in their small stature. The stranger could feel himself upon the stage among them. The bodice, itself, is a complex masterpiece, as elaborate as in a portrait by Cornelius Janssen, or by Mark Gheeraerdts. It has arched and frilled shoulders, the form of which is continued down to the waist, then gathered in a bow and the ends spread out upon the bustle, so stiff and starched that they keep in position. From the back, therefore, it is a ruff in the form of a figure eight. The collar is high and stiff, and hung with necklaces.

The ballet skirt can be rose pink, closely ribbed, and with concentric rings of white. Near the rim there is a row of green; rose pink again; then white: then black, with blue divisions and flowers in red and green; and then a rose pink edging. Two long flowered ribbons from the waist trail down upon this. And the ballerina has a coloured ribbon tied at each shoulder, and looped round at the elbow.

For other skirts can be of a red stuff flowered with green; or of a woven material that has horizontal stripes of grey and yellow upon white. Others are blue or red, accordion pleated, but of soft and pastel ground, with a wide band of white, worked flowers, and no other ornament, rather more than half-way down the skirt. These will have bodices richly embroidered with flowers, roses and tulips predominating, as though to balance with the lack of ornament below. This type, though, is more common in the Kalocsa country of Southern Hungary; where it is worn with clocked stockings and red boots.

Nevertheless, it is a costume of the ballerina sort. But the true country of the peasant ballerina lies, where we see it, in the Mátra mountains, and typically at Kazár or Buják. This is the little town near to the borders of Galicia.

II

Swanilda has stooped down to pick up the key. Her companions on the stage are the peasant ballerinas; but Swanilda wears the one ballet skirt alone. How young and gay the music! And she unlocks the door.

When we come upstairs into the mysterious room Swanilda has, already, put on the doll Coppelia's costume. Frantz, her lover, climbs a ladder and steps in at the window. Doctor Coppelius returns. And Swanilda, as Coppelia, has become capricious.

She takes up a sword and strikes the other dolls with it; the mandarin, who nods his head and hands, and the Moor who plays the dulcimer. She kicks the pages of the book of magic with her toe. Coppelius gets alarmed, but succeeds in stopping her. He is bewildered at her sudden moods and tries to calm her. He puts a tambourine into her hand. And what do we see and hear? Upon the instant there is Spanish music. Coppelia dances a fandango or a seguidilla. Aha! the patios and balconies. The dry cackle of the castanets, in rhythm, coming from the shuttered windows of the dance school of Otero. White fan and snow white mantilla. All through the heat. Siguiriyas, polos, martinetes, in the Gypsy suburb of Triana. But it has ended as suddenly as it began.

Swanilda is Coppelia again.

The applause dies down. And, with the last handclap, we see another change of mood.

She picks a plaid up off the floor, and dances a jig or écossaise. It has a twining and returning rhythm. We taste, in it, the sugar on the shortbread, and have time to see the green eyes of the dancer and her freckled face. How charming if she could wear tartan stockings and a Highland bonnet! A dance of a fishergirl among the laced pinks of Paisley! There are sweetshop windows, rose and lemon yellow, and Sunday will be the Scot Sabbath.

But it ends.

Swanilda, as Coppelia, runs behind the curtain. And we hear that curious tinkling tune again. It is the air to which the doll, Coppelia, makes her movements. Coppelius pulls back the curtain. But she is sitting stiffly there, as usual.

At this moment Swanilda glides away. Coppelius runs to the window and sees her arm in arm with Frantz, crossing the square below. The old man faints in midst of his clockwork figures. And the curtain falls.

The scene is a shady lawn before the castle. The festival has begun. A huge bell stands in the background, hanging from poles which are decked with flags. Beside it is drawn up an allegorical car filled with players. The young couples about to be married are being presented to the lord of the manor. When this is done the nobleman mounts a platform, and makes a sign for the dancing to begin.

Swanilda and Frantz are left alone.

She takes up a little bunch of cornstalks and holds it to her ear. It is a lovely moment. She listens to the corn sheaf. And we are to imagine a summer wind playing in its golden locks. As though the lovers walked by the edge of a cornfield.

"Does it not say that you love me no more?" she asks.

Frantz answers that he heard nothing.

Then Swanilda gives the corn to one of Frantz's friends. He listens to it, and says he hears quite well. This lovely pastoral is perfectly expressed in mime. It is, even, more beautiful from the stylized movements. How pretty Swanilda would be, if you were alone with her, in a corner of the golden harvest! In her short ballet skirt, walking birdlike, in the convention of the ballerina, with her satin shoes.

If she can appear, thus, before five thousand persons; why not, if you are her lover, for yourself alone? Like a painted idol. More exciting in the thought of that; and then, again, only as herself. Not, really, Swanilda: still less, Coppelia. Only the girl who mimed that rôle; but who walks with you down the summer evening. For whom you could break off a sheaf of corn, and with your own hand hold it to her ear, lifting her hair to do so. The same person, or the shades of her, through all time. In a long gown of saffron by the leaning stone; and, now, to the Hungarian dulcimer in a field of rye. It is beautiful to watch Swanilda among the peasant ballerinas.

But the little tinkling air plays once more. In its happy associations, it could be an entr'acte bell heard after long illness when we go to the theatre; or when the theatres open again and there is peace. To this tune Doctor Coppelius forces his way through the crowd and demands to be compensated for the damage done to his toys. We could see the ghosts of the lovely Olympia and Spalanzani: of Antonia and Doctor Mirakel: of Giulietta and Peter Schlemihl. A purse is put into the old man's hand, and he goes off. Oh! when shall we see him and his automaton again!

The stage clears for the csárdás.

The dancers take up their places. The men, in their long gowns, like surplices, place their hands on the girls' waists; and the girls take the men by both shoulders. This is how they dance the csárdás. The tune is first played out to its length, and given every accent. Two by two, stamping their Russian boots, the dancers come up to the footlights. But Swanilda, and a few of the peasant ballerinas, come from the country of the satin shoe. Once more, the csárdás, in all the fullness of the tune.

And then the music quickens. The dancers spin round like tops. It is the reason for those ballet skirts. The leaping tearing csárdás comes. Faster and faster. Fragments of the tune whirl and turn upon themselves. It is an intoxication. The golden cornstalks have been garnered in: the grapes have been gathered. They give themselves upon the music. And it turns and turns. New themes come in and dançe with each other. The dance of the village inn, while sunset dies along the plain. It is a fury of excitement. The cymbalon is leading. And it rises into a frenzy or delirium, until the dancers are breathless and fall upon the ground. Or outlast the music, and spin into the wings. And the stage lies in darkness. The golden sun, the golden cornstalks dead. And the csárdás ended.

ROMARIA*

It is a morning in the South, early in the year. The almond is in blossom.

But there is not long to wait. In a moment or two the key has been found and we go into the church. It is long and high, with a Mudéjar ceiling, work which is, at once, the spider and the honeycomb. From its long, thin shape it is more a chapel than a church. The walls are lined with coloured tiles, or azulejos. And there are tombs and canopies and many altars. No one ever comes here. It was with difficulty that the key turned in the door. But listen! listen! What can be that droning? It is like the wings of bees, like the wild bees in the tomb of Agamemnon. There, they come in through a crevice, and their droning is in the dome of the tomb chamber, above where the golden masks lay in the dust of ages. Here, too, it is high up, near the ceiling, close to the artesinado. It keeps to the gilded honeycombs. But no need for more. It is the droning of the nuns.

Along the walls are tombs of knights who died in battle, princes and great men in their time. This praying, praying, is equivalent to the dusting of their effigies, though none know their names, or can read what is written there. It is one sort of immortality, an earthly one, a kind of paid flattery, but better than oblivion. Or is it better to be forgotten? Perhaps it is only if a young knight lies buried that there is truth and pathos in those tears and in the waving of those wings. For that is the sound. That is the music and its meaning. But listen! listen again and think upon it! The sound is droning, droning. These are the metamorphoses of insects, little beings whom we look upon with horror, but they are changed into court ladies, virgin princesses, priestesses, and nuns.

Their grille, or balcony, is at the far end, opposite the altar. But you cannot look at them. An iron lattice with golden flowers and roses goes up to the ceiling, though the thicket stops short

* From *Sacred and Profane Love*, 1940.

139

of that, and there are but the empty panes or mullions. The droning, droning, is behind the grille and comes down, down, while they are spinning, for its sound is not of idleness, not the insects in a summer wood at evening, not a droning for pleasure but a honey-taking, yet something more slumbrous, more domestic, more continual, and less of an adventure. It is something which is perpetual, and of which no appreciable part of the whole is ever finished, yet their nature urges them to it, so that it is measureless, like the dimension of time, itself, according to the different manners of its reckoning, only a substance or an entity if you think of it like that and, really, with no beginning and no end, just time, which you can either worship or ignore. If you listen for a little while longer, the droning comes to mean all things. It can be an interpretation of the heat of noon: it can mean nothing, nothing: or it loads the air with flowers and, another moment, is suffering and telling its monotony of wasted days. It is possible not to listen to it, and to look at the monuments, instead, but it will come back to you as though you had never heard the drone before. It is never, never, silent . . . and, then, it stops.

The death or passing of this murmuring leaves the vessel empty. It takes, in imagery, the heat out of the morning. But there is not a footstep nor a movement. It is but an interval. And it begins again on a higher note, as though hurrying, and then becomes slow and slumbrous, older in tone, and but a telling of the beads, an old monotony, a murmuring or mumbling. It had, in the beginning, the ghost or the shadow of someone feminine and youthful, a higher tone and a speeding of the spinning wheel. But there are no Fates here. Nothing can happen. No future time, no present, nothing but the past. As for the living moment, it is no more than another morning. The hours go more slowly if you hurry through them. The dead are sleeping. And the young knight sleeps the deepest sleep of all, dreamless as when he was a little baby, long ago, and went from lap to lap. That was in the time of steeple hats and rat-railed shoes.

But the droning, too, is like the sound of millwaters. They are binding the golden harvest, and the lovely cornfield is but stubble. As for the millwaters, they, too, are feminine. They churn and churn. It is a turning or spinning of distaff or of

Reception of Dutch Ambassador by Sultan Achmet III, by J. B. Vanmour (1671–1737)

Dutch Ambassador crossing the second court of the Old Seraglio as the Janissaries are rushing for their dinners, by J. B. Vanmour (1671–1737)

spindle, endless and inconsequent. But no: they are the insects in their metamorphoses, winged virgins who are droning in the hive, beating their wings, which they will never use in flight. It is the oldest of old sounds, so old that the dead turn in their sleep and go to dust in slumber. They are praying, or making incantation, over old dead bones. So where is the honey in this carved and fretted hive? For, yet, there is something cloying and heavy in the air. If the nuns were dispossessed and the convent empty, you would still feel it and could listen for its murmuring. So take up the seashell and hold it to your ear! Listen in the summer wood! The leaves are never still. There is a murmuring and another, though a little, world is working. Stay still in the open field and hear the whirring of our world! This drone of wings is how they find their comfort: how they spin for another life and make ready their robe, which, first and foremost, is a winding sheet. They have to pass through dust. Like the insects, they must sleep through the long winter. It is against nature not to store up honey. Here, there is no certainty. Nothing but a promise made from mouth to mouth. How cruel to disturb them: to pull off their wings and bring them down to ground: to destroy their labours and their wasted days: to rob them of their honey!

It is a nasal droning, with the timbre of the voice of Spain. For this is a convent in Seville, one like many others, and it needs no name. Here is no imagery of the millwaters or the summer woods, for it is a convent in a noisy town; but that sad, but busy, droning brought those images before the mind. The nuns' choir, though invisible to ourselves, is a large room or boudoir from which they look down into the church. True, it cannot be comfortable, but it is more of a drawingroom than the bare rooms of the convent. It has benches and cushions and illuminated books. And they come into it as you come into a drawingroom, through one of many doors. Some are excused the droning if they have other work to do. Others are ever droning, in perpetual adoration. It is better not to be precise; not to know how many hours they pray. How quickly time must go, up there! Faster than in the street, in the world of living men and women; more swiftly than in the tomb; faster than with little children; quicker winged than the memories of old men and women remembering when they were alive;

quicker than youth itself and leading, more certainly, to nothing. It would be no part of our philosophy to make excuses for them. Their lives are wasted, spent to no purpose, but no worse for that than any other lives. The trajectory is in slow motion, but, if we quicken it, we get the picture we would wish to paint. For the sadness, the sad burden is in all those empty hours. It is their very purpose, their prayers, which are the wastefulness. Who am I, though, that I should say this? For I have never prayed, and do not believe in prayer. Unless, at least, it be a means to determine wishes and ambitions, and by concentration of purpose to achieve them. We could admire a musical instrument, and not appreciate its tone, not like its resonance, or the volume of its sound. In just that manner a sceptic can understand their prayers. To such a mind it is too much prayer that spoils the beauty of the convent.

What then could bind together these communities and keep them from the world? Is it not enough, in itself, to live in a walled garden, for the Hortus Conclusus could hold all the flowers of the spirit as well as all the flowers of the world? Separation from the world of men and women gives time to till that soil. But such flowers of the spirit are far removed from superstition. They belong to enlightenment, to a time while the light strengthens, not to nights of ignorance and darkness. But such a community could never fill its numbers. Such souls are too rare, and they have no increase. They live but once and the continuity is broken. It cannot always be creation, the giving birth to intellect and imagination. There must be routine, the accomplishment of daily tasks and duties, years when creation slumbers and the ordinary and average have their day. The philosophy, therefore, and the beauty of this virgin life, in all of it which expresses that Sacred or Divine Love is their calling, will form our subject. Their prayers are part of the picture, but not the reason that prompted us to paint it. We would have them, for our own æsthetic pleasure, at every other duty than that for which they are assembled and enclosed. From a third to a half of their energies may be increased by this, while their resolution would not be weakened by the same worship in another form. Divine or Sacred Love means other things than meditation and a mumbling of prayers. If it were music that would be a different matter;

though music, even, is but a part of it. There are so many other instruments of worship. For the cloister is more than a refuge from the world; there is opportunity in this predicament. They have come together for a purpose, not merely for escape. Our project is to intensify, or dramatize, this visual scene, making use of the evidence that has come before our eyes and completing the picture by surmise and from imagination. Of a certainty, such lives are, and have been, possible. That, to their possibility, so many daily hours of solitude and uselessness have been added, is but the proof of what could be achieved in the full practice of these hooded or these hidden energies.

They are but a half—or not so much—fulfilled. And, as with so many other lives, it is their own ends which have defeated them. This, however, is the drama. Their hardships and austerities make the dark colours of the scene, and it is not defeat if they achieve the purpose of their lives. We know, too well, that the earthly paradise we would design for them is impossible. But its occasional perfections are like the divine melodies of music. They break suddenly, and come back again. There is no reason for them. The inspired moment is after hours of working. We, the audience, no less than the artist, have to wait upon it. We must take the waiting with the rush of speed. And to no subject could this truth be applied with a more accurate meaning than in this fantasy to which we now begin to give our energies. We treat of the nuns in their needlework and embroidery, in the dispensary and pharmacy, in their singing and among the flowers of the garden, behind the grille and in the parlatorio. Such activities, as neither men nor women can be all philosophers or poets, form the painted scenery for these virgin lives. Who would not rather see them at these pastimes, against the fanciful architecture of all ages and every clime, than in the stone cell and on their knees? That, too, penitence and preparation are in the picture, but the twist or foreshortening by which we study them and draw the composition will alter that proportion and give us their lives as swift, or swifter, than they really pass, ignoring the monotony.

But we must begin with places. Let us go somewhere far away, that it may be a solitude through unfamiliarity. But, also, we must prove our liberty of choice and movement. The beautiful, in this, inasmuch as it appeals to the imagination, does not lie in what is near to hand. It is a thing of occasion, the play of locality and environment. And the shadows whom we project, when these scenes are ended, will be stronger and more individual from this contrast with the lives spent in these cages. For they are not prisons; though, perhaps, to be confined of your own free-will, or because it is the convention, is more hard than to suffer for your crimes. It is no martyrdom, when all your companions are happy and have found their solace. But we have to consider that it would be the rare soul who would feel more than a few regrets. We are not searching, here, for exceptional human beings. These souls, and their persons, have an animal similarity. They are sheep of a flock, the whole company of doves, swan princesses, or whatever simile you choose to call them by. We must impute to them not the individual, but the group, soul or consciousness. This, indeed, must be the ideal of any community who give their fortune and liberty into the common fund. They are to become alike in mind and plumage, regimented to the pious plan. Even so, that amount of their days not spent in prayer is as much, in total, as the lives and recreations of the working classes, who spend a third of their lives in shop or factory, and the rest in the train or 'bus, at home, or sleeping.

But we return to the doves of the cloister. It will be in remote places, far removed from what we conceive to be modernity, that we shall find our instances. For distance, like time, is comparative and not absolute. It if is your home, and what you are accustomed to, it is never distant, unless you are far away from it, and then, the measure is different, it is you who are remote, wherever you may be. The population may be ignorant and superstitious, but so it must be in order to support and countenance this waste. These are the vestal virgins, and it goes back to the earliest history of men that they should be honoured and set to live apart. Perhaps this sacrifice or abnegation of what was most beautiful and valuable in human beings was the beginning of all human strength, other than brute force. In this sense it was among the greatest of human inventions, a prophecy of peace amid incessant fighting. Long, long ago, it will have lost that meaning. But this most unproductive and expensive of legends has continued. It is human sacrifice with no shedding of blood. And it had its own secret of perpetuation.

The invention spread and multiplied, being so universal in all races who are not mere savages that it is not only of Christian connotation, but is found in most other religions. But it would be, obviously, a superstitious and a fickle population who most admired this sacrifice and made its embellishment into a festival. Such is the soil in which these institutions thrived. There are so many instances, and the choice among them takes us to cloisters that we would argue were both paradise and prison for their inmates.

Our first instance is Aveiro. This is a little town in Portugal, on the salt lagoons to the south of Oporto and not far, in modern distance, from the fishermen of Nazaret. It is the same water world, with those curious boats that we have mentioned; "esguichos", shaped like a sickle or a crescent moon riding on the waters; "moliceiros", with poops and prows like necks of swans, both carrying loads of salt or seaweed on the salt lagoons, and all brightly painted with most brilliant colours. The great Atlantic is but a mile or two away beyond the dunes. But the interest of Aveiro is in its convent of Jesus, or Santa Joana, called after the daughter of Alphonso V of Portugal, who was a nun here in the fifteenth century. The chapel, of which the decoration dates from two centuries later, is well described as "rutilante de dorures". That is the phrase applied to it in the French guide book, and the term is true. Nowhere else than in Portugal and, there, in few places, perhaps four or five in all, Lisbon not included, for the earthquake destroyed everything, is there this richness of pure gilding. It is the gold of Brazil, of Mines Gerães, in real gold leaf upon the carving, a soft, crumbling sand or gold, which glitters without light upon it. The carved ceiling is wonderful in this respect, and so is the altar, the carvings of which are coffered and recessed on purpose to dazzle and bewilder the eyes. It is a golden tabernacle lifted up and held sacred in these wings of gold. The chapel, thus, is not remarkable as architecture but it is incredible in gilding. Such an effect is nowhere else to be seen, save where we shall mention it, and, always, it is the gold of South America come over in the galleon.

Now the nuns, in Portugal, have been long dispossessed. They were abolished after the expulsion of Dom Miguel (the equivalent, in Portugal, to Don Carlos) by the laws of 1834.

Most of them rejoined the world, since no more neophytes were allowed to take the veil, while the sequestration of their property had reduced them all to poverty. A few nuns chose to remain, and there are harrowing stories of the appalling state of infirmity and starvation in which a few old nuns were living, as late as the 'seventies of last century, in a convent in mid-Portugal, near Vizeu. They were the last of the Portuguese nuns.

Here, at Aveiro, it is as though the doors of the convent had been sealed up in 1770. Yet the dust of two hundred years is nowhere to be seen. We could think that, as in children's stories or the libretto of a ballet, the nuns come back to it. But not at night. This is not the Romantic movement. These are not the moonlit wraiths of *Giselle*; nor *Robert le Diable* with its *valse infernale* and its ballet of nuns. This belong to another, and a sunlit, age. If they come back, at all, it would be morning or evening, or in the shuttered noon. The convent and its cloisters have been made into a regional museum. But no one visits it. Down in one corner live a peasant family. The balconies are hung with flowers and birdcages dangle from the beams. They are the peasants or contadini of the piece; actually, of course, it is the custodian who lives there. For the rooms above, besides some early paintings, have a collection which, even to an eye that has feasted long upon the rococo, in all countries, has an exceptional or transcendental charm. It is the art of the "presepio", the figurine, akin to that of Southern Italy or Bavaria, essentially a feminine art, and work, probably, of the nuns, themselves. There are dressed figures, little shrines, and painted papers. But the arrangement and handling are so exquisite that we must come to think of Aveiro as a little centre, to itself, in which there was leisure and happiness to make such things, and hands that could not be improved upon for graceful invention. The intrinsic prettiness is astonishing in scope and quantity, an art of confectionery, but ravishing in taste and tact. Painted paper, or a wooden panel, as background to a little shrine, will have a design of flowers on it that can only have been conceived of in a world in which the rhythm brought continual delights. The colours, too, are fresh as spring, or as morning or evening in their world of rococo, light pinks and blues and greens, of which those bare names give but the indication. Silks and materials are a delight and ravishment in colours and in embroidery. But it is particularly the dressing and arrangement, art of the milliner, or even of the window dresser, the angle, the neatness, the alluring colour. Not indeed, more important than cut paper; but the heaviest books are only paper. To deny this charm would be to say that painted scenery is never beautiful. Its instruments are scissors, needles, paint brushes. But, in effect, this is the world of perfectionment in little things.

This remote part of Portugal, a remote country, with the Atlantic to one side, two days' journey from Oporto, lost in the dunes and salt lagoons, how comes it that this lonely district has an art as delicate as that of Venice? It is far, too, from Braga, which was the capital of its baroque school of architecture. Quite different, also, for the buildings of Braga are whitewashed walls and sober granite, a grey green granite of which there are no quarries near Aveiro. Perhaps, in the garden staircases of Bom Jesus or Lamego, works without parallel in other lands, we would find the masculine counterpart to the minor arts of Aveiro. For they are feminine. We must believe that it was the nuns, themselves, who possessed this touch of hand and could teach the people. Two nuns, or three, out of a hundred; not the whole of them. But with a master hand who invented, who brought this flower to blossom and who set its seed. And, in the embroidery and dressing, many other hands could play a part, not only of nuns, but children. So that it was a big workshop. It was like the preparations for a fancy dress ball, but a ball for children, as though their confirming or their first communion was a festival, an orgy of doll dressing, tableaux of innocence and fresh gaiety, rosy cheeked angels with black eyes of Portugal. In the slanting sunbeams those black eyed Cupids ascend, or descend from, Heaven on the golden ladders. Their wings are plumes of Cherubim, feathers dyed and painted in the workshop of the nuns. Or their wings are gauze and muslin and, like the little Indian of the rope trick, they climb up but a little way, and credulity will hide them.

Little plays and sacred dramas were given by the children. And, if we are to be present at these in the spirit in which they were performed, an earth, and a Heaven, and a Hell, must open for us. Children were the dolls or marionettes. But their literature of religious mysticism, the hyperbole and ecstasy in the lives of the Saints, as read by the nuns—or, indeed, the religious reading of Portugal in the time of João V and his successors—was as rich in symbolic incident as any painted ceiling. We must realize that there were definite text books of emblems and symbols, so that personification was easy and the similes, as they could be called, were understood. The figures in fresco paintings, among the Southern Catholics, all had their point and meaning, and were, generally, passed by experts before the painting was begun. Thus, the whole world of imagery was universal and had become the vernacular. Dramas and Passion plays were, almost, a Jesuit invention, where, for instance, in the Roman churches enormous spectacles were staged under the direction of members of the great Galli Bibiena family. Lower down in the monastic scale, with the Capuchins, there was a preoccupation with death in its primitive symbol of the skeleton. The Cappuccini, in some instances, had waxwork figures in the vaults below their churches; but, more often, their play was with mummied bodies, as in their monastery near Palermo, where the three or four thousand dead bodies are dirty and horrid, but not frightening, except to those persons who would be afraid of moths or bats. Another of their fantasies was in the arranging of old bones; skulls and tibia, or thigh bones, all forming patterns, as with the shells or pebbles in a garden grotto.

This morbid drama had its feminine parallel acted, chiefly, by the companies of nuns. It was the dressing and decking out of the skeletons of martyrs. They have been measured and fitted with court dresses of the costliest materials, spangled suits of Spanish cut, sequinned with jewels, with rings upon their bony fingers, and glittering tiaras posed upon their skulls. They lean upon one elbow on a cushioned deathbed; or stand, propped upon their feet, held up by hidden rods and fetters. A special ingenuity, as though it were the work of certain hands, shows its invention in the artificial flowers. There are wreaths and nosegays, chaplets and fallen blossoms, strewn for the festival as though from maiden fingers.

Sinister and pathetic scenes will have been enacted in the robing room, when the skeleton had to rest upon a chair, or had to kneel before it quite stood up. The articulation of this thin and hollow dummy would be always at fault in its machinery. It will have been difficult to fit his arm into its padded sleeve; or near to impossible to drag the martyr's skirt over her skull and past her bony shoulders. Now and again, the marionettes would move or nod their heads, but it was too natural to count as a miracle. We may think that it took days, or even weeks, to dress them for eternity, to remember the last detail before it was too late, and to fix their glass cages. Such doll or death's head dressing is part, certainly, of a talent for the theatre; while it has, as well, its morbid poetry. In Sicily and Naples such skeletons can be seen; in Bavaria and the Tyrol; and in Portugal and Spain. Nearly, if not always, they will have been the work of nuns. If they could inspire a particular poetry, and we would think of Baudelaire, more especially, it is obvious, too, that a most curious book might be devoted to them. There have even been draughtsmen, or lesser artists, who have given their lives to such a task. For this martyrology would need a lifetime before it was completed, if set down in all its morbid detail with its necrophilic sadnesses and beauties.

Of such morbid obsessions there is no evidence at Aveiro. Instead, there are intoxicating prettiness and gaiety, qualities that are quite gone from us in our contemporary world. The apple greens, but of many kinds of apples, a pomology, in fact; the sugar pinks; the catalogue of blues, such are the bergère or bucolic graces. And, if we go into their workshops, we would find incessant preparation and a life as full with ceremonies and festivals as upon any isle of Bali. In some sense, indeed, but for the dancing, there are distinct parallels in the world of fantasy and legend with which they were surrounded, as in the temporary nature, the paper and plaster of their decorations, objects which would be destroyed to-morrow, for their criterion was newness. The quality of permanence is, after all, not essential to a work of art. There must be lighter things which are only good because new. Such is the particular enchantment of Aveiro; little objects, as though of yesterday, that will be gone to-morrow.

Yesterday and to-morrow, but how distant! It is all lost to us; just beyond reach, but not touching on to-day. There is, in all certainty, another night to live through before the slanting beams of morning. That belonged to the morning or evening

149

of another world, the evening, in fact, and just before the sunset. Such are the bright, clear colours, which are in exaggeration, for the midday world is not like this. They lived, not in an afterglow, but just before the colour died, in a moment of hyperbole, of exaggerated stillness, when no one moved, and all eyes watched the sunset. Perhaps the light stayed later here than in some other places, here on the edge of ocean, where the long beams lie upon the water. There is an unreal emphasis, as of a wonderful, an exceptional moment. We are watching a sky spectacle which can never be repeated, a feeling everyone will know, with its expectancy that something may happen. But indeed, it is to our own purpose to exaggerate this moment. The opportunity is our plaything.

For the whole regiment of nuns has come out for an airing. They have a collation, a Romaria, once or twice a year. Early in the morning, before it was light, you would have heard, far off, a creaking and complaining that never stopped, like something slow and trundling, moving towards you, but so slow and in such seeming agony, yet ever nearer, but never near enough to see. It was a grinding, groaning, screeching, the turning of a whetstone, a filing or sharpening, but so clumsy, so patient, so long suffering and complaining, so laborious and plodding. If you were the writer, you would have heard in memory the little piping note call of the knife-grinder, his Papageno music in the early morning, for this is how you hear him in the streets of Seville. But this has not that bird soul. It is heavy footed, dew-lapped, moving under the yoke with bowed head and in hopeless servitude. They are the peasants' ox-carts, belonging to the convent, with wheels of solid wood, the section of a tree trunk, more square than rounded, moving in slow agony and screeching on their axles. They have come for the infirm and aged of the nuns; and the peasants, who have no note of time, are waiting before daylight at the convent gate. None but countrymen could bear the screeching of those wheels.

Already, like white doves, the nuns move in the shadowy cloisters. The porteress is in her lodge. Presently, great panniers are carried down and laden on the donkeys. The dove throated morning has begun. Mules are brought to the door, and the abbess and her court ladies mount their steeds. They start off for the pinewoods with a great crowd following. There are nuns on foot; and all move slowly, for it is not far away. It is the feast day, or Romaria; and little children walk in the procession, covered with gold, and wearing cardboard wings dressed out in silks and gauzes. Behind them go their mothers, and men who play bagpipes and accordeons, or beat incessantly, the drums, called zabumbas.

The place of meeting is on a little mound or eminence. Tables on trestles are laid beneath the trees. As the procession comes past, any children by the wayside kneel down with joined hands, as if praying. It is the servants of the convent who have prepared the feast, women in peasant dresses with round, flat hats of black, of Lusitanian model, and a flap or veil at the back, descending to their shoulders. There are fish from the Atlantic, sardines taken by the fishermen of Nazaret, and the eternal codfish, bacalhau, of all Portugal. Great piles of bread and pastry load the trestles; but, more especially, there are the little cakes and sweets that no other country has in such plenty, each town or district having its speciality. Many, if not most of these, had we time to study the history of Portugal in the eighteenth century, were the invention and manufacture of the nuns. They are, in particular, the doces de ovos, sweets made with eggs: the ovos moles, especial to Aveiro, and packed in little wooden barrels: toucinho do céu, trouxas and lampreias de ovos from Portalegre and Caldas da Rainha; fios de ovos, aletria from Abrantes: doces de amêndoa, doce podre of Evora, morgado and dom rodrigo of Algarve: tijelinhas of Santo Tirso: pastéis de nata, sweet cakes of Tentugal: pães de ló, gingerbreads of Fafe, Ovar, Figuiero, Alfeizerão: cavacas of Caldas, Felguieras, Resende: the morcela of Arouca: marzipan of Portalegre: arrufadas of Coimbra: fig or almond cakes of Freixo de Espada or Moncorvo: and how many more! For this, remember, is a feminine feast. It is not the banquet of Batalha or Alcobaça, as we might read of that in Beckford. This is a sweet tooth feasting; and they drink, not wine, but chocolate. Or draughts of lime or orange, orgeat or pomegranate with pounded barley. And sweet ices in great plenty.

But it is the sight, more than the feasting, that is peculiar and strange. For who has seen a fête champêtre, but only of white nuns? They are like doves or seagulls descended on the land. And there must be a reason for it. A glut of beech nuts; or an

Atlantic storm. It is the same spot that they come to every summer, their open air refectory. To their midday meal, and they will have another in the evening, the lyric or idyllic noon succeeds. There is no siesta. No nun could sleep on such a day as this. They sit at the pinetree's foot, on the scented needles, touching the hot sand with their fingers. A warm breath, hot with resin, glaucous, dropping with the perfumed sap or gum, plays in the sighing, but now silent, boughs. It is as scented as the East, more warmly perfumed, more ambrosial, because the whole pinewood is a sleeping animal. The pine needles are its coat, its slumbrous fur, and then suddenly, in the midday stillness, it breathes out health and life. It sighs, in drops or tears of perfume, as though its breath were dew that refreshes, that is an awakening, that lies soft upon the lips and eyelids, and is summer, but keeps cool, cool, in the pinewood.

All of the nuns are talking. Many of them, in twos or threes, go to and fro slowly, in among the stems. And, to some, it is a treat, an adventure, to walk far away. They can go to the edge of the wood and look out on the world. It is a shoal of sand banks, with the salt lagoons and, if you listen for it, and at some moments more than others, the great Atlantic breaking on the shore, a coast with no cliffs so that its roar is even and monotonous with every wave that comes. Here and now, it is wave upon wave, and, then, there is silence, as though something bigger is preparing and would break upon the sands.

But the composition of this lyric scene draws us back to the little mound and to the body of the nuns. For it composes into a scene or drama with a hundred figures. The white doves have taken possession of the landscape. Their white habits and black cowls, which are in simplification of the colour, enhance the drawing. It has the magpie markings, but is more simple because the blacks and whites are even and regular. They have no pattern, no pieing as of wings and tails, and are but black for head and white for body. All the interest is in the grouping and the movement, made more dramatic because all their habits are the same. And the total experience of their blacks and whites is, in itself the key or secret of this pleasure, which is our delight in all chequered things, in the chessboard, in all parti-coloured flowers or dresses, but more exciting in pattern when it is but black and white. Their gestures and actions populate the scene.

It is a picture of movement because all the colours are the same. Their habits or liveries are identical in marking, so that it is a theme in variation, and strength and subtlety come forth from the monotony.

The groups are ever changing. It is a banquet, a festival, such a scene as the worship of the golden calf, where all the nuns are priestesses or sacred virgins. The full cornucopia would be its emblem, for there is such plenty on the trestles and in baskets on the ground. Yet it is not the harvest, nor a feast of increase, for these are neuter beings, they have no progeny. So the celebration is by proxy, yet such is its purpose, or its hidden meaning. And a curious emphasis, a distortion, underlines the action, made more obvious in the lengthening shadows and by the light of sunset. It is still more manifest when four nuns between them lift the huge panniers and unpack the viands. There are nuns, pair by pair, to each handle of an amphora. Others are carrying cloths, or great sheets, by their four corners, as it might be fishermen furling down the sails. Some walk to and fro again, their heads bowed from custom, as though they are at prayer, while they talk and chatter like a lot of children. Others hobble, like witches, on their sticks; or lean on a companion and are led by her. There are the tall and gaunt, as if their lives of sacrifice had gone into their stature; stout nuns, the Merry Wives, mere hollow shells of laughter, for their lives have cheated them; and the odd or eccentric, who are told by the folds of their robes, or by the knotting of their girdles. What are the young nuns dreaming of? For they walk together; except where one is known attendant on an older nun. But we must think that here, not in a Venetian convent, nor among the sophistications of the world, there was little unhappiness, or frustration. Of so many sisters in any family, one or two would go into a convent. It was happier than marrying, if you did not want to marry; and, in their conditions they hardly knew their suitors. It was little more than an imaginary longing, a spiritual, and not a physical state, to which the cloister was equivalent. The mysticism of their faith comforted them with its simple metaphors, its legends of love and goodness, and the simplicities of its code of sin. The nuns had no children; but they knew the pleasures and affections of this sort, being surrounded, as though of purpose, by children in their lives;

children to rear and educate, to have for companions, to prepare for the world they had, themselves, abandoned.

But now the Verbena* or the feast begins. It is easy to know the Abbess by her place in the centre and by her pectoral cross. There is a long table, and two great wings of trestles to either hand; but our theme is the effect and not the details of this banquet. For the beams of light are nearly level. They are golden searchlights played into the pinewood, but swinging slow and, where they have lifted, it will be dead until to-morrow morning. It is a feast of druidesses, but not their native oak-trees, for this is resinous and aromatic. A person in ignorance would wonder at the gathering. Why have they come here? For what reason are they at dinner in the pinewood? Their long shadows lie behind them, and the whole concourse is sinister and fatal as each druidess moves or manipulates her shade. The Abbess has become immensely tall and all the nuns are angular and bony. They appear to grow as you look at them. It gives the air of absolute antiquity, as though they were older than the trees, or than any wood which puts forth green leaves for summer. They look like creatures of the dark come out, in presumption, while it is still day, for a banquet of funguses and toadstools. Till the light dies—when there is sighing and sweet breath up in the boughs, of odorous gums and ungent dropping balsams. And then, once more, it is a simple holiday or picnic, the Romaria. But, ended. The Abbess mounts her mule again. A creaking and groaning comes from the ox-cart wheels. And the nuns go back slowly to the convent, to the columbarium, where the cells have been empty all day. Their white wings, and black beads and necks, soon make the cloisters live again. Seeing which, we may wish, and wish in vain to-day, that breaking of the silence. For they are gone away for ever, though the beauty of Aveiro lies in those tempor-ary and fragile things that have the look of yesterday, and that inspired us to the Romaria.

Any person who loves, as we do, such forgotten places, will find delight and poetry in Oporto, in the old convent of Santa Clara. This town of camellias, for nowhere else are they so smooth and beautiful as in the quintas of the Duoro, must be looked down on from above, from a church tower in its midst,

* Verbena is the Portuguese term for a picnic.

because of its tiled roofs. Each old house would seem to have
a staircase well that is carried up into a pavilion or gazebo, even
if it be no bigger than a large birdcage. There are many hundreds of these windowed turrets; indeed they, and the lichened
tiles, are the feature of Oporto. They are to be admired from
the terrace in front of the Sé, or cathedral, where you can lean
on the balustrade and see them far below you, or a few feet from
you. The harmony or contrapuntal variety in these utilities of
another age, their curious identity, and the problem of what
persons must have lived there, made me think of nothing else
than the "Clock" Symphony of Haydn. One after another, in
their different tones, I heard the ticking and the chiming of
those clocks in the midnight stillness of his adagio, broken
here, as it would be, by nasal voices and the noises of the town,
but no less magical for that. I have never seen another town
that could have this appearance on a moonlit night, such
proximity and mystery, such a serenading of cats, from their
terraces and hanging gardens.

On another steep hill amid these houses stands the convent
of Santa Clara, of old foundation, for it was built by the Queen
of Portugal, Donna Philippa de Lencastre, daughter of John
of Gaunt. No one ever comes here, and it is nearly impossible to
find the sacristan or key. To those persons who have seen it,
the interior of this church will have given an impression such as
is to be had from few other places in Europe, or indeed, in any
other land where the art of the baroque age is made credible in
its sumptuary magnificence. The gilded ceiling of Santa Clara
and its high altar could only be described as a glittering cavern,
but seeped and penetrated in its own refulgence. Here, again,
is the gold of Aveiro; or, as we know it to be, of Minas Geraes
in Brazil. Nowhere else than in Portugal is this gilding to be
seen. In the town below, down by the harbour, there is magnificent gold carving in the church of San Francisco, but it
cannot compare with that of Santa Clara. A proscenium arch,
as in a Bibiena theatre, rises over the high altar, and this, like a
transformation scene or the apotheosis in a ballet, has golden
and winged figures standing on volutes, under gilded canopies,
or alighting on the golden boughs and branches. Within this,
another proscenium frames the altar, behind which the massed
reliquaries proceed upward in diminishing tiers of dazzling,

theatrical perspective. The effect of this whole interior of Santa Clara is difficult to describe in words, but, assuredly, it is one of the major beauties of baroque art. We see it without its figurants, for the nuns are dispossessed. This is not the little world of Aveiro. They are urban ladies; or, so far as their clausura is concerned, hermitesses on a hill in the middle of a town. They could look out, as we did, from the balustrade before the Sé and hear the noises of the city. They knew the moonlight on the roofs of tiles, and, of a morning, looked down on the rabelos, the wine boats of the Duro with their square lateen sails and their gigantic rudders worked by a helmsman from a high platform at the back. There would be the country-men who came down with the grapes: peasant women of Tras-Os-Montes with round tambour hats and the capa de honras, a cloak or mantle of parti-coloured cloth, worn with a great hood, and heavy golden jewellery of Gondomar. Some-times, also, a shepherd from the mountains of Estrêla. They wear thatched cloaks of straw, like a coat of yellow reeds, and their homes are conical or beehive huts upon the green flanks of the hills, among their flocks. They are Celestial peasants from old maps or chests of lacquer, not out of place in this steep town of tilted roofs and miradors.

But we have not done with Portugal. Our subject takes us to Beja, in the Alentejo, to the convent of the Portuguese Nun. Her name was Mariana Alcoforado. She lived in the seven-teenth century, and is known to the world for her intrigue, and her letters, with a Frenchman, the Chevalier de Chamilly. We must describe, however, the approach to Beja. This is in the South, for it borders on Andalucia. For mile after mile there is a straight road across the plain. Sometimes to either side, there are rows of eucalyptus trees, with the nests of storks high in their branches, in sign of Barbary or Tartary, or the far Orient. The white pallor of this landscape is extraordinary. It is not the white of snow or dust. The colour seems to come to it from its immensity. There is no shade at all except the eucalyptus. Presently far away, a white pyramid is seen, with other simple, cubical shapes at its foot, on a hill in the very middle of the landscape. That is Beja. But the simplicity of its bare outlines is how the imagination would conceive of Andalucia. This is exactly the setting devised by Picasso for the Spanish ballet of

Don Carlos, Pretender to the Spanish throne (1848–1909)

Frontispiece to Angas, *New Zealanders Illustrated* (1847)

de Falla. We see the white walls, the simple black cube windows. The walls, sometimes, have drawings in charcoal done upon them. We could almost find the curtained door, with the miller and his wife behind it, and await the entrance of the Corregidor. It is a white square, or plaza. And, far away, through a white archway, there is another town, a simple cube or pyramid in the distance, and the blue sky. It is as though the painter, in letting his imagination escape into the endless plain of Andalucia, had reached to the far side of it, to the Alentejo.

The Portuguese Nun, Sœur Marianne, lived in the convent of the Conceição, founded two hundred years before by the Infante D. Fernando, father of the great Emmanuel I. Her grille, which suggests in simile the spokes of her fan, has been removed from the convent to the local museum. It was through this barred window that she spoke to the Chevalier de Chamilly in the true tradition of this land of serenades. The chapel of this desecrated nunnery is yet another of the baroque chapels of Portugal, not less sumptuous than that of Aveiro. Were we continuing South into the Algarve, we would find another specimen at Faro, on the Atlantic, upon the hottest shore, summer and winter, of all Europe. There must be other such chapels in the small towns of the interior, places never visited nor described in books; Elvas, for instance, of the sugarplums, Castelo do Vide, or Portalegre, again with its convent of the Conceição. But, here and now, at Beja, we go from the chapel to the chapter-house of the nuns, a high, vaulted hall which has mauresque tiles or azulejos upon its walls, only comparable to those in the Casa de Pilatos, at Seville. The lights from their metallic lustre form so unexpected a setting for one of the lesser masterpieces of French literature. Sœur Marianne must have dreamed here, against her conscience, of the Paris of Le Roi Soleil.

Outside, for the Conceição is in the middle of the town, a military band is practising through the hot afternoon. They play in a room of the barracks, once another convent or a monastery near by. I am not the only traveller to have heard them. Their programme is Albeniz, and music of the Spanish zarzuela, pasadobles, quick marches, as of "eyes-right" to the bull ring and the brave toreros, but slightly mocking, in mock heroic of the music hall; quick waltzes, estudiantinas; military

12
157

fanfares, the trumpets of Bibataubin. Never could the music of popular and legendary Spain be so appropriate as here; and, nowhere else, so well performed. It was tempting to wait until the evening, when they played in the garden underneath the trees. Here, indeed, would be a banquet and an intoxication for the senses. Not a feast, exactly, but a public bar, a place of summer drinks while this lively music lasted. Sœur Marianne, or her phantom body, would be listening at her grille. Along the white alleys, as now, there are shadows talking at the casements. They are the serenaders. Under the white archway, far away toward Spain, that other town is a mirage, a pyramid, against the starlit sky. The Chevalier de Chamilly, cloaked, is in the square and hears the music; or gone, gone, to the Castillo di Bibataubin.

Borne upon the same pinions, we come down into a crowded street, hear more music, and watch a procession of black penitents. It is the moment of the Tocado da Gloria, when all the church bells sound together. Statues of saints are sailing through the streets in clouds of flowers and glittering candles. The charivari of voices is broken by the strident, wavering cry of the saeta, the impromptu "arrow of song", of Gitano or Flamenco inspiration, uttered by the Gypsies as certain statues pass before them. Their rhapsodic voices, only wrung with penitence and sorrow, speak the sufferings of the Virgin, who is sculptured in her agony, weeping and crying. In midst of this the Tocado, at midday, is indescribable in excitement, a clashing of cymbals as loud as thunder, or the roar of cannon. Their beat and rhythm intoxicate the imagination.

A few more days in Seville and it will be the Feria, which I have only seen to the extent of driving through the town on the way to Cordoba, upon the second morning of the Fair. A light rain was falling and the majos, or cavaliers, were riding in the streets dressed á l'Andaluz, in tight trousers, short black pea jackets, with the hard rimmed sombrero, brown, grey, or black, worn at a rakish angle, and their majas seated behind them on the cruppers of their saddles. The majos have a wonderful air on horseback from their thin figures and the way they hold themselves; the majas wore white dresses, with high combs and white mantillas. Later, in the evening, there will be dancing in the casetas, or open booths, along the calle San Fernando,

between the walls of the Alcazar and the tobacco factory of
Carmen. They dance, all night long, to guitars and castanets.
The dance is the seguidilla, which in its snap and sparkle is the
fountain, the fan, and the dust of the Triana; a dry fire of
Manzanilla, or softer Amontillado; the strumming guitar and
the mechanical piano. But it is enough, surely, to have seen the
cavaliers and their majas riding in the rain on the morning of
the Feria.

DRAMAS AND DANCE CYCLES OF THE ISLANDS: THE AREÖI SOCIETY*

WE arrive in a vessel after a long voyage. Our ship is rocked by the sunset wind.

All morning we lay against the reef, grinding upon the walls of coral, casting the lead, calling out the fathoms. For the coral atoll is but just below water. Looking down, we see patches of clear white sand for floor, and fishes with spots and stripes of gold, like birds on the trees, among the branches of the corals. Of these, later. For they live and breathe in their own element. That is Poseidon's kingdom, though he is known by other names.

Over and upon this, with a long swell, the ocean lifts and hurls itself in an unbroken wave. But we are within the reef and have before us high hills and a dazzling white strand. Instantly, the canoes come out. The first is filled with gifts of fruits and flowers. In another are the high priests and their idols. The King comes last with his attendants. They are dressed in brilliant cloaks and helmets of red feathers. But the King's cloak is entirely yellow, and shines in the bright sun like gold. Climbing on board, they throw their cloaks upon our shoulders; place their feather helmets on our heads; put their fans into our hands. An hour later the hood of night comes on the land.

And so we have reached an island, big or small. No need to be precise. It is all Oceania; the coral sea of many isles and archipelagos. Oceania of the light skinned races. Not the Negritos, nor the Melanesians. But the voyage was a necessity. This cannot be written of as though we were native to the islands. Nor, entirely, as if we came from their Antipodes. We are a disembodiment; and write of what we see with the eyes of the poet or the artist, having all antiquity for our journey here, until the recent past. It is a subject for a com-

* From *Primitive Scenes and Festivals*, 1942.

position, to be judged by intrinsic, not by literal truth. We will allow ourselves, after being carried here, to enjoy the recreation of this enchanted spot. For that, we will wait for the voyages of the Areöis. That is our subject.

Meantime, for accuracy, we return to the large red feather caps, for that detail may give identity to what will become general to this coral sea. Their cloaks and helms of feathers are made, more often, of the red, yellow, and green feathers of a small bird. Another bird, *Melithreptes pacifica* of the ornithologists, inhabits the mountains and has under each wing a single yellow feather only, of an inch in length. They are caught with birdlime smeared on poles, and the pair of feathers taken from them. The yellow war cloak of the King, which we saw shining on the strand, and that became more like a cloak of gold as he was rowed nearer to the vessel, is four feet long and eleven and a half feet round the hem, made entirely of these feathers. It was formed during nine successive reigns. Dating from the antiquity, therefore, of this paradisal shore. "For the most prominent feature in the character of the islanders appears to be their love of indolence, in which the too great bounty of nature has permitted them to indulge." This much may we read, even of a hundred years ago: "and that they appear hitherto to have been an exception to that common law of nature, which has seemed everywhere else to have imposed toil in greater or less degree upon all men." Shall we continue?

But these shores of fragrance must display their population. The women dress in long, loose calico gowns of gaudy colours, preferring red or yellow; some of them wearing a small girdle or gay handkerchief tied round their waists. Over their calico gowns they wear silken shawls; with a wreath of red or yellow flowers, or an ornament of red or yellow wool upon their heads. They walk barefoot. The girls in their dances form head-dresses of living fireflies, which they impale upon slips of bamboo, and fix in such a manner that for hours they wear the glittering diadems in their hair. Their chiefs are clothed in pieces of snow white tappa, made from the paper mulberry, and allow the trains to drag after them along the ground.

Husbandmen have aprons of red dracæna leaves, ornaments

made from the pearly nautilus, and chaplets of flowers of the scarlet hibiscus. Their tattooing is plainly visible. One pattern, varying in its details, is like the crown of a palm tree. It springs from the central line of the back, and gracefully curls round both sides of the body. They, also, wear a picturesque kind of hat made of palm leaves, which, in the words of an eye witness, gives an interesting finish to their manly figures. And the fishermen, in their canoes, use long bamboo rods and lines, from which a pearl imitation of a flying fish is attached, for the capture of the bonito, dolphin, or albicore; or plunge into the water with a hand net, when they come in danger from the sharks; or their long black hair may get entangled and held fast in the branches of the corals.

That is Oceania, from end to end. Not a particular island, but the consensus of its Pacific sands. Paler than our shores, as though there were more pearl shell here. For the waves roll from half across the world, and in a million years have ground the shells into a fine white dust. They are shores of coral, too. It is, in fact, the coral sea.

And among one group of islands we find the Areöis. The Jesuit fathers describe something similar in the Caroline and Ladrone Islands. The Areöis, for we must quote again: "were a sort of privileged libertines, or strolling players, who formed themselves into a society for the worship of the god Oro, and the practice of immoral dances and pantomimes. They spent their time in travelling from island to island, and from one district to another, exhibiting their performances, and spreading a moral contagion throughout society. The numbers connected with this fraternity, and the magnitude of their expeditions, will appear from the fact of Captain Cook witnessing, on one occasion, in Huahine, the departure of seventy canoes filled with Areöis. On board the canoes in which they travelled they erected temporary altars, for the worship of the tutelary deities of their society. On public occasions they painted their bodies with charcoal, and stained their faces with a scarlet dye. At times they wore a girdle of ripe plantain leaves, and ornamented their heads with the bright yellow and scarlet leaves of the barringtonia. Their entertainments consisted in delivering speeches ludricrously referring to public events, in pantomime exhibitions, in wrestling, and in dancing during the night to the music of the flute and drum. In the constant display of these often obscene exhibitions, they passed their lives, strolling from one place or island to another."

In our eyes they are South Sea Islanders. To themselves, they are inhabitants of the living world. But, for our purposes, they are neither the one, nor the other. Not more than the personalities of universal legend. Their fruits and flowers, as much as the fragrant winds and coral shore, are the classic architecture of this myth. If we impute to them more of beauty and intelligence than they possessed, it is in the interest of the ideal, and no more, it may be, than to the eyes of their beholders.

This may be the moment, too, in which to discredit the stories of the Protestant missionaries. It was not long before, under their influence, the women and girls at Sunday service wore hideous bonnets, like huge coal scuttles, based upon the middle class fashion of the 'forties, when the missionaries first arrived. The islanders fell out of an earthly paradise into a Sunday slum. The conch shell was made silent by the harmonium. We attach little more importance to their stories than to their promises of heaven. The one, indeed, contradicts the beauty of the other. That the Areöis were immoral is not to be denied. And it may be enquired what is meant by morals, where are neither palaces nor slums: nor sound of marriage, nor funeral bell? But the wheezing harmonium must be for ever banished. It has come and gone. It came with measles, whooping cough, and colds: and other and more wasting ills. So the tin chapel is not yet put up. We could have wished it was but an interlude, a day and night in prison; but what it touched has been destroyed for ever. It has been the hand of death: and, in life, it is better not to think of that.

In effect, we land upon this shore with all the technique learned of other lotos-eating lands. It is a food that, like fancy, has no substance. True lotos eaters are, generally, more famished than well fed. But the Lotophagi are no parallel: for the Areöis led active, and not passive, lives of pleasure. In virtue of this they become a concept that we clothe, or unclothe, with our prejudices. They are the instruments of pleasure, not the audience. Here, the Areöis spread a moral contagion throughout society, journeying from isle to isle. In a paradise where there is no poverty, nor cold. Nor excessive heat: but the seasons are tempered, day by day, instead of month by month: a little rain in the early morning so that earth wakes freshened. No floods, nor gales. But, for excitement, the lightning and the thunder.

We will take the climate and the scene in order to have those skies and that brilliant light for background. For it is, precisely, "that indolence in which the too great bounty of nature has permitted them to indulge", together with the information that the Areöis "were a sort of privileged libertines, or strolling players, who passed their lives in travelling from island to island"—it is these statements that intoxicate the imagination and make the Areöis, to our eyes, brothers and sisters to the comedians in Watteau's paintings. "Their magnificent valleys abound not alone in luxuriant forests that attract and charm the eye, but also in trees bearing sufficient fruit to supply all their proper wants. The trees which produce the bread fruit, the banana, orange, coconut, and the cheremoya, seem to contend with one another for the palm of superior strength and beauty, and for the quantity of their spontaneous abundance. Their hogs require no care, and feed upon fruits which would otherwise rot and waste upon the ground; and their coasts abound in fish of every kind, which can be obtained at the price of no more labour than such as might be termed an agreeable pastime." It reads like an account of paradise.

But where to begin? Along the white strand; upon the scented hills; or in Poseidon's kingdom? So many thousands of leagues of blue weather, in every direction, into the four winds, have given to these islands a character of light that is their own. As much as to oases among the yellow sands; but Oceania is a continent of islands. A coral sea of many isles and archipelagos, with an entity as of Asia or Africa, and attributes that could be personified into a statue or a painting. Unsullied of history. So that its physiognomy has no likeness to another. A continent of islands, inasmuch as Africa is black man's land. That is its meaning, that it is isle upon isle. That it has been built up in a million years out of the blue main. The marine Indies; for where the past of poetry or painting are concerned, the Oceanians are Indian, to be known by what ocean has yielded to them, the pearl, the sceptre of narwhal ivory. There are a million wonders in half the world of ocean; and those living in their midst could rightly be called the Poseidonians.

But, here, it is not Neptune, but another god, who has given colours, also, to the trees and flowers. Not a snowy landscape lit by the prisms in the crystal; nor that which lies yellow in a grain of sand; the chalk hills; the plain of sherds and broken marble under the acanthus and the asphodel; where the blue campanula grows from cracks in the granite; the blue delphinium from the moraine; where the oleanders in the dry riverbed compose into a myth; or an almond in blossom is the antique world upon a youthful morning; where the hills and high places are trodden by the Muses; here is nothing familiar, or that has a token meaning. All things are soft and clear as in a drop of water, but of blue water, as it might be a drop of water upon the back or shoulders of the god, himself, youth or maiden, as he climbs out of the sea.

Day and night, here, are spent, half-in, half-out of water. Amphibian noons, cooled by the surf for snow. The kingdom of the trident. Their legends are of the vast spaces of the ocean. How they beached their canoes after many days at sea, and were the first to set foot upon this isle of flowers. How they plucked, at once, the jasmine for their hair. Not a bird flew away. All stayed, or came up near, as though their bidding was to wait for man. During the first years they could be struck down like flowers. Their wings were but to float them in the pleasant winds. Flight has but one meaning. It is pure pleasure. Far away, where the sun sank, there were other isles where no one died. In other ways it was the same there. They had night and day, for none feared the dark. The nights were too beautiful to lose, crowned with nocturnal blossoms that lived for this hour and only opened now. The winds, too, breathed differently, and you felt the sea plumes waving in them. The clang, even, of their feathers, now and then, and the breaking of a gigantic wave. Their paradise, in fact, was but another island, for the imagination could conceive of no more fruits or flowers.

Listen! It is a huge roller breaking. And we hear laughing and singing. The fishermen are far out upon the reefs, crossing what has been uncovered by the tide; and women and girls go with them, lit torches in their hands. They will come back with pearls. The ocean gleams and drips with phosphorus. It is easy to be a maiden and return a woman in the morning. The rosy shell of Venus is in sign of that, held in the hand, for the rosy awakening of day. All will carry back shells for ornament. Their pleasure gardens are out upon the coral, which we will see, later, pool by pool, in all their wonder. What we would have, for the moment, is laughter and singing upon the coral reef. For, near at hand, the blue moonlight shows us chieftains in togas made of snow white tappa; tattooed like the drawing of the body upon the human body, only it is an abstraction, a mere pattern of dots and lines, or an arabesque of leaves and shells, but it moves with the body, it lies upon the body, it is a sculpture to be felt by the fingers upon the living flesh, it is the lunar outline upon the solar body, a form seen in double silhouette, a flickering and pursuing shadow, a shade upon a shade. These are moonlight warriors in white cloaks, beaten out of the tree bark, and all day you would hear the hammer, hammer, of the wooden mallets. Such is the loom or distaff of the islands, for it is common to them all. There are the different qualities but this is the snowy white, without pattern. The textile of the Polynesians has another sound and one to which our ears must get accustomed for we will never hear it but upon the coral islands and it is much different from that of silks or cottons, to the point that it is the Oceanian fabric. Their ghosts would walk in snow white tappa, the cloth of blue ocean. It is grown in the sea gardens, so near to the marine that at the sound of a bare foot the tree crabs will drop like apples from the boughs and scuttle into the sands. Here, in the moonlight, we are under other branches—flowering branches—the tamanu,* with white flowers and a perfumed bark, held sacred, so that it is death to break a bough—or the coral tree, itself, with scarlet blossoms that cannot be described in moonlight, for they are blind or muted, yet burning like flames of coral in a moonlit water, until torchlight falls upon the gleaming trident, and laughing and singing, some with pearls, or some with cockle shells, the young men and maidens come in, wandering, from the reef. Then, the clusters

---

* Tamanu: *Calophyllum inophyllum*. Coral tree: *Erythrina corallodendron*.

keep their scarlet colour. It is retained, or muted, in them until the torches light the lower air.

What other flowers are there? A hundred that we could not name. But the white clematis has a sugary or spiced starlight of its own, as it trails upon the darker trees. A starlight of a few inches in density, blowing sweeter up to its petals; while the fragrance of hyacinth and jessamine mingled comes from a low shrub, the horopito, with bright green leaves as of a nutmeg tree, and waxen bells or trumpets that hang in clusters, of white, and pink, and crimson, and all shades of red. Come down to the shore, where the red fuchsia creeps out of the sands! Or but a few steps into the forest! That is another, or an underworld. Huge fungi, sprouting from the tree foot, are so broad and strong that you may sit upon them; while, upon the ground, luminous toadstools of enormous size gleam with phosphorus and shine like evil stars or constellations out of the damp.

But we seek, once more, the moonlight and the cloaks of snow white tappa. Near to them sits a queen or a princess, sceptre in hand, of sea ivory, made of the tusk of a narwhal or sea unicorn, one of the wonders of the southern seas. This monster, could we but see it, is as white as snow, marked with a few dark spots or blemishes; its belly, white and glistening, and as soft as velvet to the touch. With their tusks they break the thin ice to breathe, down in the dreadful South where the Pacific becomes Antarctic. The explorer Scoresby remarks of the narwhal: "a great many were often sporting about us, sometimes in bands of fifteen or twenty together . . . they were extremely playful, frequently elevating their horns out of the water, and crossing them with each other as in fencing." That was in the old days of the sailing ships. In our time such a sight could not be seen. The herds of narwhals are all slaughtered. This twisted sceptre came from one that drove in to shore, after a storm; or, more probably, pursued a shoal of fishes and was stranded in the shallows. Its horn was bartered from isle to isle along the coral reefs, passing from queen to queen out of their dusky hands: carried in canoes close to the triton shell, which is their war horn or trumpet blown out on the deep. You would hear, for it is still night, the voice of the triton and the splash of many oars. And the canoe comes past, at high speed, navigated by the Southern stars which lie in countless archipelagos into infinity, until the eyes can stare no longer, and a meteor glides out of the zenith, without a sound, like some portent, but dies above the sea. Another, and another, fall. They shoot, like golden bolts, out of the firmament, living only for that moment, to portend a mystery. Such was the coming of the narwhal sceptre. Listen! listen! It is the sweeping of a snow white toga. That is the noise they make. We see a shell bracelet and a dusky hand.

How wonderful are the clear colours of the morning, in Oceania, upon the Southern Seas. The pandanus trees droop their fronds almost into the waves. Here is shade, instantly, of a fern-like kind. The coconut palm is in ecstasy, dancing in every wind; while the substance of shade is as much from blossoming branches as from green leaf or hoary stem. There could be, here, such an experience as to lie down to sleep in the shadow of the orange, or the shaddock, not of their leaves, but of the fruit itself, red globe on globe, or of the swollen and distended yellow moons. At foot, the pine pricks almost out of the sand. The sunlight comes down, with no dilution, for the hills are not high enough for clouds to gather. No more than terraces, or pleasant eminences from which to take the cool. And covered, from head to foot, with trees in flower. Here, by falling waters, grows the South Sea chestnut, *Inocarpus edulis*, with dark green leaves, white flowers in season, and aerial roots, like buttresses, that join the branches to the chequered earth; a bower wherein the shepherd, but there are no flocks to watch, could look, instead, down to the coral reef.

The morning and the evening breezes, playing from the shore, waft these many scents upon their wings, so that, at dawn and sunset, and long after, while our ship is rocked by the sunset wind, every breath is perfumed. Shrill voices from the town cleave the air like darts. Far into the night. Thus, the evening and the early morning. Noon is the hour of distillation, when they wax and strengthen in the stillness, in the shade of their own leaves; a spiced breath, but it hangs upon them and is not blown away. Scent of the flower mouth is part or parcel of the noonday heat. Look how it lies blue upon the dryad body! For a maiden, naked to the waist, lies in the shade. We will have music. The earth is all dappled with its cloaks of shadow and the open sunlight. Call it golden! But it is the golden yellow of a dancer's body that is painted with tumeric and coconut oil. Not yet. We are to embark, later, with the Areöis.

And crossing from shade to shade, a girl passes in a snow white shaggy dress. Of cotton tree fibre, loosely woven, and on purpose for coolness much too big in size, hiding all her body. Like a pearl in the oyster shell; or the chrysalis in the cocoon. Within that white shagginess, her nude figure is to be guessed, or dreamed of. That is the purpose in her loose white dress. For it hides her from neck to foot.

We called for music. A dryad sings from under every tree, hidden in the bracts or flowering boughs. You have but to look between, or lift them aside, and she will be lying with her companion at the tree foot, one with an empty turtle shell strung for a harp, or the sea conch to his lips blowing a mournful and a shaggy music. Always a vibrant or a wavering music, such being the nature of their South Sea throats, or in order to be heard above the sound of sea, which is never still for long upon the islands, but like the voice within the seashell is ever hidden there. A voice, and a sea harp or sea trumpet, that is all. It is more in the melody than in the instrument. And more in the singer than in the song.

But of an isle in utter ocean, until the dancers come in pearly coronets and necklaces of flowers. Not yet. This is the long and lazy noon. There is music, and a pause of heat. For the leaves are as hot as flames; and in those colours, burning in a steady fire. The flower bracts burn like candles. There are feathery fires upon the hills, where the tufted palms grow; and a shrill fire in the groves of bamboos, given from the green rods. That and the deep heat of the timber trees; the teak with scarlet fruit or scarlet flowers; trees which are poisonous, the itchwood, or the leper tree; trees which give a black dye; the pine tree; or, for the haunt of music, the glorious barringtonia with red flowers; the banian with its flying buttresses; or the sandalwood tree, smelling warm and fragrant, which, when the traders come, will bring death and destruction to the island.

It is a scented indolence. Not the siesta of green shutters, nor of the fountain. Here, you cannot lie upon cool marble in a pillared shade. Walls that sport the snapdragon do not throw down their shadow. The hours do not chime with bells; nor does a voice call from the minaret to where merchant and beggar lie sleeping. To the court of waters, and the trellised alleys. To the mules tied up in the shade. To the honeycomb vault, and arch of stalactite opening to the orange grove. Here are no colonnades, nor dancing waters.

But it is an isle of indolence. The lustral shadows reach between the trees; flower shadows, not the shade of leaves; the form of the scarlet cone, or fiery cluster. There can be lawns of white or red sloping to the waters; or fields, more cerulean than ocean, breaking on the scarlet bough, or at the hanging fruit. A rosy soil, on which you tread the blossoms, but only in token, as though it were moonlight, for the colour comes from the loaded branch. A near shadow can be as blue as the lotus pool, and as translucent, with that same lightness as of the lotus cells, glistening in texture, as of a blue light upon the petal, blind, or matt, because there is no white on it, and it is blue through and through in all its particles, an interior blueness as though you lay within the lotus. And, near by, a tree of white flowers, smelling like hyacinth and jasmine mingled, until its difference is recognized and it becomes a person, a hand that sheds incense, a guttering candle, for it is weighed down with flowers. Here are flowers, there is no word for it, that are muted and have no smell, by that much more creamy or more velvety, as blind persons who love music or who live by touch. Each of the shades has its philosophy; those that lull; or are intoxicant; that bring discontents; or sensual longings; that are sufficient in themselves so that the imagination calls for no more than that; or by something missing are more lovely in their imperfection; that remind one of a forgotten name; or, in extension of that, are as though one is so much in love that the eyes, from too much looking, have forgotten what is out of sight; others to inspire music; or build a policy or a culture that is peculiar to themselves, as it could be, cities of the gondola; melon domes; or palaces of coral, all rustication, rising from the shadowed waters. All day you could lie in a tree shade and be no further in your thoughts. It is in the Southern Seas. Here are, in fact, no more than flowers or persons. There are no great causes.

No horror but the feasts of human flesh. We may find a

victim trussed and bound, sitting ready, his feet drawn up below his thighs, and his arms folded, tied tight so that he cannot move, then lifted on to the hot stones of the oven with leaves and earth thrown upon him, or put to the huge cauldron. When cooked, his face is painted black; and the flesh is eaten with great forks of many prongs, made of the hard wood of the casuarina, a drooping tree which grows about the burial places. Such are the cannibal hearths. You could see joints of human flesh hanging on the trees.

This is the landscape in islands that have hills, that are not the simple atoll. In New Caledonia, Tahiti, or the Marquesas; mainlands where you could make a journey of a hundred miles, or be lost three days' march into the interior. In Fiji, Samoa, or Hawaii, in New Britain; or New Ireland, off the coast of New Guinea, where the stone men were undisturbed until a year or two ago, and tilled their terraces and stuck their wigs of hair with flowers, living in plenty, having heard no rumour of the turning world. But, in order to comprehend the immense Pacific and its archipelagos, its lonely islands that may be destined to a bloody fame, and the reefs of coral, that ocean must be seen in entirety from the Arctic Aleutians down to the roaring South. Then we can return and set forth with the Areöis on a voyage of pleasure.

A map of the Pacific Ocean gives the following as the most curious in shape of the coral atolls. Aitutaki and the Hervey Islands, among the archipelago of the Cook Islands, midway, it could be said, between Tahiti and Fiji. Niafuoō, between Samoa and Fiji, is almost a complete coral circle with a round lagoon three miles across in its middle. And three islands are more curious still; Tongareva, Rakahanga, Manihiki, isles of euphony, lying north-west of Samoa. The first is nearly a hexagon of coral, in no place wider than a hundred yards or so, with a lagoon twenty miles long and ten miles across inside it. Rakahanga is a distorted square of the same pattern; and Manihiki a square with bending sides, so that it is broken nearly into a pentagon of coral. The other is Wake Island, half-way between American Hawaii and the Philippines, an isle like a coral arrowhead, with a safe lagoon within, and lying open for the seaplanes. Guam, not less notorious for its potential future, lies much nearer to Manila, an ordinary isle of hills and valleys. These islands are important enough to be inset upon the map; how many more must lie all but virgin! There are still the islands, Los Jardines, marked "existence doubtful", five hundred miles, or more, west from Wake Island towards the concealed mysteries of the Japanese Mandate. A seaplane from Wake Island, maybe, could solve this problem. There is no other quite like it in the world to-day. The Japanese Mandate extends over the Bonin Islands, the Mariana or Ladrones, and the Caroline Islands, coral atolls about which it is next to impossible to discover anything in the present for it is the policy of the Japanese to keep them, on purpose, in obscurity. Of old they were Spanish settlements and the resort of South Sea whalers. Guam is an American outpost in the midst of these. Tinian, in the Marianas, has the remains of old buildings, left by an unknown race; and when Admiral Lord Anson called there, in 1742, the isle was deserted but it was remarked of the wild cattle that: "it is not uncommon to see herds of some thousands feeding together in a meadow. They are all of them milk white, except their ears, which are generally black." The Carolines lie south of these, towards New Guinea, including Yap, which is the Japanese answer to Wake Island and to Guam. These islands, too, have ruins; while, of the inhabitants, we are assured that: "their dances are by no means indecorous, and are performed by the unmarried men and girls, who stand in a row on a plank, and with graceful movements of the arms and body keep time with their feet to the song. . . . They bathe three times a day, and anoint their bodies with scented coconut oil and tumeric."

Other wonders of the Pacific are Easter Island, Christmas Island, and the now notorious Pitcairn. The Solomon Islands are, probably, the only cannibal islands of the modern world. Their population must be related to the stone men of New Guinea, but they are thieves and prodigals, the degenerates of that antique world. Their patriarchs are different in expression from the elders of that lost nation. Where shall we sail next? To the frightful landscape of the Galapagos, four thousand miles away, and half of that across an open ocean? A scene like Pluto's underworld; isles of the damned, for their arid hopelessness breeds suicide; igneous rocks whereon the maned lizard creeps; where the droppings of the sea-birds make a nightsoil many fathoms deep. Or south, a thousand miles, to Easter Island, where the giant images stand upon the coast in mystery. No living person knows the whole Pacific. Melanesia, Micronesia, Polynesia, could be called three continents of islands. In respect of arts and customs New Ireland may be the most interesting of the whole Pacific Islands. Its natives were masters of what could be termed outrigger sculptures, wood carvings into which the image or fantasy of the war canoe had passed, so that they are made for speed and lightness, encased, often, in an open framework which suggests the bounding of the craft upon the patterned waters; some great amphibian gliding in the reef pool; or even, in extension of imagery, a bird flying, or static, but in the symbol of its powers of flight. New Ireland carvings are to be known at once. They are not dramatic and obscure, like negro sculptures, suddenly sensual, and exquisite by moments and by feeling, but always of the animal in man. Negro carvings can be nearly great art, through intensity and meaning. But New Ireland carvings have, as it were, the flying fish for canon. It is an imagery of much fin and wing, with scale and ridgeback, and the dolphin tail, which delights in springing over the billows and enjoys the resistance of the waves. All this, in terms of the tutelary deities. So that they are more excitant and poetical than wrought in terror. What must have inspired them are the forms and colours of the coral reef.

It is among the Melanesians and Papuans, and principally in New Britain, New Ireland, the Solomon Islands, the New Hebrides and New Caledonia, that the dance and the savage arts have come to their fullest development. These groups of islands follow in a curve the Western coast of Australia and are, as it were, in parallel to the tribal ritual of the aborigines in Queensland, or throughout that continent, dances and initiations, arts of the masquer and of metamorphosis pursued with the intensity of total war, all else subordinated so that the drama or dance cycle can play through the seasons. The shadow life of these savages is more complex than slum life, or life in a council house in any modern town. Nearer, too, to the realities than in a city of wet pavements and back windows. In comparison, Hawaiians, Tahitians, who are Polynesian,

and live in an earthly paradise, have the languor of the
South and are less serious in their pleasures. They are Sicilians
of the Southern Seas. And, in fact, of another race. Down
South, where it is colder, there were the Maori warriors;
while Hawaii, Tahiti, the Marquesas, are the temperate isles,
far removed from steaming Papau and equatorial heats of the
Melanesian or Negrito. But, in those tropics, the primitive
savage still flowers in his prime.

It is here that an anthropologist can spend a lifetime in an
island; where a river pours the rains of Papua into the coral
sea; or in an unknown archipelago, moving from isle to isle,
watching the kitchen middens rise, as it might be a hundred
thousand years ago. Not in a whole lifetime could be exhausted
the treasures of the land or sea; for a language must be learned,
and another tongue is spoken but a few miles away; the
shadowy taboo must be explored, which is the subconscious
given phantom form; and their involved imagery of belief and
superstition be co-related and its shadow illusions understood
and explained. Works, such as *Drama of Orokolo* or *Stone Men
of Malekula*, are in evidence of this.* The time traveller could
have no experience to compare with these. They are the
complete antithesis; while an aeroplane passes over the coral
reef and is gone before the next wave breaks.

Concerning life in the coral pool it would be impossible
to be both sober and exact. For the fishes surpass in colour
all that the imagination could conceive of. Blue and silver,
ultramarine, or scarlet, striped, pheasant marked, or golden
spotted with drops that are of liquid gold and fade while the
eye looks at them as the fish is caught; fishes that are the
macaws of the coral grove, but in greater variety; that bask
or glide, or flaunt their parrot skins; or are singular in shape
as well as colour; monstrous and creeping, or shooting like
Xiphias through the olivine, for the waters are of every colour
beside the blue of Amphitrite. Their form is of a million ex-
periments to devise beauty and swiftness; but, as well for pure
ornament, for there could be no other purpose than their
mutual pleasure. The entire conspectus of these South Sea

---

* *Drama of Orokolo,* by F. E. Williams, and *Stone Men of Malekula,* vol. i, *The Coral
Islet of Vao* (4 vols. in all), by J. Layard; two of the most interesting anthropological
works published in our time.

fishes must be impossible of attainment, for many species are in variety beyond number; nor, in a thousand years, could it be feasible to search all the coral reefs and be certain which are peculiar to what set of islands, for they may be as restricted in their habitat as the Birds of Paradise. Some may haunt one reef only; or be found in their millions all through the coral seas. Their colour mutation is no mere development of new shades and markings. But it is as though from the full palette the most opposite colours had been chosen, and growth, from the beginning, had been for clash and contrast, a sort of shadow scheme, if the light and luminous took the place of shade. Not in dun colours, but in blues and scarlets for the *poissons-perroquets*, cockatoos of the coral reef; so individual it could be a suit of colours dyed for one fish alone, until another gleams above the floor of snow white sand. Others have their fins prolonged into a pair of scaly wings; into fringed oars or rudders, according to their motion; they sail, or fly, or float, or skim upon the waters. The commonplace, the vernacular of fishes is, here, all gold or silver. They are netted, splashed, or striped with it; or, like the macolor, one of the kakatoes, are all black and grey and white, but so disposed that is in the colours of the whale or dolphin, but as pretty as a golden carp. A hundred painters, content with these wonders, could not portray them in a thousand years; and, as well, there are the different sorts of shells from the Red Sea, across the Indian Ocean, from Amboyna in the Moluccas to the Galapagos.

The true and veritable Poseidonia, the kingdom of the islands lying half across the world from Africa to the Americas. Seas of the pearl sceptre, the chambered or pearly nautilus; the latirus, which, when dry, is dull and colourless, but, upon being wetted, as though in its own element gleams like a rainbow; terrestrial molluscs which, like little painted shells, climb into the trees; two hundred species of achatinella in the Sandwich Islands, which are their habitat; the spotted or banded land shells of Papua and the Solomon Islands, belonging, in the language of science, to the trochiform group of helices, known as geotrochus, their lips brilliantly tinted with scarlet, rose, or yellow; the bulimi of the forests, one of which, from the isle of Guadalcanal only, is of a delicate greenish straw colour, with the edge of the lip bright vermilion; glittering fish hooks made from the pearl shell of the haliotis iris; the shells of New Caledonia, which are more wonderful than any; canoes that are patterned or inlaid with shells; the clam shells that are big enough to use for fonts in churches; and the *Triton variegatus*, war horn or trumpet of the islands. They are found on the beaches and in the pools, and, as a rule, their beauty lasts. This is not so with the fishes. They lose their colour when they are lifted from the waters. They are as far from their own element as meteors that fall upon the earth. In a moment they have lost their fire, and die dully, as the light dies.

There is the truism, also, that shells do not journey for long distances, unlike the migrant shoals. They may have their summer or their winter pastures, and change a tropic for a temperate isle. Their lanes are by instinct along and under the blue main. It is impossible, in fact, to know them all or to calculate their numbers. On a day, at any coral shore, they may appear in their nations. How, therefore, to make them tally with another shoal a thousand miles away! A race of fish may be so rare as to appear extinct; and then be found, in multitude, where they have wandered in the waters. The hidden droves of the deep seas must be included, which are unknown save for what the net brings up. This is of no more moment than the arrow that falls upon the plain. The huge depths are untroubled and hold to their secrets. It will be impossible ever to explore them thoroughly. They are dark pits or caverns illumined by strange gleams. But what necessity is there to look down into those valleys! The coral ramparts come up from the bed of ocean. Not exactly. It would be more true to say they are forts or breakwaters built by the madrepores upon the summits of marine mountains. Bastions of coral a hundred or two hundred feet in height. Not more than that. Coral-capped mountains, for the sheer cliff or precipice may fall for a thousand fathoms, and near the shore be as deep as the Himalayas. It is upon this outer rampart that the ocean lifts and hurls itself in an unbroken wave. It is deep blue, and curling over, breaks into a roar of foam, white as foam, or as the blue hair of the sea god. Thousands of rainbows shine along the spray, as though ten thousand fountains were splashing. Within the atoll the coral artisans are found, for the outer fortifications are formed by their slaves or peons. Here, in the lagoon, are brain coral (for it has the shape of that) or mœan-drina; astrœa; and the branching madrepores and explanaria; corals that are all shades of colours, not alone the red and white, but browns and yellows, pink and vermilion and deep blue. Bright red, yellow, or peach coloured nulliporæ; the pearl-shell eschara and retipora. Such are the coral groves and coral branches.

Where to choose to study this! The first coral reefs are in the Red Sea; and from the East coast of Africa to the West coast of America there are coral isles. The Cocos or Keeling Islands in the Indian Ocean, eight hundred miles to the South of Java, are as typical of any; or Christmas, halfway from there to Java, where Captain Cook lay to, in 1777, for turtles, "perhaps as good as any in the world". Near by, the Indian Ocean is six miles deep. There are the Maldive atolls, below Ceylon; the Nicobars which were famed for shells; Celebes; Amboyna; and so into the Pacific. The Great Barrier Reef, a thousand miles long, runs parallel to the coast of Queensland and nearly touches on New Guinea. Sometimes, but ten miles from the shore; or, in places, a hundred miles or more. It is here that the waves break upon the longest terraces of coral. But the madrepores never build out of the water. Their labours are done when the reef, at low tide, is an inch or two below the surface. So that you can climb out from a boat and walk along it. And, in places, the broken pieces detached by the waves have been piled up, like blocks of cement where a pier or breakwater is unfinished; while, upon these, the softer corals have been powdered into sands, and the seaweed and the guano form a soil, until it is a little coral island. Months, or years, could be lived upon the Barrier Reef. Or but a few moments, in imagination. There is no time for more. It is the primitive world, not in its scenes and festivals, but in the untainted mornings. We are far enough from the savage men to keep them, in contemplation, across the Coral Sea. Opposite are the Louisiades, where the communal houses are built down to the shore, and the men are all fishermen.

The catamaran is poled along the shallows. A raft, made of planks lashed together; or they push it in front of them, wading upon the reef. They are savages of bestial feature, with frizzed-out mops of hair, their ears and noses slit for ornament and pierced by a piece of shell. A man of thirty is like an old man; black as a negro, but of the Papuan race, which means more hirsute, and with a sloping or receding head that expresses cruelty or cunning, filed and blackened teeth and the mouth of a carnivore, or cannibal. All his ancestors have fed on human flesh. He is an eater of raw fish; an ichthyophagite; the man of the kitchen midden, collateral of the beachcomber along every shore, groping for shellfish with his hands, but, the next moment, throwing a line which is baited with the pearly nautilus. A primitive of the coral seas, where the green iceberg never comes. An amphibian, for half of his days and nights are spent in the shoal water. His catamaran could be lying off Golconda's coasts, it is so heaped with shells. Many of those, in the antique world, would be bargained for by Kings. One of their number, *Cypræa aurantia*, "the morning dawn" or orange cowry, when found upon the reefs is so rare that its wearer is given the dignity of a chief. The philosopher may wonder why the most beautiful is the rarest. But the savage is old enough in wisdom not to be astonished. He finds other shells little less wonderful, which are so common they are no concern of his. They are thrown, one by one, where the waves wet them, or they even crawl along the boards. In the meantime, we will have it night. He baits his hook again with a bit of pearl shell. It is low water and he wades upon the rocks. A meteor falls across the sky. There are a myriad lights burning and no heat from them. It is the Southern starlight. This warmth of the waters is no part of that. But the planets throw down their fires which lift into long lines upon the swell. And so it is for long hours in the catamaran until the morning.

The thought of those curious nights and days takes us to one more locality before we set out with the Areöis. It is to the Sulu Islands in the Philippines, between their Southern mainland, or Mindanao, and North Borneo. In the Celebes Sea. And the sound of that gives us the high eaves of the houses, built side by side, their huge gables hanging above them like tents or crooked steeples, like the poop of a junk or the fo'c'sle of a galleon. Not all shaped alike, except in principle, so that they could be as many boats drawn up on a beach, out of the monsoon wind. These houses of Celebes or of the Sulus are a fantasy of shipbuilders, and the ribs of their eaves are carried through. They are boats, keel upwards, and the ribs have sprouted into horns or antlers. It is a wooden architecture influenced by pirate seas and by the deer or ante-lopes of the forest. By affinity, if not, directly, through sug-gestion. Seas of the lateen sail, for the junk has sailed here from the China Seas. The war canoes, with foam at their prow, are oared upon another ocean. Here, in a storm, a huge junk has been shivered on the reefs. And, on a lacquered noon, the lateen sails have often come and gone. The water towns are upon the far shore; floating cities of the sampan with their own joss houses and their dens of infamy. Thousands of souls are born, and die, upon the river. Beyond these islands it is the China Seas; so that their Southern winds are from the Pacific, but the weather can change and blow down to them from Bantam China or Cochin. The Malay seas, the haunt of Malay pirates. Beside Borneo, but the archipelagos lie from here to Honolulu. This is the last mainland, for Borneo is big enough to be the terra firma, so that the Sulu Islands are between several worlds, and it is here in obscure corners that fishing villages are built on stilts into the sea and every conceit of seafaring finds expression along the shores. For the seas could be said to be more fertile than the land. They are more punctual than the cornfields, and have not to be tilled or sown.

Here, then, are the Sea Gypsies, round and about Sibutu, the nearest of the Sulu Islands to North Borneo. The southern-most of all the Philippines. The Sea Gypsies are born in the sailing canoe and pass their lives in it. Having no villages, nor houses upon land. Their sails are made of matting, and they know the ins and outs of all the winds, how and when they freshen and exhilarate from isle to isle. Or creep, turtle footed, as though they trailed in weeds. There are the steady winds that, month after month, would speed you out to ocean, and offer no return. Rare winds, once in a lifetime, that break the laws and blow back whence they came. A North wind breathing out of the South, in prelude to an earthquake and a tidal wave, when an island, like Krakatoa, could be blown out of the bed of ocean. They do not even pitch the tents. They are wanderers upon the seas. Their stolen food is there for all to steal. And their sea voyages are mostly made by night. Dawn comes to meet them upon another shore, rising like naked

Venus out of her pearly shell, and wafting to land upon the catspaw calm in the opalline or milky waters. Where else could you find Gypsies walking upon the coral reef? Or their naked children paddling upon the rocks? What signal or indication will they leave behind them to guide their friends? Broken coral stems piled up into a pagan altar? A mound of oyster shells? And with what intent?

That the dappled herds—only they are dipped with gold and vermilion and deep blue—have moved away? That the golden fin no longer waves above the sand? Sometimes, like the Gypsies, they have destroyed just for destruction's sake. A coral pool has been entirely pillaged. The fronds and coral stems have been chipped down with the hammer. Or so it would seem. The broken shells, from which their inmates have been gouged away, float upon the calm, as sordid as the ship's refuse upon which the seagulls feed. They are like the cracked eggshells that the cuckoo has thrown down from the nest. It is, of course, in hyperbole that we call them Sea Gypsies. They are a tribe who have taken to the waters. But like breeds like; and there are points of similarity in the nomads of the coral reefs. They move by stealth. The fraternity do not meet by chance. They are liars and dissimulators. And they will spread false news. They will come ashore at some village, bringing triton or cowrie shells hidden in a piece of matting. By fire of personality they barter these for other things; and, always, the purchaser loses in the bargain. And they are off to sea before he knows this. That contrast between the Gypsies on the road and the motor car that passes them, or the aeroplane overhead, is present here in the difference between this naked poverty and the primal colours of the coral sea. There is no taint upon the fishes or the seashells. Was there, once, a golden age when *Cypræa aurantia* was as common as the cockle shell? Has the race perished? Or were they, purposely, made few in number? If they show themselves, they will be stolen. In this they are blond children whom the Gypsies kidnap.

And there are lights and music. It is the embarkation. Men and women and young girls climb, laughing, into the canoes. There are many farewells; but no tears, for they will come back again. It is but a journey from island to island, and the wind will carry them all night. No need to use the oars; or more than dip a hand into the milky waters. It cools the pulse. For the night is warm; and there is music without end.

The Areöi Society, in sixty or seventy canoes, take the sunset wind and are gone. But we go with them. It does not matter where. As long as there is music, and at dawn and all night through we have the scents of the paradisal islands. And more than music. Or that much more which music brings. For there is much else besides; and we would talk of it in our own symbols. What is there in the colour of a skin? These are the Tahitians, and the women are no darker than Sicilians. The Sicilienne could be danced here. Forty or fifty Siciliennes promised long ago, and unfulfilled. By the net of waters. Against the netted foam. But not the Sicilienne alone. That measure must mingle with the other music. As dew falls, even out upon the waters.

We will not exaggerate the beauty of the songs; but, as with all music, it is what it seems to be. And we will have it in our idiom. This is a troupe of players and comedians, with flowers at the wrist and neck, and in coronals of flowers that will keep fresh until the morning. This is the primal world in decadence. And there are parallels in all the full blown flowers of decay. Music, itself, is first and last of the arts. If ever there comes a lull, listen, and you will hear the conch shell blown in the prow and at the helm! That is primitive music. It is, thus, the wag-gons or the moving tents are kept together. It is the long horn of the shepherds in the mountains: the bucium* that echoes along the valleys.

Dew falls upon the sea trumpet. Dusky goddesses, in plenty, dip their wrists into the water. You could see a dark hand below a moonlit wave. And the goddesses, or Columbines, are in gowns of calico. Many of them wear the scarf or handker-chief of the rumba dancer. Or the snow white shaggy dresses that we saw. Others wear dryad blue: and are naked to the waist. A lute is held in a hand of amber—for we would have it a lute—and amber fingers touch the strings. What shade of petal are the lips that sing? A shell ornament glitters at a shadowed ear. The figure is a smoky column rubbed with rose

---

* This is the Roumanian name for the bronze trumpets, eight or ten feet long, blown by the Wallachian shepherds.

and jasmine oil. It is rare to meet with this upon the waters, as the armada moves above the madrepores and knocks at mullions into which the moonlight falls. For all night long it is the coral reef.

Who would not disembark upon this dazzling white strand? And watch these shadows become living girls and women? Here! Ah! here, the Sicilienne can begin. But we do not call it that. This is the youth of the world and there are no complications. So it may be many other things besides. How can it be a Sicilienne with waist and breasts of amber? With a body rubbed yellow with tumeric? And another smells of sandalwood. Like the opening of a little box or casket. But a pillar, none the less, of naked sandalwood. Another has stained her face with a scarlet dye, but it is no more than rouge upon her skin of cloves. And her limbs and body are not altered by it.

Such are the dryads whom we watched beneath the boughs. But the men are actors or musicians. Some wear their feather helmets in the moonlight. In a moment we will have dance and pantomime. Where are the moonlit currant bushes? Like those bunches that are dipped in sugar. No! No! it is not that. And here are neither asphodel nor myrtle. Not ilex: nor the tamarisk. These are the South Seas. What is fanciful is not architecture but the structure of the shells. Can we have the mime of the nautilus; or of the shell of Venus? For we see this as a huge composition of goddesses or women bathing. But upon the coral shore. That is the difference. There is this much in the colour of a skin. It is thus, and thus, that the moral contagion spreads throughout society. But no one dies of it. We are alive but once; and in this mood would pass our lives, strolling from one place or island to another.

THE MARIENKIRCHE OF LÜBECK*

In the old and Hanseatic town of Lübeck, so far into the Northern world that it faces upon Sweden and is the natural port from which to sail into the Baltic, there rises the high-pitched roof of the Marienkirche. It is a great building of brick, uncompromisingly Northern in its details, the triumph of a separate or Baltic school, with its vessel filled from floor to roof by the tombs of the merchants. It is as full of these as a ball-room is of mirrors; and something living of so many men and women who are dead and gone still attaches to the statued silence so that it is not altogether the vault or charnel house. Their statues were set up in this hall to keep each other company and to wait together. It is, therefore, but the diversion of an hour in their long vigil when, sweet and dulcet, the celesta and the string of bells begin, not high in the tower, but low down from a hidden balcony. This proceeds in richness, but of nothing Eastern; more like the heavenly harmonies in a choir of angels, or so I heard it, thinking of an early picture. But this grows and swells in artifice, pealing more loudly, and of a sudden enriched again by the silver trumpets. They die away in a glissando of bells and new artifice begins of syrinx, clarion and shawm, of timbrel, gittern and shuddering cymbal. All the vessel of the church rings and echoes in the counterfeit. The tombs lose their terror and listen in contentment. It is the ring-ing of silvered armour: it is far off bells heard in the lonely wood when your feet are still: the blackest cherries, thick as starlings upon the trees, and pressed like wine to make a winter cordial: it is a prosperous wind in white sails and the slicing of the waters: tales of bright dresses and black faces: the voice from the high tower: painted wings of birds: the red gold globes upon the dark-leaf trees: exotic notes: and fading, dying the little syrinx, little voice out of the reeds: so dies this organ on the air into the stillness of this empty church. It is the organ of Buxtehude (1637–1707).

* From *Dance of the Quick and the Dead*, 1936.

183

EMBARCATION OF DON CARLOS*

To a person who has passed a great deal of his life in Italy, the other alternative of Spain has a peculiar and understandable fascination. This may have begun, so far as I am concerned, on a certain day in Venice, in 1907 or 1908, when I witnessed on the Grand Canal a scene that I shall never be able to forget. The floating ease of an afternoon spent in a gondola was enlivened, of a sudden, by much noise and stir coming from the water-gate of a near-by palace, the Palazzo Loredan. The iron gates were thrown open, a wooden gangway was put down, and an immensely tall old man with a square white beard, dressed, if I remember right, in black, but wearing, certainly, an immense black sombrero, came down the steps and, leaning on the arm of a little black page, crossed the plank into the waiting gondola. The negro page followed him and stood in the bows of the boat, while six gondoliers in magnificent liveries lifted their painted oars, in stripes of red and yellow, and in an instant the gondola slid out from the shadows into the sunlight and was gone. To our enquiries, we were told that this was the Pretender to the Throne of Spain. It was, in fact, the embarcation of Don Carlos.

* From *A Background for Domenico Scarlatti*, 1935.

THE ARMADA, OR SHOAL OF MAIDENS*

This farthest and latest of the Indies, the Antipodes, is true to its fame of feathers. Chieftains of ancient blood wear mantles of the particular plumes that are their prerogative. The loose effect of these immensely increases the width of the shoulders, so that their aquiline features, tattooed faces and tattooed bodies seen where the robe hangs open, carry them into the semblance of bird men. Those cloaks of feathers are like wing sheaths, with the wings folded back and shut, ready to open. The feet of these figures would have to be talons, and this necessary illusion is sustained in the lines and circles of their tattoo marks. That other race of bird men, the Red Indians of the North American prairie, never attained to this toga'd and senatorial calm, in part because their feather regalia was of plumes strung wide apart and fluttering, and partly for the reason that the epitome of their pride was the Redskin riding his horse. But his steed was a light, wild horse, in no way resembling the Gothic horse, the *destrier* or *percheron* for our plated armour; while the wing feathers of the eagle made a line of flags or kites tied to his back and never a box of wings nor the spread and soaring splendour. Besides, the prairie is to be compared in nothing with this coral shore. Neither are the maple woods, not even in autumn in their shrouds of fire, to the orchid and epiphyte forest below the hills of snow. For their forest of spruce or larch is a monotony unlit by flowers. The Redskin may trail in Indian file, hour after hour and never speaking, while the maple woods like the dying dolphin faint in their million flukes and expire in flame, but it is only a background, a thin sensation to his fierceness, never a landscape. For, here, the Maori warriors have a static calmness against their setting which is like the ghosts of great men, the shades of the *Iliad*. The unruffled plumes exaggerate their stature and in their right hands they hold sceptres of jade, the symbols of their kingly power.

* From *Dance of the Quick and the Dead,* 1936.

185

In their feather mantles a difference of structures is to be noted, for the plumes of these Antipodean birds for all their bright colours resemble long, straight hairs more than wing plumes, and the straight combing of the long feather strands down all the length of the feather mantle to the feet makes the height of the wearer more gigantic still. There is never a green, nor a blue among these cloaks. Their astonishing variety in colour and pattern is always red, or black, or yellow. And it is not always of feathers that they are made. Almost the only other material available to them was dog's hair. This was woven into a stiff felt and dyed in tremendous blacks and yellows with the juices of herbs or tree barks. It was ornamented by knots or tufts dyed in red; or, on occasion, the whole mantle was of white, a ribbed and combed white, like a cloak of straw bleached into the pallor of snow. But, in general, they were of black or yellow, trembling in tier after tier down to the ground like a crinoline, or as if starched and stiffening to the feet. The whole robe shook and trembled as they walked, with a rattling like the wind in ears of corn.

It may be imagined with what majesty these figures moved, sceptre in hand.

The gravity of these sceptred shades was enhanced by the laughing and volatile character of their women. It was the women who made these elaborate robes or mats; and while only the highest chiefs by the exertions of their whole tribe could obtain plumes enough for a feather mantle the common dress of the nobles was woven by the women from the fibres of the native flax. The most valuable of these robes was the *Kaitaka*, wrought out of a species of Phormium cultivated especially for the purpose, the fibres of which almost attained to silk in their softness, and we are told that a period of two years was often devoted to their manufacture. Both winter and summer robes were composed of flax; the winter robes, being made of the dried leaves, were warm and impervious to the rain and gave the wearer, when sitting down, the appearance of a thatched haycock. The black-string mat, called *Koroai*, was a black dress thickly ornamented with black strings, or filaments, about a foot long, which hung down gracefully over the folds of the drapery. Another kind was adorned with tufts or bosses of coloured wool, and had black strings here and there at intervals, or scarlet feathers. Often the winter cloaks were thickly covered with strips of flax leaves, rolled up into tubes, and dyed black at alternate intervals, resembling the quills of a porcupine; it was these that dangled and produced a loud rustling noise as they jostled together at every movement of the wearer.

The *topuni* or war cloak, consisted of a large flax mat into which was fastened at every thread a lock of dog's hair dyed in different colours, giving the exact appearance of a beautiful fur. The patterns were often of pure white, or of black and white hair arranged in narrow stripes. These war mats had a shaggy collar, composed of strips of fur about six inches long falling over the shoulders. We have to think of the heads of these warriors as adorned with feathers, or with the blossoms of the clematis, the crimson metrosideros, and the green hoya. Amongst the feathers employed for this purpose those of the tail of the Neomorpha were of black, tipped with white, and small carved boxes were used by the chiefs in which to keep them. Bunches of the white feathers of the albatross were worn in the ears; or the wings of the eagle, or hawk, were fastened to either side of the head, giving an effect like the winged cap of Mercury.

Their death heads, for this was the effect of tattooing which obliterated all expression save one of staring fierceness from the features, were stuck with flowers. The spectres dwelling on this far off and Stygian shore had the appearance of living in a transitional life. Their wars and feastings were left to them; the clemency of the climate gave them flowers and plumes of air for their adornment; and when their purgatory was atoned this shore would know them no more. They had a terrible solemnity which came from their slow tread and lack of expression. The filed and sharpened teeth, gleaming white from afar out of their darkened skulls, were never parted in a smile. Yet, for all this carnivorous and cannibal taint, they were no naked savages. These carrion men, condemned to this purgatory and to the devouring of each other's souls, came forward in their cloaks, the insignia of their septs. We are to imagine that such mantles made their only clothing. The naked warriors, whenever not engaged in battle or in the games of war, draped themselves in these cloaks as does an athlete between the rounds of his contest. And, as fighting was their only life, the Maori warriors relapsed as to the rest of it into that curious and solemn impassivity that we have noticed, so that it is scarcely an exaggeration of image to call these mantles for their ease by the name of death cloaks. They were funeral finery, the trappings of the tomb.

But we will complete the historical possibilities of this antipodean world by mention of the hunting party upon which the Maori warriors might well have been engaged. It is, perhaps, the strangest of all such expeditions, the world over, this journey through the forest of epiphytes, of trailing orchids, to the cold foot of the snow hills. Their object was a gigantic bird, the Moa. This creature was to be found in plenty at the period when the first Maori arrived, and for a long time they were killed for food until such bulky and probably stupid birds reached to the point of extermination. Even so, it is probable that a few were still in existence at the time of Captain Cook's first voyage, and to this day several tolerably well authenticated stories have been afloat, from time to time, of whalers and sealers, and more recently of gold diggers in the South Island, having obtained glimpses of gigantic birds. But, more than this, it is even certain that bunches of its feathers were not long since in possession of some of the old chiefs as ornaments, and the spot were the last Moa was killed is still pointed out by the natives. Fragments of enormous eggs have from time to time been found, and some fifty years ago an entire egg was discovered. It appears that a man, in digging the foundation for a hut, suddenly came upon this egg, together with a human skeleton. The body had been buried in a sitting posture, and the egg must have been placed in the hands, as the arms of the skeleton were extended in such a manner as to bring it immediately opposite the mouth of the dead man. The egg was ten inches in length and seven in breadth, the shell being brown in colour, and rather thicker than a shilling. The Moa, it may be said at this point, was no less than eleven feet six inches in height, or even, according to some authorities, thirteen or fourteen feet high. The legs of this giant, which would have to our eyes the thickness of a steel girder, reached to higher than the heads of its feather-crested hunters. It was, according to tradition, of a red colour.

There is a fascination in conjecturing the disturbance of this prehistoric ghost from its lair, and in wondering what kind of croaking or cackling cry it can have emitted. We may imagine the furious darting of its head, and the futile flapping of its embryonic wings. This roc, or fabulous bird, in its terror made vain and ineffectual attempts upon the air, that paradise out of which it had fallen. Its only safety was in the open country where it could outrun its pursuers; but some of their number headed it back into the bush, and it stood at bay waiting for the spears. This giant bird represented an antiquity of which its own bones were the only memorial; and in the slow agony of its death there is portrayed the cruel extinction of anything that has become useless and unnecessary. There is not a soul left to pity it: but a curious picture comes into the mind of the Maori standing near to it in its dying struggles and striking upwards with their clubs to reach its head. The straight red hair of the monster, for its feathers were more like straight hair, were dyed with blood. But the eventual plucking of its feathers was more horrible still, when the bird was trussed and gutted for the feast, its huge legs drawn up like cranes beside the body or laid out straight, and more than six feet long. The breaking of its knee bones called for as much strength as the cracking of a skull. The traveller from another world, who having landed from a ship found his way to their bivouac, would have known no sane explanation of this enormous fowl roasting in the embers, or of the roc's egg stolen from the nest and littering the ground with splinters of its broken shell. No supper of aeronauts, even of that sort who might be imagined to dwell in the higher reaches of the air and only occasionally to come to earth, would have found for themselves a winged creature on such a parallel to their calling. And this brings us to the ghost-like figures round the fire, who rustled in their cloaks of feathers every time they moved. The stainings of that magical yolk were on their hands and clothes, so that this race of bird men proved their cannibal proclivities even in this feast.

Next morning, nothing but huge bones lay upon the ground and the Maori had gone down from the mountains to the sea-shore. The shadow of a jade sceptre fell like moonlight upon the paler bodies of the young girls. They passed all their leisure upon the beach, amusing themselves, when not in the water, with flying kites made of leaves and throwing mimic spears formed of fern stalks; or sailing their little flax canoes down the rivers and watching them tossed about by the waves of the sea. For dancing, their bodies were painted a golden yellow with tumeric and coconut oil

But their main recreation was in the sea, for they swam like fishes and would move in a school or shoal out in the deep waters, breaking the placid bay. It is easy to imagine them running in chorus upon the sands and swimming out to a schooner of which the white wings had just shewn above the headland. They would sport like dolphins round the bows and draw the sailors to the wooden sides. In a moment they would catch the end of rope dangled in the water and swarm up it, one after another, to the deck. They came up out of the sea a second time upon the ship's sides, straddling on the rail. First, their smiling faces with the clianthus, or another flower, dripping at their ears; then, other girls, more of ocean, with white feathers of the albatross; then, smooth shoulders and lower heads crowned with flowers.

By now, the first and most daring rode astride upon the rail, and in a breath stood on the deck. One after another they came up gleaming from the water, rode the wooden rail, and in a moment stood like the pillar of a rainbow upon the deck. Those gleaming, shining pillars played like fountains; while flower-wreathed heads and glistening shoulders climbed up again and again out of the sea and became limbs and bodies pouring water down. Two or three girls at a time rode like naked Amazons upon the rail and leaped down to join the rainbow. And, as air dried the spray upon them, their burnt and nectarine colour came back, like the flush of shame or shyness upon their cheeks. By this, all their number had emerged out of the sea and the hindmost, finding no room to stand, showed as whole statues upon the rail, holding with an uplifted arm to the shrouds. These ropes, like the ribs or stays of this wooden ship, felt the cut and swish of the waters and the dying speed, drawing down to anchor. But the sudden invasion of these nymphs had so disconcerted the crew that, without touching them, and hardly having laughed or spoken, the whole school or shoal of sea maidens climbed like acrobats into the rigging.

This ascent was a ravishment to the eyes. Their savage figures made a bewilderment of lovely forms. Some climbed the ladders, and stretched as if they climbed a face of rock for the rungs were well apart, flattening the body; other girls swarmed upon a rope, hugging it close and tight as if it were a lioness gnawing and licking a bone. The rigging was a core upon which they climbed in both directions, their bodies facing each other through the meshes, so that a figure seen from the back was the echo to another body climbing directly in front of the eyes. The shrouds of the schooner were as populous as those of the glass ships, made early in the last century, that are crowded with sailors, blue mannikins manning the yards to the topgallants, like a ship dressed for review. Here, also, the ropes were rods of glass or of fire, crossing the bodies and not hiding them; when, of a sudden, each figure stood up to its height, alone and with no support, and leapt from every altitude of the rigging down into the sea.

Some fell from the highest yard-arm, straight down, feet foremost, passing in front of the eyes like a statue falling, dislodged and dropped; other girls leaned over, bending their bodies and, when taut enough, like an arrow from a bow shot down into the hollow sea. More and more bodies dropped, too quick to count, and there were pairs of girls who stood for an instant face to face, or even back to back, and fell linked in each other's arms to the ocean. In a moment not one was left, and the school or shoal with wild play of foam headed for the land.

If we place this crowded scene of spray against a landscape resembling that of the coral atoll there will be only this difference that its inner solitude is not invoked. But so little change is entailed that no more is meant by it than the act of walking for a few paces to look on the salt waters instead of the sweet. And what we see is the emergence of this school or shoal. All their voices are talking at once, and they pass the headland like the dolphin herd playing through the swell.

They deviate to where a blue wave lifts and climb with it, their bodies tossing as flowers upon it, and lie helpless in the crest of it until it breaks and shivers; or leap below its backbone in a lovely arc and lie still for the foam to come. Their game is the coolness of the breaking waves. Some turn to meet this, holding up their arms so that all the force strikes upon their bodies. They wait for it, treading water, and it lifts and thrills them. Others reach to it and climb upon its back, close to the white mane, held high enough to see the sunlit shore. This is a sip of honey and no more. They stand just for a moment and the cataclysm comes, hurling them from heaven into the glaucous twilight below the waves. Or, if it overtakes them, lie sideways as if for the chariot to pass by. And, all this time, the school or shoal advances until their feet touch the ground and after a stroke or two they stand.

At the first smooth shoulders coming from the sea a loud and warning conch shell is blown from the shore. It is a sea voice, as if a bearded mouth, dank with weeds and spray, blew into the whorls and flutings of the shell. This rumbling of the marine conch echoes and reverberates along the hollow shore. It is a sound unknown to our ears and only familiar to mock Indians of the Antipodes. At once, the response rises out of the sea in this returning shoal. No catspaw of wind, far out in the blue main, could have brought the sea god more quickly to the surface and to skim the waves. His train, waist high and grounded in the shallows, tread the first corals of the atoll. Their figures on the stepping stones sway and hesitate, falling up to their shoulders into the coolness, and then finding foothold upon a higher ledge that raises them to the knees out of the water. They are on dolphin back, or standing in the chariot; yet, by analogy of melancholy, it is once more the stepping stones and that distant ghost moves among them, answering the conch shell. Till now, she cannot be distinguished from the rest, where all are uniform in hue and shape, pouring like rainy statues, like the bronze statues of the fountain, in rainbow spray.

But, at least, if these are figures of a magical fountain, the spell has been lifted from them. The school or shoal of maidens has come ashore upon the atoll. One after another they are only ankle deep, wading out of the water, while the emptiness of the coral isle has nothing to distract the eyes from those dripping and shining figures. Their play is against two horizontal bars, the line where the sea meets the sky, and the disk or circle of the atoll. Within this, the sweet waters of the lagoon make another ring.

The simplicity of the setting could not be improved upon for this play of sculpture. The foam-born figures loom large and larger; and in their wet freshness it is as if wrappings of weeds, of sea-green tresses crackling in their pods, had been taken from them at the water's edge. It has left a stain of iodine upon their limbs, or it is the verdigris brought out by water playing upon bronze. The marks of it are indelible upon the skin, like the pourings of some essence, or some essential oil upon them. Its tarnishings are the only ornament in this stern reality.

For it is the Indian pantheon, or arcana of all her nymphs and goddesses. This remote and only imagined shore, given that appellation because of the part ever played by the Indies in poetry and imagination, is the scene of this emergence straight up out of the sea. It is prolix and many limbed, like the Hindu fancy, but corrected from that redundance by a classical purity that draws its strength from the canons of savage beauty. This is the discovery of the age we live in and its implications affect every utility of the modern world. It is timeless, with no ties of place or date. Against the simple lines of the atoll and the ocean this alphabet spells forth its syllables in new and endless combination. Their sudden appearance from nothing, out of the sea, is the measure of their divinity and inspiration. Compared to this, how slow and languid is the near past, of wine-coloured velvet, with the tones of a virginal stealing upon the ears and a lapdog at the feet of Venus, in a lute-livened noon under the brocaded boughs. That was long ago, the age of Titian; too long ago, yet not long enough. For this is more bold than that Italian ease.

The cosmogony increases and gives birth. Their paradise of the primitive mind blossoms at the sea's edge, as it might be the primal invasion of flowers upon the protozoic land. It is coral, built up out of the sea in a million years of toil, now brought to fruition in the miracle of a moment. And, to anyone, who witnessed this, his own phantoms would mingle with the crowd. But even before this, it is the dispersal of the images of every other age and culture. The constrictions of their needs and fashions were the perversions of this primal form. If its rediscovery is the fine metal of our age, here are the auriferous Indies, untrammelled and undismayed.

The pedestals of coral lift their statues in every attitude into the open airs. It is an invocation of sunlight and the cool sea, for still they run with water which shines upon the copper of their skins; but we impute the ghosts of flowers to answer the curves of their bodies in this empty atoll, putting the sword of a cactus or the almond bough beside them for their recoil from the painful points or an excuse for their allurement. And yet this emptiness of background makes the true poignancy of our Antipodes. It is another world still untired and in its youth; also, our own adolescence, something sighed over and not always enjoyed. Here and now, it is offered us again, burning all in a moment. It becomes incarnate, growing downwards from those flower-wreathed heads.

In only a moment this school or shoal of maidens will be gone. But this is that intermediate moment, the one other sensation in life between the pangs of birth and the agony of death. They only offer themselves for an instant of time, and then will be gone as swiftly and suddenly as if the sea took them back again.

Already the fountains have ceased playing. The bodies of bronze and copper drip no more with water, and their return to earthliness is the affirmation of their strong and athletic grace. If, each in each, these were the figures for a fountain, they had been chosen for strength and delicacy, narrow in the hips, but with arms muscular enough to lift a full amphora to their shoulder; or even, in the manner of a dancer, to support a body of their own weight and carry it to the jet of waters. Held in the heart of light, and with water running from their limbs, that pair of figures would be the climacteric of this pagan vision on the atoll. But, even now, this is played and performed. The nymphs and goddesses of the arcana, like dancers or milkmaids of the Indian god, portray the pleasures of poetic heat. But it is not the fabled India, for they are pagans and have no belief. This is their link with our own age, and part of their loveliness to our eyes.

For the last time we look upon this dolphin herd who sported in the waves and, come ashore, have played the fable of adolescence in a manner and with an ease to which our millenniums of false beliefs have unaccustomed us. They are unfettered; but our own epoch having broken its chains is too old to profit by its liberty. Thus, the two ages are of mortal contact to each other: each would kill the other at a touch. We should die in a desert of the mind, while they would perish of our sophistication. Like statues of oiled bronze the nubile Oceanians display

194

their graces to the empty atoll. They are as alike as animals of a breed, in savage similarity, as alike as the dolphin-herd among the waves, their only differences being forgotten in the next snaring of the eyes. They show, in fact, that fixed or semi-rule of resemblance which makes everyone at the masqued ball so alike as to be indistinguishable because the visible expression is masqued and so there is no key to their character. It is, then, that minor differences assume dramatic importance; and now, in this last moment of the arcana, the many-limbed anthropomorphic goddess sheds her divinity and disperses it among her devotees.

Our noon of the clianthus is drawing to an end. The Oceanian solstice has accomplished its purpose in preparing a solitude and peopling it from the sea. We have already said that, to anyone who witnessed this, his own phantoms would mingle with the crowd; and the last sacrament of this vision, or serving round of its godhead, discovers a ghost among the sunburnt bodies of the atoll and imbues her with the skin of saffron and the gilded hair that makes her paler than her sisters, until, by contrast to their dark bodies, her colour becomes warm and smoky, as if there were smoke or fire of sulphur under the surface. In fact, that ghost of the inner lagoon has crossed from the sweet to the salt waters. This is a symbolical act: it makes her unattainable among the crowd in which she is willing to lose her identity, and it is the sign that she prefers the group-soul to her own individual soul. In this general anonymity the unmasking, indeed, is still to come. But this Oceania, which was our refuge, dies anew, of inanition. Farewell to the clianthus, and to the paradise inspired by its red husks! Those lovely forms loom for the last time, larger than life, in the manner of figures upon the screen that advance on the audience till the moment of contact and then stride like giants over our heads into limbo. Life and intelligence are disseminated from their eyes and from their smiling mouths; while their material or venal person is represented in no more import than as it might be by the petals opening from the calyx. Their virginity of contact is that of flowers blowing upon the wind, in apparent carelessness and happy among their sisters. At the same time, the more than burning metal of their colour, together with the cut of their petals, is designed for attention, not calculated for neglect. It is with shuddering impact, shuddering the soul, that they answer the summons of the marine conch. And the Oceanian evening opens to them its archipelagos of light, flowering meadows unbreathed and unattainable but shuddering before the eyes, while nocturnal scents come upon the cooler air and the last rumbling of the sea shell dies in its throat of pearl.

URSARI*

THEY are here. The fanfare is sounding. And here are Ursari, bear leaders, like the family I saw as a boy at Eton, in 1914. That, too, was a fateful year, a year of death. They appeared, suddenly, one winter evening, just as it was getting dark. It is a long time ago, now, but they could never be forgotten. They were a man and two women. He seems, at this distance of time, to have worn a comical fur cap, a coat that I cannot remember, and some form of leggings. He did not wear shoes: his feet were bandaged, as it were, or wrapped in rags. The women, who were young girls, were dressed in a way that has left no impression, but they had perfectly round faces. Their faces were so round that it must be a tribal characteristic. On being asked who they were, and whence they came, their answer was only, "Bohémians". This meant little. And they could, or would, say nothing more.

They had with them two bears. The man played a bugle, while he led one bear: the other, which was the smaller of the two, followed the elder girl. Her sister beat a drum, or tambourine. Both bears walked upright on their hindlegs, wore muzzles, and were led along with a rope or chain, being menaced all the time with a stout cudgel. Now the bear has wooden stupidities, wooden virtues. Something could come out of his tragedy, if he could ever learn. But he can learn no more than to walk upright, and to dance. This he is taught by putting a heated tray under his feet, so that he lifts his paws.

I remember, so well, the trumpet and the drum, the round faced Romis, and the slow dancing of their animals. Where had they come from? And whither were they going? They were, probably, Gypsies from the Carpathians. Or they may have started from the Caucasus and seen the Caspian and the fair at Nijni. But what does it matter? My companions had forgotten them by the morning, and they never came back again.

*From *Sacred and Profane Love*, 1940.

197

THE WANDERING SINNTE*

Even as we write this, we get the smell of ten thousand camp fires.† It is the smoke of a tramp's fire, ten thousand times repeated, which, itself, comes from the rags they wear, impregnated by the smoke, tinged, also, by the food they are cooking, everything stolen, even the funguses that no one else dares eat. These come up in a night, after rain, with domes and phalluses that are like an evil Kremlin, a Kitai Gorod, a Tartar city, spawned when only owl and bat and spider are awake. The encampment is in a plain, a stony meadow by the river, a field of bones and rags and refuse heaps. Now, it is black with tents of sacking. The last stragglers arrived at sunset. Their bundles are but just dropped upon the ground.

Certainly there is a magical feeling, or anticipation, in the air. From the town of tents comes a noise which is the clattering of cooking pots and this, in their thousands, is as loud as many kettledrums. And, here and there, deep voices of the Gypsy patriarchs, talking in few syllables to the naked children. These bearded elders might all be sons of one mother, so alike are they, and not one of them, were there light to see, would have a white hair on his head. When Gypsies grow old, they get darker, one sign, so it is thought, of their Indian origin. But you can only see from fire to fire across the acrid smoke. The plain stretches far away, as far as the sunset itself. And the red hot bars of that seem never to grow pale. But the night begins with shade after shade of darkness, as though by successive turnings of a screw. It will not rain, yet. It is hot and sultry, with sudden strange winds blowing out of nowhere.

All is wild and remote, where poet, painter, or musician, have never been. Instead of Spain or Hungary we give you Ursari (bear leaders), Calderarii (tinkers or coppersmiths),

---

* From *Sacred and Profane Love*, 1940.

† The historical truth of this scene is the camp, or parliament, of 40,000 Gypsies at Belgrade, in 1867.

198

Lingurarii, who live by carving wooden spoons and bowls, and, wildest of all, Laeši and Netoši. Each group has its chiefs or patriarchs, its Buljubasas, who ride on horseback to give themselves authority.* In this town of tents there may be a hundred or more of these Gypsy Kings. The whole race of their subjects, in all their different sects, are the Ciganje, or would call themselves the Ciganje Rom'njiči, which means Roumanian Gypsies. These older men, grandfathers or patriarchs, are in the likeness of shepherd kings, Hyksos, which might well be a word in their own language. Often, in the mode of ancient or savage kings, they have a silver mounted stick, or sceptre, their wand of office, a heavy staff which they carry with them, and which is ever by their side. For the monarchs of the tent have it in their blood to be conspicuous. It is not their pretence to lead an ordinary life. To be stared at is necessary to their profession. Out of rags and tatters they have to create a personality. And this must have its measure of pride and arrogance. But, also, the circumstances of their lives keeps them from the drabness of the slums. In appearance, they are Shepherd Kings, but their Arcadian realm has been transmuted. They have lost their flocks and herds.

Here comes a Laješ,† or horsecoper, insolently swaggering, with long hair down to his shoulders. He wears a heavy belt of leather, studded with brass nails, has the trousers of a Mameluke, and munches, munches, at a hunk of bread. His long stockwhip is in his other hand. Others, clowns on horseback, come galloping by. Nothing more clownlike than when one of the Laeši catches at a pony and jumps upon its back; but he becomes then, immediately, someone magnificent out of the plains. All Asia, Scythia, Tartary, are behind him. The Laeši, more than other Gypsies, show their Indian origin. They are fakirs, wantons of religion. When Bacchus invaded India, the Laeši will have joined him and been his vanguard, darting like dervishes into the crowd; and, again, campfollowers, stragglers in the dust of his triumph.

Many of them have veiled or hypnotic eyes, set at a slanting angle in their heads. By merely looking at you, or so it is said,

---

* They were allowed to wear the full beard, a sign of nobility, long red mantles, coloured boots, and the Phrygian cap.

† Pronounced Laets, or Laetsi in the plural: as, also Netotsi for Netoši.

a Laješ can force you into buying a lame or broken-down horse. As for their physical appearance, like virtuosos they have set themselves apart. They have an indescribable insolence and swagger which are implicit in their very walk, are full of wild jokes that resemble the pleasantries of the executioner, and the next moment, are making off as fast as they can run, seeing the police, or someone they have cheated. The funny turn in any troupe of acrobats is always, as one might say of music that is in their idiom, in the Gypsy rhythm, this, because of the baggy ill-fitting clothes of the clown, so unsuited to acrobats, but, with that, the more surprising when they prove such agility and daring. In the same way that the black mask of Mezzetin, even in the most delicate paintings by Watteau, is the black face and black beard of the eternal tramp, in the likeness it must be said, of Jackson, the first and only tramp cyclist, so we see the Gypsy in the clown who is an acrobat. But the young men are warrior clowns, actively and potentially dangerous.

And here are Romis, Gypsy maidens, fourteen years old and up to twenty. They have, always, long skirts trailing in the dust and have run after you, begging, in every suburb and banlieu, in the Barrio de Santiago and at The Seven Towers. This is because the Romis are ever, and always, the same. There is no need to praise their dark skins and fiery glances. They are on every road, on the outskirts of every town. Some of them are mere children, but carry babies of their own. They belong to every tribe; with heavy necklaces of golden coins, dangling earrings, or no more than a shawl's soiled fringe against their tawny necks, but always, in every movement, are women of their race. They have no home, no country, but come forth, fixed like this in type, from a whitewashed cave, or from a tent of canvas propped upon sticks. They need no mirrors, and own no clothes but those they wear; yet the genius in their blood gives them personality. Along the dusty alameda, or in the lane between the hedges, the coins that are thrown to them are to pay for that, but their own sentiment is disgust or contempt for the gâjos. They will never sell themselves; and have learnt every deceit and trickery, being perpetual outlaws.

They could have come here from the combes and dingles.

But, also, and this is more interesting in theory and in fact, from the whitewashed caves. Aloe, or prickly pear, are their curtains, fences, clotheshorses. It would be Guadix, or the Cuevas de la Vera, both near Granada, and in a landscape that is apocalyptic, and should be sown and tilled by skeletons. We can see those, more than lifesize, leaning on their sickles, met with at some corner of the blood red field, in a lane of the harvest; or, even, sitting in the shade for their siesta meal, by great flagons of wine and flat loaves shaped like a landsknecht's cap.

But the plain is African, in spite of the pomegranate and the orangetree. And the Gitanas are as dark as the Chleuh women of the fondouks. Here, too, they sing and dance; and Flamenco music, as mysterious as themselves in origin, comes more easily to them than the waltzes or boleros of the wine shop. If those are two cave towns, two capitals of the troglodytes, we should think, also, of Triana and the Albaicin, names of music, the one a dusty suburb, but leading, at long distance, to the Sierpes and to the court of orangetrees below the Giralda, the other consisting of the hill of caves opposite to the Alhambra. This race who, when they settle, have always loved to establish themselves in the shadow of some tumbling castle, or even in the very ruins, here, in Granada, have those red walls and towers and their hidden courts of stalactite and filigree always before them, high in the air across the valley. Upon the hill of the Alhambra, night and day, there is music coming from the Albaicin, music which must be heard in breaths and snatches. It is their speech, or vernacular, more than it is melody. Probably it is spoilt, now. We should have stood here thirty or forty years ago, and heard Canario, Gagancho, or Chorrojumo the Gypsy King, in siguiriyas, polos, martinetes. Or in the saeta, the arrow of song, intoned as the groups of sculpture are borne past in the Holy Week processions. All that is gone, or nearly gone. Instead, we would have the Gitanos of Almeria, living in the ruins of the Alcazaba. Or the Gitanos of Murcia.

This town of tents, which we have pitched in the lost Balkan, has every kind of nomad, but in their old character, for this is long ago. And this capital, this metropolis, has only stood here for a few days. It might move to anywhere to-morrow. But, since it once existed, it can be geographically assigned, for, but for this, it has no positive significance and might be moving, like the slow shadows on the plain, being a town without streets, or fountains, or the fronts of churches.

Was this their parliament; or the Moldavian horse fair? Have they come here to choose their king? Or are they collected like the flocks of starlings? We would hazard that their whole gathering is instinctive. It is waste of time to dispute the reason. And we must look at them closely, before it is too late. We must allow ourselves the freedom of day as well as night. It is as though in this darkness, which is lit by their fires, we can see them in any light we please. They have come here from every end of the world; of a certainty no contradiction, or impossibility, for their wanderings have taken them much further than we could know. It is nothing for them to return home after ten years, or more, and then, to no fixed point, but only to make enquiry of other wanderers and overtake them, at sunset, somewhere in the plain. But, as well, in addition to those of their race who never cease from journeying, there are others who move according to an established and definite rota, though always of instinct, never written down. Some have settled themselves and, by assimilation, sunk, dully, into the slums of the big towns. Here, however, from Moldavia, they were slaves not long ago,* except for the wildest of them, the Netoši, who move by night and hide themselves by day. We would like to write, just at this period, of Podolia, of its pears and apples and its orchards of black cherries, but that would give no warning of these wanderers, who would be gone by morning. And, of course, in Kiev, they had a suburb of their own. There were Gypsy musicians in cafés, and who would be hired to play in houses. Moscow, too, had its famous singers and violinists, but they and their music, however stimulating or nostalgic, are too sophisticated for our purpose. We return, therefore, to the tents.

Most of these Gypsies, we have said, would call themselves Ciganje Rom'njiči. That term is, however, wider in its implications than even the extended limits of the modern country of that name, for it includes the Balkan, old Turkey, and the Ukraine. In all those countries the language of these wanderers

* The monastery-owned Gypsies in Moldavia were freed by the law of Prince Mihailu Sturza, in 1845; the privately owned Gypsies not till 1855 in Jassy, and 1856 in Bucharest.

would include many words and phrases of Roumanian origin. Their second language, spoken a little, in some patois, by every one of them, would be Roumanian, this, because that country was, for so many centuries, their centre of dissemination. Coming out of Tartary, many hundred years ago, this was their first taste of the West. The natural conditions of Moldavia exactly suited them, while the serfdom to which they were submitted reserved them and, as it were, compelled their increase. It became their native land, to the extent that far-off India and Tartary were forgotten by them. The first syllable in the name of their adopted, or enforced, home land came to be the most important, or key syllable of their own tongue, as though in confusion of their origin and history. From here, they wandered into near-by lands and, having once escaped, were free of the near Orient. From now onwards they could call themselves Turkish, or Russian, or Bulgarian, but in nearly every instance they had come from the Carpathians. In many cases they will have forgotten that language, or will feign not to understand it, but always, in so far as they have any roots at all, that land for many centuries has been their home. It will be noticed, also, that, where their genius for adaptation is concerned, this particular background or origin has not given them opportunity to become anything else than their primitive or rudimentary selves. They have not traversed Europe. They are still on its borders. In Spain, or Hungary, they have coloured the background, but become a part of it. They have taken the Hungarian tunes and played them in their own idiom, adding a frenzy or delirium which was not there before. Music of this sort is both of the Tziganes and of Hungary, not the one without the other. What could be subtracted, or taken away, from it, is its Gypsy manner: Then, the Hungarian would remain. But remove that, and the other would be but ornament and could not stand alone. Against all this the Ciganje, who have no villages, nothing but their tents, and who have not known any other world but this, must appear in what is nearest to their natural element without extraneous influence, or anything but what they are, or were. To what extent, then, are they Roumanians? That first syllable, which has always haunted them, moving with them into any country of the world is, in reality, of little import. These, it would be more true to say, are the Ciganje before they became Tziganes, or Gitanos. In this encampment, moreover, all are not Christians. There are many Moslems, not that either religion would be genuine, or of more importance to them than as a base for superstition.

What wonders of personality and of appearance surround us upon every side! Here, in the Ciganje town of tents, you are among inspired actors who have been born with a natural gift, or genius, for the picturesque. Their temperament has no other outlet than in interpretation of the rôles of beggar, tinker, thief. This is their only opportunity. But we can walk among the Wandering Sinnte. And we must, at the beginning, see with the eyes of men and women who have never lived within four walls. Some of them have been kept in prison. Others have but begged from door to door. The women go up to every stranger to tell his fortune, and push their way across the threshold of the houses. While this happens, the men hawk their copper pots and cauldrons, or sell their wooden spoons or bowls, or lead the dancing bears. Their begging, and it is in this that they are different from other beggars, is always mixed with curses. It is the advantage of their secret tongue, that they can say what they please and none will understand.

Besides the dramatic use made of their tawny looks, the Ciganje have invented the sudden attack. They collect in the outskirts, and then storm the town or village. But they have, also, another and more ingenious stratagem which works according to a different system. It could be described as invasion by infiltration. All day long, from early morning, they work through a village. They are an army of stragglers, with no beginning and no end. The plan is never to appear in sufficient number, or near enough to each other, to rouse the fury of the villagers. Upon such feast days of the rags and tatters the town or village appears as if attacked by a troupe of comedians. It is in this connection that we cannot but name Jacques Callot. But the Wandering Sinnte were unknown to him. Long acquaintance with every vagabond and strolling player had given him the power of instantaneous or static rendering of their characteristic movements and gestures. All those who know his *Balli di Sfessania* will agree with this. In little, in not more than an inch or two of space, he gives us the whole Italian Comedy. His was the epoch of sword and plume. Its rags and tatters, as displayed in the strolling players of his time, have more than an affinity, they are, indeed, in close relation to the Gypsy finery, that is so near to destitution. And a day of ceaseless beggary and insolence would end, often enough, in the forcible punishment or imprisonment of the offenders. They were continually driven out from towns, whipped beyond the parish bounds, or penalized otherwise, and painfully. It was like a revenge upon comedians who have been too funny.

Afterwards, if there was no such retribution, they would gather in the tents. There had to be a share-out of the spoils. The encampment would be some miles away, along a trail made known by the fluttering of rags that had been tied to bushes and to the boughs of trees. Coins would pass from hand to hand. Rags and tins, found thrown away, would be examined carefully, as if to price or put a value upon them. It is a thieves' market among thieves, a "marché aux puces" among the fleas and vermin. Till long after sunset the stragglers would come in.

This people have nothing of the peasant in them. Their nerves, indeed, have states of feeling which could never be found in men and women who are chained to the soil. For their poverty, which may be more extreme, is not imprisoned in one place. Peasants, it could be argued, are in the same relation to the seasons that the animals are to man, dependent upon them, with no power to alter them, not certain, nor with real knowledge of their masters. But the wandering Gypsies never blame their mode of life. They wander from instinct, which is higher, or lower, reason than stark necessity. They are nomad beings, with a sensuality which is abnormally soothed, or fired by music. The lion and the serpent love music. Those are not peasant animals, like sheep, or cows, or pigs. This is their difference. And it applies, also, to the Wandering Sinnte. The young men, who are spare and thin, might in their trickery and their air of proud disdain belong to the race of the desert lions; while their maidens, are, certainly, the pythoness, the snake goddess who works by enchantment and must not be approached or touched.

Their music is the only art they have, but it is not all the Ciganje who are musical. Many of them have no ear at all. But it is magic to them because they do not understand it. Not one of them can read the notes. They cannot explain how it is done, or what it is that they are doing. It is a magical process, and that is all. Also, it is the one art of which there is no visible or outward body. It is carried in the mind, or in the blood, taking up no space, with no weight or substance. And it works by enchantment. It is a finer and more fiery drunkenness, affecting young and old, potent in a breath of time, and dazzling the senses. But the violins are cheap and ill-made; and yet the character of this music is helped by its blocklike notes and by the wailing scraping of the bows. It is street music, but of the poorest hovels, and, then again, pastoral, but always, by some curious alchemy, conveying even by its bare outline a picture of the background that gave it birth. This faculty, also, has its double or shadowed meanings, in the sense that not only can this be read into, or magnified out of, its sound, but, also, that process is not in exaggeration, for such was the authentic truth of its origin. They are peasant tunes, and it is impossible to decide how much of it is the peasant, and how much the soil. But, at least, it is indigenous, like trees or flowers that are native and grow there to perfection. By that, they give character and become, themselves, the personality. By such is one land recognized and made different from another. But here, in this case, as always with the Ciganje, they are tunes that have been stolen. And the Ciganje have made them of their own.

For the Kelipen has begun. As soon as there is music, that thing which was missing has come back to us. It is a miracle, like the fire of the Epiphany, the feast of tongues. They fly to their cymbals and violins. In one corner, a band of children, of Ciganje boys from five years old to fifteen, play as if inspired. They are at that age when music is inexplicable, when it means everything or nothing, but when its very mysteries are an intoxication. At the first notes of music, some of the younger Laeši get up from the ground and go to look at the horses that were given them in exchange, this morning. This pleases them, and they start imitating castanets by cracking the joints of their fingers, which are always long and charged with electricity. Still uncertain, they begin throwing their hats into the air, and follow this up by strutting about like peacocks. Everyone who is not dancing is hammering or banging. So many of them are Calderarii, coppersmiths, and their pots or cauldrons lie ready to the hand. The reason for this noise is in their excitement, and

as an accompaniment. Their ears hear nothing inappropriate in
this din of sound. Its alternative of utter silence comes suddenly
and with no warning, like those feelings that communicate
themselves, in mystery, among the animals. It runs from heart
to heart and stills all other feeling. But the town of tents is too
drunk with drink and music to keep silent. Everywhere, in
every corner of the encampment, there are individual groups
dancing to the cymbals and violins. There are no crowds to
watch them, because they are their own audience. All are taking
part. It is a miracle that works racially, to the mass, not to the
separate person, for the individual, the separate entity, no longer
exists, or has to be informed. He knows straightway. This
magical intoxication is in touch with all of them, so that it is
natural to wonder whether other crowds have ever enjoyed
themselves, so universal and wholehearted is their absorption.
They are lost in the music. And it has beauties such as other
crowds are blind to. It has no religion, nothing of the spirit.
It is music, as music, and has no other meaning. It is, therefore,
a pleasure or intoxication, a drug on which these human dregs
are living. The older men are all drunken; the Hyksos, as we
have called them, the Buljubašas, having reached a state of
frenzy. The young men stand, swaying in each other's arms. At
the same moment, the Romnia are dancing in the openings of
the tents. Suddenly the music dies.

Before it finishes, another air is taken up, on one violin only,
as if in suggestion, and all the others follow it. At first, slow and
mournful, as though in lamentation, and then changing in
mood. But there is a strange flickering, far down in the sky.
For the town of tents is to disappear in fire and water. The first
signs of the storm are no more than the flashes in a summer
night. They are signals—but in sign or manual of what portent
—or are pointless and soundless; but look! again! again! they
flare upon the sky. They are messages of our own world, at no
great height into the heavens. For we are, indeed, upon the
earth. We are born, and die, upon it. The lightnings are its
emanation, the surcharge of two vital forces. It is war; or the
play of such giant forces that it looks like battle. And, of a
sudden, there is wild and tremendous lightning, an illumina-
tion of the night in the shape of some animal leaping or bounding across the sky. And utter silence. It is forked lightning.

Then once more, that leaping and flashing, followed by the thunder's roar. And rain falling like a storm of hailstones. In a moment the Kelipen has ceased its frenzy. Everyone has run or crawled for shelter. The tents are packed full. It is midnight and noon in one, lit up, violently, again! again! again!

A PICTURE OF ROUMANIA*

THE first impression of Bucarest comes from the wide extent of space that it covers. This is because there are so many houses standing in their separate gardens. Owing to this, Calea Victoriei, the main street of the capital, is as long as Oxford Street and Regent Street put together. You can dine at a restaurant just across the road; or you may have to traverse the entire extent of the town in order to get your dinner. It may take, in a taxi, nearly as long a time as it does to go down the Grand Canal in a gondola. Bucarest, then, is a town which is protracted and drawn out. So are the hours kept by its inhabitants; only you would not think so, for they pass so quickly.

It is a question of temperament, and climate. In the summer it is as hot as India. No business can be done between midday and five o'clock. It is at that hour, or later, that the shops open for the afternoon, and they do not close their shutters till nine or ten. You dine, therefore, at ten or eleven, and no one would think of going to bed till three or four. This, again, explains the multiplicity of restaurants and cafés and, in its turn, accounts for the popular music which is incomparable and haunts the mind. Not that the climate remains at that temperature for ever. The autumn, which is the most beautiful season of all, lasting, sometimes, till early in December, is followed by a winter of deep snow and sledges. It is, in fact, the climate of Seville and St Petersburg—for thinking of Bucarest and its languorous delights it must be St Petersburg and not Leningrad—it is the climate of Seville and St Petersburg in one. And this is the reason for the tempo of Bucarest, which is different from that of any other town.

I had been advised by many persons, when going to Roumania, to see the country first and the capital last. Bucarest, according to this opinion, was no more than a bad copy of Paris. Actually, in Bucarest, there is nothing whatever of Paris, except

* From *Roumanian Journey*, 1938.

the one or two inevitable dress shops. The Chaussée Kisseleff may a little resemble the Avenue du Bois; but plane trees lining both sides of a road do not make a copy. It is the Chaussée Kisseleff, called after the general who governed Roumania during the Russian occupation of 1832, that leads straight into the Calea Victoriei. You can walk for nearly an hour down these two streets and the character of Bucarest will begin to form in your mind.

It is not only the larger houses that stand apart in gardens. Nearly every house has more space allowed to it than in any other town. This permits of much waste of room in courtyards, outhouses, stables, and so forth, and, of course, increases the picturesque leisure of the place. Of dire poverty there are, unfortunately, some signs. No town can rapidly increase till it has a population of seven hundred thousand and not bring misery with it. But new buildings are springing up on every side. If you look down at Bucarest from one of the roof gardens of its modern flats, there are sights and sounds of rebuilding in all directions. And some of the buildings are more than creditable specimens of the modern style. Luckily, owing to the generous scale upon which the city stands, this rebuilding has not entailed much destruction of the old. The character of Bucarest is, in fact, enhanced by new improvements, though there must come a point, before long, when improvement becomes spoliation.

Now the Calea Victoriei is not the magnificent treelined boulevard that the foregoing remarks might justify in the imagination. It is as narrow as Bond Street, and with more than one curve in its length. The first beginning of it, from the direction of the Chaussée Kisseleff, is disappointing. It is nondescript and meaningless. There are only small houses and no shops. It is like a quiet street in some country town, except for the line of passing motors. Then, gradually, the finer houses begin, one ministry after another lines the road and you pass the Royal Palace and the National Theatre, until you come, in the end, to the quays of the river, the Dâmbovița, or the Dumbovitsa, if it is written as pronounced. Such is the geography of Bucarest. It is simple enough; and anything else there is of interest lies to right or left of the Calea Victoriei in a narrow area to each side.

The character of Bucarest is in its personality, not its monuments. Even so, there are three or four churches that should be
seen. The church, for instance, of the Colţei hospital, belonging
to a monastery that has been destroyed, is an interesting
example of the bastard Byzantine of the eighteenth century. It
has good frescoes and much gilt and carving. Other churches
are the Biserica Doamnei, built by one of the Cantacuzene; the
Stavropoleos; and, more especially, the church of the Patriarch
Antime, dating from 1715 and containing some admirable carving. Outside the town, and requiring a special permit because
its buildings have been made into a prison, is the monastery of
Vacaresti, the most interesting sight of Bucarest, with a good
stone porch, fine twisted columns in the interior and a frescoed
decoration which is most interesting. A painted view of Jerusalem, occurring in midst of this, is no less than a landscape in
the modern naïf manner, by the ancestor, it might be thought
of the douanier Rousseau. And that is all that need be said
about the ancient sights of Bucarest, for they amount to little,
and that little is altogether overshadowed by the contemporary scene.

Or this statement may be qualified, at least, to include its
inhabitants past and present. This is a land where, till recently
works of art consisted, in the main, of costumes and carpets.
Anything more permanent was destroyed in the ceaseless petty
wars and was, in any case, no safe possession with the Turks in
sight. More than this the Turkish Empire, which in material
riches was the greatest power in Europe during the sixteenth
and seventeenth centuries, has left its oriental influence upon
the land and its inhabitants. The Turks had inherited the legacy
of splendour in dress from the Byzantines. There was even one
body of the Sultan's bodyguard, the peiks, a branch of the
tressed halberdiers, whose uniform had come down in direct
descent from that worn in the household of the Palæologi. They
wore a truncated, conical hat, surmounted by a triple plume.
The Sultan in his progresses through Constantinople was attended by a court, the splendid variety of whose costume defies
description. When, in the eighteenth century, the Phanariot
Princes, Greek families of the Phanar or Greek quarter of
Constantinople, were sent to rule the two principalities of
Moldavia and Wallachia they brought with them the customs

and dress of their native city, informed, it may be, by certain traces of French culture and manners. Especially, they imported with them the dresses of the Sultan's court. Our digression is in order to account for the extraordinary costumes to be noticed in all old family portraits in Roumania.

But this brings us to a general consideration of the old noble families, or Boyars, of Moldavia and Wallachia. The Cantacuzeni may be all but proved in descent from the Byzantine Emperors of that name; Brancovan, Kretzulesco, Philippesco, Stirbey, Vacaresco, Baleano, are families of Wallachian origin; Catargi, Balsch, Callimacki are from Moldavia; the Ghika family were originally Albanian; Mavrocordato, Soutzo are Phanariots from Constantinople; while the Rosetti, Moruzi and the curiously named Regoli di Roma are Phanariots of Italian origin from those Greek islands that were formerly Venetian, such as the island of Naxos. It is this tradition of inherited wealth and luxury that make of Roumania a different land from the neighbouring Bulgaria, from old Serbia, or from modern Greece. At the same time, the complexity of the different races from whom the modern Roumania is formed could not be more evident than in this complicated tangle of descent.

During the eighteenth century Jassy was the capital of the Phanariot princes sent to reign over Moldavia. Jassy, in all the two principalities, was the most important town. Bucarest was small by comparison. The Boyars, whether of Moldavia or Wallachia, must be thought of as living, with a horde of servants, in what we can only call a temporary accommodation. With very few exceptions, nothing like the great town or country houses of Western Europe were to be found. A house was built to last a few years and was renewed with every generation. Its riches, as we have said, were in carpets, in fine costumes and in jewels. At the end of the eighteenth and beginning of the nineteenth centuries there were built, in Moldavia, a few country houses, like Bozieni, or Stânca, in Russian Paul I "Adam" style, resembling "colonial" houses in America. Of old castles, or villas, there are none. A Phanariot prince only reigned at the whim of the Sultan, his liege lord, and was in perpetual danger of losing his life, if sent for to come back and account for himself to his master. Their temptation, therefore, was to make as much money as quickly as possible. Many of them reigned more than once, and for as many as three or four times. Such were the curious conditions of Bucarest, and still more of Jassy, during the course of the eighteenth century. The Boyars of more native descent kept as much as possible upon their estates. In the two capitals it was a completely oriental existence. As late as 1818, there is an account by an English traveller of an audience with the reigning prince, at Bucarest, in which he is described as being carried into the room, in the old traditional manner, supported by the arm of a servant under each of his shoulders, as though he were too important a personage to walk. These were the manners and customs of the old Turkish court, or even of the Court of Pekin. It was remarked, too, that the Phanariot princes had no standing army. This was not allowed them. Their state consisted in a multiplicity of servants, and in a few heyducks or Albanians gorgeously arrayed. I am even told, by Prince Matila Ghyka, that a Phanariot Prince, of the Mavrojeni family, made his official entry into Bucarest riding in a sledge drawn by a pair of stags with gilded antlers.

If the oriental, or even Byzantine, ancestral background to the capital is stressed it is because only in comprehension of this can its present unique features be understood. It is because the past of Bucarest, or that part of the past of Bucarest which devolved on it from Jassy, is of as much moment to its present psychology as the past of Rome or of Madrid, of London or of St Petersburg, is to their present tendencies and their appearance. But, also, and we cannot deny this, its picturesque details have been irresistible and have cried out aloud for inclusion.

Perhaps the most interesting memorial, in Roumania, of this time is the portrait by Liotard, which is the property of Prince Jean Callimacki and hangs in his house in the Chaussée Kisseleff. This is a rarity, too, among Liotards for it is a painting in oils and not a pastel. It will be remembered that Liotard, who was a native of Geneva, had established himself for five years in Constantinople where, it is said, he grew a beard and adopted the Turkish dress. He was invited thence by Constantine Mavrocordato, the Hospodar of Moldavia, of Phanariot family, and proceeded to his capital Jassy, where he remained for ten months. This was in 1742–3. In Jassy he painted the portraits of the reigning prince, his wife, his son, that of the Patriarch of

Jerusalem, who was upon a visit there, the portrait of Prince Scarlati and many others, all of which would seem to have been destroyed in the great fire that burnt down the palace of Jassy —all, that is to say, except the portrait that we are now considering. The painting of Prince Constantine Scarlati is, though, preserved in a contemporary engraving done from the drawing in sanguine that was a preparation for his portrait. It seems unlikely, however, that the painting we reproduce is that of the reigning prince. The young man that it represents is beardless, which must mean that he was painted in extreme youth. The probability therefore is that the tradition of the Callimacki family is correct and that the person portrayed is the son of the Prince, Alexander Mavrocordato, known as Delimbey, "the mad", who was to reign at Jassy many years later, 1782–5.

This portrait is a really charming thing. Especially, perhaps, because of the rose-coloured pantaloons that the young man is wearing. But, here, another point arises; that it was not Turkish costume that Liotard adopted for himself. We are expressly told that he grew his beard and started to wear his peculiar costume, by which he was to become known all over Europe, while he worked at Jassy. It is, therefore, the dress and beard of a typical Moldavian Boyar that he affected; and in the portrait of himself, in this guise, we have the perfect representation of the dress of such a person. This is borne out in other portraits inherited by Princess Callimacki from her Vacaresco ancestors; one of which is here reproduced, for it is full of character. It represents an old Boyar, blinded in one eye, and wearing an immensely tall fur headdress, decorated with a red plume that was the insignia of his office. This, again, was an inheritance from Turkish or Byzantine tradition. Those persons who have seen the mosaics in the Kariye Djami at Istanbul, will remember the kneeling figure of the Grand Logothete Theodore Metochitis presenting an image of the church to Christ, and wearing an immense striped turban that was the badge of his rank. This personage died in 1322; and the court costumes worn in Moldavia and Wallachia until 1848, even after the change of rule from Palæologus to Osmanli, are in the same living tradition.

It is most curious, therefore, to be shown the picture of a young lady, painted somewhere about 1810, and be told that it is the daughter of one of the Boyars, whose portrait is repro-

duced. This portrait, moreover, which has some of the handling
of a Goya, is remarkable for the beautiful diamond sprays worn
by its subject. Nor, in spite of the fact that it is so manifestly of
the decade 1800–1810, is this portrait at all conventional in its
dress. Not only that, but the young lady has the joined eyebrows, the sprincene inbinate, which were so much admired in
this country and that must seem, to us, as peculiar as the traits
of Hindu or Rajput. This again is of the pure Orient and has
not its equivalent in any Western land. We are told that this
trait is still to be observed in a few old families, particularly
the Stirbey.

But these old portraits, which will soon become a new interest
to anyone who sees them, must be experienced in a house that
is literally full of them, in what we might term the family
museum of Monsieur Mano. This gentleman has collected
every conceivable portrait of members of his family during this
time, and where they were inaccessible he has caused copies to
be made, or has copied them himself. The results of his energy
make one of the most interesting collections in Roumania.
They are not less absorbing to the student of costume, or of the
history of taste. Several more female portraits are to be seen, by
the hand that painted the oriental Goya just mentioned. These
are of rare beauty, and take, indeed, a high rank among late
eighteenth-century portraits. But, in this house, the paintings
of men are even more remarkable. It is almost inconceivable
that these Boyars in their furlined robes and immense fur hats
should date from the early years of the nineteenth century.
There are fur hats that must have been four to five feet in
height, and, in the case of a tall man, adding this to his six feet of
stature, there is a total of ten feet or more, a bearded Colossus,
in fact, of altogether fantastic appearance. The young men, in
a date equivalent to the bucks of the Regency, invented a
bulbous form of headgear which came into fashion, a fur hat
shaped a little like a Greek priest's hat, only more completely
rounded, so that it had more of the appearance of a Russian
bishop's mitre. But this was the last decadence, the last flowering of tradition. In the next generation, as we have said, this
characteristic costume went out altogether, after a slow development during what may have amounted to as many as fifteen
centuries.

Underneath the fur robes magnificent brocades were worn. Once more, this is of Turkish or Byzantine tradition. These silks and brocades are often very well rendered in the portraits, and their flowered materials deserve the attention of any competent professional designer. But the painters of these portraits remain a mystery. One painting in Monsieur Mano's collection is signed by a name that is something like Hayer, written in German characters. It is probable, therefore, that the artist was a Viennese who must certainly, to judge from the quantity of work that he executed, have lived for a considerable time in Roumania. But this subject, altogether, is one that deserves investigation by some one who has time, and who is living upon the spot. Whether it is the same hand that painted the Goyalike women is unknown. All those, at least, are by the same artist. As the Boyars are painted, as if by an identical person, at all dates between 1760 and 1820 it is evident that there must have been more than one painter at work, and more than one generation, even, of painters. The Boyars insisted upon a close and exact representation of their features and the significant details of their costumes. Even in spite of these dead rules there were painters, probably from Vienna as we have said, who had enough personality to achieve these most interesting portraits. They are an important part of the history of Roumania and the names of their authors should be restored to knowledge. There is, by now, hardly another part of the world in which painters of their accomplishment, and with such obvious claims to attraction and interest, would be allowed to remain in oblivion.

While this subject is under discussion mention must be made of, perhaps, the only other artist who has left any traces in Roumania. We refer to Louis Dupré, a pupil of David, and author of a delightful book, *Voyage à Athènes et à Constantinople*, published in 1819. This folio has coloured lithographs that are masterpieces of the art and is unique, besides, as being the only representation in art of Ali Pacha of Janina and his more than peculiar court. He is to be seen, there, floating, narghilé in hand, in a reverie, it may be, of future tortures to inflict upon his friends and enemies. He glides along in his painted caique, upon the waters of the lake of Janina, attended by two Greek or Albanian youths with curled locks and suspicious beauty. At the end of his volume Dupré gives a drawing of the Moldavian

Hospodar's encampment, and mentions drawings that he made of various families, including the Soutzo. It is more than probable that portraits by his hand may still exist in Roumania. His stay in the principalities was of short duration, and he returned to Paris, dying at an early age, in 1837. Louis Dupré is admittedly, an extremely minor artist, but he was a clear and beautiful draughtsman, especially of costume.

And, after Dupré, the list of foreign artists who have visited Roumania is completed with another Frenchman, Raffet, the military painter, who travelled in Moldavia with his patron, Prince Demidoff, in the 'fifties and has left many lithographs, in black and white, of Moldavian scenes. It is more than probable, too, that diligent search would yield drawings by a much greater man, Constantin Guys, who came out as war correspondent to the Crimean War, for the *London Illustrated News*, and is almost certain, in the course of his duties, to have visited Jassy, for the headquarters of the French army were at Varna, upon the Black Sea. It is sad, if this surmise proves to be correct, that Constantin Guys arrived in Moldavia less than ten years too late to draw the costumes that were worn until 1848. It is certain that they would have had an appeal to his imagination. Also, he would have drawn, inevitably, the heyducks and the Albanian bodyguard, together with the French fashions that were worn by the emancipated youth of the time. The principalities, in those days of transition, must have formed a wonderful spectacle to those who had the power of appreciation. Also, the horses and carriages of Bucarest were subjects that might have been specially invented for the pencil of Guys.

There is more than one description of the capital during the middle years of last century in which the extraordinary contrasts are noticed that were to be observed in its streets. Horses and carriages that would have been the pride of Hyde Park or the Prater would pass within a few feet of hovels that were not fit for animals to live in. A lady and gentleman dressed in the height of Parisian fashion would walk side by side with a half-naked Tzigane. There were Armenian merchants, Turks and Greeks, Jews and Russians, each to be known by his distinctive dress. Later on in the century, after 1881, the year in which Bucarest was declared capital of the kingdom, the increase of

its importance and wealth did not diminish but rather accentuated these living contrasts. A luxurious social life came into
existence, careless or oblivious of the intervening poverty. The
reflection of this is to be seen in a curious book, rare even in its
own country. It consists of a collection of the social paragraphs
written in French, for the fashionable newspaper of the early
'eighties. Every week there was a gala night at the opera and a
performance of *Norma*, of *Ballo in Maschera*, or of *Don Pasquale*, was made the occasion for magnificent balls and supper
parties. The sophistication of the language in which this odd
book is written, with its account of the jewels and the dresses
worn, of the flowers and the table decorations, is given an im-
petus, or is lifted to another plane, when these hidden discrepancies are realized. This little book is a complete exotic
or oriental commentary on fashion; it is not literature but
near literature, or, more exactly, notes for literature. In the
same way that there are books which could not have been
written without the help of a manual of dates, or of a guide
book, this scarce little volume has a distant, or menial, relation-
ship to Marcel Proust. This is the material upon which he fed
his intelligence, and perhaps the embryonic touch of Monsieur
de Charlus revealed in its author may account for its quality.
The heavy perfume of its pages, which are so meaningless, and
so strewn with cyphers, clings to every picture that the mind
can evoke of Bucarest in the eighteen-eighties.

Bucarest, as revealed there, is a compound of many things,
Russian, French, Viennese, Turkish, Phanariot. The fashion
and luxuries were French; music for the ballroom came from
Vienna; the extravagance and prodigality were Russian, for
that country is neighbour to Roumania; while everything that
was of the Orient had its origin in the background that we have
sought to establish in the preceding paragraphs. We must think
of the Chaussée Kisseleff on a summer evening when the carriages were driven at a furious gallop from end to end of the
avenue. Everyone knew to whom each equipage belonged;
while the demi-mondaines of the capital drive alone in their
segregated glamour, the cause of varied feelings to those persons whom they passed. Their pace was swift, but not headlong,
for it was the gilded youth who urged their thoroughbreds to
full gallop, being the same persons who, in the next generation,

own racing motors and thunder along in the full noisiness of the
exhaust pipe. Such was the fashionable glitter of a summer
evening during the 'eighties and 'nineties, and for the first
decade of this present century, during, in fact, all the best years
of a lifetime. It was an atmosphere, we may conclude, that had
not its like in any other capital of the West, owing to its hints
of the Phanar, or even of Cairo, its South American languor,
the Mexican luxury of its caparisons and harness. Meaningless
it may have been; but we are thinking only of its appeal to the
eyes.

But the present in Bucarest, the continuous present which
consumes the living, has still a quality that must be put into
words. This is the total of those different things that give it
atmosphere. The popular music plays a great part in this; but
music we have not yet come to. There are the primary or superficial traces of the Orient, the glass of water, perhaps, and the
sherbet of roses that you find at three or four o'clock of the
morning in your bedroom. This is the legacy from a not distant
age when pure water was a luxury. In Turkey, and in the
country in Greece, a glass of good water is still the greatest
luxury that can be offered. As for the sherbet of roses, this is
a spoonful of sticky paste, of the colour of pink roses, lying upon
a glass saucer. Its taste is delicious, like the scented airs of
Kazanlik, the valley of roses under distant Rhodope, where the
attar is distilled; or sometimes the sherbet is changed for a
conserve of cherries or blackberries. These sherbets are made,
of course, in houses and cannot be bought in shops. I have been
told, too, that in some old Roumanian families a paste used to
be made from lotus petals, but this waterlily sherbet seems to
have vanished into the past. If these last attentions of the long,
hot evenings are in living proof of this remoteness, so are the
pair of Albanians attached to the house in which we stayed.
Their lives, which seemed to pass in easy sinecure, were
patterns, we are told, of fidelity to their masters. In no other
country of Europe are these heyducks still to be found, save in
Roumania, where five or six families still maintain them. The
two Albanians of whom we are speaking might be described as
octavo editions of King Fuad of Egypt, himself of Albanian
descent and of exactly the same physical type. There had always
been Albanians in this household. When they wish to retire

from service, and go home, they send back another of their family or clan in their stead, so that the supply of Albanians is inexhaustible. It must, all the same, be a long and roundabout journey from Bucarest down the Black Sea, through the Bosphorus, to Athens and Corfu, and thence to Tirana or to Elbasan.

Many enjoyable hours can be spent in Bucarest looking for carpets. Down by the river, the Dâmbovița, there are carpet stalls where the wares are exposed for sale in the open air, as at a fair. Here, it is sometimes possible to find a pretty rug for the equivalent of as little as six or seven shillings. These would be native rugs of the simplest patterns; but, also, some extraordinary relics of the last century are to be discovered, floral patterns of inconceivable hardness and complexity, or elaborate woven frames surrounding a poodle or a St Bernard dog. The better rugs and carpets are, naturally, in the dealers' shops; but, although their prices are far from high, an exceedingly good Oltenian rug costing no more than ten pounds in English money, the supply is very limited. After a long search in the shops of Bucarest only four Oltenian rugs could be found for sale. This is because the area of manufacture was always small and most of the good specimens have, long ago, been bought by collectors.

Roumanian carpets fall into two main divisions, Oltenian and Bessarabian. The Olt is a river coming from Transylvania and running through the neighbourhood of Hurez and Cozia, due south, into the Danube. It drains the chief watershed of the Transylvanian Alps and is a region of pastoral valleys, in that district from which the carpets came. The great period of their manufacture would seem to have been from 1790 till about 1860. Their colours, often enough, are in wonderful harmonies of red and blue, rivalling in softness the colours of the finest Ghiordes, only it is a bold softness of pure reds and blues. The patterns are, in simile, like strewed flowers; they are a pattern of flowers as thrown upon the ground, not held in bunches or formally arranged. They are flowers, singly, or tied together in twos or threes, with a border upon another ground of smaller bunches symmetrically arranged. The intervals between these groups of flowers, in the main design of the rug, are kept to the bare ground of the colour base and are not worked over with

Maori chieftains, from Angas, *New Zealanders Illustrated* (1847)

Maori warrior, from Angas, *New Zealanders Illustrated* (1847)

the minute interlacings and arabesques of the Persian rugs. The Oltenian carpets, then, are bolder and less finished in design than the rugs of Turkey or the Caucasus. On the other hand they are both softer and more bold in colour, so that by many tastes they are preferred to any but the most valuable of Persian weaving.

The Bessarabian carpets are entirely different, and are, perhaps, better known in England. Bessarabia, it will be remembered, was a Russian province from 1812 to 1918. Its population—it was, before 1812, part of Moldavia, and touching upon Poland, the Ukraine and the Tartar provinces—is, ethnographically, a different mixture from that of Wallachia, of which Oltenia is part. Bessarabian rugs are slightly later in date than those of Oltenia, for their period extends from 1815 until about 1860. They are to be known often by the black ground upon which their design is worked, and this, in its detail is sometimes not unlike an English needlework carpet of the Georgian period, only greater use is made of the black background and the floral patterns are more successfully bold and unconventional in design. In fact a good Bessarabian rug looks as though it came from a land of carpets; an English needlework carpet, in spite of its beauty, always suggests that it was the recreation of the ladies in the house for which it was made. Another influence in Bessarabian design came from the neighbouring Odessa, where the émigré Duc de Richelieu, founder of that city, imported, it is said, one of the directors of the Savonnerie factory from his native France and established him in a local carpet industry. There is a breath, then, of the sophistication of the French Empire in some of the more elaborate of the Bessarabian rugs; and yet the finer examples are unique in their way and to be recognized at a glance. Of these it may be said, at once, that there are more to be bought in London than can be seen in all Roumania. They were collected by Russian amateurs before the war and had found their way to London and Paris long before Bessarabia had become, again, a part of Roumania. It is almost hopeless to look for Bessarabian rugs in Bucarest; but the Oltenian are still to be found, though rarely and with increasing difficulty.

Besides the possibility of fine rugs the antique shops of Bucarest contain the expected icons, silver work of no particular merit and, of course, peasant costumes, though not nearly to the extent that these are sold in, for instance, Budapest, where the multiplicity of peasant shops, beautiful as are the dresses and headdresses of Mezökövesd and Boldog, have become so numerous as to constitute a definite nuisance. Indeed, in Bucarest, by contrast, this industry has not been carried far enough, and some enterprise is badly needed by which the lovely costumes of Rucar, the Saxon dresses of the Siebenbürgen, the Ruthenian costumes of Bucovina, the distinctive Szekler dresses, the Suabian costumes of the Banat, all the wealth of Roumanian peasant art, which is the most rich and copious in Europe, should become available for purchase and for study. Equally, there can only be said to be the beginning of a museum of folk art. Its few rooms, in the Chaussée Kisseleff, contain no more than the first scratchings of the surface. There is surely, here, an opportunity to do for the peasant art of Roumania what has been accomplished for Northern art in the wonderful Nordiska museum at Stockholm, or in the open air folk museum outside Oslo. The rugs of Oltenia, or Bessarabia, are only a fragment of this enormous peasant creation, though they constitute a part which can fit admirably into the most civilized surroundings. This art of weaving is only a portion of an enormous belt of such creation, extending from the Black Sea to the Baltic, giving on its way the Houtsoule crafts of the Polish mountaineers in their remote corner near the Bucovina, and ending with the elaborately embroidered aprons of Lithuania, or the rjivy rugs of Finland. The Nordiska museum, which has extended its activities to demonstrate all the peasant arts of the Baltic, might be balanced and completed by a museum in Bucarest covering the whole area from the Bucovina to the Danube, for this is the richest part of the world in peasant costumes, peasant architecture, folk lore, and, it may be added, in folk music and folk dancing. The time is not, yet, too late. It is a still living art; and without much difficulty or expense a museum could be assembled that would be, in its kind, one of the wonders of old Europe.

This would seem to be the moment, too, in which to speak of the wonderful collection of paintings by El Greco that are in the possession of the Royal Family. Numerous persons are now familiar with these hitherto unknown pictures owing to the El

Greco exhibition in Paris, in the summer of 1937, where they were the centre of attraction. These paintings, which are nine in number, are distributed among the various Royal palaces, at Cotroceni in Bucarest, and in Foïshor, Peleş and the smaller Peleşor at Sinaia. Their history is that they formed part of the collection of King Louis Philippe, sold after his death, and then resold in 1879. They were purchased by King Carol I, without the realization of their real value, for El Greco was then a forgotten painter, together with a number of indifferent late Italian paintings, in order to furnish the Roumanian palaces with a garniture of old masters. They had been gathered together for Louis Philippe by that mysterious character, Baron Taylor, who may have been his illegitimate son, a figure of mystery who makes an appearance in Borrow's *Bible in Spain*. Borrow, too, we must remember, was one of the first persons to appreciate the greatness of El Greco and he prophesied, in the 'thirties, the high estimation in which the "Burial of Count Orgaz" would one day, be held.

The most striking of these nine paintings by El Greco are a lovely "Marriage of the Virgin", a late work dating probably from the last decade of the painter's life, after 1600, and a large "Adoration of the Shepherds", also a late work, most wonderful in colour and with huge soaring figures of frightening effect, a picture which is very similar in style and handling to "The Annunciation", in San Vicente, at Toledo. A portrait of an ecclesiastic; a "Martyrdom of St Sebastian"; and one of the not uncommon paintings of St Martin, on horseback, dividing his cloak with the beggar, are, also, in the Royal collection. Very curious, indeed, is the small sketch of the "Legend of St Maurice and the Theban Legion". That painting, which is, or was, the wonder of the Escurial, is quite different in this version. The colour of that incredible masterpiece has, here, lost its fire. More peculiar still, the warriors of the Theban Legion are no longer in Roman kilts but are shown in Elizabethan trunk hose. The little boy in the foreground, holding a helmet, has become the image of the small orange seller in the Bull Ring at Seville, in the drop scene painted by Picasso for the Russian ballet, *Le Tricorne*. This version, in fact, cannot be described otherwise than as disappointing, in spite of its intensely odd and curious effect. Some authorities have suggested that it is a copy by Jorge Manuel Theotocopuli, the painter's son; but it seems more probable, owing to the different features and altered dresses of this version, that it is a very late painting by El Greco conceived of, perhaps, as a kind of sketch from memory, for the original painting, it must be considered, had never been engraved. If Greco wished to see, again, that supreme work of his genius there was no other course than to go over from Toledo to the Escurial. This may have been, then, one of the replicas, in little, of his large paintings, for a contemporary writer tells us that Greco had, in his house, a finished sketch of each one of his big compositions. No fewer than three small versions of this subject are mentioned in the inventory of Greco's studio, taken after his death. "St Maurice and the Theban Legion", in its Roumanian version, is an odd and weird work which adds little to our understanding or admiration of El Greco. "The Marriage of the Virgin", or "The Adoration of the Shepherds", are, contrary to this, two paintings, knowledge of which is necessary to all admirers of El Greco. They are late pictures of his most interesting period, and take an important place among those most extreme productions of the human spirit. They are, needless to say, the greatest works of art in Roumania.

The paintings by El Greco may be described as one of the invisible attractions of Bucarest. Even if they are not seen, it is interesting to feel that they are in the air. There is nothing incongruous in their presence in this town. Its aspect, which is unlike that of any other European city, most exactly suits their provenance and origin. If Bucarest be as essentially Roumanian as Toledo was particularly Spanish, there are other human elements, as well, which give a spiritual similarity to both towns. What was Moorish, in Toledo, is Turkish or Phanariot in Bucarest. It is not a question of architecture, or the comparison between Toledo and Bucarest would, at once, become ridiculous. But Bucarest is nearer to Turkey than Toledo to the Moorish town of Granada. So many persons, now living in Bucarest, have their connection with the Phanar. This would have been, had the Cretan painter aspired to ancient descent, the boast of his proud claim upon the Byzantine tradition. The Phanar was the civilizing, if corrosive, influence upon Roumania during the whole of the eighteenth century. Even the churches of Bucarest, in their bastard Byzantine style, have their frescoes based upon the strict formulas of the schools of Mount Athos, conventions which were familiar to the painter since his Cretan childhood.

And there is even living, in Bucarest, a rich colony of Sephardim, or Spanish Jews, the descendants of those driven out from Toledo and from Granada, still speaking Castilian, and forming part of that Sephardim population to be found in great number at Salonica, at Brusa in Asia Minor, and throughout the ancient Turkish Empire generally. The Sephardim, who are the aristocrats of the Jewish world, have families as ancient in origin as any of the noble families of Europe. Their history, which has never yet been written in detail, is a wonderful subject for the historian. That they should still be speaking Spanish, after an exile of some four hundred and fifty years, is astonishing in itself. Their family lore, with its extraordinary ramifications, can have no parallel in the traditions of any other race. It would be interesting to know what legends still persist among them of their ancestry in Spain. The strict education of the Sephardim Jews, their petpetual intermarriages which have fixed their physical type to so remarkable a degree, their rules of family, the history of their synagogues, these are some of the mysteries of the Sephardim. In Salonica, which is in some sense their capital, for they have even newspapers printed in Spanish, the Jewish women wore a particularly beautiful costume until the middle of the last century. This will have been their costume as worn in the fifteenth century in Spain; and it is probable that the colony of Sephardim in Bucarest had, also, their distinctive dress. Spanish folk tunes, or tunes with an unmistakably Spanish flavour, have been collected within the last few years among the Spanish Jews in Rhodes. This proves the inalienable tenacity of the Spanish influence upon them. It is remarkable, too, that the Sephardim of Bucarest, in contradiction to the general political tendencies of their race elsewhere in the world, are reported to be warm in their support of the Spanish Rebel Junta.

But, now, we will confine ourselves to the physical appearance of Bucarest. Its huge area, and the leisurely spacing of its houses, are still of the Orient, while skyscrapers, more in model than in fact, and blocks of modern apartment buildings rise in every direction. Bucarest is described in old books of travel as being a town of woods and orchards. There are churches, or rather chapels, now standing in its busiest areas of commerce that, until the middle of the last century, were hidden from view in midst of a patch of forest. In fact, the churches and monasteries now engulfed among its modern streets must have seemed nearly as remote as the little convents still existing on the outskirts of the town. Most of these, which are the attraction of the country round the capital, stand upon the edges of small lakes or lagoons. Such are the convent of Tigăneşti, some twenty miles from Bucarest. A few miles farther in the same direction the forest of Snagov has, in its midst, a lake, upon an island in which stands the monastery of the same name. There are others of this character, at Pasărea, or Comana, an equal distance from the town; none are of any great architectural interest, but all are picturesque, while the first two, at least, are romantic because of their situation by the blue waters of those still lagoons. Any convent or monastery the approach to which is by boat gains that much by its isolation and seems, more than ever, to exist in a sphere of life of its own. Equally a lake, which has little to recommend it except its waters to bathe in, has its surfaces broken, in these instances, by the reflection of cupolas and domes, while the music of bells, of the Eastern ritual, to the wooden mallet's stroke, comes over the long waters through the mists of evening.

In other respects the environs of Bucarest are not worthy of the town. A dusty, dry plain, with many marshes, stretches for an immense distance down to the Danube. Only in one direction does the scene improve, where a road, with an appallingly bad surface, leads to Mogoşoaia, the country house of Princess Marthe Bibesco. The beauty of Mogoşoaia is a tribute to the skill and good taste of its owner. An outside staircase, and a pillared loggia in the style of those of Hurez, make of this house the unique essay in its style. The material is a close, whitish brick, not unlike the brick architecture of Lombardy. At the other side of the house there is another loggia, and a series of flowered terraces go down to the lake, which is full of lotuses. The interior of the house, which we were allowed to see by the kind permission of its owner, is simple and beautiful, and must be the ideal retreat for a torrid summer. Of the Venetian architect who is said to have worked here and at Hurez I could see no traces. But the house contains a bedroom with splendid Empire furniture that belonged to Madame Tallien, from whom the Prince is descended, and in every detail in the interior the touch of an assured taste is revealed. The house, too, has a chapel, nearby, with an exceptionally good interior in that sub-style of late Byzantine which is known as the Brancovan, from Constantine Brancovan, 1688–1714, who was the great builder of his generation. It was this personage who built Hurez; and if that convent is the most charming and attractive in the whole country, Mogoşoaia must be its equivalent, where the Roumanian country house is concerned. It must be said, though, that as it stands, Mogoşoaia is entirely the creation of its present owner. Before that time it had been empty and derelict for many years.

The excursion to this house occupied the afternoon of one of our last days in Bucarest. But before we close this subject, or, at least, end any individual day with a description of the music that is the recreation of every evening there, another and most curious subject must be mentioned. In this city which has had so many polyglot influences, and in which the peculiarities of its character derive in so large a part from the Orient, there are the few remnants of one of the strangest and most extreme religious sects that have ever existed. One of the first features noticed by the stranger in Bucarest are the cabs, or droshkies, driven by Russian coachmen, wearing long black velvet caftans and a peaked cap, black in winter and of white linen in the summer. These Russians are often magnificent specimens of humanity, and their horses, in a land where it is better not to look at the horses, are glossy and well-cared-for. Generally they are a pair of a particular and valuable breed, known as the black Orloff, though these fine horses are not to be seen, now, as often as formerly. These cabdrivers belonged almost entirely, in old days, to the Russian sect of Skapetz, or the Skoptzi, a sect who made it their practice to mutilate themselves.

The origin of these fanatics is obscure and undetermined. They were one of the numerous sects of dissenters from the Russian Church, of whom the Starosti, the Old Believers, are the most famous. A short digression into Russian history is necessary in order to explain these matters. They are concerned with the Patriarch Nikon, the reformer of the Russian Church during the reign of the Czar Alexis (1645–76). The Patriarch Nikon, is should be said, was a gaunt and terrifying figure, seven feet in height, whom we may imagine in his monastery of the New Jerusalem, or Voskresenski, daily repeating the curses in the 109th Psalm, with a nude hermit by his side. This was the perpetual and typical action of his extraordinary career. It was the Patriarch Nikon, in the middle of the seventeenth century, who drove the Starosti into exile in the Northern or Arctic forests, where they built their characteristic wooden churches. They were known as Pomortsi, or Dwellers by the (White) Sea. Others of the Starosti fled to the southern confines of Russia and crossed into Bessarabia, where their descendants are still found, as will be seen in the ensuing chapter. If the general body of Old Believers were so numerous, at one time, as not to merit the name of a sect, there were other, and smaller, numbers of them who broke apart and adhered to the wildest extremes of religious fantasy. Such were the Khlistovstchina, Jumpers or Flagellants, and the Bezpopovtzi or priestless. These rejected marriage, and believed that suicide by voluntary starvation or burning alive, which they called purifying by the immaculate baptism of fire, was the most meritorious action that a believer could perform. Two thousand seven hundred died thus, in 1687, in the Paleostrovski monastery. Some readers may be reminded, in this, of a scene from Moussorgsky's opera, *Khowantchina*.

Another division comprised the Beglovestnie, those dissenters who simulated dumbness, and though tried with the most fearful tortures by Pestel, the Governor of Siberia, in the time of Catherine the Great, could not be induced to speak. Other votaries of silence were the sect of the Beatified Redeemer, who lived constantly absorbed in the contemplation of the holy portrait, which was supposed to produce heavenly bliss and ecstasy. Most extreme of all were the Stranniki, or Wanderers, who considered they must flee from the wrath to come by being homeless and houseless, and, especially, by dying in the open air. Moscow, which the Orthodox Church considered to be the Third Rome, coming after Constantinople, was centre and headquarters of these various sects. Archbishop Dimitri of

Rostov, in his book upon the different sects, written early in the eighteenth century, mentions no fewer than two hundred of them. The Russian Church, in fact, persecuted all the sectaries and, not least, the Skoptzi.

Many of those mentioned are, now, extinct; but the Skoptzi, the most uncompromising of all, are still surviving. It is supposed that they had long existed in Russia, but did not form a religious body until 1765, when their doctrines were preached in the provinces of Orel and Tula by a fanatic called Kondrati Selivanov. Their dogma consists in the literal translation of such texts as "If thine eye offend thee, pluck it out", with others of the same import. The necessary operation was performed with steel and fire by the hands of this fanatic, himself. Eventually, he appointed a deputy, Silova Ivanovitch, who operated upon the converts in Siberia and Eastern Russia. Selivanov was exiled to Siberia where he gave himself out to be Peter III, the murdered husband of Catherine the Great. Her son, the Czar Paul I, caused Selivanov to be brought to St Petersburg, but deciding that he was an impostor caused him to be imprisoned in an asylum, an interesting decision when the mental balance of the Czar, himself, is taken into account. Selivanov was eventually released and placed in the monastery of Suzdal, in the Upper Volga, or of Spasso Euphemius, it is uncertain which, where he died in 1833, at well over one hundred years of age. The doctrines of the Skoptzi found a number of adherents. Many rich merchants were members of the sect. The jewellers and moneychangers in Moscow and St Petersburg, in Odessa and in Riga, were members of this community, and would offer large sums of money to induce converts to join them. For a time, under Alexander I, the Skoptzi even flourished. In that curious age and under that most mysterious of Czars, who later, it would seem, became a hermit, himself, and went to live for fifty years in the Siberian forests, there were even instances in which officers of the Guard became converted by their soldiers and took the irrevocable decision by which they joined the Skoptzi. It is even claimed that Field-Marshal Count Souvarov became a Skapetz. In 1856, it was estimated that there were thirty thousand of them in Russia; while, in the Urals and on the confines of Armenia, whole villages had nothing but a Skapetz population.

These various details should give the background of fanaticism in which the Skoptzi had their origin. They were exiled to the farthest corners of the Russian Empire; or crossed the frontiers into neighbouring lands. Of their present condition in Russia I can find no mention, in any account published during the last twenty-five years, but it is to be assumed that they must still exist, though the cult is likely to be extinct as far as its proselytyzing energies are concerned. And having said so much about the origin of the Skoptzi in Russia we, now, return to Bucarest, where this discussion was prompted by mention of the Russian or Bessarabian droshky drivers. We have described their fine black Orloff horses and the long black velvet caftans that give a look of Russia to the streets. Until twenty or thirty years ago the droshky drivers were almost always eunuchs of the Skoptzi sect. Their practice is to marry and have two children, or, at least, a son, after which they submit themselves to this cruel operation which alters all the rest of their lives. The story that this operation is the culmination to a licentious orgy I take to be very far from the truth. On the contrary, after having done their military service, and had the requisite children by whom the future of their tenets is assured, they carefully undergo an operation at the hands of a surgeon, but, it is natural, in circumstances of deep secrecy. It is said that, according to the strictest tenets of their creed, their wives, also, go through an operation which is directed to the same purpose, of stopping procreation, and that, at this time of sanctification, even their domestic animals are emasculated. This would only be the case in rare instances of fanaticism.

The interest of this peculiar creed lies in the metamorphosis of its victims. Practically none of the present droshky drivers in Bucarest are Skoptzi, but it is still possible, upon careful inquiry, to discover some old adherents to their faith. I was taken to a suburb of the town where several whole streets of prosperous-looking houses were pointed out as having been the homes, until a few years ago, of the Skapetz cabmen. Side by side with the houses were the stables for their horses. This was a relic of the days when Bucarest had as fine equipages as any town in Europe. Every person approaching middle age remembers these Skapetz cab drivers who had the status of confidential servants and, being in possession of many persons' secrets, could be relied upon never to divulge them. This inquisitiveness, this passionate passive interest, were the signs of their physical condition. In no instance is anything but good to be heard of them. They are given the character of pathetic and deeply religious persons condemned to this fanaticism by their beliefs.

But there is still a small quarter, even in this area, which has altogether changed its inhabitants, where you can see the Skoptzi. We stopped at a stableyard, where some personal inquiries were made, and in a moment the old cabman Vassili emerged. He was tall and heavily built with a completely smooth and hairless face, ageless features and the high-pitched voice that was to be expected. Like the few remaining Skoptzi of Bucarest he was prosperous, and had let out most of his stables for a garage, only keeping one carriage and a pair of horses. He was born in Moscow and had come to Roumania with his parents when a child. The next day we saw him driving in the streets, where he is still a well-known character. When asked his age, with a touch of that pride and mystery that are noticed in all accounts of the Italian castrati singers of the eighteenth century, he refused to answer until a correct guess was made. He was, actually, sixty-eight years old; but was not sure of this within a year.

Round the corner we were in midst of a whole street of them. All are prosperous, living on the rents of their stables, and, in a few moments, we were drinking Russian tea with them and eating honey underneath a pergola of vines in someone's garden. There were eight or nine of these metamorphosed beings, all with the intense inquisitiveness of their kind. They will not drink or smoke, and an inquiry after one well-known Skapetz was answered, sadly, with the phrase "he is lost to us". The meaning of this was that he drank and smoked and had, therefore, forfeited their friendship and his own chances of salvation. All these Skoptzi, being old men of between sixty and seventy, had been born in Russia. Only one of their number had the appearance of middle age, but he avoided conversation, and so deceptive are the effects of their condition that he may have been as old as any. Their intensely religious atmosphere is most impressive.

The cruel mutilation they have undergone alters their

physique in a variety of peculiar ways. It is this which should interest the student of psychology and, also, it may be added, the medical profession. They become large and feminine round the hips and can, with a little acquaintance, be known, at once, by their disproportionate limbs, which seem curiously articulated, by a shambling walk, and even by the shape of their backs. More curious still, after several generations who have mutilated themselves, it is said that these physical characteristics appear even in the normal individuals who have not submitted themselves to emasculation.

No history of fanaticism, and one has never yet been written, can ignore the Skoptzi. But it is palpable that their character has been grossly misrepresented. The sacrifice of their virility is, for them, the supreme renunciation and must have been attended, in the past, with the death of by far the larger proportion of its votaries. There was no greater sacrifice that they could make. The pathos of all religious belief could not be played to more bitter effect than by such ruthless protagonists. The Skoptzi are not vile and sensual but are pathetic to a degree that is hardly to be believed. Human beings have, it is probable, never had a more terrible illusion to trick them into felicity and ultimate salvation. But their appearance in Bucarest, in the middle of the last century, coincides with the extinction of all that was Byzantine in the neighbouring Turkey and is, therefore, a fictitious reinforcement of the Orient into a country that will never cease to be of the Orient, as to a large part of its idiosyncrasy. The old and tortuous Orient is not real without the eunuch. The very presence of the Skoptzi is like the wind that never ceases to blow out of the steppes. But this vilified sect have the virtues, also, of the Quaker or the Moravian. The exposition of this must wait till a later page of this book. It must be sufficient to say that they deplored, in Bucarest, that no new converts ever came now, to increase their number. In Bucarest they are nearly extinct and in another ten years there will be none of them left. But the Skoptzi still flourish in another Roumanian town, in Galaţi, and it is in Galaţi that we must describe a visit to their homes, and the impression of true religion, and almost of sanctity, that is shed about them in their pathetic lives. At the present time, the Skoptzi claim to have 340 adepts at Jassy, of whom 180 are women, as many more at Galaţi, many fewer at Bucarest, and some 500 scattered along the Delta. In all, they are numbered at 1500. In my opinion this is an underestimation.

It was in the knowledge of having seen some of the most curious individuals left in Europe that we came away from that suburb of low houses. Row after row of those one-storeyed dwellings stretched in every direction; but the Skoptzi had gone, and no stranger could ever find his way back to them through this maze of little streets. And here, walking in twos and threes, were the typical Russian peasant women, looking, even, like the peasant dolls of childhood. Their heads were hooded in white shawls that entirely hid their faces, they had blue cotton dresses printed with white or red flowers, and, of course, heavy wooden clogs. Because of their hidden features they were like painted wooden ghosts. These were the wives of the droshky drivers, with, it is probable, the wife of a Skapetz among them. And, in another moment, this suburb of old Russia was entirely left behind.

Life in the poorer quarters of Bucarest must be far from unpleasant. Food is plentiful and extremely cheap; in fact Roumania has a cheaper rate of living than any country in Europe. Bulgaria, or Jugoslavia, may approach to it in these matters, but the greater fertility of Roumania produces crops to which those colder countries cannot aspire. Chickens are the equivalent of tenpence each; turkeys are a little more expensive. They have excellent fish, fresh water from the Danube and salt water from the Black Sea. There are a variety of fruits, from the apples of the colder north to water melons, ending with those huge gourds that have flesh the colour of blood oranges and are a favourite food with the populace, that are typical, therefore, of the extreme south of Europe. Yet this town which had such tropical heat during our visit in September, lies pale and noiseless, in winter, under a thick covering of snow. Sledges make their appearance, and the cold of St Petersburg has succeeded to the fire and languor of Seville.

It must be because of this variety of foods, and for the torrid heat, that Bucarest possesses an altogether inordinate number of summer restaurants. The same thing is to be seen in the places where many of the population of Bucarest spend their summer. The road, for instance, between Predeal and Sinaia, a distance of twelve miles, appears to be lined on both sides with open-air restaurants, over the greater part of its extent. In Bucarest they are to be found in all quarters of the town. The names for these garden restaurants is grădină. Dinner, though it is difficult to call it dinner if it begins near midnight, will begin with a glass or two of ţuica. And now we come to the Roumanian cuisine. This, to gourmets, was the surprise of the Paris Exhibition. The Roumanian pavilion was thronged, night after night, for this reason. It is probable that, after pre-Revolutionary Russian, the Roumanian is the best native cuisine in Europe. Dinner, in even these inexpensive grădinăs of Bucarest, will consist of ciorbă, a fish or chicken soup made with sour cream; and will be followed by carp, perch or sturgeon. Other dishes are mititei, a compound of grilled sausages; tocană, veal with a tomato sauce; sărmala, rice balls with chopped meat, wrapped in winter in a cabbage leaf and in summer in a vine leaf, similar, in fact, to the Greek dolma; a tender saddle of lamb; or muşchiu de vaca, filet de bœuf, always excellent. There are, as well, fleiça, beef roasted on a spit; or ardeĭ umpluţi, paprika pods filled with rice and minced meat. Poussins roasted on a spit are a speciality of Roumania. Other things which can only be described as delicious are a pilaff of quails, and the crayfish, or queus d'écrevisses, which are cooked in a variety of ways, with saffron or paprika, and have better flavour, even, than the crayfish, or kraftor, in Sweden. Roumania, also, has its own caviar, which they prefer fresh, though this does not make instant appeal to those who are used to the salt beluga or molossol. The fresh caviar is infinitely more expensive, having been brought the same day from the Black Sea; but it must be said that the Roumanian salt caviar is only just less good than that of the Caspian. There are a great many dishes that are eaten with a sauce or dressing of sour cream. For dessert there will be fresh peaches and fraises des bois, or wild raspberries; bunches also of the small white grapes; and, of course, Turkish coffee.

The wine in Roumania is generally, or universally good, but never exciting. A wine is but seldom to be met with that can be thought of as a discovery. Individual proprietors only make enough for their own needs, and it is only the rich vineyard owners who will take trouble over their products. On the other hand, the wine seems never to have the heavy sulphurous taste of most of the wines of southern lands. No similarity can be noticed between Roumanian and Sicilian or Southern Italian wine. There are wines made with imported Tokayer grapes, but possessing quite a different flavour from those of Tokay. As a rule, though, the red wines are more interesting than the white. The Crown wines are usually to be relied upon; as are those of Cotnar, Odobeşti, or Drăgăşani. These are, perhaps, the best; there is not much to choose between the others. Many of these wines could probably be much improved upon with care, by the selection of the best vintage years, by careful maturing, and so forth. But these processes require many years before they can be brought to perfection and, in the meantime, the Roumanians seem content to drink the wine as they find it. A tolerable brandy is made, resembling the Greek cognac. Many home-made liqueurs are distilled upon country proper-ties; good cherry brandy, particularly and, also, peach or apricot brandy. Finally, it must be said that Roumania seems sadly deficient in mineral waters, Borsec being the invariable reply to every inquiry. There must be many excellent waters in the mountains; but, either these have not yet been exploited, or else it is that the Roumanians prefer to drink the local water with their wine. Perhaps, until this custom has stopped, their wine will never receive the attention that it deserves.

Persons who have spent a two-months holiday in Bucarest have assured me that, on leaving, they have realized there remained twenty or thirty of these small restaurants or grădinăs, to which there was not time to go. And if there is this bewilder-ing choice of food the same thing is true of character and locality. There are, of course, the expensive restaurants to be found in every capital; places like the famous Capşa, which well deserves its reputation, and has a confiserie and sweet shop attached to it that has, perhaps, no equal in Europe. But the true character of Bucarest is to be found much more in smaller places of less international repute. A summer day, which is divided into two by the siesta, a device, incidentally, that gives the illusion of prolonging human life, could find no more pleasant ending than dinner to the accompaniment of music. This, indeed, is the culminating pleasure of Bucarest. It may be said, in a phrase, that there is as much music here as there used

235

to be in Naples when the festa of Piedigrotta still brought out, every year, the new songs that were to sweep like fire all over the Italian peninsula within a few weeks.

This music is of many different sorts. The expensive restaurants have American bands, as good as any to be heard in Paris or London, and playing the new tunes that have only been surreptitiously released and are still played, as it were, by the favour of the conductor. The players in these bands are all of Roumanian nationality. No one would know that they were not American. If this music has to exist it must, at least, be as good as possible, and this is our excuse for mentioning these places. There are, as well, the bands that play Viennese waltzes; and the fact that so much of the present Roumania was part of the Habsburg Empire will sufficiently account for the ease and grace of their performance. Gypsy bands also abound, but are not as good as in Hungary. The Roumanian Tziganes have not yet developed a sophistication that can be adapted to the restaurant life of a big capital. Their performances are rough and uncouth. To be properly heard they should be listened to in the remote country where their genius keeps to the soil and invents those tunes that are collected by Bela Bartók and by Kódaly. In them, the true Roumanian speaks; but it is in a dialect that is not understood in great cities.

There is at least one grădină where a Russian orchestra can be heard. This particular band is of superlative merit, in its kind. They sing the tunes that were sung in Moscow before the Revolution, many of which are familiar tags, as hackneyed as the cheaper Spanish tunes that are the commonplace of circus or bull ring. One Russian singer, living in Bucarest, was mentioned, who had an extreme renown before the Revolution; but this person was, unfortunately, ill and could not be found. This band, probably because in Bucarest they cannot actually be said to be in exile, possessed a quality that I have never heard before in a band of their description. The banality of those Russian Gypsy songs, and the songs which go with drinking toasts, had never appealed to me before, heard now, for the first time, away from the Russian restaurant or tearoom of conventional exile. There are some Russian tangos, such as the well-known "Dwe Gitare", that have a peculiar nostalgia in these circumstances. The origin, too, of that traditional song is

Maori warrior in dog-hair cloak, from Angas, *New Zealanders Illustrated* (1847)

Maori chieftain with jade sceptre, from Angas, *New Zealanders Illustrated*
(1847)

mysterious for, if it is a tango, it can hardly have been composed before the War. Many of them come, of course, from Russian musical comedies; but nearly all are, now, anonymous. One of the best known of all, which passes, always, for a Russian Gypsy song, is, in reality by the Spanish violinist Sarasate, who died some thirty years ago, and it is to be recognized in his "Zigeunerweisen". Perhaps he may have heard this air in Russia. If that is so, then this tune and many others of its kind may be nearer sixty than thirty years old. Later on, at Vâlcov, on the Black Sea, we were to hear many more of these Russian tunes, and some of them, we were told, had come lately from Russia.

But the real beauty of these evening entertainments are the Roumanian songs. By now, after three weeks in the country, the dawn of them had broken upon one's mind. They come, at first, only with the recognition that they have been heard before. A day or two later they are in your mind and you cannot remember where you have heard them. Next time, it is that the tune is in your ears and you cannot quite get it. Like something unattainable it hangs beyond the reach. That very evening a band may play it, but, when you get home, you have forgotten the way it went. It comes back to you in the middle of the night, and next morning has gone from you again. In the end, when I knew these tunes, I could be kept awake thinking of them, such is their impalpable nostalgia and the mystery of their quality.

I have compared them with the songs of Piedigrotta, but this is a comparison in popularity. It does not attempt a description of their merits. They are the popular songs of a great town and have nothing in them of Moldavia or Wallachia. This is not peasant music; it is the music of the inn and the grădină. Neither does it show any American influence. But many of these tunes, again, are a mystery as to their origins. Some of them, people remember in their childhood: others, that are just as good, come from the latest revue, at the Carabus, for instance or from some other summer theatre. There is nothing whatever of Vienna, nothing Hungarian, still less Russian, in their style. Neither are these the French chansons of the music halls, although their purpose approximates more to that than to anything else. They are partly that, and in part the popular song, as of Piedigrotta, where the new tunes were tried over for the first time, every year, and still the old favourites never died. They are less sentimental than Neapolitan songs, not set out expressly for the tenor, nor giving him the high notes that all Italians would want. On the contrary, they are better when sung by a woman's voice. It does not even appear that their composers are at all well known or popular. There must be new songs, every year, for the revues, and the best of them blend irrevocably with the old. It is, thus, a convention that has been in existence for a long time. Its mannerisms are perfectly well known and, in fact, in order to be a good song the new must fit exactly within these limitations of the old.

To the many persons who will have heard the band in the Roumanian pavilion at the Paris Exhibition it must be said that the virtuoso who played upon the syrinx or Pan pipes would appear to be unique of his kind. There is no one else in Bucarest who plays upon that instrument. But that particular band, which is famous, consists principally of Tziganes, and they played Gypsy music. Neither can I say that I altogether admired his performance. The Pan pipes, besides their Papageno qualities, possess, as it were, a propensity to impertinence, and the shrill whistle which terminates every tune comes to spoil all that has gone before. Also, the noise of it quite overpowers the band. Even so, this first introduction to Roumanian popular music will have been a revelation to many people. Nothing of its kind has ever reached Western Europe before, though its true quality may have been forced or obscured by that too exuberant performer. I find that my view of this instrument was shared, also, by Liszt. In his book, *The Gypsy in Music*, talking of the Gypsy musicians of the Danubian provinces, he says: "There is, also, great use made of an instrument consisting of several pipes placed in a row, similar to that which we call Pandean pipes, the honeyed tones of which would quite sufficiently cancel the verve of their orchestra, without the further effeminating effect produced by the equally free use of a kind of mandoline." And yet the effect of these Pan pipes is, surely, to be heard, transcribed and reproduced towards the end of Liszt's Tenth Rhapsody.

This is the only good popular music that I have ever heard in the knowledge that it was living. New York, or Harlem, are of a different order. This is living music in the sense that it was alive in Vienna in the day of Lanner and of Johann Strauss. It transmutes every memory of Bucarest. The point of these songs is that they are like images or clichés of the town, giving you its feeling and atmosphere within a breath or two of its air. At the same time, I wish it had not been necessary, in order to illustrate my meaning, to write the names of Lanner or of Johann Strauss for they infer an entity that is entirely alien to that of which we are speaking. This is much more the café chantant of Degas; but as if its cafés were at no inordinate distance from the Black Sea, or even from the Bosphorus. It is essentially the music of a southern land. If the fados of Lisbon were all that they are said to be, this music would be their equivalent.

Towards the end of a few days in Bucarest this music will take up an extraordinary share of one's unconscious attention. For most of the day, or night, it is at the back of one's mind. This, indeed, is the true nostalgia, in music, for the import of these tunes is undeniably sad and disillusioned, in spite of their words, which may have an entirely opposite meaning. The hot September nights always hold the echo of them from some café. They seem to utter, cynically, their message of the little chance there is in life and the small meaning there is in happiness. All the same it is a land of summer heats and fruits. The climate, as in songs of Naples or Seville, has circumscribed their shape. By now their burden becomes unbearably sad. Yet, since this is its expression, and it has none other, it would be useless to seek for an explanation. The message of it is in the music.

For night after night this can continue. "Ionel, Ionelule", that masterpiece of disillusionment, though, a moment later, it may be fraught with another meaning altogether, can easily become an obsession. It opens like the popular songs of Seville or Valencia; and then in a moment is itself again. This is its nostalgia. At every reiteration it comes back again. On the last night of all, just before I fell asleep, I remembered it once more. And then, immediately, the strains of it came from the open air café next door, in the Chaussée Kisseleff, from under the trees.

It was four in the morning. There was no other sound but the footsteps of one of that pair of faithful Albanians, enjoying his sinecure of night duty and listening, no doubt, like myself, to the music. Outside, the long avenue lay quiet. How curious it seemed, lying there, to think of the Chaussée once full of carriages, of the Skapetz coachmen, of those Laetzi, at the fair, only two days before. This was Bucarest, a town that is like none other. And, once more, the refrain came back incarnating the nostalgia of my thoughts. All, all was implicit in that tune.

HURDYGURDY*

This is to be a musical experience without parallel. All, who would listen, must come with us to a town consisting of a wretched street, a mile long, unpaved, and very wide. A Jewish town, entirely, to judge by the inhabitants. We will, even, give its name. It is Mohilev, in White Russia, upon the far or left bank of the Dniester.

There are no roads or railways. It is 1835; and all country-men, over a certain age, still think and talk of Napoleon and his pride and fall. The Poles, who form a large part of the population, and are the peasantry and gentry, look upon him as their saviour. The Russians only recall the barbarity of their own sufferings, and how the Cossacks slew with sword and lance and set fire to buildings where the French wounded lay. That was twenty years ago. What everyone remembers is the cold and hunger.

Meanwhile, the past has slipped back again. That means, for many of those concerned, a subsistence that is little better than starvation. It is as if, and there may be comfort for us in this parallel, the tyrant, or hero, had struck a sudden and murderous blow, without warning, and been driven reeling back into the snows. But, in fact, it is again as it used to be. Only with burned villages, where the war has been, and many men maimed.

But, come, walk into the town. It is an October evening. We have passed a row of windmills. For the wind blows here out of China and Tibet. There is nothing to prevent it. Much else, besides, comes out of that limitless distance. We meet great waggons driven by men in long gowns with long beards. Shall we say the snow is falling? No! the sky is the colour of the cheeks of green apples.

The houses are one-storeyed and like the shacks of mining towns. Only old and dilapidated when new built. Of grey wood

* From *Splendours and Miseries*, 1943.

and plaster brightened with flat paints. Each house is a shop and has its goods for sale. In some, the oil lamp is already burning in the dark back room. But the peasant population cannot read or write. For their sakes there are shop signs all along the street. A great jackboot, of rusty iron; a long shirt or caftan made of tin; the barber's cup for bleeding; a golden bowl or pestle for the apothecary; a gilded fish; a gilded goose; all tarnished; how they must crank and rattle upon a windy night! If you walked here, under a stormy moon, you might imagine these to be the creaking trumpets of the rag fair. For, in fact, there is little for sale that is not second-hand.

But it is the busiest hour. There has been rain, and the street has big puddles that reflect the sky. Nevertheless, men dash from one side to the other, ankle deep in mud, holding live chickens, but half starved, or mended garments. If a coin were dropped, it would sink into the mire. No one could find it. But they are so poor they live by barter. A peasant brings a few eggs or a dried fish and, in return, takes away a cup or plate or printed handkerchief. The traders or pedlars are all dressed in black, with high boots, and fur caps, but their gabardine is soiled and green with age. For the number of its houses the town is swarming with inhabitants. The children are their parents, in little, dressed no differently, and the boys wear the same black curls below their ears. Some, though, are red haired, and show the Tartar in their cheek-bones. The red bearded Jews, who are always tall and thin, are like the magician in a fairy-tale. Or like the wicked uncle in the pantomime.

This enormous population is so miserable that it longs to move. Not that it has ever known a settled home. Is it the Tartar strain in them that makes them nomads, only wandering from town to town? They are swarming, like the ants. When they are ready and when the barriers are down, they will migrate to Vienna, to Berlin, to Whitechapel, to America. If we could see this town towards the end of the nineteenth century, a particular horror might attach in our minds to some of the Jews, red bearded ones among them, who, above their top boots and tattered coats, wear a tall silk hat, tilted back above their ritual curls. It is the top hat of the age of prosperity, of the bank and stock exchange, worn jauntily, could we forget the fox, the showman, the wizard in the children's story, and implying no more than that the wearer looked forward and saw himself on Broadway or in the Mile End Road.

No sign of that, this evening. The secret police will but herd them towards the Austrian or Polish frontiers. And leave them there to starve, or pick a living up out of the gutter. Where were their ancestors a hundred or two hundred years before? We do not know. Spread everywhere from Lithuania to the Crimea. The red ants driven before the swarming black ants, that is all. Swarming, and then migrating, like the lemmings. Driven on by their misery, and in the end, into the emigrant ship. But not yet. Not for another human generation. Some of these children whom we see this evening will take their families to America. But, until middle age, they will live upon the serfs, and pick up their living second-hand.

Down to the left, beyond the houses, flows the Dniester. Through the empty plain. This is so huge that in the distance it is another colour. Here, it is like mud, desiccated, but bleaching grey for winter. Far off, as though from every weed upon its surface, it is a velvety or mossy green, rubbed thin. Deep down runs the river, very broad and slow. I have seen it sixty miles higher, at Hotin, which is a slum, not a town of Jews, in Roumania, upon the other or near bank of the Dniester: and at Mohilev it will be no different. It flows quietly, for it is very deep. Suddenly, the town ends, there is a steep drop, and the river flows below.

We pass soldiers in their long grey coats wandering stupidly, in amazement, even in Mohilev, for they are moujiks out of the Northern birch forests and have only known the wooden towns. They are conscripts and may never get back to their homes. It must be a market day. The peasants are spending their money. But the black gowned Jews outnumber them. And it is the Jews who go hungry. The peasants are well fed. But it is as though the whole town is too poor to afford a light. And it has grown darker. You can catch the sunset in the pools of rain. Lamps are lit, at last, and they must be naphtha flares; here and there, when the light can shine on tin or china or cheap enamel. Where obscurity helps business, there is no light at all.

We have the feeling that we are many miles from home. It would be a nightmare to have to sleep here on a filthy floor, and we are to imagine that we shall return, before it is too late, to a small manor or country house a few miles away where we shall sup on beetroot soup, thick with cream, on partridges from the October woods, and the sharp berries of the season, and afterwards, round the wood stove, listen to music, and talk of our extraordinary experience. We do not live here, but are foreigners, travelling, perhaps, to Kiev or the new city of Odessa, handed on from country house to country house, in the manner of that day; journeying like Lamartine, who had the same adventure as ourselves, and described it. Perhaps the confidence of that safe comfort at the end of the day helps us to exaggerate the squalor of the scene. Were we forced to spend the night in it we must shut our eyes to the shades and undertones of this remote and miserable slum.

Was anyone happy or contented? We see characters who could be Jewish comedians, and many others from the Yiddish theatre, where, it could be said, genius is often hidden under grease paint. Here and now, in embryo, for their opportunity has not dawned. Remember, this is a hundred years ago! Probably, in any such community of black gowned men, there must be those who can mimic, or create character. For they never come out of it into the fields. It is as far as they go if they are seen at the edge of the beet fields, bargaining, where the black raven hops. Where the magpie flies off. They are never to be seen digging, harvesting, nor herding. You will see a black gowned man riding on a peasant's waggon, and it means that he has possession of the peasant's holding. They are, eternally, the middlemen. They buy up the eggs; they do not set the hens. A Jewish child is never goosegirl. Rather, they are the sparrows, the mice, the rodents of the town. In big cities they congregate in dark cellars, where mushrooms might grow. They do not spend money on the exterior of their houses. But, in fact, in this town they are so miserably poor they have nothing to spend at all.

The children of the Jews are curiously bird-like in their similarity. Palely precocious, and at the age when their features alter, it is to be felt of them that they are only growing into the plumage and physiognomy that is natural to them. The lamb turns into the sheep; or the squab with its huge beak and scraggy neck becomes the painted pigeon. But, in their early youth, it is as though they might turn into something different. And so it is with the ringleted children of the Jews.

Mohilev is a town in which to search for musical or dramatic talent. A town of many towns; for their frontier extends from Wilno to the Golden Cheronese. It is enough if, in one place, there should be a Menuhin. Yet how could there be a chance of that? At this moment they are imprisoned in the ghettos. They are fermenting, seething, boiling, in their slums. For, where this race dwells, there are always slums. There are never the carved and painted wooden houses of the peasants. Those rustic houses are like wooden boxes. Their eaves are carved with the fretsaw, and then painted. The peasants walk like peacocks in their embroidery. Could we see a village on a wedding day the headdresses of the young girls would be like the crowns of princesses in a fairy story. Their kakochniks or bridal crowns are in a hundred patterns according to locality; a Northern Orient in which the women go unveiled. But the Jews, by comparison, never beautify their houses nor their persons. They are nomads of the unpaved streets. Of the back rooms. And, in big towns, of the basements. As middlemen and sellers of second-hand clothing their trade is drabness. Their racial instinct is the quick return. They move from one town to another town, but it becomes the same. Yet it is impossible not to pity them. Deep in themselves they are discontented, dreaming of New York or Johannesburg, of Broadway or the Rand. As yet, unheard of; but they feel that in their bones.

But Mohilev, or Hotin, a hundred years ago! The carriage wheels sink up to their axles in the mud and filth. It could not, properly, be described as mud. For mud is formed from soil or humus. It should have clay or chalk in it. But this is the dust made liquid and coagulated. The accumulation, down the years, of animal and vegetable detritus. Grey with poverty, and swollen with cabbage stalks, with garbage, and the nameless refuse of the drains and sewers. Which, in Mohilev, are the gutters and the whole width of the slimy, pollulating street, that seems to flow with mucus, with expectoration. There is the knowledge, here, which it is impossible to suppress in our minds, that their food is slaughtered in another way. It is the sign of their religion. Perhaps the Kosher slaughter house may be more merciful than the poleaxe of the peasant, but we think of the Jews in imagination, sitting down to milk-white veal, bled white and pale, according to their ritual. There are tanneries in Mohilev, and we smell the hides and skins. But the carriage step is put down and we must walk across that open sewer. For a little time it is impossible to look up, until we are so mudded that it does not matter. Then the swarming misery takes possession. And we hear the shop signs swinging in the wind. Idly, idly, like men hung in irons upon the gallows tree.

What can be the average of life in Mohilev? Many children, and little babes, must die. There are many old men, who have flourished like the weeds. In stony places. Or rather, in between the stones. Except that here are no stones. The shacks are built of wood and plaster. But there are funguses that grow upon old bits of wood, and there is the mildew that spreads upon the plaster. How else could they live? They have crept in between the bricks. They have sprouted in the crevices. They crawl forth into the grey light of Mohilev, and go back again.

For all its vitality this town is inanimate and imprisoned in the past. The Jews are so orthodox and conservative. To-night, as we see them, it is a medieval ghetto. The barriers are still up. The world is not yet open. There are no hospitals. What happens to the sick and ill? For an answer, come to the crowded cemeteries. Count the Jewish headstones. There are many, here, with more room space than they had in life. They lie, at last, in their own beds, and have not to seek their living. In the distance there are the golden domes of the Russian churches. Not in Mohilev, but in the villages upon the plain. This flowerless mud is neighbour to the orchard and the grove of birch trees. The priest and the Rabbi pass by upon the street. The one is an ignorant and drunken peasant: the other, bred for generations in the slums. But his roots are in the earth; while the Jewish Rabbi is like the weed upon the wall. His community are of their own planting, without invitation, and can be uprooted. But, like the weeds, they seed themselves anew. They spring up in waste places, and choke the sunflowers near the peasants' cabins.

Nor weed, nor sunflower has any colour, here and now. It is autumn, and the sunflower rattles its dead leaves. The plant is withered to an iron skeleton; an iron standard which has been hit and twisted, scorched even, and the tin head droops, for it is like a head of painted tin, until you touch it. Here and there, the heads have fallen, burnt out by their own flames in the summer. The yellow corolla has gone black. By that curious alteration in dead things, if you pick up a dead sunflower, it is flat and heavy, a wadded or stuffed disk, that is all, and then the seeds drop from their cells, and we have that analogy which we noticed in another place with the dead flies of the window casement, with the smoked out wasps' nest, or, in our time, with the radiator of the wrecked motor car, or the shattered aeroplane of modern wars. So much for the dead sunflowers of the backyard. They are the roses of the Ukrainian gardens.

A child comes by holding a bunch of weeds, like groundsel. Probably he has a linnet in a little cage. Another may feed a crust of rye bread to a whiskered mouse. Children's games go on. But the mud is too thick to trundle a hoop or spin a top. They have to be games of guessing, or little riddles. You would not find the wooden hobbyhorse. But the children are starlings if their elders are the crows. They gather, we mean, in the branches of a tree. You hear a hundred voices chirping, all together. Or so it seems. They are collected together at the corner of the street. And they dart off with a movement of a hundred pairs of wings, and dipping, all together, cut another angle, and are gone. They are round the corner, out of sight, or but a few steps in front of us; and then are gone again. So it is in autumn fields, and in the hedges. Soon they will be gone altogether, to another clime.

But it is a hundred years ago. The old evening darkens. Down towards the sunset, it fades like a sheet of red-hot metal. Tighter, tighter, into darkness, like the turnings of a screw. That is how it fades. We will not have it that it is quite dark. The huge plain is so empty that the dark will come up, all at once. The wind, blowing towards the sunset in the West, comes from unknown lands in the utter distance. Here are no safe woods and covers. It is because of this such cruel things have happened in their history. We have not had the Tartars on the plains, or the winds out of the North and East. From the tundra, where mammoths are found in the cold cliffs of the river. Or listen to it! blowing from all imaginable Orients, in semitones and quartertones beaten with the palm of the hand upon the sheepskin drum.

Could it be music that we hear? Ah! it must be ancient music of the dulcimer, and a thrilling and strange excitement seizes us because of the sunset and the fever in the air. It is not the mouth organ, nor the street violin. There could not be pavement music in this far off town, so long ago. Yet they must be street musicians. It sounds like a little band of instruments that accompany peculiar and special tones. Ah! it is nothing. Do not listen so intently! But we have known a hurdygurdy bring magic into a London slum. We cannot help but listen who are the slaves of music. This does not turn and grind. It is not music of the handle. It is not mechanical. What can it be? For it begins again. Now harsh and vibrant, and then melting. That is the mystery of music, for this is of the sort that suddenly intoxicates. It steals upon the senses. It does not work immediately and at once, though that can happen, but not here and now. For we heard it in the distance. We must come nearer in order to be entranced. To the next street corner, hurrying reluctant, for the dread of disappointment. But it begins to assert itself. Oh! stop still and listen. It is a peculiar instrument we have never heard before: or not played in this manner. For those are the hands of genius. There is no faltering. The notes break or impact in their peculiar way because it is an instrument, half harmonica, half dulcimer, akin to the cymbalom, and its special qualities are described in the word claquebois. Listen! listen! the like of it will be heard no more. For this is the transcendental player. Probably the greatest, untaught musician there has ever been. Upon an ancient, rough instrument of which he is the virtuoso. He is, in fact, playing in the street.

What we see is a bearded man in a long black caftan, seated at his instrument in the middle of a crowd. His foxskin cap is on the ground. Behind him, four men, much alike, as though they are his brothers or near relations, hold their violins and basses ready. When we come up, he is sitting with half-closed eyes, waiting for inspiration. Then he looks down at his dulcimer, and tests it by preluding upon the strings. During the course of this we feel that he has seen us. He draws us, by that, into the orbit of his hypnotism, although it was not a direct glance, but he has taken notice of the strangers, and allows time for the drug to work. A moment, also, for us to stare at the extraordinary appearance of this man of genius. He lifts his head and gazes into the air again; then, with a sudden movement raises both arms, and looking down at the dulcimer, brings down both hands in unison, and strikes with the pair of hammers together. The four musicians take their cue from him, and follow.*

This Jewish musician is Michael Joseph Gusikov, but, before we remove him into a room (his own bedroom), a concert hall, an opera house, or to anywhere else that we should like to hear him, and attempt to explain his untutored genius and the extraordinary effect it had upon his listeners, we should look at him again. He wore, always, the clothes of the wandering Jewish musician of his land. Because he was that, by profession. The fact of the many distinguished persons he had met, made no difference to him. He wore the beard of the Russian Jew, looked poor, and, indeed, was very poor. He has the sunken cheeks and high cheekbones of the Slav, and is very pale. In fact, he is dying of consumption.

This is his history. He was born at Sklot, a little town near Mohilev, where his family had been musicians for upwards of a hundred years. His father played the cymbalom, or dulcimer, an instrument with cords of metal which were struck with a pair of hammers, and which was in use among the Jews of Russia and Poland. At the age of seventeen he was married, according to Jewish custom. He could not read a note of music, but learned several instruments, and played at weddings and village dances, and made occasional, short journeys to Moscow. Soon after he was twenty years old, he could play the flute, his chief instrument, no more because of his consumption, which gave him fearful fits of coughing, and made it painful for him to draw in his breath. This disaster plunged his family into misery and starvation.

But, in this mortal predicament, Gusikov, who was formed by nature to be a great musician, set to work to make a musical career possible for himself. For this purpose he chose a musical instrument of the street or village fair, and resolved to introduce

---

* Bihary or Czermak were alternative in my mind to Gusikov for this study of illiterate or instinctive music. But the material and background of the Hungarian Tzigane are well known, by now; and also, even from the meagre accounts that are left of him, it will be apparent that the Russian Jew was the greater player. Probably, indeed, the most wonderful genius of his kind there has ever been.

such improvements into its tone and range as would make it capable of the most subtle shades of execution and interpretation. This instrument, called Jerova I Salomo by the Jewish peoples, was of most ancient origin and may have come from classical China and India and their schools of music, but the use of it had spread in medieval times among the Tartars, the Cossacks, the Russians, the Lithuanians, and as far as Poland. It was formed, somewhat after the manner of a marimba, out of a number of slats or strips of pinewood upon a bed of straws, struck, we would imagine, as though it were a clavichord, but capable of a deeper and louder tone than that because it was a bigger instrument, and, in any case, played with a pair of hammers like a cymbalom. Originally, this instrument was tuned upon the major or Chinese scale.

Gusikov increased the number of the strips of pinewood to two and a half octaves, disposed chromatically, not in the order, alternatively, of semitones, but arranged in a particular way in order to facilitate his execution. He contrived to isolate the vibrations of the wooden notes, and make them more powerful in tone. Three years were spent by Gusikov, from 1831, in perfecting his instrument. But, at length, his preparations were complete, and in July 1834 he set forth with his four brothers or relatives to Kiev and to Odessa, where he performed in the opera house and was heard by the violinist Lipinski, who has left an account of him. At this time he was heard also by Lamartine, who was travelling through Southern Russia. It was due in large part to the encouragement of Lipinski that Gusikov undertook his journey to Western Europe, appearing with wild success in Vienna, in Milan, in Germany, in Paris, and in Brussels, where his health completely broke down, and it was evident that he was dying. And he died at Aix-la-Chapelle, in 1837, at thirty years of age, when about to start upon his journey home.

The repertoire of this transcendental player consisted entirely of Russian, Polish, and Jewish popular melodies and folk tunes. Further accounts of his genius are given by Mendelssohn, who heard him play in Germany; and by Fétis, the musical biographer, who made friends with him, saw him continually during the four months that he was ill in bed in Brussels, and dying, and took down from him, personally, the facts and details of his life. Fétis gives a warning that his description of Gusikov, short though it be, is genuine and authentic, and will be found different in some respects from others. He must be referring to the *Biographie Universelle* of Michaud, which claims personal knowledge of Gusikov but gives a ridiculous account of him, and is responsible for the sensational story according to which Gusikov died in a concert room at Aix-la-Chapelle, upon the platform, in the act of finishing his recital. He claims, also, that Gusikov could read music, that he was well known in Italy as a virtuoso, and that a concerto written by him for clarinet was given with great success in the San Carlo theatre at Naples. The truth is that Gusikov was entirely obscure and had never performed outside his native Russia until he came to Western Europe a year or two before he died. In the end, Michaud describes the instrument of his invention, or perfection, as being of the nature of a harmonica or xylophone. Michaud, it is evident, was unmusical and insensitive. It is better to trust to the musician Fétis, to Lipinski, to Mendelssohn, to Lamartine. All these are agreed upon his genius. According to them, Gusikov was of the sort that appears once, and for ever, and is gone.

We are in the presence of, probably, the greatest untaught or impromptu musician there has ever been. But, in fact, this description is not accurate. For he was a musician by heredity; while no one who could play upon his variety of instruments, and could devote three years of his life to the perfecting of so special and subtle an instrument as that upon which he made his fame could be called unskilled. Gusikov was a musician in the medieval or Oriental meaning of the word. He could not read music, and it was not necessary. Indeed, it was not written down. The music he played was composed by instinct and instilled by ear. It would never be charged against the poets of the sagas, and of the old epics, or the ballads, that they could not read or write. It was their particular poetry, and it even gained because of its special conditions or restrictions. The poems lost nothing in beauty or subtlety because they had to be got by ear. In the same way, folk music, epical or lyrical, in its hundred sorts, loses nothing because it has not the sophistication of print and paper. Rather, the opposite. It loses when it is written down. Many of its nuances may be impossible to transcribe, while performance from the printed copy, in the concert hall or music room, must lack the fire and vitality of the original. Street music, if divinely inspired, or the music of the fair, indeed, all popular music when it bears the mark of genius, spoils and tarnishes at the hands of those who have been trained in schools.

Circumstances, of race and environment, brought it about that the airs played by Gusikov were music of the street, more than of the mountains or the plain. Hurdygurdy tunes, coming out of nowhere, such as would be heard in little towns, together with the grand or epical embodiments of nationality, for this is one of the regions of the world where folk music is part of the history of the land. The focus for these tunes was the fair of Nijni-Novgorod, six hundred miles to the East, upon the Volga. Most of them anonymous, of unknown origin. But Gusikov will have brought back with him, too, the popular airs of Moscow. He will have gone to hear the Gypsies who made their living by singing and dancing in the guingettes and cafés-chantants of the suburbs, and who sang both in their own language and in Russian. He will play the germs, or first ideas, of many tunes we know, together with airs of Tartar or even Mongol origin. Polish and Jewish tunes from the fairs of Poland and Lithuania. Some, also, which approach the Hungarian, and could be mistaken for Hungarian airs. The true historical analogy of Gusikov is, of course, to the bards or rhapsodists of Russia in the Middle Ages, and he represents a survival of this into modern times, but in conditions made exceptional by his peculiar genius, by his special instrument, and by the flowering of his talent due to the consumption that killed him young.

But enough of this.

We watch him putting his instrument together, in public, before his audience. He does this in order to show how simple are the means from which he draws such great effects. In the same way a magician demonstrates how much he can do with nothing. For his instrument is only a dulcimer of wooden slats or notes lying upon ropes of straw. But they are strung or balanced with the extreme of care, almost as though the instrument is made anew each time he plays upon it.

His black caftan is like a primitive form of the frock coat of the virtuoso. It accentuates his thinness. We notice the pallor of his face, and the habitual cast of melancholy upon his features. He never smiles. We wonder, having heard him in the distance, and by rumour, what the character of his music will be. For his face is utterly impassive. And, according to the nature of the airs he plays, we shall hear him in the street at Mohilev, or in the humble bedroom where he died.

Now he begins to tune the notes and strike them with his fingers, listening in rapt attention, and then again, as though disdainful or indifferent. Those are moods of creation. He takes up the hammers, and now he plays a prelude, but only to test his instrument. It is a sip or taste of the intoxicating liquor. There comes another preluding, this time for display of speed and power, a sweep of all the notes at full force, dying away pianissimo, so that the whole of his magical world lies open in its strangeness from end to end, as it were, from masculine to feminine, in tones that we have never heard before, deep and angry, but fading into enchantment among the strands of straw.

But he breaks off, suddenly, and lifts both hammers into the air. It is the beginning. He brings down his hands together, and strikes with both hammers, this time in a tremendous shake or rattle. It is the typical opening with the cymbalom, a sort of throbbing or quivering like the swaying of the python, a shivering from head to foot, even as when the priestess of the oracle, who has bathed her body and her hair in the waters of the Castalian fountain, shakes the sacred laurel tree and eats the leaves with which she crowns herself. In fact, it is to give a moment for the narcotic to get to work, and it is succeeded by a pause which is indescribable in excitement while he waits again, with uplifted hands, and then begins, softly, to play one of the tunes of the Balagani.

A little, early, hurdygurdy waltz.

They are the tunes belonging to the painted wooden booths that were set up, on public holidays and festivals, for the performance of strolling players. The booths used to spring up in a night in the square of the Admiralty, at St Petersburg, for the Mid-Lent Fair. During the rest of the year the actors toured the country. There were Balagani, too, in Moscow.

And they came to every small provincial town. But the fascination of the Balagani consisted in the prodigious talent of its performers. There were Italian and French dancers who were in actual descent from the Commedia dell' Arte; and families, like the forebears of the Legat brothers, who were to become famous in the Russian theatre. But the French or Italian genius had become acclimatized. We can only trace its origins in the skill with which the wooden booths are painted, and in some of the characters of the pantomime. Also, in the music. For that is in the Russian idiom, but now and then, as in this little waltz, taking on a foreign form. It is, indeed, not far removed from the simple waltzes or ländler of Haydn, such a tune as, sometimes, forms the trio in the minuet of a symphony, but composed on this occasion for a musical clock, shall we say, and taken from that, or the mechanical organ, to the Russian fair-ground. Then born anew, and become the waltz of the Balagani, upon the hurdygurdy.

Shrill notes are mingled with it, as when the ballerina dances while she plays a bugle. It is not so much that the tune is mechanical as that it is a primitive waltz, in wooden or archaic form, turning, turning, within a little space. Written, where, and by whom? No one knows. Where they make the hurdygurdies. But it has been altered a little in order to fit it to that wooden box upon a stick, and the changed notes have given it the Russian nationality and idiom. Is it our imagination? Can it be but the creaking music of the hurdygurdy that is identical in every slum? How appropriate upon the straufiedel or cymbalom! Listen! listen! it is the Balagani in every wooden bone. It plays in slums and below the painted palaces. Young persons walk here with their governesses, and carriages come by, painted green, with outriders and postillions in scarlet cloaks. They halt for a few moments, and drive on. But, chiefly, this waltz is an interior drama, within the wooden walls. Open, in front. Taken down, and put up again, on all the fairgrounds. And it ends, as abruptly as it began.

But the musician has not changed his mood. With no longer pause than for another tune to come, he gives us one of the gods of comedy, descended to the muddy street, among the litter of the crowd. Standing on the boards, outside the frame, in the light of afternoon. For a moment only, and then he leaps on to the stage. But we see him by the wooden arch which imitates the colonnade. He has altered much from Bologna or Bergamo. For he is neither Pierrot, quite, nor Harlequin. He has the flaxen, peasant hair, the linen shirt of the moujik, the linen trousers, and the Russian boots. Perhaps you would only know he was a personage of comedy from his collar, which is like a ruff, and from his wig, and painted cheeks. But none of the characters drink wine from a straw fiasco. They drink raw spirit. Their simulated drunkenness is more heavy and animal. Such is their metamorphosis amid the white lights of the North. We know that in the music. We can hear it.

And, preluding softly, he plays a tune that is entirely Russian in accent: a popular song. This he might play, in bed and ill, with his instrument upon his knees, as Fétis heard him in his room in Brussels. For it requires no execution, but the expression lies in its poignant phrases. None the less, we are in Mohilev in the open street.

Ah! this is different and nearer to the bone. Those others had wooden bones. But this is flesh and bone; or, at least, it bleeds. How can it be that this bare simplicity has such effect? For it is the bare bones of music. You can listen, and wonder how the heart beats in it. If he plays it once, or twice, or three times, it may resolve itself into mere notes at first or second hearing. That is the mystery of music. It may be the guile of the virtuoso to allow it to be bloodless, once, and let it drop, lifeless and uninhabited, into your hands. Or it can be your own fault. But it returns. And, this time, it may miss another of the listeners and be dead and lifeless to his ears. Such are the cold hours of music. The chill dawn. This is when he strikes to light a fire. But it catches. The sparks begin to kindle. The next time, the blood begins to flow. We get the sacred tingling of the skin. The god comes down to earth and there is magic in the air. In the streets of Mohilev. No one moves. It is impossible to stir or speak. It is too strong and overpowering, even in its weakness and simplicity. And what is it? Ah! no one can tell. There must be something animal in us that is entranced by music. A dumb nature, of which this is the word.

But he puts down the pair of hammers. These are but preludes to test the instrument.

255

For a few moments he tunes the notes, while two of his band of musicians kneel beside him, and without a word from him, repair the slats of wood and tighten them in order that they should take the greater strain that he will put upon them. It is, even, necessary that he should begin softly, but his months and years of practice while he made the instrument and perfected it have taught him how to strengthen his tone. At first, it is no louder than a virginal or glass harmonica, partaking of both natures, if that be possible, and intended, therefore, for effects of infinite subtlety and concentration, like the music of a world in little, all things in proportion, so that a street song is the whole of ragged poverty in the motes of dust, that glitter, and the entire theatre and its actors are in a wooden booth that is no bigger than the hurdygurdy. You hold the stick in one hand, and turn the handle with the other. And, thus, you move with slow steps along the slums.

But we are to hear his instrument, like the cymbalom, lead the other instruments. It is tuned, now, and upon its mettle. Even the notes that he touches with his finger have the heroic twang. It is the dulcimer of Asia, no more, in little, the music of the Balagani. No more, the hurdygurdy. We are to hear tunes that have come, at a horse's pace, across the plains. From both the sunrise and the sunset. Part of the thrill of excitement is the pause and the anticipation, and he knows, cunningly, how to play upon this. By making another adjustment at the last moment, when all was ready for him to pick up the pair of hammers and begin. Almost as though he wants a little time in which to mesmerize his audience. There are virtuosi of the concert platform who achieve this by looking round among their auditors. It was said of Liszt, by one who heard him: "He knows well the influence he has on people for he always fixes his eye on some one of us when he plays, and I believe he tries to wring our hearts. . . . He subdues the people to him by the very way he walks on to the stage." But the musician whom we see before us now hypnotizes by being impassive and expressionless. He has long hair and a long black robe, and looks straight down in front of him. In fact, the pause is for his personality to impress itself. This strange being, nurtured in poverty and misery, and belonging in dress and appearance to the ghettos of the Middle Ages, who

played at dances and village weddings, is the genius of untaught and instinctive music. He attacks the heart and blood
more than the brain. He entrances, and then intoxicates.

The moment has come.

Lifting the pair of hammers, so that we see his wide sleeves
tied at the wrists, he pauses, to get the time, and strikes the
bass notes, which roll like kettledrums. It is another instrument
altogether. The loud and resonant dulcimer, rattling, rolling,
in announcement. For this is how the cymbalom begins, imposing silence.

But his hammers run right up the instrument and dividing,
perform another shake, in bass and treble, both together, and
still louder; and then, in short runs or rhapsodic openings,
drumming fortissimo, with full force of both hammers, up and
down the whole gamut of the notes, display the two and a half
octaves, from end to end. Then, joining together, with both
hammers upon the middle notes of the keyboard, he gives a
last great shake or rattle to the cymbalom, and the prelude
ends with single, struck notes, in both directions, that give
forth the masculine physique, the male architecture of the
dance.

Now it comes. In a short stabbing phrase, slow and solemn,
rattling from end to end, with another shake, and another
phrase that bows low, as in the genuflection of the dance,
quickening, ever so little, then slowing down to the formal
conclusion. The other instruments come in. It is the Ukranian
tune, "The Stork";* and now, softly and swiftly, the dance
begins, as though with every kind of step worked into it, in
endless variation, with fresh entrances, ever quicker, quicker,
gathering as it goes. This he does with but half the force of the
dulcimer, for the point is speed and nimbleness. But the major
opening returns. We listen, unwilling to move or stir, to this
most intoxicating of dances there has ever been. And the tune
comes back, turning upon itself, faster, faster, and dies away,
in magic, into the body of the dulcimer.

With only the interval of a moment, as though the dazzling
effects of his preluding were necessary no more, he begins to

* This Ukrainian dance, "The Stork", was used by Tchaikowsky for the finale of
his second symphony. It is among the most thrilling movements in all music, but,
of course, altered or adapted by the composer from its original form.

play an air of different character. He contrives that his instrument should imitate the plucked strings of the guslee. He gives us the music of the Kalieki and Kasiteli, street singers, beggars, mostly, and those who sing in chorus, on the pilgrimages. It is an archaic music, grand and primitive, like the sweeping of many harps. Dating from an age when music was near to plain chant. Religious in tone, but with the nip of strong drink in it. This is music of the great rivers and the plain; Dniester, Dnieper, Don, and Volga; but the next tune comes from the birch forests, because it is less assured and more credulous. The horizon is hidden by the trees; but the tune is fanatical in meaning. Probably a hymn of the Raskolniki, or Old Believers; even of those who have been driven from their homes to the Arctic shores and call themselves Pomortsi, or dwellers by the sea. For there are Old Believers in this part of Russia, too, not far from Mohilev, and their religious choruses are characteristic of them.

Next we have a curious Chassidic tune, one of the ecstasies of the Chassidim. This is a sensual poem, of many thrusting ornaments and regurgitations, but in the Babylonian mode, it might be, so obscure and ancient is its form. Passionate, though, and ecstatic; more physical or, indeed, sexual than any other music, for it translates so easily into symbolism, and the flowers are ugly. Thus, Rabbi Israel Ba'al Schem, in his white robe, walked with his humble disciples in the Tatra hills, and it was the first time that the Jewish nation had invoked the trees and fields. After this, a wailing lamentation; then, the blowing of the shofar, or ram's horn trumpet; and he plays a Hebrew melody which could be of any place or time.

The secret of these extraordinary performances of natural music must be, in part, because the dulcimer is an unaccustomed instrument to our ears. This music would be prosaic on the piano or violin. But it has been necessary to create for it a vehicle which is capable of the highest degree of virtuosity. This is no simple dulcimer; the secret of it died with Gusikov. It is, of course, remarkable that a dying man should be possessed, physically, of such powers of execution. The reason is that nervous energy need not fail until the end. Perhaps, also, where it is an instance of tuberculosis, the very nature of that disease makes it that the powers or faculties of display are

retained by the dying man, till long after they are any good to
him. Certainly his feverish or febrile health affects his genius.
We should never hear another performance that is like this. A
healthy man, it may be, would not be capable of these superb
strengths and subhuman subtleties. The gradations of tone are
exaggerated to the point of being drugged. It is when a
musician of genius throws the whole of his nervous and physical
life into his music that such effects are possible. We shall see
how quickly he can intoxicate; and, in another moment, make
us weep.

But he is, again, the musician of the rustic dance and village
wedding. What can be the history of these melodies? Are they
composed by any one person; or do they take shape, imper-
ceptibly, as they travel, and are they the work of many hands?
For the same tune alters as it goes. It can be found in different
villages in another version. It can be like the same story with a
different ending. This changes its meaning. But the lesson of
that has not been lost upon the virtuoso.

Looking up, for a moment, from his instrument, he begins
a simple, poignant tune. It is compact and square, and whatever
that may be, it has but that one meaning, which is as personal
as though it were a portrait. Nothing else could be intended.
But it is a peasant portrait; like an image upon a wooden panel.
It is full face, and looks straight out before it, with flat shoulders,
and arms straight down at its sides. Only in the first few bars.
Then we hear in it the red fire of a primitive sunset, upon black
earth. We see cabins or shelters or fresh boughs, where the
crowd eat or drink at the huge horse fair in the plain, while the
music turns into the discordant music that they listen to. Black
lambskin caps and shaggy sheepskin coats are worn. We are
looking for a race of strangers in the crowd. We shall know
them by their springing, limbered step. Here is one! He has the
insolent and peacock tread. Wearing a travesty of a beggar's
rags, with bared chest and brass-studded belt, long hair to his
shoulders, and mesmeric gaze. He has companions in the
crowd, but they keep away from him on purpose. For their
trade is cheating. The music has turned into a Ciganje tune.
And it ends with a run or glissando upon the dulcimer, played
without the hammer, by the fingers of one hand.

But he plays the same tune again, and it is entirely different.

259

Now, wholly in Ciganje rhythm. With wild runs and ornaments hidden, before, in the body or fabric of that sheepclad
tune. Without the addition of a note, but changing the time
and altering the meaning. Fire, or sparks, are in its footsteps.
Impossible to let it bear images, for there is such entrancement
in its time and measure that the tune hypnotizes in itself, and
has no suggestion but its own peculiar tread. The runs or
shakes are like flourishes. That plain tune is in another language,
a secret tongue of chicanery or subterfuge. With one finger of
the right hand he runs from end to end of the keyboard, as
though, for this sacred trance, he would tear the cymbalom to
pieces. Loud and shrill, like the run of the Pan pipes which are
equivalent to bird whistlings or interjections played by the
Danubian shepherds where the river becomes a swamp of huge
willow trees, down by the delta, and storks and cranes and
pelicans are seen. It must be in imitation of the Pandean pipes,
which he may have heard once or twice and no more.* But now,
the glissandos sound soft and smooth for the expiring of the
tune, and it dies into the great plain as the mists come up.

But we are to hear music of another order. Tunes, or their
prototypes, that will be sung, in another generation, in the
night cafés and restaurants of Moscow. Under the gas-lit
chandeliers of the Novo-Troitski Traktir or the Moskovski
Traktir, where the Gypsy women singers of Moscow danced
and sang. Not in hovels, but in all the luxury of gilded mirrors
and plush sofas, among the barbaric wonders of Russian
cooking, sparkling Crimean wines, and champagnes from the
Don. Tunes to which we would listen, all night through, and
never tire. Not so monotonous as the Hungarian Gypsy music,
which is too formal in its beginnings. Many accounts have been
left of these famous Gypsy women singers. They sang both in
Russian and in their own language, and there were among
them artists who have never been equalled. No one could pass
any length of time in Moscow without being seduced by these
melodies, and carrying away the memory of them. The
audience, consisting chiefly of rich merchants, was quite
different from that of the capital, St Petersburg. They called
for the same tunes, over and over again, which they remembered all their lives. Melodies that evoke no imagery, and, in

* Compare Fanica Luca, the Roumanian player upon the Pan pipes.

fact, mean nothing else but the drug which is in their sentiment and rhythm. But this is, indeed, a craving which must be satisfied.

The long opening notes of the tune are repeated, two or three times over, like the casting of a net, which is thrown again and again so that nothing can escape it. Also, the musicians must mesmerize themselves. They have to feel it working in them. It quickens. The violins begin their wild leapings, and the abrupt changes of key which are the means by which they work upon the nerves and gain their hold upon them. By now, we can understand that old legend of the Orient according to which the rules of music were formed in order to tame the wild animals, and to bring harmony into the world. For it snares the senses. It is the formula of the drug that it must be repeated again and again monotonously. The primás or first violin ornaments the melody, and then plays it, in variation, against the cymbalom, while the spell works in himself, in the other musicians, and in the audience. Then it seizes him, and he leads the orchestra, playing at furious speed in counterpoint against them.

So it is among the Magyars, but, here in Moscow, the fabric of their orchestra is the balalaika, led by the cymbalom. We have the slow melody again, again; then the chorus comes, and the Gypsy choir begins to sing. After which a famous singer, one or other, takes up the song. The night music spreads contagion. Were you to walk into the crowded hall of the Moskovski Traktir, shaking the snow off your coat, or go up into one of the private rooms above, you would find half-drunken men and women laughing, and others sitting, weeping. Upon summer evenings it is the same, in the cabarets outside the city.

Here and now, we hear these tunes upon the dulcimer, and can predict the future for them. But they are played in primitive or embryonic form, not vulgarized. It is impossible they should die. By some magical alchemy, they are crowd emanations or impersonations. By the rule of numbers they must always have existed, as melodies, and can never have been written down. In the sense that they were complete already, and only needed to be gathered like the mushrooms in the field. We have said that they are exhalations or interpretations of a mood; but, in fact, they can create the mood. That must be why some tune comes into the head for no reason when we are thinking of nothing in particular. But, as regards the composition of these melodies, they do not always visit the brains of those who are prolific of such things. Did we know the true history we would find that they come, impartially, to rustic musicians who have been visited before, and to those whom the god inhabits, this once, and never again. It is quite arbitrary. There are empty shells that murmur continually, and that bear his echo in them; and those may be persons who cannot read or write, and are, in all else, of low intelligence. Others may have a knowledge and an instinct surpassing that of most musicians. For fire and inspiration, when they play, there is nothing to be compared to them. This must be because it is still a wonder and a sacred mystery, beyond logic and beyond explanation.

The process is sensual and physical, and nothing else. We have to submit to it as the hooded serpent to his charmer. We have seen that one of the secrets is repetition or reiteration, and that it must begin slowly and gently, as though to rock or lull the senses. The ornament or arabesque is a part of it. Probably the purpose of that is to distract what is more critical or resistant, in order to cast the spell behind it. This is equivalent to the voice of the anaesthetist; or to what the hypnotist may say while he bids us stare upon some glittering object in order to fix the focus of the eyes. There must be submission of the will and senses. The slow prelude, or lassú as the Magyars call it, can be drawn out, delayed indefinitely, until the trance begins to show. It may, even, be that the secret lies in mastering the hours so that they merge into one another, and none of the audience have the will to get up and leave. They are willing to spend the whole night in listening. In effect, this music could be a drug put into their glasses that destroys their resolution. A narcotic that works collectively, as in the hegemonies of insects, where all obey instinctively, and no individuals are outside the spell.

We are listening to "The Scythe" and "The Goosekeeper"; two romances which, in later years, were favourites in the night restaurants of Moscow. And we hear their real character upon this rustic instrument, where, by rusticity, we intend wooden houses and a far horizon. The tunes are potions or medicines that must be mixed with wine. But, in their simple state, we assist at the gathering of the herbs. In a dewy morning, while the rye is green. How can that be, while this simple tune turns in upon itself ? But it is as if the mere notes had a taste in them. In that, they are minor enchantments, like a vision in the crystal or upon the wall. It hangs upon the notes, so that the picture does not exist without the music. So soon as he plays, it stands out clear before the eyes, and this could happen ten or twenty times, always the same. Precise in detail, fixed, and yet it fades with inattention, for before the end of the tune we can listen to nothing but the melody. And, as it dies, the picture comes up for a moment, but dies, also, like a taste upon the tongue.

How is it that the Russian accent can inhabit but a bar or two, and be unmistakable in that? In the opening phrase, merely, of a song. That is enough. So that if it broke off, there, and went no further, there would be no mistaking it. Is it because music is a sort of shadow or parallel to speech? But let the song continue to its end! When the chorus comes, after the verse, the mystery appears again, immediately, in the shape and content of the strophe. It is not enough to say that the music follows certain racial and acknowledged lines. It is the timbre and meaning of those rules, themselves; which accepts the explanation but carries it no further. The definition, that is to say, is a matter of fact; it states the formula, but does not tell us why, and how, it works. We know the ingredients, it may be, but are not told the secret of their quantities. That is withheld, as are the savours of the earth and of the rain. It is those which give the flavour, and no mathematical formula can imitate them. Can it be because the sensibilities have been bred and nourished in these lands? Would another human race, inhabiting the same country, work in that same idiom? Certain curious traits of resemblance there would be, ghostly parallels or identities, but no more than that. Music, then, must be the ghost of speech, when it comes spontaneously, to simple souls, in inspiration: when it is born in minds that cannot read or write. But, also, it can be in the form of a riddle, that is meaningless, yet full of meaning. There can be themes that are like an epigram; a play of words; a catch; an apothegm. Freaks, like a double fruit, or the rose that has two hearts. We shall find instances of this magic. But, later, among the immortals. Not, here, in this blossoming of the plains.

The player is a Jew bred to poverty and a life of misery. We must shudder when we think of the room in which he spent his childhood. Of the slum street: excepting, always, that it was a slum of the Middle Ages, and an Eastern slum, at that, but with full rigour of the cold added to it, so that for winter raiment, the rat, the cat, the fox were skinned. But, in all things, the nationality of Gusikov must be considered, for it makes him different from the Gypsy players of the cymbalom. The genius of the race which excels in tragedy, and which interprets but does not create, found in him its opportunity. Fétis, describing Gusikov, speaks of the habitual melancholy expressed in his features; and mentions his pallor, which added to the interest aroused by his prodigious talent. To this, we could add, for our part, his distinctive Jewish dress, in which he appeared condemned to the slums, the serf of the filthy streets. And, also, to be in some sort a student of alchemy, in the long gown of the priest or wizard.*

A musician of his race, even if he could not read the notes or write down music, even though he were an instinctive and not a learned player, would be possessed of more intellect than a Hungarian Tzigane. But it is with those that he is comparable in temperament. Of the famous Bihary we are told, by Liszt, that: "When an orchestra alternating with his played at a hall he used, almost as soon as they had finished, to take up the same themes but with a new vigour . . . they no sooner came to his hand than they became Bohemian." The performances of Gusikov, when we remember that he was a dying man, called for an altogether incredible expenditure of nervous and physical energy. But we should compare, for this, the accounts of how Chopin, another consumptive, had to be carried upstairs and into the room in order that he should be seated at his instrument, during the concerts that he gave in London, and elsewhere in this country, in 1848, a few months before his death. Even so, he had not to limit himself to the more simple items of his repertoire, but was able to give a full exhibition of his powers. Chopin's songs, which were Polish and Lithuanian airs that he adapted, were of the type

---

* A portrait of Gusikov appears as frontispiece to a little book by the Viennese music publisher Schlesinger. It was printed in 1839; but I have failed to find a copy of this.

of melody played by Gusikov, who, once again we say, performed nothing but Russian, Jewish, and Polish popular tunes and dances. But these took on, immediately, a character of his own, and became the vehicles of his mind and personality.

O, what a miracle! This is the damp mists, distilled, from a clearing in the forest. No! no! it is pure music. You must not move or stir. It is leagues from anywhere, too little to be found upon a map. But its beauty is in perfect form. This you would never be given by a Tzigane player. Those have the fire: but not milk, not crystal, not perfection. Not milk of the udder; but the milk of plants and flowers. Weep! weep! Not because it has a meaning, but because it comforts and assuages. It is as though the fingers of it touched or stroked our hearts. You will be awake when you remember this; and yet its message is of sleep. It tells you that you can sleep and dream of what you will. That is the way to die: when your hand is upon the flower. For the music forgives and understands. How can that be? Ah! do not ask. It is in the phrase, and is as clear as speech. It comes again, with no other meaning. There can be no mistaking it. That is its message. In a language that has no need of words.

And another, and another. These are not folk songs, but they are taken from little plays and dramas composed in popular style, and performed at fairs up and down the country. And they come back to us as popular songs and dances played in the Tzigane style, like the tunes heard by Sarasate and transcribed by him for his violin. We can never tell, precisely, whether those are Russian or Hungarian; the truth being that they are theatre music, of no defined frontier, but with the restaurants and cafés of Moscow as their capital. Here and now, we hear them before they reached the glitter of the gaslights. This is the music that transposes men and animals and makes them weep. For no reason. It is a spell or an enchantment. You may lose the focus, for a moment, in listening to the notes, separately, but not surrendering to the tune, a sensation like that of moving swiftly past a fence or row of palings and counting them one after another, in isolation, until the eyes get weary and the stakes or hop-poles flow by, once more, in their patterns. In fact, you may break the magic, but can get back to it. Or, even, it allows you to drop out, on purpose, and pulls you in again. For the magic lies in the playing, not in the tunes themselves.

This is a song of the mushrooms in the woods. With no words; and, were there words, we should not understand them. It tells of how the mushrooms held a diet, a parliament, and went to war with the mushroom known as the borowik, the pine-lover, for their leader. With but a pair of wooden mallets, tipped with felt, the damp, lonely wood becomes alive. Ah! but it is not the picking of mushrooms. What we have in the music is October and the hunter's moon. It is a ballad in rustic accents. And the melody, after it, is so haunting and beautiful that we must dwell on every phrase so as to remember it.

Next, a little drinking song which sparkles, when shaken, as though from the flakes of gold leaf in the Danzig brandy. And a song of the linden flowers, a summer song, for the Poles take their name for the month of July, lipiec, from the linden trees, and drink a miot or honey mead in that month which is flavoured with the linden flowers, so that it is in our own tongue a flowering mead and we would celebrate this hydromel that swims with flowers. If there be wine, it is the Hungarian tokay, but mead is the national drink. Those are meadows of the red agaric and the chanterelle, or fox mushroom, from Northern parts of Poland or Lithuania, at the edge of the great forest, where the fields are damp and shaded from the trees. Here is nothing Russian. It is a different paganism, of another ancestry. We have village mazurkas and kolomyjkas coming from Ruthenia, down near Galicia, which is close to the Dniester. In order to bring back those tunes it is but necessary to cross the river.

There can be a mere phrase, of which it is not possible to bear the poignancy, that brings tears. The master of such emotions is Schubert. It has been written of the great Anton Rubinstein that he could play some simple piece by Mozart or Schubert and reduce his audience to tears. But the divine genius of those composers almost suffers from the fact of their having been human beings, having lodged, and fed, and done hack work for the publishers; it would be an advantage, positively, if those melodies were anonymous for then we have the assurance, almost, that they existed in nature. The ancient instrument, and its particular and unique development into a perfection that will never be heard again, this, too, helps the music. For the more beautiful of these melodies have a natural or rustic spontaneity that could never be imitated by the masters. On occasion, too, a depth of meaning, as though dug into the soil and into the whole human past; or, again, sacred and wonderful because meaningless, or beyond meaning, in that manner of a riddle or conundrum, of an epigram or rebus, even, the theme being equivalent to a nugget or a meteorite of mathematical and magical properties giving forth sparks and radiations, capable, musically, of being read backwards or in contrary motion, split into variation, and then continued, telescoped, as it were, in double counterpoint, or submitted generally to all the devices of the contrapuntist. This, in the hands of the greatest musical genius there has ever been, is a subject to which we shall return on another page hoping that the remarks and reactions, even of an amateur, may bear a little contribution to the sacred mystery. For this instant it is the lesser magic, but that is no less wonderful in its spontaneous flowering. Nearer, too, to the human emotions because it has no encumbrance. Laughter and tears lie as near together as flesh to the bone. They are contingent; or spring up in one another's footsteps as though their seed was carried on the winds.

Why should such gifts come, unsought, to ignorant minds; or be borne, as at this moment, from the hands of a dying man? Ah! this is something that we shall never hear again. The subtle genius of his race is inhabiting these others. The outcast, who has no home, possesses them and speaks their secrets. It is the hour of exception when all things are tranced. Persons, who are under the spell, will empty out the money from their pockets on to the table in order that he should continue playing. Meanwhile, they sit weeping as they listen. They are persons who keep quite alone, and do not move or stir. Such is the effect of music. It is an intoxication, certainly, or an hallucination. They are possessed by music, and are, mentally and physically, under its dominion. They are in his power completely. If he belonged to the race of vagabonds it would be all fire; the slow flame, and the raging, all consuming fire. For that is the Gypsy style. In their own language, and none other. All that they play becomes Bohemian, and uncontrollable. But this musician is priest or wizard, and not dervish. He is not the naked fakir who walks into the fire: who, in frenzy, tears and eats the living goat, stabs himself, gashes his own flesh, and lets the serpent bite him.

This Jew with the dulcimer has more subtle magic. It may be that because he has lived in houses he is more understanding. Those others, who are nomads by blood, cannot know the pathos of those little things that are personal belongings. Their fire is inarticulate: it is of the blood, but not of the heart or brain. Therefore, it is animal and not spiritual. It is communicable, by mass, as are sensations of fury or of panic. It requires incessant heating of the blood, for it appeals to passions that must never cool. Therefore, their ornament and the headlong, vertiginous speed with, immediately, the preluding of another melody upon the violin or the cymbalom, already foreshadowing another climax in its long-drawn phrases.

The children of the tawny race are precocious, and at an early age they are in love. From birth they are young animals. It can be seen in their springing walk, and in the manner in which they raid the villages as if to rob them. Music, to them, is a sensual pleasure like the purring of the cat that stretches up, in ecstasy, and treads with velvet paw, and jumps into your lap. It is instinctive, like the displaying of the golden pheasant when he arches his back, or tautens it to one side, and running up and down with leaping step, with flashing eye and golden hair, stiffens and distends his cape or mantle, hissing, meantime, as it might be a serpent, in order to mesmerize the hen. His display is a dance of courtship, nothing else. But the hen pays little heed to his magnificence. The cock bird displays, or shows off, for his own pleasure.

This is the attitude of the Gypsy, in music, towards other races and the secret, also of his own sensations. He makes use of it as a means to hypnotize. It is his frenzy or delirium; but to himself, as well, an ecstasy of enjoyment. He does not, even, have to learn as other men. When a violin is first put into his hand he imitates by watching the fingers of the other players, and has to get the tunes by heart. To the Gypsy, and to the Jew, as well, music was a means of sorcery. A method of obtaining mastery, and to be enjoyed as such. The child prodigy, who is a Jew, is no uncommon phenomenon, but occurring, nearly always in Eastern Europe. At twelve years of age they have learned everything there is to learn. They may never play as well again; probably because they lose their souls by constant repetition of what is already flawless and cannot be improved upon. We have to consider what music can mean to a child prodigy. And our argument points, perhaps, to the limitations of the violin. If it were another instrument he might never tire of it. The clavichord, the harpsichord, perhaps the lute, are instruments capable of lifelong improvement and exploration. Those are personal instruments of fresh discovery and endless beauty, as, in this instance, was the straufiedel or cymbalom of Gusikov. His ancestors, before they begged their way from slum to slum, could have been minstrels in the Tartar camp.

Most of our music is Italian. Its line of beauty is from the Mediterranean. Even if it comes from the green fields, or from the stone walls and border towers; even if it be a madrigal, a fantasy for a chest of viols, a pavane, a galliarde, or divisions on a ground. Its greatness, when it flies with wings, is in an air which is Italian, though permuted behind the mullions on winter nights of wind and snow. Toccata, pastorale, or passacaglia, all are Italian, in origin, and by name. But this is music from another world. Blown by the long winds out of the kibitkas or the tents of felt, moved with the nomads to where the grass was sweet and the wilderness was pied with flowers. There you could have heard this instrument, or its counterfeit. The germ of this music was no Italian serenade, but an epic upon the harp and sheepskin drum, played at the moment when the conqueror lifted up his victim's skull, and drank from it. Such was the frenzy, or the seizure in this music. Its time for love was when the khanum stood in her golden gown, stiff with gold, and with her train held up by her maidens. Behind her mask of white lead or antimony, which was white with the cosmetic, and like a mask of paper. In the distance there were four towers of skulls, built up as high as you could throw a stone, a row of skulls, and then a row of clay. The countrymen told how, at night, a bright light seemed to be burning on the tops of all the towers of skulls. Behind that, the sky was pale and greenish and entirely empty.

The cymbalom, in spite of the extraordinary resources of his

particular instrument is inadequate for so consummate a performer. It is the same sensation that is given by the greatest
pianists. The single keyboard is not enough. In much of his
music we hear the Berecynthian rattle. This was the giant
cymbalom or dulcimer carried by the Scythian Horde in the
vanguard of their battles. It was the ancestor, too, of the music
of the Turkish Janissaries. Their bells and drums and cymbals
were in imitation of its sound. Called Berecynthian after the
clashing cymbals, drums, tabrets, bucklers, of the Corybantes,
who were priestesses of Cybele. In fact, the giant cymbalom
was the consensus of that noise. But, in the Scythian horde, it
preluded among the horsemen.

The musician stood, erect, in a waggon that was a ten-
wheeled chariot, and played while it moved along the steppe.
He played them into battle, and at the feasting afterwards,
when they ate horses roasted whole, entire, served up with
their heads, and drank fermented mares' milk. At such nomad
feasts the musician was sometimes an "Indian", which is to
say he may have been a Gypsy, and at other times he was a
wandering Jew. He went everywhere with the Tartar warriors
and formed part of their military establishment. When great
towns were captured, musicians rode at head of the procession
for the triumphal entry. They played the Tartar Horde into
the burning ruins. Historical survivals of this practice were the
Gypsy violinists who accompanied the Wallachian voivodes on
their wars. It comes down from Attila and his Huns, and is
true of all the great nomad conquerors down to Tamerlane.
The Mongol, Batu Khan, who brought Gypsy coppersmiths
from Central Asia with his army when he invaded the Danubian provinces, in the twelfth century, which was the earliest
irruption of the Gypsies into Europe, had "Indian", that is
to say Gypsy, or Jewish minstrels with him. No certain
description of this instrument has come down to us. It is but
a legend: and a name for intoxication and delirium.

But we hear wild cries and the beating of the cymbals. Then,
sharp blows, as it were the striking of an anvil. In imagination,
these give sparks of flame. It is the nomad coppersmiths, or
armourers, who come forth from their dark tents and take up
the din. They have the long hair of the fire eater or snake
charmer, and wear rags that are singed and blackened by the

flame. At that early date they are still Indian. The shadow of
the great Indian sun is upon their skins. For their burnt bodies
are the colour of their copper cauldrons. Now we hear a loud
twanging, as of strings or wires that are tried, and then tight-
ened. The same note is struck again, again, but with the fingers,
which are more sensitive than the plectrum. Those chords
suggest a race of archers. They must have bow rings made of
bone or ivory. From every direction there comes the neighing
of mares and stallions, and the bleating of herds of longhorned sheep. But, above that, comes the testing and the tuning
of the strings. It must be a huge instrument, and there is
more than one of them.

The ten-wheeled chariots have the mares attached to them,
for part of the music is the stamping of the hooves. Now, loud
and tremendous, it begins. The players, like charioteers, are in
long white gowns. But there are no fillets on their foreheads to
bind their hair. Their hair flows, loose and long, upon their
shoulders. They are the furies, urging into war. They move
their whole arms, as though they strike with blacksmiths'
hammers. It is a giant dulcimer: the tremendous shakes and
arpeggios sweep the air. There can have been no other such
preluding. Two or more of the huge dulcimers sound forth
together and strike out the theme, with that terrific rattle which
commands and exults. Long as a death rattle, and leading into
that. The waggons move forward. The horses paw the earth,
and rear up on the rein. At the same moment all the tents are
down. The Berecynthian sistrum is not one instrument alone,
but the giant cymbaloms or dulcimers, and trumpets, drums,
and copper cauldrons. But the players of the dulcimer are
possessed by fury, as though they ran amok, or slew in frenzy.
It is darker, darker; and to more of the long tremendous
shaken rattlings the whole Horde moves on.

Now, with the fingers of one hand, he sweeps the notes. It
is part of the *Midsummer Night's Dream* of Mendelssohn, as
though played upon the virginals or clavichord. Preluding, in
magic, with glissandos, up and down the scale, in the manner
of the cymbalon or dulcimer. A magical underworld opens;
as if to that wave of the fingers, as if they held the key. It is
curious how, in this, he speaks with a foreign accent. A
nocturne: ah! but this is the greenwood of Arden upon

Midsummer Night, while the nightingale is singing and there are little, mysterious noises that no one can explain. It is so exquisite that everyone is in tears. The little dance dies down. The glissandos come again. We hear the last notes played, which mean the ending. And the echoes of this magic die away. It is impossible to move or stir.

Then, like someone who is dying, who puts out his hand, he takes up the hammers of the dulcimer, but as though the room was in darkness, or in a dying light, and preludes upon the notes. We are in that street of Mohilev; or near by, in the little town where he was born. For the music has the intonation of the spoken word: and these are the last words of a dying man. There will be no more. Only a phrase or two, and it is ended.

The whole town is in darkness as we drive away.

RELIZANE*

W H E N we got to Relizane it was noon, and noon is the hour of rest. The heat was formidable, desperate, and what wind there was panted in little gasps just loudly enough to stir the dust. It would begin like a quick gust of temper, would spring round upon its heel, whirl up into a spiral, and be gone like the snuffing of a candle. And soon it would come again, near by, as though there could never be peace or calm, as if the leaves had never given shade at mid-day, as if all living things had not the ghosts of shadow, their own ghosts of their own height, to hide in.

This town of Relizane is a French colony, and so it has a square, or *place*, in the middle of it, and here stood the only hotel in the town. But what was this upon the ground? It was trussed like a chicken. It moved. It walked. It rather hurried. There was, as well, the clumsiness of the grasshopper about it, for its legs were jointed the wrong way, and their ends, where the feet should have been, were stunted and withered. In fact, they were not feet; they were knobs of flesh, all dusty and stained from the road. They were trailed along it; they were never used.

Instead, he used his hands, and they were protected with wooden soles, tied over the wrists with a band of leather. This was how he walked, dragging his legs behind him.

This terrible being, who was young—not twenty years of age—smiled up in a happy way out of the dust, as though there was some good joke at the traveller's expense. He knew no better of life than this, and could not suspect on whom the joke really rested. But it seemed irresistibly funny to his half-idiot brain, and he found it difficult to compromise between a smile of welcome and a roar of laughter.

The grin made his face round and young, and it credited him with a little more sense than he really possessed. His skin was

* From *Touching the Orient*, 1934.

yellow and dusty, with marks, like scratches, on his face where the dust had been rubbed; in fact, his colour was that of the true Algerian. And he wore a newly bought fez, which, somehow, added an additional horror to all his circumstances.

There was every sign that he would wait outside while the travellers ate their luncheon in the hotel, and, with this to look forward to, we walked in. It was a commercial hotel. The walls were covered with coloured engravings given by manufacturers of cheap goods, and a few of them had calendars attached. It might have been any hotel in the French provinces, somewhere sufficiently far south for the flies to be troublesome.

This pest was very evident in the dining-room, but it was crowded, in spite of this, with Frenchmen who were resident in the colony, who hung up their hats every day on the same hook, and bowed every day, in the same direction, to the same fellow-guest.

The proprietor had greater pains to spare for travellers who had arrived in their own motor-car, and he came towards us, menu in hand, with a peculiar mechanical slowness of gait. He was lethargic, leaden of step, and seemed unable to raise his head from his chest. He shuffled towards us in slippers, never lifting his feet from the ground. But the heaviest thing about him were his eyes. The eyeballs were immensely swollen, and showed such an area of white round his pupils that he was given a perpetual stare. It was difficult to believe that he could shut his eyes.

His personality seemed to be embedded in, as it were, a film of white wax, under which he could just be seen moving. He made one think of the larva of an insect, of a grub in its cell. He was comfortably established, and would feed on the food so close to his body.

But he was ill, very ill, very lethargic, very sluggish. His life must be a trailing misery to him. So the iron of Relizane was entering into the soul. There was not a thing about the town that was not horrible.

It was not easy to eat, until the sight of the black scullions brought a sort of reassurance with it. And there were some barefooted negresses in bright colours, with folded red turbans, who came in with dishes of food and never spoke a word, but gave their due of domestic atmosphere to the scene. Dark skins

can never look dirty beside pale ones, and, indeed, the sight of
a white person in the kitchen of this hotel would have been the
final horror of Relizane. The stained table-cloths were as nothing to this possibility.

Luncheon over, there remained that person to be confronted
who was waiting outside the hotel. He had been joined by
others; and now we were told that something had gone wrong
with the motor, which would mean a delay of half an hour.
There was nothing to be done. The only course was to climb
into the motor and wait.

The most extraordinary fantasia of beggary played itself
before the eyes, and it would be impossible to imagine a more
complete epitome of misery from its sharpest and most dramatic angles. This was what mean whites had brought to the
indigènes, and, in recoil, it was springing back upon themselves,
as shown in the sleepy-sickness of the white hotel-proprietor.
That was almost the least of these possible evils. For, at any
rate, it was a dulling, a padding of the senses. He was only just
conscious out of that film of white wax. He could shuffle round
to his customers, could speak to them, could even add up their
bills. Probably he was born in Relizane, for as a settlement it is
some eighty years old; and, if this was so, he was being paid
back for some of the faults of the older generation. They had
much to answer for.

But there was no time to think of him, for these evils before
the eyes claimed every moment of attention. While this lasted,
nothing else in all the world existed.

The first beggar had been joined by five or six more, and
they huddled close together, each odiously near to his hated
rival. This suggested that they lived as much upon each other
as upon the spectator, and soon the truth of this began to
play.

The original beggar was the oldest of them all: the others
were hardly more than children. It did not seem as if a single
one of them had the strength or the ability to hold himself
upright. They were all crouched in the dust.

The next one to catch the attention had withered arms, and
his hands, by that curious atavism of the idiot and the imbecile,
were long and thin like a monkey's, but flat and twisted, with
no life in them, as though this was a monkey whose fingers had

275

been caught or crushed in some trap or machine. It must be hard for him to feed himself with those hands that could hold nothing.

The other children were just as bad. One was thin as a rake, with ribs showing through his shirt; teeth, preternaturally big, that could be seen, or so it seemed, through his drawn cheeks; and skin like dusty parchment unduly stretched. Another was a speechless imbecile, whose guttural, uncouth sounds in their more ordinary mode of idiocy were even somewhat of a relief before the more extravagant horrors of the rest.

For they were covered with sores that the flies did not neglect, or were crippled in such violent fashion that their parents must have twisted back their limbs, soon after birth, as you break a stick for the fire, that does not quite part, but hangs down beside itself, with nothing but the bark, or skin, to join its severed pieces.

The whole lot of them were now sharing in the joke, and it kept them so amused that they never looked up at us. They felt our eyes on them instead.

The joke was of the eternal sort; it was probably months, or even years, old.

The one of them whose sores were the worst flourished a stick in his hand. He had begun to wave this about as though he meant harm with it, and presently, at his bidding, they all shuffled themselves nearer to that thin child with the yellow parchment skin. He was playing with a rosary of wooden beads, the sort the very poorest Mohammedans hold in their hands. This must have been his only possession, other than his clothes; but he was so stupid that he did not know it was in danger, and kept telling the beads idly with his fingers. It was just a facet of their joke, just a little thing touching its circumference, only an episode.

Another moment, and he was given a nasty hit on his hands and the rosary was wrenched away from them. Immediately his face curled up and he began to cry. But he never moved, or made the slightest attempt to get away from them. He sat perfectly still, and nothing in him had altered except the expression of his face. The corners of his lips turned up, as if with the taste of something bitter, and presently—but only presently—the tears came. His crying was of an ugly, chatter-

ing sort, but the others were not going to allow him to mono-
polize the attention for ever.

Instead, they moved on to the idiot-child who could not
speak, and, at once, their plan revealed itself. He could not
talk, but they were going to make him cry. A good hit in his
ribs with the end of the stick soon accomplished this, and it
was a hearty, ordinary cry, perhaps the only normal thing it
was in his power to do.

Meanwhile, the original beggar—the one who had been
there all the time—was dreading trouble. He started to tremble,
to shake all over, from head to foot, as if the blow had fallen
already. It was like a kind of palsy. It made one wonder if he
had not been shivering all this time unnoticed, because of the
worse horrors he had wrong with him.

Another bully had come up and joined them, and his powers
of evil were only held in check—were only delayed, as it were—
by an atrophied leg, strapped down, as if he was kneeling on
one knee, on to a wooden stump. What speed he had was the
result of hopping on the other leg; and he seemed to think
that he was late for the fun by the hurry with which he arrived.

He might have been the brother of the bully with the stick;
and the pair of them, together with two more who seemed to
have nothing worse wrong with them than a nest of sore places,
were now the only ones still appreciating the joke. The others
saw it from a different side.

The next thing was going to be a quarrel between the two
bullies for the possession of the stick. The newly arrived bully
had the advantage of mobility over the other, and he hopped
about in a way that reminded one of boys on a football-field
when they play about before the game begins, and one of them
will keep his foot on the ball while he hops on his other foot.
They were both roaring with laughter, showing their white
native teeth, and apparently enjoying themselves.

But they closed and grappled with each other, and the stick
had changed owners in a moment. The new bully had been left
out of the fun. He was going to catch up and enjoy himself.
His way of doing this was to give a hard knock to every one of
them. And the crippled wretch who had been crying for nothing was given a real pain to weep for.

But the others, when they were given their second hit,

stopped crying. The bully knew who were the weak ones, and, while the others had gone silent from anger, he gave more blows to the dumb child, and hit, again, the hopeless cripple and the shaking yellow child. The others had begun laughing once more: it was very funny to be on the safe side of the trouble.

What use was it giving them money? If one gave to the weak, it would only be taken away by the strong the moment one's back was turned. If things were nasty, now, they would be far nastier, then. There would be an orgy of bullying; but it was impossible to resist giving, and so the most appalling of them got a handful of coppers.

Meanwhile, the three weakest of them were still crying, and there seemed to be no reason why they should stop, having once begun. They were born into the world crying.

As for the child with the yellow parchment skin, he was still shuddering, but dryly, for his face showed no sign of tears.

But the war, having died down, now began all over again. Apparently the results had not been good enough. The skeleton child with the yellow skin knew what was coming and wept out loud. Even those who had stopped crying kept silent and looked serious. This time the bully meant to hurt them.

He had already struck a blow at one child when the door of the hotel opened and a Frenchman came out. He went up, at once, to the bully, took the stick away from him, broke it in two with his hands, and threw it away.

Then the whole truth dawned. They were blind, all blind. There was not one of them who could see.

But the Frenchman was not sorry for any of them. He kicked at every limb he could reach.

They squirmed away, touched at the wall, and were gone. A moment or two later the motor was repaired and we left the town.

We saw a huddle of rags down the corner of the next street, and, in the midst of it, stood, or as near as possible stood, the two bullies. They were sharing out the coppers.

So another truth was apparent. They were a concert-party. It was organized brutality, and they had not cried for nothing. But that, also, was the bully's part of the business. They had to see to it that the tears were genuine.

And, before they had stopped quarrelling, we were a mile or two from Relizane, on the road to Oran.

SHADOW*

Let it be August, the ilex month.

How still it is! Not a leaf is moving. Holly and privet line the walks—but now the deep wood comes. Here are husks or ghosts of bluebells, the corpse of blue hyacinth, unburied and rattling its dead bones. To one side, the hanging wood falls in soil of leaf mould to a breathless lake.

It is enough, enough. This must be no known solitude.

Come deep into the wood and lose yourselves. For, now, the enchantment will begin. Who is there who could walk into a wood and never listen nor look round? There are so many mysteries or silences, so many sighings in the leaves. Think of your own youth, which is going, or has gone. One has passed you with noiseless footfall; or has dropped behind. Who is there, that would not weep for this? It is the world, our world, and it withers in a day.

And yet, it is only August, the pompous high meridian, the Augustan month. The August noon burning on the water. For there is the whole day to waste. The August noon glittering on the waters, the flashing of the oars, when it is too hot to look. For we have to come here to think of this, away from poverty or riches. And who is this first phantom? A tall thin young woman in a pellisse of green sheepskin and a wide-brimmed hat, who walks between the hedges upon the smoother grass. She has long, thin hands, and jet black rings and bracelets. She has sloping shoulders, and picks her way among the fallen twigs. And from her shadow the wood leads on into poetry. For her love is poetry, she lives within a phrase. Look at her once more for there will never be her like again among women!

This is the world of those who have transcended life, and been kept outside it. Of those who will never live again, for they have an immortality that is not physical. In this wood, this place of waiting, one will not speak to another: all are solitary.

* From *Sacred and Profane Love*, 1940.

Their own world holds them. For her, the goatfoot waterfalls leap from rock to rock; the reflections in the water of cupolas and gables are the lake, itself, become a Georgian stables; the shadows are manteaux espagnoles over the long and the light summer land. Her ghost is a personal spectre: but why should I not speak of her? This is my master from whom I learned and there can never be her like again. But look into her features and see their tragic bones, her Dantesque profile in the mirror pane. We wrote in communion with one another and mine will always be the freedom of her world.

But we must open and be less melancholy! For this is the world as it has been, and as it might have been. Let us go quickly to where we breathe its air. Once more we may find that tall thin young woman, lying, this time, under a fruit-tree that is in blossom and reading a book of poetry in the long, lush grass. Or sitting, it may be, in the garden of a London square. The pear tree is in flower and the long grass waves above the page. How lovely to be young and to feel poetry running in your veins! It will be Swinburne or William Morris that she reads: August, or In the Orchard, from *Poems and Ballads*; Anactoria; Golden Wings, or The Blue Closet. Such are poems of pear or apple blossom to be read in the springtime of one's life. But, as well, the Fleurs du Mal darken this paradise, as though with lines of rain. It is poetry of the blood's decline. And her own images begin to form. Metaphors of a bony personality, of hard dry brilliance, nothing soft nor milky, of dogskin leaves and furry buds, of landscapes and persons that have never been before. And then, Ah! then, my world begins to grow. This wood leads on into infinity. I wander in the orange grove and feel the red gold globes. I hear a barrel organ, and know they dance to it. Then, Actæon, stag antlered, comes out through the trees; we hear the horn of Orion: Krishna dances with the milkmaids: Midas and his men pick cherries, standing on long ladders: Cupid and Campaspe play their game of cards for kisses. Fantasies of the hot South come like tunes from the mind that made them. For, now, it is another world. And we have the whole earth before it sinks, or burns.

FESTIVAL AT NOLA*

I. NIGHT AT SANTA LUCIA.

"Rends-moi le Pausilippe et la mer d'Italie."—GÉRARD DE NERVAL

U PON such a night as this it is impossible to sleep. All Naples sings: or strums the mandoline.† It is because the god of music has persisted here, but lingers only in the trembling of the lute string. The mask of Pulcinella is scribbled on the walls. A man runs past in rags; and the mules and horses are thin as ghosts from the knacker's yard.

Here are booths of amulets and sacred emblems. There is a smell of wax. These are the candle shops. Little plaster statuettes show saints or sinners writing in the fire. We are among the statues. You will see wings being fitted to a wooden doll. Gods and goddesses are for sale in the workshops. And, at the corners, there are barrows for old clothes.

Here are water melons, "Redder than the fire of Vesuvius", as the peddlars cry them: apricots, "There's cinnamon inside": pears are "Ladies' thighs. We adore them!" grapes are "Gold, not grapes": nuts, "As fine as quails' legs". Here are booths of lemonade with festoons of lemons. Here are the stalls of pizza, flat pancakes cooked with cheese and tomatoes; and bladders of goat's cheese, or mozzarella. Men, old and young, and a few women, drink sanguinaccio, made from chocolate and pig's blood, which improves the constitution.

* From *Primitive Scenes and Festivals*, 1942.
† The Festival of St Paulinus, at Nola, is described in *Siciliana: sketches of Naples and Sicily in the Nineteenth Century*, by Ferdinand Gregorovius, translated from the German by Mrs Gustavus W. Hamilton (London, G. Bell & Sons, 1914), pp. 111–123. It is taken from *Wanderjahre in Italien*, published, in German, in 1853. My account of the festival is based upon this. The translation by Mrs Gustavus W. Hamilton is, in itself, a work of art. A few of her sentences and phrases I have quoted in entirety, because it is impossible to improve upon them. My account of the festival, indeed, is a picture based, as it were, upon a sketch by Gregorovius. This is the place, perhaps, in which to remind readers, not only of the *History of the City of Rome* by Gregorovius; but, also, of his *Roman Journals, 1852–1874*, translated by Mrs Gustavus W. Hamilton (G. Bell & Sons).

281

Here are stalls of syrups: and flower stalls of roses and carnations. You cannot see the sky for strings of washing.

It is a phantasmagoria: an hallucination. What we see are living phantoms. For this is ninety or a hundred years ago. Here are the Pulcinella theatres, with Pulcinella's house at the entrance, whence the snapping tones of the mannikin are heard above the siren waves. For stone steps descend down to the water's edge, and it is an open paved foreshore, as it could be the stage of a huge theatre set for a crowd scene. A sea piazza for a marine festival. The lazzaroni sleep, everywhere, upon the pavement and the sea wall, in their rags and stocking caps, the cap of a tarantella dancer. The mask of Pulcinella upon the wall becomes the symbol of the town.

It is Santa Lucia, the fishermen's quarter down by the waters of the Bay. Here are the oyster stalls. But, as well, all kinds of shellfish are offered in this horn of plenty. It is like a fair or market. Here, too, the nymphs of night cast their nets for strangers. This is the city of Parthenope, a siren or sea nymph whose naked body was found upon the shore. These are her daughters.

This is Santa Lucia of old Naples, long pulled down.

To-morrow, we rise early. But who could sleep to-night? We can see the volcano and the rock of Capri. It all lies before us. In their season there are cliffs of violet and narcissus where Procida and Ischia float upon the milky seas. With vales of lemon and pomegranate trees. The goatherd stays upon the mountain, looking down:

> *To isles of fragrance, lily-silver'd vales*
> *Diffusing languor to the panting gales:*
> *To lands of singing and of dancing slaves,*
> *Love-whisp'ring woods and lute-resounding waves.*

It is late: but there is no end to the music and the singing. In this town of the volcano and the tarantella. The town of Southern superstition. The urn into which Campania pours her grapes; where the Bay loads the cornucopia with shells and fishes.

We hear, all night, the twang of the guitar. Through the open shutters, from the balcony. While the bells of many convents, some cracked, some strident, strike the restless hours.

Here is the tunnel, hewn by convicts. And the tomb of Virgil. The oleander, even in the darkness, blooms before the palace of pink walls. In wooden tubs at foot of the great stair. But we would have no palaces. We would, sooner, the oyster stalls and fishing nets. And the mask and cap of Pulcinella.

The early morning is virginal, but sordid. On the way to the railway station, through the mean streets, we meet the galley slaves, guarded by soldiers, and marching two by two, clanking their heavy chains. Some are wearing blood-red, the colour of fraud and infamy. Turning a corner, we see Vesuvius and the Bay. It is June 26th: the morning of the festival at Nola.

II. FESTIVAL OF ST PAULINUS

For an hour, or a little more, the train goes through the Campanian plain. On every side are vines as high as houses. Nola is twenty miles from Naples,* and not far from Aversa, the birthplace of Pulcinella; whose image, or prototype, works in the vineyards in soiled white linen coat and cap and trousers. In the dog days of August he may be nearly naked in this classic land. For it was at Nola that Augustus Cæsar died: and the peasant still drinks red wine from a two-handled amphora of terracotta. But Nola has its own Campagna, where the vines are trained on stunted elms and apple trees, and there are terraces of lemon and pomegranate trees. They are apples, indeed, of a special and late sort, that taste of lime and honey. Never hidden for long, we see the cone and plume of smoke from Vesuvius.

But the excitement grows. It is not enough that the flat-topped houses of one storey are the home of Pulcinella. For we are approaching the most extraordinary of all festivals in a

* Nola was an important town in classical antiquity. Hannibal was defeated here, by Marcellus; while Augustus Cæsar died at Nola in A.D. 14. At the present time it is a town of some ten thousand inhabitants. St Paulinus was born in Gascony in A.D. 315, his father being a Roman Prefect of Gaul. He was converted to Christianity at Bordeaux, and having been made Consul was appointed to Campania. He became bishop of Nola, and was famous as a poet and religious author. He died A.D. 431, and is buried in the Church of S. Bartolommeo in Rome. Whilst he was Bishop of Nola, the only son of a widow in that town was taken by the Vandals into slavery in Libya. St Paulinus set out to rescue him, and became a slave himself. It was upon his return to Nola from servitude that he was met by the inhabitants of Nola, dancing and carrying obelisks in front of them. The festival was celebrated, ever after, on June 26th. St Paulinus was made the subject of a Latin epic by Saverino de Rinaldis, in imitation of Virgil, called the *Paolineide*. This poem may contain further clues to the festival.

Mediterranean land. And the roads have become long clouds of golden dust. Through these dash the calessos and carricolos, two-wheeled open carriages going at full gallop, crowded with anybody who can cling to them. Cross-gartered peasants in the peaked hat of Fra Diavolo; monks and priests; children beyond counting; and peasant women wearing the striped dresses with puffed sleeves of the district, and the mucador or headdress of the country, a veil folded in classical manner upon the back of the head. As to the galloping horses, they have loud and jingling harness, their manes are twisted with flowers, and pheasants' tail feathers nod above their necks. Crowds are pouring in from Naples and from all Campania to the festival.

We have arrived at Nola. But no one can walk at his ordinary pace towards the town. All are hurrying, or running. The railway station is a little distance from the walls. And here the fair and the great festival begin. More than ever it is a phantasmagoria, an hallucination. One must go carefully and forget nothing of what is to be seen.

The walls of the town have been covered with gigantic pictures, painted in a frenzy, where the masters of old Italy have come down to the gutter, working all night and for a day before. Decorations for a slum inferno; painted wings of houses; Cupids of the mean lodgings; a garlic-eating Harlequin; the family of Pulcinella; the volcano and the golden Bay; and the "gran Foca marina", the monster, or sea-calf, shown to the public in an ancient tower. Musicians and town criers make incessant fanfares and trumpet blasts, as though for a circus entrance, and the effect of this perpetual repetition of an opening phrase or flourish is both exciting and pitiful. These fanfares, which will linger for long afterwards in the memory, sounding suddenly, for no reason, in the silence of the night, are so many frantic appeals to be heard above the others, and not to be allowed to starve. They are military ghosts: trumpeters dying on the field of battle, who with their last breath lift the trumpet to their lips. Yet pariahs, street Arabs of the Neapolitan slums. Tritons, too, who play their conch horns before the shell of Amphitrite, the sea-goddess, who, in metamorphosis of the fair is none other than the "Gran Foca marina", the sea-calf who is an exhibition in the tower. With a hired band of music to proclaim her, she journeys from town to town, and came to

Nola, last night, drawn in a tank of water on a waggon. Mute goddess, who lifts her seal-like neck and looks pitifully around her in her prison tower. The trumpet blasts that surround and accompany her can mean nothing to her animal mind but cries for food and cries for love. Her mammal soul, and the souls of ten or twenty men, are in a drove, a finny herd, together.

Every kind of stall has been set up at the entrance to the town. Their purpose is to catch the crowds before they get into the streets. The hucksters are calling out with all the force of Southern lungs. It is not exactly a market, for the crowd pours through it in one direction towards the town. Most of them are carrying little coloured flags, and have bought emblems or amulets of St Paulinus, as well as food and flasks of wine. But, as well, every conceivable object is for sale. Green umbrellas, pigs and sheep, strings of sausages, mortadella, cheap crockery.

But a strange and wonderful sight makes one breathless and gives the sacred tingling to the skin. It is announced by the trumpet and the drum. Something moves: it is a curtain drawn aside. The actors come out on to a trestle, and the curtain falls back behind them. We behold another race, of Areöis, of strolling players, who spend their lives in travelling from town to town, exhibiting their performances, and spreading the contagion of the stage. Some instinct tells one they are of different race. They are standing on two planks set up on trestles before their booth or theatre. There is no time to stay. The crowds press us on. But it is something that will for ever haunt the memory. Four or five actors and two women, or soubrettes. Of a race apart, as it could be priests or temple prostitutes. Where are they now? Still travelling with some fair? For the circus music does not change so much. But it is wonderful to see them in the sunlight of an early morning amid the fanfares and the frenzied voices. A mandoline hangs by a ribbon from a nail. Columbine, the dove, the gentle singer, lifts it down and holds it in her hands. It is impossible to hear her; but she begins to sing. The other dances, and holds a tambourine. There is a clown, a comic Bacchus, camp follower of his Indian triumph; a young man who is poet or pierrot of the company; and a person cast for tragedy. Their voices are quite lost in all the din, so that it could be one of those common nightmares in which you call for

20   285

help and cannot make a sound. No one listens: or looks at them
for longer than a moment. Everyone is hurrying, or running
past.

We are carried on, as though to an assault upon the town.
Looking back, we see them work their blandishments; but all
in vain. No one has the strength, or patience. All press forward
into the town; entering through a breach in the walls or fortifications, a place where those have just crumbled and the fallen
stones lie, one upon another. Not a gate or solemn entrance
into Nola. But there are many lanes and alleys leading from it,
into which the crowd disperse to find the quickest way to the
piazza. For the Piazza del Duomo is the centre of the festival.
But these alleys are dark. The sun has not yet come down to
them. And in their silence, where there is no other sound than
that of hurrying footsteps, we hear behind, in front of us, and
to every side, the noise and music of the fair.

But, of a sudden, noisy and discordant music bursts upon
the ear. Of a curious, halting, swaying rhythm. As though it is
moving slowly forward. Tottering from side to side. Can this
be imagination? In the distance there are shouts and fanfares.
Furious blasts of the trumpet; and the fevered sensation that
every window in the tall houses may open like a showman's
box, a Punch and Judy theatre. With gaunt and bright movements of which we will not know the hidden drama. But it
grows louder and steadier. It is coming in our way. We are to
see the pagan mystery.

Here it is. Down this side street, and moving towards us.

A tower, or monster, tottering in its steps, in midst of an
immense crowd. Taller than the houses to either side; and
rushing one in ecstasy or delirium from Campania to India.
For it is entirely Indian in this moment. Yet, not. It is a tower,
or obelisk, of five storeys. We recognize Corinthian columns
in every storey, and a frieze and niches. But the whole obelisk
glitters, or coruscates, red and gold and silver. The columns
are bright ruby red with tinsel; and, in their shadows, red like
Bengal fires. The tower is gold paper and gilt paint, figured
with saints and angels on a golden background. Paladins, also,
in gold and silver armour, troops of cherubs, painted genii,
false draperies and curtains, golden arabesques and flowers;
while this painted population hold in their hands gilded palm

leaves, wreathes of flowers, and the spilling cornucopia. Many of the saints are dressed like Roman warriors; or wear the golden buskins of an actor. In the lowest storey of the obelisk there sit a choir of young girls, virgins, dressed in white, and garlanded with flowers. Above them, on a level with the first floor windows of the houses, there is a band of trumpets and kettledrums, with triangles and cornets. The obelisk is borne upon the shoulders of about thirty porters; and has just begun to move. It had been waiting, and is now ready. It advances. Tottering; and swaying like a palanquin.

It has passed us, and moves slowly on, standing higher than the roofs of the houses, with an extraordinary sound of creaking and fluttering, a straining of ropes, and a shaking and jostling of its many statues. Down one street, and then another, this huge obelisk proceeds, directed, it would seem, by instinct or the group soul of the bearers. At its apex, a saint with a golden nimbus glitters in the sun, above the tiled and lichened roofs. We follow, walking in the crowd. And now there is a burst of music from a different side, and the summits of another and then another obelisk appear above the housetops. All these moving towers are proceeding in the same direction towards the cathedral.

What are these gigantic obelisks?

They are the guglie di San Paolino. The guglia is a form of religious monument that is peculiar to Naples, and found no-where else. A marble obelisk in several storeys, or we could call them members, topped by a statue of the Madonna or a saint. Their shape is that of the flame of a candle, the jet of a fountain, and up all their height they have masks and bas-reliefs, and balustrades and statues. There are three of them at Naples.* The guglia del Gesú, outside the church of Il Gesú Nuovo, with its façade of stones cut into diamond points, is the most elaborate of all, and springs sixty or seventy feet into the air, surmounted by a statue of the Virgin, an exuberant and bubbling monument of marble, diamond-shaped, itself, in plan, and set at an angle to the Gesú. Nothing in architecture is more

* The other two guglie in Naples are that of San Domenico, in front of the church of that name; and of San Gennaro, which is in a piazza at back of the cathedral. Their date is, approximately, 1690–1730. There is a connection between these Neapolitan guglie and such monuments of the Austrian Baroque as the Trinity column in the Graben at Vienna, designed by the Italian theatre painter, Burnacini.

287

expressive of the vitality of the Neapolitans than these baroque obelisks. Here, at Nola, the marble of the guglia (which means lily) has been metamorphosed into an obelisk that moves, and is inhabited by living persons. It is a tower with motion. A triumphal car, a juggernaut made from a pyramid, a living fountain.

As to the origin of the guglie di San Paolino it is probable that some form of triumphal car had been used in the festival since early times. They were, as we shall know presently, made anew every year by the different Guilds of Nola, and we may assume that they followed in their decoration the fashion of the day. They will have been late Gothic, according to the Neapolitan Gothic of their time; and have gone through the various phases of the Renaissance to Baroque. But, when the guglie were set up in the square of Naples, the inspiration communicated itself immediately to the inhabitants of this provincial town, and the pattern became fixed. They designed a guglia that could be carried through the streets; that could tower up above the houses; that carried living persons, singers and musicians; and that gave such opportunities to the carver and the gilder. At the time when we see the moving towers of Nola, in the last days of the Kingdom of the Two Sicilies, the type had been followed in its deviations for a hundred years and more. Being so essentially Neapolitan, the spirit of it faded with the passing of their independence. A few years later it had lost its force. We see it, therefore, in its prime, when Campania down to the city and the Bay was a land of singing and of dancing slaves.

The guglie of Nola are constructed in this manner. A high wooden scaffolding with canvas sides is set up in the street close to the house of the head of each Guild. The screen of canvas keeps the work secret, and protects each obelisk and its artificers against the weather. And so the guglia begins to grow; hidden on three sides, and with boughs of myrtle and green branches on the fourth, where the obelisks nearly touch upon the houses. The work continues for six months. By early June the guglia has begun to rise above the roofs. It is growing like the Indian mango tree.

Each Guild, or Arte, makes its guglia. And every one of them is to be known by the principal statue on its front. Judith glittering with gold, holds a dripping head of Holofernes upon the obelisk of the Husbandmen or Reapers. But this group of sculpture only fills the niche upon the middle storey. Upon the highest floor of every guglia there stands an angel swinging a censer; above this a golden cupola or a gilded flower; and, on top of all, the statue of a saint. On the guglia of the Husbandmen or Reapers it is St George with the cross of Malta and a white flag in his hand. But besides this, as a distinguishing sign, each obelisk has an emblem hanging from the frieze of its main storey. The Husbandmen and Reapers have a sickle; the Bakers two huge loaves; the Butchers a joint of meat; the Gardeners a pumpkin; the Tailors a white waistcoat; the Cobblers a shoe; the Grocers a cheese; the Wine Merchants a fiasco. And, as well, each obelisk has a man to walk in front of it, carrying a particular emblem. A silver pillar is borne in this manner before the obelisk of the Wine Merchants; and on this pillar lies a wine barrel, held by two little statues of St Peter and St Paul. The Guild of Gardeners is more fanciful. It is preceded by a handsome youth who holds a cornucopia, and smiles upon the crowd.

Standing in the Piazza del Duomo we see, and hear, the coming of the guglie. From every quarter of the town the obelisks are on the march. Each has a choir in its lowest storey; and above that, the cornets and kettledrums, the triangles and trumpets. There are nine obelisks in all. They advance, tottering in their steps, and halt every now and then to give a rest to their bearers. No sight could be more thrilling than the convergence of so many marching towers. Several streets lead into the Piazza; and one or more obelisks, to their own music, advance down every street. The giant of giants belongs to the Guild of Farmers. It is one hundred and two palms in height; or between sixty and seventy feet from the shoulders of the bearers up to the golden nimbus of the saint. As it comes forth into the square we see the living actors in the lower storeys, and young girls or boys above them in short tunics and helmets of gilded paper, holding in their hands gilded wands or golden bulrushes. Above and around them are the hundreds of golden statues, big or small.

The greatest of the obelisks is preceded by two little pasteboard towers, in which sit children crowned with golden wreaths. Behind them, a pasteboard caïque, or pleasure boat, on which a boy sits, cross-legged, in a Turkish costume, holding a pomegranate flower. After this comes a galleon, floating in a little painted ocean. At the prow there is a young man in Moorish dress; and on the poop a statue of St Paulinus kneeling at an altar. At the back the towering guglia of the Guild of Farmers comes forth with bursts of music, and as it appears in all its height there is the detonation of ten thousand crackers, thrown down not only on the Piazza, but in all the streets that lead to it. The church bells ring their loudest, and flocks of pigeons fly round, volleying their wings, and casting swift shadows out of a cloudless sky. Every balcony is full of people, and hung with flowers. Below, nearly all the crowd are carrying little banners of gold and silver paper; while we begin to hear, at once, the music of as many obelisks, marching, one behind another, into the square.

The giants of pantomime are now visible in all their strangeness. Like so many, marching, golden fountains. The gilded saints at their summits, balanced by the golden jet, are theatrical and extraordinary in their attitudes, praying, preaching, or bestowing blessings. Some gaze from their pedestals, in ecstasy, into the sky; or look down from their giddy height upon the crowd. One is a kneeling saint, borne on his totem pole down every street towards the altar of the Duomo. Another stands like an Indian fakir on his mango tree. One rolls in triumph upon his gilded car. Another strides the golden lotus petal. For, in symbol, they are Indian; and the procession of these towers is like some Hindu festival. Not in its decadence, but it could be a thousand or two thousand years ago. They could belong to that sect of Brahmins in whose name it is denoted that "their covering is the air"; or to those others who are "clad in white", or "saffron yellow". And we would think of these towers, accordingly, as waggon-temples built to receive the god for his yearly visit of one day only in the golden month of June. In reason of this the guglie di San Paolino are so many pagodas by their multitude of idols. Of that legendary India where Krishna, a lovely youth of Ganges in a yellow robe, played his flute and all living beings were entranced.

The procession of these Stylites on their plllars is purely pagan as a spectacle. It is thrilling and intoxicating like a draught of pagan wine. We are carried back to the arcana of the ancient gods. We are to see other mysteries. But the discordant music of so many bands grows loud and louder. Nine towers are advancing; and there is time to see the different nimbus to each statue of the saint. For none are alike. A wild fantasy has set the constellations on their heads. There is the simple nimbus, a circle like the bands of Saturn, or Orion's golden belt. A half-moon nimbus in emblem of the months above the pagoda of the Gardeners, for the weather alters with the new moon. A fuller moon, that is like a sickle, above the Reapers' golden tower. A golden barley moon above the Bakers' wain. A circle of golden stars upon the great obelisk of the Guild of Farmers, which, in their golden multitude suggest the sheaves of corn. But, also, there are other fantasies of the golden nimbus. One pagoda—could it be the obelisk of the Tailors ?— has the statue of St Paulinus in a shepherd's or a pilgrim's dress, with staff in his hand and wine flask at his side, wearing a rakish tricorne or a corded hat, and the nimbus behind his head is the stylized counterpart of that. The obelisk of the Wine Merchants has its statue backed with a sunburst of golden rays, as it could be the smiling face of Bacchus looking down upon the vines. And it is not only golden. It has strips of mirror set in it, which glitter like diamonds. At each halt of the obelisk, as the bearers set it down, the nimbus sparkles or trembles in its fire. It burns with a steady light; and again, flashes as the march proceeds. It has advanced into the square. This golden rocket hangs, in perpetuity, upon the air. And, round it, the lesser fountains leap, continually, to their appointed height.

All nine towers, tottering and swaying, are to be seen at once. And so many mysteries are contained in them. Each obelisk is in the pattern of the guglia, that Neapolitan invention which was derived from the great machinery of the old Italian theatre, with its "clouds" and the "heaven" or "Parnassus" of its transformations. The guglia belongs, in fact, the the school of Bibiena, and is related to the huge funeral catalfalques, or to the staged mysteries of the Passion erected in their churches by the Jesuits. But here, at Nola, the guglia is not static. It has been given movement. It is a living monument that moves and . . .

For we will know in another moment! It is Indian in its exuberance. This pagoda has its idols of the living and the dead. We are in the nodding plain of India, among its temples. Indus, Ganges, Brahmaputra roll their waters. It is a sacred spell, or an intoxication. But, as well, the nine towers, the nine obelisks of Nola, are nine holy mountains. A sacred Thebaid of a night and day. These are its crags and pinnacles. The cliffs of Meteora, the Cappadocian mountains hollowed out with grottos. There are hermits upon the summits of the hills. Not the nymphs of old, who cried out aloud upon the rocks; but holy anchorites, the athletes of religion, advancing on their pillars. For the nine towers are tottering forward. They are coming out, all nine of them, into the square.

And the tallest tower of all sets out dancing to the music of its band. A man with a conductor's baton stands in front of it, and gives the time. In the beginning it is as though it is about to fall. It totters, while its population of the living and the dead rattle in their bones. Then it steadies. The obelisk lifts its feet and dances. It treads the measure. The thirty bearers move in rhythm, stepping this way and that. The colossus dances: or it could be a huge elephant and its howdah. Dancing in this manner, each obelisk takes up its place before the Duomo.

Now comes the counter-dance. With two men to beat the time, one obelisk dances against another, in a solo dance and counter-dance of swaying towers. One moment they are leaning towers or campaniles, at a slant, in different angles, in outward perspective, sloping from old age, or in a subsidence of the soil beneath the ancient city; but then they come together into time, and bow in rhythm. They shake and tremble, as though seized with the ecstasy, while they dance side by side. They move apart again and dance, one against another, in cross rhythm to the music of their choirs and bands. And now they dance in pairs, the whole nine of them changing partners, a dance of giants who are clumsy in their movements. We can hear the music of four obelisks at once, while the other five towers hide behind them, and we only know the stamping feet, and that the piazza is full of dancing pyramids. The dance and counter-dance of each pair of obelisks lasts for a few moments, for as long as the bearers can support the weight, after which each tower comes to a standstill and the trumpets play a wild flourish to announce the end, and the start of a new mystery.

About twenty men and youths begin to dance round each

obelisk in turn. Each puts his hands upon the shoulders of his neighbour, making a ring or circle in midst of which two solo dancers move in counter-rhythm, with a third youth whom they lift up in their arms. While they dance with him, he is in a lying or recumbent posture, but goes through the motions of dancing with his limbs. He grows more languid and more lifeless. He droops: he shuts his eyelids: he is dead: or sleeping. The music quickens: and the circle dance round him, faster and faster, to a quickening measure. And now comes the mystery of the festival. For the dead or sleeping youth returns to life. He smiles and lifts his head. He raises himself upon his shoulders. He has awoken. He stretches his arms. And, with a sudden movement, he strikes his castanets in the air.

This dance is performed in front of every obelisk. No one can explain it. The meaning has been lost far back in antiquity. It has been suggested that the rites of Adonis are portrayed in it. In the Adonia, the festival in honour of Adonis, celebrations were held for two days, the first of which was spent in howling and lamentations, the second in joyful clamour, as if Adonis was returned to life. This youth, we would recall, was the favourite of Venus. He was killed by a wild boar, while hunting, and Venus, after many tears changed him into a flower called anemony. He was restored to life by Proserpine, on the condition that he should divide the year between herself and Venus, living six months with each. This is symbolical of the alternate return of summer and winter.

But the rites of Adonis are identical with those of the Egyptian Osiris, which, also, began in lamentation and ended in rejoicing, when Osiris returned among the living. Osiris was a legendary King of Egypt, who brought the fruits of civilization to the earth. He was murdered; and Isis, his wife, wandered through the world seeking for her husband. He was magically restored to life by his son Horus, and continued to rule the land as King of the dead. It has been written that nothing could give a clearer idea of the power and greatness of Osiris than this inscription, in hieroglyphs, which has been found upon some ancient monuments: "Saturn, the youngest of all the gods, was my father. I am Osiris, who conducted a large and numerous army as far as the deserts of India, and travelled over the greatest part of the world, and visited the streams of the

293

Isther, and the remote shores of the ocean, diffusing benevolence to all the inhabitants of the earth."

Osiris, we may add, is more generally given as the son of Jupiter and Niobe. It is stated that after his golden reign in Egypt, Osiris resolved to go and spread civilization in the other parts of the earth. He left his Kingdom in the care of his wife Isis, and of her minister Hermes or Mercury. The command of his troops at home was left to the trust of Hercules, a warlike officer. Isiris was accompanied upon his expedition by his brother Apollo, and by Anubis, Macedo, and Pan. He marched through Ethiopia, where his army was increased by the addition of the Satyrs, who made dancing and playing on musical instruments their chief study. Afterwards he passed through Arabia; and so to India, or its borders. As to Saturn, his, also, was the golden age. During the festival of the Saturnalia, held in Rome, which is not far distant from Nola, the chains were taken from the statues, to intimate the freedom and independence enjoyed by mankind during the golden age. It was permitted, too, for slaves to ridicule their masters. The festival, itself, had been instituted by Janus, the most ancient king who ruled in Italy, in gratitude to Saturn from whom he had learnt agriculture.

Whether the march of Osiris into India clashed with that of Bacchus, we are not told, and can but conjecture. It is more probable, indeed, that Bacchus was identical with the Osiris of the Egyptians. The festival of Nola would seem to be in classical descent from the Baccanalia or Dionysia of the ancients. Or, equally, from the Saturnalia or Adonia. It had become involved, somehow, in the return of St Paulinus from his slavery in Africa. Or was made the occasion or the excuse for that. When he came back to Nola, so the legend runs, he was met by the citizens, dancing and carrying these obelisks or towers before them. It would appear, then, that an old feast of fertility, of a golden age, held in a Roman provincial town, took on a Christian meaning and survived till modern times. The youth who returns to life is none other than Adonis, in the guise of that only son of the widow of Nola, who was carried by the Vandals into slavery in Libya. St Paulinus set forth to become a slave in his stead and rescue him. Hence the dancing obelisks: in time, influenced in their shape by the guglie of near-by Naples. The Indian or Hindu aspects of the festival are brought about by the circumstance that the feast itself, in origin, was something of an Indian triumph, considering the legends of Bacchus or Osiris; and by the fact that the prolixity of both ornament and imagination in Southern Italy, during the Baroque age of the seventeenth and eighteenth centuries, produced effects in sculpture and in architecture that are almost Indian, as many authorities have noticed when discussing the Neapolitan churches, or the churches and palaces of such towns as Lecce, in Apulia. Here, in Nola, it is not a church, nor a palace. It is the whole procession that is Indian.

The nine towers glitter in the blue Campanian sky. Preceded by many monks of all the Orders, and by bishops and deacons in the mitre of Osiris, amid the shouts of thousands, they start upon a round of the whole city. The church bells ring their loudest; while a myriad crackers, thrown down and bursting, make the sound of innumerable instruments of percussion. Perhaps the crackle of the castanets when Adonis, the sleeping youth, raised his hand was the signal for this.

The gilded galleons dance before them. And so the procession sets out. The huge obelisk of the Guild of Farmers is the first to move. Its bearers take away the props of wood and lift it to their shoulders. It sways and totters, and begins to march. Behind it comes the pyramid of the Husbandmen and Reapers; and the heroic figure of Judith, holding the head of Holofernes high before her, appears to shake and tremble. Obelisk follows Obelisk: Cobblers, Tailors, Gardeners, Butchers, Bakers, Grocers, and Wine Vendors. All advancing. A procession of pyramids, of obelisks, of marching towers. The whole town seethes, and roars, and surges with excitement.

The rites of the golden age are restored, for a day and night. Osiris, the son of Saturn, comes to life. He has returned from India. The chains are taken from the statues; and images of the gods are carried in triumph. It is his golden reign. He is met with dancing towers. There is magic in the air. It is a festival of fertility. Why does the youth in the caïque, which is borne along, hold in his hand a pomegranate flower? Why could the statue of Judith be holding a sheaf of corn, and not a severed head? Or the obelisk of the Gardeners be preceded by a youth who holds a cornucopia? Why had dead Adonis a castanet in his hand? We meet a troop of children who have gauze wings upon their shoulders; and a full brass band plays the March from Moïsé in Egitto. The shepherds' bagpipes, the pifferari or the zampognari, that come up at Christmas from Calabria; is it imagination? Do we not recognize their sound? And we hear, upon all sides, the rhythm of the tarantella. They are dancing in the wineshops; in the streets; in the vineyards. The wreathing, twining tarantella danced among the vines, in sight of distant Vesuvius. The tambourine is struck in frenzy. It is midday: the golden noon has come. There is the firing of cannon from the barracks. And a fanfare of bugles. Wherever we look, an obelisk, a pyramid, walks or dances. The Stylite gods are carried in their towers, with choirs and bands of music in their lower storeys.

The tower of the Reapers or Husbandmen emerges. A golden sickle is its emblem. Will it not march with its flail into the harvest? It must be a statue of Priapus upon the obelisk of the Gardeners. He is the god of orchards and of gardens, born to the goddess Venus after she had gone to meet Bacchus coming back in triumph from the Indies. Or some say Adonis was the father. What, then, of the tower of the Wine Vendors? And of the seven others?

It is a delirious and haunting dream. Are the actors still shouting on the board outside their theatre? Noises of the fair mix with the festival. Booths or shops were open on the day Adonis died. Someone haggled for a pomegranate; for a clutch of eggs; for a lark in a wicker cage. And so it must continue. What is that droning? Will the nine towers go toppling down? Ah no! it is the golden age. Or the noon of that, declining to a golden sunset. With singing and dancing, and crashing of cymbals. The pagan gods have been restored to life. There go their palanquins, in the streets and squares of Nola.

FINALE IN FORM OF A BACCHANALE*

THE antique magic is in the air again. Forget the present and the future. Nor, in particular, is this the past. Like music, it must live in its own melody and make its shape. The ram's horn trumpet blows. It is the Bacchanale. The breath winds long and steady in its twisted volutes, more pastoral than the conch shell which calls the tritons and divinities of ocean. Again and again it blows. They come from teeming India down the dusty plains, gods rubbed with sandalwood and powdered blue, youths of the cassia flower with towers of jasmine in their hair, the sacred milkmaids, the rout of the flowering precincts, male and female, and dark cupids. Their tamed animals are led along, peacocks which dance to music, the striped tiger and the purring lion. It is their ecstasy. They close their eyes and listen motionless; or start to weep. The living gods are carried past, mute and ineffable, their followers in frenzy.

Some walk slowly with iron barbs in their flesh, dragging great weights with them, quilled like the porcupine with hooks and wire, in a halo, a palisade, the points all trembling. Some hold the trident and come forward, dancing. Others are naked, but for ashes, with circles and ugly signs painted on them, the wild men, the sacred vagabonds who sleep beneath the trees. They are Brahmins in yellow robes, whom none may touch, who perform miracles, those who control their breath and are suspended between life and death; others who, by fasting, hover over their bodies and are rapt in contemplation. The long sleep of the lotus tank and the slow unfolding. The inscrutable smile, and darting and swaying of the serpent neck. Language of the wrist and hand to hypnotize the senses, for such are the flower-soft Indies, now advancing. Monks, in their colleges of red or yellow, where the pearl-red pillars look towards the mountains. The ponds bear on their surface the blue lotus. It

* From *Sacred and Profane Love*, 1940.

297

is the Abbey of Nalanda. Time was nodding, nodding, in those flower-hung days.

But there are contingents, too, from across the Indian main. Their ships of sandalwood churn the foaming ocean. And the flowers and winds are different. It is another world. Their men and women have the pose of dancers and move with hieratic step, but softly as animals. Their king rides on an elephant, and none may pronounce his name, it is so holy. Before him march a company of Amazons, and in the procession there are carriages drawn by goats. It is a circus triumph, but the visitors are of another creation from ourselves, with a different tread, passing us like flowers blown by.

And the scene alters to the lacquered Indies. It is the land of the palanquin. There are golden plains and the pale shadow of the ginko. But we take it in its islands, far from the rites of the Shaman and their Northern fogs. There are mimed plays and antique legends danced to music of the gamelan. To our untrained ear it is the only music of the Orient: announcing a god out of the waterfall, out of a moonbeam, a sea god glittering in his pearlshell armour, always an entrance and a diminishment, a dying off, as though the bells and gongs died down in another world, of unknown crops and harvests, where the temples are built up in a day and destroyed at the golden dawn, being but scenery for the sacred trances. The gamelan, too, is music of the child actor: the sacred serpent coiling from the ground: a myriad heroes and divinities with supple limbs in the long drawn epic: poetic images interpreted by the wrists and hands, after which the dancer is a child again. Suddenly the wind of inspiration seizes on young and old alike, and all descend into the nether world and come back, fainting, in poetic stupor. They lie prostrate on the earth, and for an hour or two are senseless, in the way of persons who have tasted death. This is their formal ecstasy: while the dying gamelan announces a new drama.

We have, as well, the third or mock sceptre of the Indies, submissive races who bowed their necks and died. They amble along the wide causeways, bringing fruits and flowers that are unknown, to market. The shell trumpet sounds thrice from the high pyramid, and priests, who do not change their raiment, and whose long hair is matted with the gore, plunge a jade knife into the victim and hurl his heartless body to the crowd below. In a distant land of this continent there are golden figures of the sun and moon: golden images of the fruits and flowers: and, for clue to the country, llamas, lifesize with golden fleeces. The stone walls of the temple are joined without mortar, and the work of giants. Within are virgin priestesses. In another place a huge pole like a ship's mast is set up. In their yearly festival, Indians, six at a time, climb to the top of this and, standing perilously for a moment, lash the long ropes to themselves and leap towards the earth, spinning, like lunar satellites, around their parent maypole. Head downward, in feathered headdress they revolve, until the rope unwinds its length and brings them down to the crowd who wait below and lift them from their sacred ecstasy and lay them on the ground, their Dædalian flight accomplished.*

But there is the crash of cymbals and of tambourines. These are milky lands of the violet and the cyclamen. Music, itself, is a bacchanale in shape, starting, again and again, and returning in its form, crowned and wreathed in flowers, shaking the lilied thyrsus, garlanded with ivy, the fig leaf, and the vine. It is the return from Bacchic India. The world was taught the use of wine, the cultivation of the earth, and the manner of making honey.

There are signs of India. The priests have put serpents in their hair, and in the wildness of their looks feign madness and the sacred frenzy; while virgins carry baskets filled with gold and fruit, and snakes wreathe and crawl from these to daze the senses. The hiss and coil of serpents are in the music, which darts and trembles in its rhythms, and proclaims the theme. Their prisoners accompany them, though it was a conquest without bloodshed. There are tumbrils loaded with purple grapes, beside which walk the captives, behind the chariot, and the lion and tiger.

When men were taught to till the earth, and the use of wine and honey, this was all, and enough, for most of them to know.

* It has only lately been discovered that the juego de los voladores, or flying game, is still practised by the Totonac and Otomi Indians. Drawings of these are to be found in two Aztec codices, those of Porfirio Diaz and Fernandez Leal. It was seen by Bernal Diaz and described by Fray Juán de Torquemada. The flyers used to be clothed as various birds. Cf. *Mexican Mosaic* by Rodney Gallop (Faber & Faber, London, 1939).

What they have learned since is mostly folly. The arts came from the vineyard and the olive grove. They learned letters from the patterns of the constellations, to foretell the truth, and translate the dead. These are mysteries, still, and no one is the wiser. The lyric moment is still a mystery between the vine and the olive. Sacred and Profane are two schools of thought, two hemispheres, two continents, a heaven and a hell, in accordance with the winds that blow.

But the music grows louder. The living have no time to think. They must take one side, or other. The siren and the time signal have been music in their day; but the bacchanale will drive away the present and the future. Here the crocus grows beneath the cedar tree in a vernal forest giving on the vines. All the airs are perfumed and sigh sweet with resin. The music thrills and empties in the hollow valley. Here Sacred and Profane meet together in the dance, which loudens with the shaking of the lilied sceptre and beats with the tambourines and crashes with the cymbals. There is one god, or many gods, but all are worshipped here. Or no god at all, but what the music means. Is there not word enough in the vineyard and the cedar breath? The creaking tumbrils pass by in a dream, while the bacchanale comes back again in louder triumph.

Where, then, is wisdom? In the arts, and not in war. In the cold and in the heat. In this music and its lilies. In shocks of corn and in the golden locks of children. In the arts and in the senses. In the bright wing and in the golden leaf. In night and day, or sun and moon, but not among the dead. In this there lies no difference: Profane or Sacred: Sacred or Profane.